GENERATIONS

SERIES IN
CITIZENSHIP STUDIES

· · · · · · · · · · ·

EDITORS

Marc W. Kruman
Richard Marback

GENERATIONS

....

Rethinking Age and Citizenship

EDITED BY RICHARD MARBACK

Wayne State University Press
Detroit

19 18 17 16 15   5 4 3 2 1

Library of Congress Control Number: 2014936774

ISBN 978-0-8143-4080-6 (paperback)
ISBN 978-0-8143-4081-3 (e-book)

Designed and typeset by Bryce Schimanski
Composed in Adobe Caslon

*To the colleagues, friends, and graduate students who helped
to build the Center for the Study of Citizenship
and made this book series possible.*

CONTENTS

PREFACE TO THE SERIES

Since 2003, when the Center for the Study of Citizenship held its inaugural conference, the center has developed a reputation for cutting-edge multidisciplinary and interdisciplinary scholarship. In effect, it has helped to forge a new field of study and then steadily elaborated upon and within that field, promoting research and conversation about citizenship in its many permutations. In a variety of settings, especially in its conferences, the center urges participant scholars to focus upon the creation of a single, emergent field of study and is encouraged to bring disciplinary learning to bear on the construction of a new academic discourse, in much the same way that cultural studies emerged from bits and pieces of anthropology, literary criticism, history, linguistics, and other established disciplines.

As the center's conference advanced from a one-day program aimed at junior scholars to the leading global conference in the field, it revealed the richness, breadth, and depth of disciplinary and interdisciplinary work in citizenship studies. It became clear that this creative and original scholarship required a distinguished publication outlet. The field already enjoyed an excellent journal, *Citizenship Studies*, and a fine book series on citizenship and constitutionalism, published by the University of Pennsylvania Press, but more was needed to build this interdisciplinary field. The center has teamed with Wayne State University Press to establish this book series, which aspires to move beyond familiar disciplinary boundaries. We aim instead to use the book series as an instrument to further advance, define, and perhaps redirect the emergent field itself.

We plan to publish both monographs and anthologies that advance the study of citizenship. Although originally intending to publish monographs, the intellectual coherence of the center's conferences made it clear that publications drawn from the conferences would make valuable books that were more than conference proceedings or essay collections. That is the case with the series' first volume: *Generations: Rethinking Age and Citizenship*. Age is a primary marker of citizenship. It is crucial to obtaining full political citizenship in a community and in shaping political, civil, and property rights. Yet the intersection between age and citizenship (or lack thereof) has varied across time and space. This is especially the case when thinking of how to define and identify citizens by "generation." This volume examines the relationship of generations and citizenship in the past and present. It explores how citizenship—membership in communities—is experienced temporally by age and how membership in a particular generation influences the experience and identity of citizenship.

Marc W. Kruman
Richard Marback

Wayne State University
Detroit, Michigan
June 2014

ACKNOWLEDGMENTS

Publication of this volume would not have been possible without the contributions of a number of people. I want to thank Rayman Mohamed and Julie Novak, both members of the faculty advisory board of the Center for the Study of Citizenship, for their help in evaluating initial conference proposals from which these published essays are drawn. The conference itself was a lively exchange of ideas, thanks to the energy and enthusiasm of those in attendance for their thoughtful and thought-provoking discussions of age-related issues in the study of citizenship. The conference itself would not have been a success without the efforts of Timothy Moran and Ann Marie Wambeke, both doctoral candidates in the history department at Wayne State University, nor Renee Bricker, a recent graduate of the program, and now assistant professor of history at the University of Northern Georgia. Publication of this volume would not have been possible without the hard work and generous support of the staff at Wayne State University Press. Thanks especially to Jane Hoehner, the director of Wayne State University Press, and to Kathryn Wildfong, editor-in-chief, for their leadership and support with developing the Series in Citizenship Studies of which this volume is a part. Finally, everyone involved with the Center for the Study of Citizenship, with the conference, and with this publication knows that none of it would be possible without the tireless efforts of Helen Callow, who simply does everything.

GENERATIONS

INTRODUCTION

· · · · · · · · · ·

Rethinking Age and Citizenship

RICHARD MARBACK

In an episode of Aaron Sorkin's *West Wing* (2005), a group of middle school students visits the White House of President Bartlett to press their case for lowering the voting age. Among the reasons they give in favor of a lowered voting age is their vested interest in decisions about uses of limited resources that cannot but have consequences for them and their futures. Among the reasons communications director Toby Ziegler gives for not lowering the voting age is the inexperience and immaturity of adolescents, to which the students respond by remarking maturity is not necessarily linked to chronological age. Their exchange continues in this manner throughout the episode. The students have reasoned arguments they believe no one is taking seriously, and Toby Ziegler resists their claims out of hand. In the end, though, he softens. So impressed by their clarity and determination that he arranges for a representative from the group of students to attend a presidential press conference on the federal budget deficit. Called on by the president, the student asks, "Do you think the budget deficit is especially unfair to younger Americans?" President Bartlett responds, "Absolutely. We're passing on a crushing debt to our children. That's not something a responsible parent would choose to do. As adults we're not shouldering our responsibility and your generation has a vested interest."

However fictional the exchange, the issues it raises are quite real. The fictional President Bartlett's response echoes statements made again and again on the campaign trail by real elected officials, such as Congressman Andy Harris of Maryland, who said, "I ran for Congress to pass on the American Dream to the next generation. If we don't seriously tackle the spending problem, our children and grandchildren will not have the same opportunities for success that we all enjoyed" (Harris 2013). As the real deficit debate reveals, we are all well aware that the decisions of one generation of citizens cannot but have consequences for another generation of citizens. At the same time, as the fictional *West Wing* debate on voting age requirements reveals, we assume a great deal about how age and aging figure in deciding who does and who does not have rights and responsibilities to decide the intergenerational consequences of public problems such as the budget deficit. As I argue in this introduction and as the essays in this collection demonstrate, we better engage issues important to us all, young and old, by more carefully considering the burdens, rights, and responsibilities of citizenship in terms of their intergenerational distribution.

While a fundamental issue such as the budget deficit is shot through with a rhetoric of one generation's obligations to another, the finitude of human life and the fact of our intergenerational interdependence have not figured so productively in thinking about who we count as citizens having the right and responsibility to debate issues of public concern. Quite the opposite. The frailty of infancy and the infirmities of aging are, for thinkers from Plato to Hobbes and beyond, unfortunate facts of a person's transient existence. In this line of thinking people only become citizens when in their lives they have matured to the point that their interests can rise above selfish attention to mere existence, when they have gained the autonomy to deliberate and decide collective concerns. Much philosophical discussion of autonomous, deliberative citizens, in the traditions of Jürgen Habermas or John Rawls, is carried on in an abstract language uninflected by human aging, a language intended to clarify the ideal conditions supporting just deliberation.

Within this tradition the ideal sovereign citizen is viewed as not driven to act by the immediacy of appetite or need. The ideal sovereign citizen is instead understood as motivated by an ambition to deliberate fairly and decide justly. Such motivation does not simply emerge. Habermas's discussion of communicative action and Rawls's appeal to the original position both aim at explaining the economic, political, and social conditions necessary and sufficient for the citizen's unencumbered capacity for participation. Anyone applying these reflections on the ideal conditions supporting sovereign citizenship faces the challenge of preserving those conditions throughout the intergenerational interdependence of human community.

The challenge itself has long been recognized. Aristotle's description in the *Politics* of the organization of society at every level from the home through to the polis is a thorough account of the intergenerational ordering of human relationships that supports, as it is supported by, the autonomy of sovereign citizens. Aristotle's autonomous head of household who rules over his wife, his children, and his slaves, manages financial affairs not for the goal of accumulating wealth but for the purpose of cultivating virtue (POL 1257 [Jowett]). There is in Aristotle's account a pragmatic rationale: "For, inasmuch as every family is a part of a state, and these relationships are the parts of a family, and the virtue of the part must have regard to the virtue of the whole, women and children must be trained by education with an eye to the constitution, if the virtues of either of them are supposed to make any difference in the virtues of the state. And they must make a difference: for the children grow up to be citizens, and half the free persons in a state are women" (POL 1260b [Jowett]). Aristotle's organization of society is simultaneously spatial and intergenerational. People are born, live their lives, and die, yet the basic structuring of their lives into households enables in every generation the presence of a limited number of citizens who possess the deliberative freedom to decide their community's collective concerns.

Placing children under the guidance of a head of household charged with preparing them for their adult roles as citizens is by itself not the entire story. Among other things we must decide the point at which those children become adults and citizens. Necessarily, experiences of human growth and rituals of maturation influence such decisions. Association of chronological aging with the cultivation of abilities individuals must possess if they are to participate in making decisions for their community—abilities such as autonomy, articulateness, and a capacity for judgment—has long presumed answers to questions about the relationship of age and aging to the nature of citizenship. Age restrictions on voting, for example, as well as restrictions on holding public office, have long historic precedents reaching back at least to ancient Rome, where the voting age, as well as the age of military service, was between seventeen and eighteen. As M. I. Finley makes clear, limited life expectancy in the ancient world made childhood nothing more than "a preparatory stage for adulthood, to be traversed as rapidly as was biologically reasonable" (Finley 1981, 159). For the Roman-born citizen, preparing for adulthood involved preparation for military service and public life, a matter of extensive education and preparation that did not end with reaching the age of enfranchisement or conscription. In his *Institutio Oratoria*, for example, Quintilian extends the education of the orator beyond the traditional studies of grammar, then rhetoric, then philosophy, into a lifelong preparation of the *vir bonus*, the cultivation of the character of the good citizen who speaks well.

Debate on the nature and role of citizenship has largely followed the precedent of associating the maturity required of a citizen—a maturity measured by the capacity for such things as autonomy, duty, and judgment—with a society's organization of the citizen's prior experiences of maturation. Jean-Jacques Rousseau's *Émile* (1979), in which he lays out a lifelong educational experience intended to cultivate the person's capacity for concern for others, comes immediately to mind. Such extensive cultivation of the capacities of one individual is of course realistically impractical for uniformly and consistently educating all youth to become citizens. Instead, less demanding chronological markers of maturity, such as voting age restrictions, provide time for at least some opportunities for maturation, such as enrollment in civics education classes and experiences of volunteerism, opportunities intended to cultivate a person's capacities for sovereign citizenship.

It is no exaggeration to say that the greatest challenges of citizenship are challenges that the precariousness of human life poses to the goal of ongoing citizenship education. As Plato argued in his *Republic*, "we must find out who are the best guardians of this inward conviction that they must always do what they believe to be best for the commonwealth. We shall have to watch them from earliest childhood and set them tasks in which they would be most likely to forget or to be beguiled out of this duty. We shall then choose only those whose memory holds firm and who are proof against delusion" (Plato 1971, 414). Plato's is of course not the only response to the problem of educating future citizens. John Dewey directly commented on the relationship between the "social continuity of life" and the human realities of birth, life, and death in his argument for educating the citizens of a democracy: "Mere physical growing up, mere mastery of the bare necessities of subsistence will not suffice to reproduce the life of the group. Deliberate effort and the taking of thoughtful pains are required. Beings who are born not only unaware of but also quite indifferent to the aims and habits of the social group have to be rendered cognizant of them and actively interested. Education, and education alone, spans the gap" (Dewey 1944, 3). The perennial challenge of consistently educating the next generation for citizenship was captured recently in the report of a survey conducted in 2003 as part of the Representative Democracy in America project. From the results of their survey of the "civic attitudes, knowledge and participation of young people," Karl Kurtz, Alan Rosenthal, and Cliff Zukin conclude without qualification, "The older generations have failed to teach the ideals of citizenship to the next generation" (Kurtz, Rosenthal, and Zukin 2003, 1). As Peter Levine argued in *The Future of Democracy* (2007), such a failure has consequences for us all.

While it is clear that we ought to concern ourselves with educating each new generation of citizens, we should not lose sight of the fact that faith in the educational opportunities available at any given time can lead older, more experienced generations of citizens to the erroneous conclusion that youth are either not yet prepared for citizenship or too inexperienced in their role as citizens. Responses at the time to the student protests of the 1960s provide stark reminders that one generation's construction of citizenship education does not necessarily presume even the potential for competence in the next generation. Wayne Booth's concern for the intergenerational miscommunication on college campuses in the 1960s—which prompted his *Modern Dogma and the Rhetoric of Assent*—is a case in point. He explains his motivation to write *Modern Dogma* came when, "In the late sixties I became puzzled . . . by the inability of most protest groups to get themselves heard and by the equal failure of what one of my students called 'establishment protestees' to make their responses intelligible" (Booth 1974, ix). The institutional soul searching needed to bridge this generation gap was attempted as early as 1971 with the publication of *The Prospect of Rhetoric*, a report that noted the divide separating an "establishment rhetoric" from a "rhetoric of revolution." The authors of the report were clear that "a most alarming weakness in higher education is its failure to make students sensitive to the ways they are using language and other symbols, and the ways in which language and other symbols are being used to deal with them" (Bitzer and Black 1971, 211). However successful we have since become in our efforts at tailoring instructional opportunities to meet the educational demands of students, one caution we can take away from the student protests of the 1960s is that the human reality of educating children as citizens one generation at a time can invite both the distain of an older generation whose preparation for citizenship may be too long past and the disillusionment of a younger generation who are faced with the emergent demands of contemporary civic engagement.

Miscommunication and the distrust that follow arise in part from the fact that it is within a narrow window of human life that people of the same age, who have shared similar experiences of maturation, come to form a citizenship cohort, a group of people whose age and education have prepared them to take on the rights and responsibilities within a given community at a given time. In popular culture something of a generational citizenship cohort is captured in Tom Brokaw's narrative of the men and women who came of age to serve in World War II, *The Greatest Generation* (Brokaw 1998). Even in *The Greatest Generation* the idea of a generational citizenship cohort is porous. Differences in race, class, and gender create within a single generation different affiliations and senses of what it is to be a citizen. The experiences of women such as Mary Louise Roberts, who served as a nurse in North Africa, and Jeanette Gagne Norton, who saw her newlywed husband off to war, differed from those of white men such as Thomas Broderick, who parachuted into Holland, black men such as Johnnie Holmes, whose all-black tank battalion faced racial discrimination despite its battlefield performance, and Japanese Americans such as Daniel Inouye, who fought in Italy, and Nao Takasugi, who languished in a Japanese internment camp.

Whatever might be said about the greatest generation as a citizenship cohort should not distract us from another fact about the lived reality of citizenship: that opportunities for participation change as people live into old age. Specifically referencing the greatest generation, Jennie Sweet-Cushman and her coauthors find a nuanced answer to the question they ask in the title of their contribution to this collection, "Is Participation Decline Inevitable as Generations Age?" In their survey of people fifty-five and older, Sweet-Cushman and her colleagues found that despite the obvious hindrances the infirmities of aging place on physically demanding forms of civic participation, the population they sampled did in fact maintain its levels of participation in those civic activities that were less strenuous. Their findings suggest, among other things, that we ought to find more ways to expand opportunities for participation among old people, an especially pressing issue as the general population ages.

We would fail to fully grasp the role of aging on citizenship if we merely accommodated for the participation of an older generation. As several contributors to this volume argue in their essays, differences within a single generation as it comes of age matter to a society's collective experiences and expectations of citizenship. In "Appreciation and Elevation of Labor," Jane Fiegen Green describes how young laborers in nineteenth-century New England used literary magazines to set for themselves avenues to citizenship distinct from the traditional avenues of affluence and gentility. Focusing on access to citizenship in nineteenth-century Indian schools, Amy Grey argues in "The Spectacle of a Farmer Bending Over a Washtub" that Native American graduates from the schools rejected their education in a Jeffersonian ideal of citizen as yeoman farmer. Instead they selected from their education those elements that allowed them to craft a citizenship that incorporated their indigenous values regarding the environment.

While it is clear that all children of the same generation do not construct for themselves the same identities as citizens, we are less clear on how the citizenship identities they do fashion can be influenced by such age-related experiences as migration and movement across national boundaries, experiences that are shaped by intergenerational forces. Children are born all the time to parents who are expatriates, guest workers, illegal immigrants, or even holders of dual citizenship, all of which are circumstances that create opportunities for contention over a child's citizenship status. In this regard, two contributions to this volume address issues of citizenship as a birthright. Yuki Oda, in "(Re)Claiming US Citizenship," argues that the repatriation struggles of Mexican Americans from the Great Depression on must be seen within the larger frame of a perceived "immigration problem" that included not only Mexican migrants but Asian migrants as well. Another facet of the problem of repatriation is taken up by John W. Hink Jr. in "He Wants to Take Them to Russia!" an analysis of several postwar court cases in which immigrant parents of children born in the United States attempt to relocate those children to countries behind the Iron Curtain. Where Oda describes repatriations in terms of US policies consonant with Japanese internments during World War II, Hink describes how the Cold War encouraged courts to protect the American birth citizenship of children born to parents with citizenship from countries under control of the Soviet Union.

Challenging the priority of national citizenship, Saeed Khan, in his chapter "The Negotiation of Citizenship among Pakistani Youth in Great Britain: Intersections, Interventions, and Interactions," describes how the legal status of British citizens who are of Pakistani descent creates the opportunity in today's global environment for a bifurcated citizenship identity. Torn between their national identity as British citizens and their international identity as Pakistani, Khan makes the case that the experiences of these youth point us toward a new understanding of the possibilities for global citizenship.

Pauline Stoltz discusses the impact of international conflicts of one generation on citizenship experiences of subsequent generations. Her chapter, "Children, Postconflict Processes, and Situated Cosmopolitanism," brings postcolonial theory and feminist theory together with childhood research in order to fashion a robust heuristic for understanding the struggles faced by children whose ancestors were forced to migrate from Indonesia to the Netherlands during World War II. Getting at similar experiences through a different research methodology, Enzo Colombo, in his chapter "Complicating Citizenship: How Children of Immigrants in Italy Represent Belonging and Rights," draws out of interviews with immigrant youth the terms through which they describe their sense of themselves as Italian citizens who are nonetheless different.

As important as these observations about the influence of older generations on younger generations are, we should not allow them to lead us to ignore the intergenerational forces younger generations can exert on the citizenship experiences of older generations. Taking account of intergenerational relationships that shape experiences of citizenship invites reflection on not only the formative years of youth but on the other end of the human life span as well, when people find themselves faced with transformation or contraction of their citizenship rights and responsibilities. Again, while it has long been taken for granted that full citizenship is achieved only after reaching a certain age—an age that provides a span of time adequate to the task of educating future citizens in customs, duties, laws, and rights—it does not follow that people who have reached the age of full citizenship will retain their rights and responsibilities as they continue to age. Today especially, as people live longer, their abilities, motivations, and opportunities for participating in society as full and productive citizens change as well.

In this regard it is worth noting debate on the citizenship status of persons living with dementia. Ruth Bartlett and Deborah O'Connor (2007) have recently drawn critical attention to the fact that people with dementia are denied their status as citizens because they are presumed to not possess the deliberative abilities associated with traditional notions of sovereign citizenship. For Bartlett and O'Connor the injustice of excluding persons living with dementia from decision making in public life resides in the fact that those persons have political interests in such public issues as health care policy and the workers' rights of health care providers, interests that are best served when those people with dementia are understood as persons who are citizens with rights as well as responsibilities. Recognizing that an issue of representation is inherent in considerations of the citizenship status of persons living with dementia leads us to reassess and potentially reimagine the nature of citizenship itself. One example of such a reimagining of rights and responsibilities is offered by Clive Baldwin (2008), who proposes grounding the citizenship status of persons with dementia in a narrative linking of their personal experiences with their political concerns.

Reasonable debate over reimagining notions of citizenship that are more inclusive of people with conditions such as dementia would need to take account of a broader historical understanding of citizenship autonomy. Such an understanding would involve asking how and why within the institutional organization of industrialized countries such as the United States citizens of retirement age come to be seen as no longer vital citizens. As Tamara Mann argues in her contribution to this volume, the making of old people into a distinct class of citizens in the United States draws on scientific discourses in which aging is described in terms of disease and decline. In her chapter, "From Personal Care to Medical Care," Mann describes how in post–World War II America federal focus on aging as biological decline played a role in creating the category of senior citizens, citizens whose interests in medical care was mobilized to pit them against younger generations, thereby dissolving bonds of intergenerational cooperation.

The fact that citizenship can be defined by a younger generation in ways that bracket off an older generation does not necessarily mean the rights and responsibilities of an older generation are always left to the generation in power. As Jessica Robbins-Ruszkowski documents in her contribution to this volume, a generation of Poles who came of age in communist Poland has taken an active role in public life in postcommunist Poland, putting pressure on the constructions of citizenship of a younger generation. In her essay, "'Active Aging' as Citizenship in Poland," Robbins-Ruszkowski explains how a generation that has come of age since the end of the Cold War has a distinctly different conception of citizenship compared to a generation of Poles who lived through Eastern Bloc rule. Robbins-Ruszkowski shows how the older Poles create civic opportunities for themselves in the new European Union through their participation in such organizations as the University of the Third Age where their participation in classes grounds their civic identities.

All this is to say that once we begin to see citizenship in terms of a process of aging, the process of a person's development along a life course from birth to death, we begin to see that what it means to be a citizen varies with a person's age, even after that person reaches the age of maturity. Citizenship, then, is not static but is rather dynamic, it is something developed over time and learned in interactions with others, many of whom belong to other generations. Children learn what it means to be a citizen in their homes with their families, in schools among peers and with teachers, as well as in their communities. Old people learn what it can mean for them to continue to be active citizens within the intergenerational networks of their lives as well. As I suggested above, these are not normative experiences we should take for granted. More important though, as each essay in this volume shows, conceptions of what it means to be a citizen that focus on the general capacities of autonomy, identity, or judgment fail to grasp the age-specific variations of autonomy, identity, and judgment that significantly shape the human experience of membership in a community. Which is to say we acquire our very capacities for citizenship over time and within the bounds of generational experiences.

Allowing for age-specific variations in the nature and experience of citizenship requires us to make allowances in our definitions of citizenship for changes in abilities, interests, and priorities that attend the aging process from youth to old age. Allowing for age-specific variations in the nature and experience of citizenship also allows us to recognize that old people can take as much of an active civic role in their communities as young people. While the contributions to this volume invite us to expand our understanding of citizenship so as to include the abilities, interests, and priorities of multiple generations, they also caution us against ignoring the inevitable conflicts that arise when the abilities, interests, and priorities of one generation are brought into contact with the abilities, interests, and priorities of another. I would argue that the caution against taking intergenerational conflict for granted ought to be seen as highlighting the need to examine more closely the rhetoric of old age that has labeled old people demented, eccentric, or frail, and in so doing justified the waning of their roles as active citizens.

Examined more closely, the rhetoric of old age as decline reveals important generational disagreements that bear on people's understandings of themselves as citizens, differences in understanding that beg for our attention because it is within these intergenerational tensions that we find the fullest expressions of citizenship. As Youcef shows in "Old Beurs, New Beurs, and

French Citizenship," the conflicting experiences of different generations of Algerians living in France is informed by different experiences of colonial French rule, resulting in a strain on those intergenerational bonds.

I draw out the theme of citizenship experiences emerging out of intergenerational differences in my contribution to this collection, "The Challenge of ANC Youth from the Soweto Uprising to Julius Malema." There I describe how the imprisonment and isolation by the apartheid government of a generation of freedom fighters that included Nelson Mandela took away from the black youth of South Africa one generation's model for citizenship. Absent the role models of an older generation, the black youth of South Africa developed a notion of citizenship that remains at odds with the generation of Mandela, Thabo Mbeki, and Jacob Zuma, a generational divide that persists in postapartheid South African politics.

Overall the essays contained in this volume highlight for us the fact that there are, at any given moment in time, multiple generations, each with its own emerging experiences and conceptions of citizenship, declining experiences and conceptions of citizenship, and what I would characterize as prevailing experiences and conceptions of citizenship. Experiences and conceptions of citizenship that are emerging, prevailing, and declining come into contact to coalesce and conflict with one another around the issues that concern people most. How people of different generations ultimately decide those issues for themselves is very much a matter of how well they manage to orchestrate their varying ambitions for and experiences of citizenship into a process productive of everyone's participation. A more productive intergenerational exchange would do more than either set a minimum voting age or extrapolate an ideal notion of citizenship from the range of age-specific affordances. A more productive intergenerational exchange would allow for people of all ages to articulate for themselves their relationships to one another. We begin to approach the challenge of this intergenerational exchange by taking up the terms of Peter Levine's contribution to this collection, "Civic Renewal: Theory and Practice." Levine provides a useful overview of the main themes involved in the study of citizenship. Among the themes he elaborates are the epistemological, moral, social, and pragmatic benefits that accrue through our civic engagement with each other. The benefits Levine discusses are available for citizens of all ages and appropriate to a framework for thinking of citizenship that accounts for generational issues as well as intergenerational engagement.

From this introduction to the task of rethinking citizenship through experiences of aging we can now see how a labile definition of citizenship grounds in generational issues. For people of all ages to most fully exercise their rights and responsibilities as citizens, we must not think of those rights and responsibilities in normative or static terms. Instead, as Levine alludes to in his essay, we must all strive to make the fullest experience of citizenship available to people across their life spans. This would involve, among other things, intergenerational public discussions inclusive of the old as well as the young. Such intergenerational engagement would encourage what Amartya Sen has described as promotion of human capabilities. As Sen defines it, "The capability approach to a person's advantage is concerned with evaluating it in terms of his or her actual ability to achieve various valuable functionings as a part of living" (Sen 1993, 30). Adapted to the purposes of evaluating people's abilities to function as citizens across the life span, a focus on capabilities would involve the presumption that citizenship is in and of itself a valuable part of living. From the view that citizenship remains valuable across the span of a person's life, it follows that our accounts of what it is to be a citizen would follow less from reflection on rights and responsibilities all should share and more from considering how persons of differing ages can most fully experience their citizenship as a central part of a rich and meaningful life. As I have presented them, the essays in this volume take up the task of rethinking the terms of citizenship from the perspective of the value that being a citizen has in a person's life. Among other things, the authors of these essays encourage us to take on the task of not only keeping the terms of inclusion open to changes in capability that attend aging but also keeping the deliberations about inclusion open to people of different ages with differing capacities for participation.

One challenge to such a rethinking of citizenship is the challenge many of Sen's critics have brought to his capabilities approach. That challenge is one of gaining some clarity on what values citizenship has for the very young and the very old while also developing insight into the distinct range of capabilities that matter most for participation across the life span. While we may not yet have good answers to the challenges aging poses to conceptions of citizenship, we do have within this collection of essays a debate and discussion of issues that follow from recognizing how capabilities and experiences of citizenship change over the course of people's lives as well as across generations.

Throughout this introduction I have suggested how each essay in this volume contributes individually to discussion of the intergenerational nature of citizenship. To conclude I suggest the contributions made to our rethinking of citizenship by the resonance of the essays in this volume with each other. From among the many potential themes, I have organized the essays in this volume to focus on four. The first theme, "Age, Cohort, and Generation," contains the essays of Levine, Green, Grey, and Hink, which, when read together, invite reflection on the means by which young people become citizens and continue to exercise their civic capabilities. The second theme, "Young Age, Globalization, Migration," encourages us to broaden our thinking about location and movement. Khan, Colombo, and Stoltz show us how we can, and why we should, account for age-related experiences of location and movement in our critical engagement with issues of globalization. The essays by Oda, Marback, and Youcef that are collected under the third theme, "Generational Disparities and the Clash of Culture," show us if age-related experiences matter to our accounts of what it is to be a citizen, then the relationship of one generation's experience to the experience of another generation is necessarily significant to our overall understanding of citizenship. The fourth and final theme, "Later Life, Civic Engagement, Disenfranchisement," contributes to the ongoing conversations through which we are reformulating ideas about maturity and citizenship. Sweet-Cushman and her coauthors, along with Robbins-Ruszkowski and Mann, describe why and how old age is a construct the remaking of which is central to our revisions of what it is to be a citizen.

To return to the intertwined issues of voting age and budget deficits with which I opened this introduction, our discussions need not be constrained by presumptions about the arc of citizenship from birth to death. As the essays in this volume show us, our discussions must also imagine terms for enlarging our capacity for citizenship in the face of exclusionary, age-based constraints that impact each generation differently and that aggregate over time into narrowed notions of who is and who is not a citizen. Through these discussions we put ourselves into the best position to address the consequences one generation's decisions have on another.

WORKS CITED

Aristotle. *Politics.*

Baldwin, Clive. 2008. "Narrative(,) Citizenship and Dementia: The Personal and the Political." *Journal of Aging Studies* 22 (3): 222–28.

Bartlett, Ruth, and Deborah O'Connor. 2007. "From Personhood to Citizenship: Broadening the Lens for Dementia Practice and Research." *Journal of Aging Studies* 21: 107–18.

Bitzer, Lloyd, and Edwin Black, eds. 1971. *The Prospect of Rhetoric.* Englewood Cliffs, NJ: Prentice Hall.

Booth, Wayne. 1974. *Modern Dogma and the Rhetoric of Assent.* Chicago: University of Chicago Press.

Brokaw, Tom. 1998. *The Greatest Generation.* New York: Random House.

Dewey, John. 1944. *Democracy and Education: An Introduction to the Philosophy of Education.* New York: Free Press.

Finley, M. I. 1981. "The Elderly in Classical Antiquity." *Greece and Rome,* 2nd Series, Jubilee Year, 28 (2): 156–71.

Generation Citizen. http://generationcitizen.org/.

Harris, Andy. 2013. "Reducing the Budget Deficit." http://harris.house.gov/issues/Reducing. Accessed July 25, 2013.

Kurtz, Karl T., Alan Rosenthal, and Cliff Zukin. 2003. "Citizenship: A Challenge for All Generations." National Conference of State Legislatures. September. www.cpn.org/topics/youth/k12/pdfs/NCSL_Citizenship.pdf. Accessed July 25, 2013.

Levine, Peter. 2007. *The Future of Democracy: Developing the Next Generation of American Citizens.* Medford, MA: Tufts University Press; Hanover: University Press of New England.

Plato. *Republic.* 1971. Translated with introduction and notes by Francis MacDonald Cornford. Oxford: Oxford University Press.

Rousseau, Jean-Jacques. 1979. *Émile; Or, On Education.* Introduction, notes, and translation by Allan Bloom. New York: Basic Books.

Sen, Amartya. 1993. "Capability and Well-Being." In *The Quality of Life,* edited by Martha C. Nussbaum and Amartya Sen. Oxford: Oxford University Press.

The West Wing. 2005. "A Good Day." Season 6. Episode 17. Originally aired March 2, 2005.

PART 1

···················

Age, Cohort, and Generation

I

CIVIC RENEWAL

· · · · · · · · · ·

Theory and Practice

PETER LEVINE

At its heart, civic engagement is a combination of deliberation, collaboration, and relationships. It means talking and listening, taking common action, reflecting together on what we have done together, and through that process, developing trust, loyalty, and mutual hope for other people who are not our friends or our clients but our fellow citizens.[1]

Civic engagement, so defined, is a necessary tool for addressing our most serious social problems. By engaging as citizens, we understand our situation and potential solutions, we sort out right and wrong, and we actually address or mitigate problems while building power. The benefits of civic engagement, in short, are epistemological, ethical, and pragmatic. That is the thesis of my book titled *We Are the Ones We Have Been Waiting For: The Promise of Civic Renewal in America* (Levine 2013).[2] In this chapter, I offer a skeleton of the book's argument, emphasizing a few of the points that may seem to be the most in need of defense.

EPISTEMOLOGICAL BENEFITS OF CIVIC ENGAGEMENT

You don't need to listen to other people if you are correct. The great African American antislavery campaigner Frederick Douglass refused to answer arguments in favor of slavery, understandably viewing the whole discussion as offensive (Sanders 1997, 361). Douglass was right that slavery is evil, and he had a winning strategy for ending it. He did not need to listen to slavery's apologists, except perhaps to find weaknesses in their political coalition.

But most of the time, we cannot know that we are right. Other people's information, values, strategic suggestions, and expressions of interest, identity, and desire may improve our views. So what we get out of deliberation is a chance to learn.[3] In this volume, Richard Marback gives an example from the South African freedom movement: "An older generation [of antiapartheid activists] . . . imprisoned together on Robben Island, learned from their experiences . . . a lesson in the decorum of deliberation. [Nelson] Mandela explains, 'In the struggle, Robben Island was known as the University. This is not only because of what we learned from books. . . . Robben Island was known as the University because of what we learned from each other'" (211). Discussing and exchanging ideas was not only a way for life-sentenced political prisoners to reclaim their spiritual lives, it was also an essential lesson in governing from which they drew when they became the leaders of democratic South Africa. Marback observes:

> It is obvious enough that participation in a democracy is a matter of interactions with others, interactions through which people make claims on each other, claims that are necessarily limited and limiting. In such circumstances, whatever people end up deciding together is more often than not more than an aggregation of what each individual wanted alone. Citizens of a democracy, people who rule themselves, are bound to decide together, and so they are bound to attempt to influence each other if they are to fashion just decisions from their deliberations. The important point here, which often gets overlooked, is that if people are bound to attempt to persuade each other, then people are also bound to be open to persuasion. What this means is that self-rule is a matter of deciding when and where and how to accept the persuasive influence of others. (220)

Deliberation is most fruitful for learning—and "deliberative democracy" is a most attractive and realistic political ideal—when talk is embedded in relationships among citizens and connected to their common work. One reason is motivational: we are unlikely to want to talk and listen unless doing so strengthens relationships and leads to action. Another reason is epistemic: we will not know enough to talk *well* unless we gain experience from acting together. To put this point in slogan form: deliberation without collaboration is empty, but collaboration without deliberation is blind.

People do talk, but three troublingly common phenomena are: (1) unreflective people banding together in ideologically homogeneous groups that reinforce their prejudices, (2) diverse groups who avoid any mention of public concerns or issues in order to preserve harmony,[4] and (3) discussions that neglect valid options because a premature and narrow consensus prevails. Our goal should be to move actual communities, networks, and associations in the direction of greater diversity, wider choices, and better listening (without asking them to sacrifice all their passion and solidarity).

Fortunately, people are already motivated to *work* together on public problems. Work has been linked to democracy in the United States since the Jeffersonian Republican Party exalted yeoman farmers as the ideal citizens (see Amy Grey's chapter in this volume.) Today, one quarter of the adult US population reports volunteer service within any given year; half of us say we belong to at least one voluntary association; and we give 2 percent of our disposable income to charity. People need special incentives to participate in formal deliberations, but they are already quite busy working together. But our work is often disconnected from our talk, and vice versa. Thus our goal should be to embed a greater degree of reflection and more diverse discussions in this common work. The tangible experiences that people obtain in service or in their paid work can inform their discussions, and their discussions can move them to serve or work better.

On this definition, "deliberative democracy" does not mean an array of new institutions that look rather like juries or legislatures and that produce decisions (although some of those would be valuable). It looks more like a busy, heterogeneous civil society, composed of networks and associations, in which there is a relatively high frequency of actual listening among people who do not start by agreeing. This theory blurs the distinctions between decision making and implementation, talk and work, and state and society. The goal, after all, is not to democratize those special moments when the government makes formal policy decisions—leaving bureaucrats to implement the decisions and the private sector to follow regulations and pay taxes. Rather, the goal is to democratize the whole process of shaping our common world. To that end, it is just as important to infuse talking and listening into the daily work of the public and private sectors as it is to deliberate periodically about formal policies.[5]

Imagine, for example, that neighbors love a local stream and are concerned about its health. Thanks to them, a pedestrian footbridge is built over it to provide access and to reduce car pollution. It does not matter much whether they cause this bridge to appear by voting at a town meeting to fund it, lobbying the local government to build it, persuading a private company to donate it, or physically erecting it themselves. So long as the bridge was their idea and the fruit of their collective discussion and effort, several advantages are likely to follow: (1) Because they designed it, it will meet their needs and reflect their talents. (2) Because they made it, they will feel a sense of ownership and will be motivated to protect it. (3) Because they are formally equal as neighbors—not ranked in a hierarchy—each will feel a sense of dignity and status. (4) By combining discussion with collaborative action, they will develop skills, relationships, and political power that can transfer to other settings. And (5), in shaping their public world together, they will gain a feeling of satisfaction and agency. As the philosopher Hannah Arendt wrote, the Americans of the revolutionary era "knew that public freedom meant having a share in public business, and that the activities connected with this business by no means constituted a burden but gave those who discharged them in public a feeling of happiness that they could acquire nowhere else" (Arendt 1963, 119).

None of these advantages is guaranteed, nor would I ignore arguments, tensions, and downright failures, which are common enough. But some of the benefits are, as Arendt knew, impossible to obtain in other ways. If you work in a construction company, you may take appropriate satisfaction in the bridges that you help to build, but they are generally not your ideas or your property once you are done. If the local government asks you for input, and you propose a new bridge, you may feel that your intellect and values have been respected—but the government fundamentally ran the process. It is when you have been part of initiating change in the world, combining talk with some kind of action, that you can attain full civic satisfaction or "public happiness."

The bridge is just a metaphor. We need not burden the earth with unlimited numbers of new structures. Restoring nature is equally valuable, as are various forms of nontangible and nonpermanent goods: events, performances, ideas, cultural innovations, and educated children.

MORAL BENEFITS

When we talk and work together about public concerns, a whole range of phrases and concepts is likely to emerge. Imagine, for example, that the topic is a local public school: how it is doing and what should change. In talking about their own school, parents and educators may use abstract moral concepts, like *fairness* or *freedom*. They may use concepts that have clear moral significance but controversial application in the real world. For example, *fairness* is a good thing, by definition. It is not the only good thing, and it can conflict with other goods. But the bigger challenge is to decide which outcomes and policies actually are fair.

Other concepts are easy to recognize in the world but lack clear moral significance. We either bus students to school or we do not bus them, but whether *busing* is good is debatable. (In this respect, it is a very different kind of concept from *fairness*.) Still other concepts have great moral weight and importance, but their moral significance is unclear. You can't use the word *love* seriously without making some kind of morally important point. But you need not use that word positively; sometimes love is bad, and the same is true of *freedom* and *achievement*.

People string such concepts together in various ways. They may make associations or correlations ("The girls are *doing better* than the boys in reading"). They may make causal claims ("The math and reading tests are *causing* us to overlook the arts"). They may apply general concepts to particular cases. Often they will describe individual teachers, administrators, events, classes, and facilities with richly evaluative terms, such as *beautiful* or *boring*. Frequently, they will tell stories, connecting events, individuals, groups, concepts, and intentional actions over time.

Moral concepts are indispensable. We cannot replace them with empirical information. Even if smaller class sizes do produce better test scores, that does not tell us whether our tests measure valuable things, whether the cost of more teachers would be worth the benefits, or whether the state has a right to compel people to pay taxes for education.

But moral concepts are heterogeneous. Some have clear moral significance but controversial application in the world. (*Fairness* is always good, and *murder* is always bad.) Others have clear application but unpredictable moral significance. (*Homicide* is sometimes *murder* but sometimes it is *justifiable*.) Still others are morally important but are neither predictable nor easily identified. (*Love* is sometimes good and sometimes regrettable, and whether love exists in a particular situation can be hard to say.) A method that could bring public deliberation to closure would have to organize all these concepts so that the empirically clear ones were reliably connected to the morally clear ones.

That sometimes happens. For instance, *waterboarding* either happens or it does not happen. The Bush administration's lawyers defined it in obsessive detail: "The detainee is lying on a gurney that is inclined at an angle of 10 to 15 degrees to the horizontal. . . . A cloth is placed over the detainee's face and cold water is poured on the cloth from a height of approximately 6 to 18 inches" (Office of the Principal Deputy Assistant Attorney General for John A. Rizzo [CIA] 2005, 15). Waterboarding is, in my considered opinion, an example of *torture*. Torture is legally defined as a felony, and the reason for that rule is a moral judgment that torture is always wrong (in contrast to *punishment* or *interrogation*, which may be right). Therefore, waterboarding is wrong as well as illegal. This argument may be controversial, but it is clear and it carries us all the way from the concrete reality of a scene in a CIA interrogation room to a compelling moral judgment and a demand for action. The various kinds of concepts are lined up so that moral, legal, and factual ideas fit together. There is room for debate: Is waterboarding torture? Who waterboarded whom? But the debate is easily organized and should be finite.

If all our moral thinking could work like that, we might be able to bring our discussions to a close by applying the right methods—usually a combination of moral philosophy plus empirical research. But much of our thinking cannot be so organized, because we confront moral concepts that lack consistent significance. They are either good or bad, depending on the circumstances. Nevertheless, they are morally indispensable; we cannot be good human beings and think without them. *Love* and *freedom* are two examples. To say that Romeo loves Juliet—or that Romeo is free to marry Juliet—is to say something important, but we cannot tell whether it is good or bad until we know a lot about the situation. There is no way to organize our thinking so that we can bypass these concepts with more reliable definitions and principles.

A structured moral mind might look like the blueprint of a house. At the bottom of the page would be broad, abstract, general principles: the foundation. An individual's blueprint might be built on one moral principle, such as "Do unto others as you would have them do unto you." Or it might start even lower, with a metaphysical premise, like "God exists and is good." At the top of the picture would be concrete actions, emotions, and judgments, like "I will support Principal Jones's position at the PTA meeting." In between would be ideas that combine moral principles and factual information, such as, "Every child deserves an equal education," or "Our third grade curriculum is too weak." The arrows of implication would always flow up, from the more general to the more specific.

I think most people's moral thinking is much more complex than this. Grand abstractions do influence concrete judgments, but the reverse happens as well. I may believe in mainstreaming special-needs children because of an abstract principle of justice, and that leads me to support Mrs. Jones at the PTA meeting. Or I may form an impression that Mrs. Jones is wise; she supports mainstreaming. Therefore I begin to construct a new theory of justice that justifies this policy. Or I may know an individual child whose welfare becomes an urgent matter for me; my views of Mrs. Jones, mainstreaming, and justice may all follow from that. For some people, abstract philosophical principles are lodestones. For others, concrete narratives have the same pervasive pull—for example, the Gospels, or one's own rags-to-riches story, or *Pride and Prejudice*.

We must avoid two pitfalls. One is the assumption that a general and abstract idea is always more important than a concrete and particular one.[6] There is no good reason for that premise. The concept of a moral "foundation" is just a metaphor; morality is not really a house, and it does not have to stand on something broad to be solid. Yet we must equally avoid thinking that we just possess lots of unconnected opinions, none intrinsically more important than another. For example, the following thoughts may all be correct, but they are not alike: "It is good to be punctual"; "Genocide is evil"; and "Mrs. Jones is a good principal." Not only do these statements have different levels of importance, but they also play different roles in our overall thinking.[7]

I would propose switching from the metaphor of a foundation to the metaphor of a network. In any network, some of the nodes are tied to others, producing an overall web. If moral thinking is a network, the nodes are opinions or judgments, and the ties are implications or influences. For example, I may support mainstreaming because I hold a particular view of equity; then mainstreaming and equity are two nodes, and there is an arrow between them. I may also love a particular child, and that emotion is a node that connects to disability policy in schools. A strong network does not rest on a single node, like an army that is decapitated if its generalissimo is killed. Rather, a strong network is a tight web with many pathways, so that it is possible to move from one node to another by more than one route. Yet in real, functioning networks, all the nodes do not bear equal importance. On the contrary, it is common for the most important 20 percent to carry 80 percent of the traffic—whether the network happens to be the Internet, the neural structure of the brain, or the civil society of a town (Barabasi 2003).

I suspect that a healthy moral mind is similar. It has no single foundation, and it is not driven only by abstract principles. Concrete motives, emotions, and judgments (like love or admiration for a particular individual) may loom large. Yet the whole structure is network-like, and it is possible for many kinds of nodes to influence many other kinds. My respect for Mrs. Jones may influence how I feel about the concept of the welfare state, and not just the reverse. I need many nodes and connections, each based on experience and reflection.

I do not mean to imply that a strong network map is a fully reliable sign of good moral thinking. A fascist might have an elaborate mental map composed of many different racial and national prejudices and hatreds, each supported by stories and examples, and each buttressing the others. That would be a more complex diagram than the ones possessed by mystics who prize purity and simplicity. *Purity of Heart Is to Will One Thing*, wrote Sören Kierkegaard, and the old Shaker hymn advises, "'Tis the gift to be simple, 'tis the gift to be free, 'Tis the gift to come down where we ought to be." A righteous Shaker would do more good than a sophisticated fascist. But even if complexity is not a sufficient or reliable sign of goodness, a complex map is both natural and desirable. It reflects the complexity of our moral world, it reduces the odds of becoming fanatical, it hems in self-interest, and it is resilient against radical doubt.

Four conclusions follow from this discussion. First, we should banish a certain kind of moral skepticism that arises from thinking that moral conclusions always rest on foundations, but alas there is nothing below our biggest, most abstract ideas. For example, you may believe in the Golden Rule but be unwilling to say *why* it is true. You may feel that there is no answer to the "Why?" question, and therefore morality is merely prejudice or whim. Your moral house has a foundation (the Golden Rule), but the foundation is floating in air. Fortunately, our whole morality does not rest on any such rule, nor must a principle rest on something below it to be valid. The Golden Rule is part of a durable network. It gains credibility because it seems consistent with so many other things that we come to believe. If it or any other node is knocked out of the network, the traffic can route around it.

Second, moral thinking is influenced by worldly experience, by practice and by stories, and not only by abstract theories and principles. I wrote that it "*is* influenced" by experience; I have not shown that our thinking *should* be deeply experiential. But at the least we can say that there is no reason to put abstract thinking on a pedestal, to treat is as if it were intrinsically and automatically more reliable than concrete thinking. I can be just as certain that I love my children as in the truth of the Golden Rule (Lichtenberg 1994).

The business leader who enters public debates having struggled to meet a payroll while paying taxes speaks from authentic experience. So does the soup kitchen volunteer who has faced a long line of homeless people with insufficient welfare benefits. The imprisoned elders of the antiapartheid struggle brought one kind of experience to the South African debate; the youth of Soweto brought a different perspective—and the whole movement became stronger when the two were able to learn from each other. (I draw this example from Marback's chapter in this volume.) In general, civil society functions best when many kinds of people bring their experience into a common conversation and then take what they learn from discussions back to their work, in an iterative cycle.

Third, we can handle diversity. If individuals' conclusions derived from the foundations of their thought, we would face a serious problem whenever we encountered people who had different foundations from our own. It is hard to tolerate them, let alone deliberate with them. The existence of a different foundation can even provoke vertiginous skepticism in our own minds. If my worldview rests on utilitarianism, and yours depends on faith in Jesus's resurrection, perhaps neither of us has any reason to hold our own position. But if our respective worldviews are more like networks, then they probably share many of the same nodes even though they differ in some important respects. What's more, each person's network must be slightly different from anyone else's—even his twin brother's. Thus when we categorize people into "cultures," we are crudely generalizing. There is actually one population of diverse human beings who are capable of discussing their differences even though they may not reach agreement.

Finally, expertise plays a limited role in reaching good decisions. The moral network in my mind cannot be—and should not be—radically simplified by applying any sophisticated methodology. I can learn from experts about causation and about how we should define various concepts and principles. But at the end of that process, I will still have my own moral network map, nourished by many sources other than the experts, and I will have to make decisions both alone and in dialogue with my peers. There is no substitute for thinking together about problems and solutions.

The most important intellectual resource for citizens to possess is a set of considered judgments about how public institutions should run. People can and should disagree about that question, but everyone's judgments should be based on informed and reflective thoughts about how to balance equity, participation, minority rights, voice, and efficiency; how much to reward innovation and hard work versus protecting people against failure; when to preserve traditions and when to innovate; how much to demand of individuals and when to leave them alone; what to do about the lazy and the disruptive; and how to relate to newcomers and outsiders. They should also know how to participate in constructive debates about such issues when people disagree.

To some extent, those matters can be discussed in classrooms and informed by readings. But much of our civic learning is and must be experiential. From Jefferson's idea of ward republics that would manage "the small and yet numerous and interesting concerns of the neighborhood" and give "to every citizen, personally, a part in the administration of the public affairs" (Jefferson to Samuel Kercheval, June 12, 1816) to Tocqueville's observation that juries and voluntary associations were schools of government, to John Dewey's notion of democracy as a set of learning opportunities, our wisest thinkers have always understood that the American system depends on knowledge and virtue that must be learned through experience. Our problem today is that such experience is sorely lacking.

ON CIVIC RELATIONSHIPS

Participants in politics and civic life frequently say that they prize relationships with other participants. Civic relationships generate power, they build communities, they reflect values and principles, and they are intrinsically rewarding. Very often, civic engagement is a consequence of relationships. As Jennie Sweet-Cushman and colleagues write in this volume, "Citizens are more likely to be engaged—especially in the more demanding types of participation—when they are invited to do so. The potential for being asked improves when individuals are embedded in networks where recruitment occurs" (245). In turn, taking collective action strengthens networks and relationships.

In 2001, Doble Research Associates conducted focus groups for the Kettering Foundation on the topic of testing and accountability in schools. That year, the No Child Left Behind Act codified the national movement toward regular measurement of students and schools and promised parents choices if their schools were deemed to have failed. In short, the relationship between a public institution (the school) and its citizens was defined in terms of information and consumer choice. But in the Doble focus groups, parents were highly resistant to the idea that testing would improve education. For one thing, they wanted to hold other parties accountable, starting with themselves. A Baltimore woman said, "If kids don't pass the test, is that supposed to mean that teachers are doing a lousy job? That's not right. I mean where does the support come from? You're pointing the finger at them when you should be supporting them." Another (or possibly the same) Baltimore woman explained, "When I think about accountability, I think about parents taking responsibility for supervising their children's learning and staying in touch with teachers." This respondent not only wanted to broaden responsibility but also saw it in terms of two-way communication (Doble Research Associates 2001).

Many participants wanted to know whether schools, parents, and students had the right values. They doubted that data would answer that question. And although the Doble report doesn't quite say this, I suspect they envisioned knowing individuals personally as the best way to assess their values. The focus groups turned to a discussion of relationships:

First woman: People don't know people in their communities any more.

Second woman: That's right. I was raised in an area where you knew everyone. That's just the way it was. But you don't know your neighbors anymore.

Third woman: I have neighbors that lived next door to me for nine years and they don't even wave or talk to anybody in the neighborhood. (Doble Research Associates 2001)

And so on—the conversation continued in this vein. Note that this was supposed to be a focus group about accountability in education. One Atlanta woman summed it up: "What we've got to do is develop a stronger sense of community between the schools and families in the community." I suspect that she envisioned a situation in which school staff and parents knew one another, shared fundamental values, and committed to support one another (Doble Research Associates 2001).

Similar results emerged from focus groups conducted ten years later, after American parents had gained access to a deluge of new data on test scores and school spending. According to the Public Agenda and the Kettering Foundation summary, "Typically, people know almost nothing about specific [accountability] measures, and they rarely see them as clear-cut evidence of effectiveness. For most people, the best evidence that a system is working is its responsiveness and the personal interactions they have with it. 'You can't even get a human being on the phone' is perhaps the chief indicator of failure" (Johnson, Rochkind, and DuPont 2011).

Implicitly, these citizens understand the concept of "social capital." In fact, when the Harvard political scientist Robert Putnam revived that technical term in his scholarly article titled "Bowling Alone" (1995), he hit such a chord with the public that within a year he was featured in *People* magazine. Depending on one's theoretical framework, social capital can be understood as a public good or resource that people *produce* by engaging civically, as a *measure* of their engagement, or as a *precondition* of active citizenship. In any case, it means the strength, distribution, and quality of relationships in a community. Thus in the book version, *Bowling Alone*, Putnam defines social capital thus: "Whereas physical capital refers to physical objects and human capital refers to properties of individuals [such as their own skills], social capital refers to connections among individuals—social networks and the norms of reciprocity and trustworthiness that arise from them. In that sense social capital is closely related to what some have called 'civic virtue.' The difference is that 'social capital' calls attention to the fact that civic virtue is most powerful when embedded in a dense network of reciprocal social relations" (Putnam 2000, 19). Before Putnam, the most influential scholar of social capital had been James S. Coleman, who had found that young people benefited tangibly from "the social relationships that exist among parents," the structure of those relationships, and "the parents' relations with institutions of the community" (Coleman 1988, S98, S113). If social capital predicts important outcomes, such as success in school, then enhancing relationships becomes a promising strategy. In keeping with the work of Coleman and Putnam, many grassroots organizing groups now explicitly aim to reform education by strengthening relationships that involve educators, parents, and students themselves (Warren, Mapp, and the Community Engagement and School Reform Project 2011, 26–30).

In traditional issue-based organizing, an organizer "already has an issue such as education reform in mind." He or she may believe that a particular change in official policy (such as more or less testing) would benefit the students. But "in relational organizing, an organizer builds a one-on-one relationship with individuals, trying to know everything about these leaders and members—even things that might at first seem to be irrelevant to education reform. The ideas for campaigns come about more slowly that way, but some argue that groups engaging in relational organizing can be more successful in the long term" (Su 2009, 16).

Even in Saul Alinsky's day, community organizing was explicitly concerned with creating and building relationships among diverse residents of poor neighborhoods. Alinsky, however, was skeptical about relationships with the government, which he treated mainly as a distant target of public pressure. His skepticism was evident in his writing and in his daily practices. The Industrial Areas Foundation (IAF), which he started, would never take government grants, because Alinsky wanted to retain its fundamental independence. However, in the decades after his death, the IAF has broadened its conception of relationships to include government officials and corporate executives. Carmen Sirianni and Lewis Friedland report that "IAF 'accountability nights' with public officials have undergone a significant shift, from confrontational meetings designed to embarrass and expose leaders in the 1970s to forums designed to consolidate incipient relationships in full public view" (Sirianni and Friedland 2001, 51). More generally, the modern IAF now teaches a "relational" view of organizing and of power" (Warren 2001, 177–78). Similar ideas pop up in other networks. Helen Johnson, who organizes in Mississippi, observes, "The whole idea of community organizing is really about relationship building" (in Warren, Mapp, and the Community Engagement and School Reform Project 2011, 139). Often community organizers say that when they seek new recruits, they are looking for people with a "relational" sense[8] (Szakos and Szakos 2007, xvii).

This vocabulary is not limited to community organizing but is also seen in kindred fields, such as civic engagement for youth. Sistas and Brothas United in the Bronx works on school reform but devotes time to cultivating relationships among youth and between young people and adults. Nathaniel, a teenage organizer, reports, "We have fun things. We do trips. And, on a personal level, we chill with each other. . . . We definitely relate differently." And one of his colleagues observes that these relationships have made her "able to understand people better, not only personally, but what they're trying to say when they speak at meetings" (Su 2009, 85).

Of all the strands of civic renewal, formal public deliberation seems the most remote from "relational" politics, because individuals are recruited to talk for a limited time and then disband. But participants in juries and policy deliberations often develop strong emotional ties. Further, the organizers of deliberations tend to believe that their own role is to strengthen relationships among citizens. Thus Harold Saunders describes the West Virginia Center for Public Life, which organizes statewide deliberations on public issues, as having a "relational paradigm" (Saunders 2005, 150).

For democracy, reciprocal relationships of concern and support are not sufficient. A *civic* relationship has the following specific features: (1) Unlike a family tie, a deep friendship, or a romantic partnership, a civic relationship is nonexclusive. In fact, a community's social capital is higher if a broad and dense web of relationships connects diverse residents. Citizens ought to expand and diversify their own relationships; exclusion and partiality are problematic in civic life. (2) Although civic relationships involve identities, interests, private concerns, and personal stories, they are not *simply* personal. For a relationship to be "civic," it must involve talking, listening, and working on public issues or problems. (3) A civic relationship need not be "civil," if that implies politeness and frequent expressions of positive emotions. It can rather encompass sharp disagreements. But the relationship must be predicated on the value of the other person as a fellow citizen, seen as someone who should be encouraged to participate in the common life.

YouthBuild USA can serve as a model of the core values defended here. It enlists young people who have dropped out of high school, assigns them public work (building houses for the homeless), engages them in conversation about strategy and policy, invests deeply in their individual development, and emphasizes loyal relationships among the participants and between participants and staff. Previous research has found positive effects on employment and education, and our evaluation found dramatic gains in leadership and community service (CIRCLE 2012).

As one graduate told us in an evaluation interview, "All the staff—it wasn't just one person—but they would sit down and have a one-on-one conversation with you throughout the year. It wouldn't be just a classroom, you know. If they saw you outside, they would just stop and ask you how it's going. It wasn't just asking the question, and not really caring. They actually listen, they actually respond."

PRAGMATIC BENEFITS

I delivered this chapter first as a lecture in Detroit. That was an apt and challenging location for such a discussion. Detroit faces problems of great scale and depth. The city's population is about half what it was in 1950, the exodus compelled by a permanent closing of factories and the service industries that once supported factory workers. Detroit's high school dropout rate is 75 percent. Michigan incarcerates five times as many people as it did in 1973 and spends 20 percent of its general fund revenue on prisons. Detroit's traditional industry has contributed badly to global warming (Citizens' Research Council of Michigan 2008, v). These are densely interlocked problems that involve individual behavior, governmental policy, corporate decisions, and vast forces such as deindustrialization and automation. Most Americans do not demonstrate much concern about these problems, let alone a willingness to sacrifice for solutions. Most available diagnoses and responses are controversial, raising divisive questions of ideology. No political movement or party offers plausible solutions. Several aspects of Detroit's crisis (such as massive incarceration) are not even seriously debated at the national level. A lack of civic engagement does not explain Detroit's problems, but—in the absence of national will and leadership—active citizens offer the only hope for recovery.

I don't happen to know the city, but I would always begin an analysis by looking for local assets and productive projects, rather than simply listing problems. Evidently, many important civic experiments are underway in Detroit. A group called Declare Detroit seizes the highest ground: "Cities are the greatest expression of civilization. Great cities are filled with people who exercise their talent and creativity as the catalytic risk-takers, doers, and leaders who forge the dynamic marketplace of ideas that grow places into prosperity. We are the people who believe in cities and pledge to align our energies for the benefit of Michigan's largest and most storied city, Detroit." The declaration proceeds to list twelve principles that are general and abstract, yet carefully constructed to acknowledge Detroit's assets and uniqueness as well as the need to move forward. Almost seventeen thousand people have become "friends" of Declare Detroit's Facebook page.

Organizations with manifestoes and Facebook pages are insufficient to reverse Detroit's crisis (which is also America's crisis). The question is whether they exemplify a form of civic renewal that, taken to a larger scale, *would* be sufficient. Here I sketch two examples to show why civic engagement is up to the task.

First, the proportion of residents who were engaged in various kinds of civic work predicted the change in unemployment rates in American states and large cities during and after the Great Recession of 2008. After accounting for the major economic factors thought to influence unemployment (demographics, dependence on the oil and gas industries, housing-price inflation, and residential mobility), civic engagement emerged as a stronger predictor of communities' resilience against unemployment.[9]

No statistical model based on cross-sectional survey data can demonstrate causality, even if it incorporates many control variables. It is entirely possible that civic engagement is not the reason that some states and cities weathered the recession well. Yet the hypothesis that civic engagement improves labor markets is quite plausible.

For one thing, participation in civil society can develop skills, confidence, and habits that make individuals employable and strengthen the networks that help them to find jobs.[10] Middle school and high school students who participate in service learning during class or who serve in school government succeed much better academically than peers with similar backgrounds (Dávila and Mora 2007). Many individuals owe their employment to fellow members of social or civic groups or have learned their most marketable skills in national and volunteer service.

Furthermore, citizens who participate in civil society expand and strengthen social networks in their communities. Individuals often find their jobs through networks, especially ones that are diverse.[11]

Meanwhile, participation in civil society spreads information. Attending meetings, working with neighbors on community problems, volunteering, and receiving newsletters from nonprofit organizations are examples of valuable ways of learning about local issues and opportunities. In Chicago neighborhoods, local and frequent interactions within neighborhoods spread information about job openings (Topa 2001). It seems plausible that in communities with more civic engagement, information flows better, and hence it is easier for individuals to find jobs or educational programs, for businesses to find partners and employees, and for citizens to hold government accountable.

Participation in civil society is also strongly correlated with trust in other people. Most studies find that trusting other people encourages individuals to join groups, and participating in groups builds trust (Sønderskov 2010). In turn, trust is a powerful predictor of economic success because people who trust are more likely to enter contracts and business partnerships, and because confidence in others is a precondition for investing and hiring (Fukuyama 1995).

Yet another potential explanation for the link between civic engagement and employment involves the government. Communities and political jurisdictions with stronger civil societies are more likely to be governed well. Active and organized citizens can demand and promote good governance and serve as partners to government in addressing public problems. Thus states with more civic engagement have much higher performing public schools, regardless of the states' demographics, spending, and class sizes (Putman 2001). Italian regions with stronger civil societies handled an increase in responsibilities much better than those with weaker civil societies (Putman 1993). American cities with stronger civic organizations are better able to make wise but difficult policy decisions (Berry, Portney, and Thomson 1993). Cities are also more likely to have adopted environmental sustainability policies if they have more civic participation in the form of petitions, demonstrations, and membership in reform groups and civic associations (Portney and Berry 2010). In the current economic crisis, governments that benefit from better civic engagement may be able to reduce the scale of unemployment through more efficient and equitable policies.

Finally, civic engagement can encourage people to feel attached to their communities (Knight Foundation and Gallup Survey 2010). The proportion of people who report being attached to the places they live predicts economic growth. Perhaps liking and caring about where one lives increases the odds that one will invest, spend, and hire there. A related hypothesis holds that the strength of local civic infrastructure, such as the availability of civically committed religious congregations, and the availability of local associations and informal venues such as barber shops, boosts attachment and investment in a community, which in turn increases civic engagement and local economic investment.[12]

The statistics cited above do not suggest that Detroit lost more than half of its job base because citizens were insufficiently engaged in civil society. Automation and the shift of factory jobs to the developing world are responsible for that trend. However, given two cities in similar economic circumstances, the one with more civic engagement will prove more resilient and more likely to recover from an economic crisis.

Unemployment—whether acute during a recession or inexorably chronic in cities like Detroit—is one example of a wicked problem. Civic engagement seems to offer a solution. Another example is the incarceration crisis.[13] At first glance, the huge number of prison sentences seems to be the *result* of citizen action. Draconian sentencing laws often begin with referenda or with legislative votes that respond to popular pressure. The phrases "populist punitiveness" and "penal populism" are used to describe an international phenomenon: politicians seeking approval by posing as tough on crime and denouncing lawyers and other elites who would coddle or protect criminals.[14]

In fact, accumulated evidence suggests that when citizens deliberate, they arrive at merciful or nuanced decisions. For instance, when judges disagree with jury verdicts, it is generally because they think the jury was too lenient.[15] Capital punishment is a popular policy in the United States, yet juries reach capital verdicts in very few cases (Dzur 2012, 60). When a random sample of British citizens deliberated about criminal justice policy, the participants shifted markedly against the proposition that incarceration reduces crime and became much more protective of defendants' rights (Fishkin 1995, 215–16).

But public deliberation is now rare within the criminal justice system. The severe and inflexible penalties referenda require strongly encourage plea bargaining, which is one reason that the proportion of felony cases that go to trial has dropped from one in twelve during the 1970s to just one in forty recently (Oppel 2011). Ninety-seven percent of criminal convictions in the federal system and 94 percent in the state systems result from plea bargains and not trials (*Missouri v. Freye* 2011, 2). The people (using the ballot box) have chosen to remove the people (convened as jurors) from criminal law.

Why would they do that? In 1964, three-quarters of Americans said they generally trusted the government and 53.4 percent said they generally trusted other people. By 2010, trust in government was down to 30.4 percent, and trust in other people had fallen to 34.6 percent, both having lost ground steadily over the decades.[16] Distrust of people of color, especially young African American men, is particularly acute and directly relevant to the incarceration problem. (In fact, "distrust" is much too soft a word for public attitudes toward young black people.) If we trust the government but not our fellow citizens, we might be willing to let judges set sentences. If we trust our fellow Americans but not the government, we would be less eager to incarcerate citizens and more protective of the jury system. Trusting neither, we are tempted to require the state to put other people in jail without trials.

A minimum sentencing law is a simple, understandable rule imposed on a complex system. It is a classic example of the prevailing view of accountability as external and driven by numbers, rather than deliberative and determined by arguments. It transforms criminal cases from transparent public events, full of explicit moral rhetoric and judgment, into bargaining sessions managed behind the scenes by lawyers. That is a recipe for even lower trust, which encourages even more Draconian sentencing laws. The resulting crisis of incarceration is largely invisible because citizens do not serve on juries or even read about jury trials. Even though criminal justice is officially public business and transparent (in the sense that one has a right to obtain court records), it rarely impinges on public consciousness.

In Oklahoma in the 1990s, the League of Women Voters saw the state's incarceration rate—the third highest in the nation—as a serious public problem. They also recognized that politicians were afraid of any reforms that could be depicted as weak on crime. So they organized a series of meetings across the state that involved nearly one thousand citizens who held diverse views. Many participants expressed anger about the costs of incarceration and favored prevention and rehabilitation. Politicians and reporters attended these meetings and witnessed the prevailing mood, which changed their estimate of what would be popular. The league then recruited participants to advocate a bill that would reduce certain felonies to misdemeanors while devolving some authority over sentencing to "community boards with citizen representation." The bill passed by wide margins. It reflected deliberative public opinion, and it created a mechanism for the kind of sustained public engagement in criminal justice that might restore public trust (Leighninger 2006, 127–34).

The sentencing reform legislation was later repealed after lobbying by law enforcement officials. The state chose instead to reduce costs by expanding private, for-profit prisons (Campbell 2011). In 2008, companies that run such prisons spent almost $69,000 on Oklahoma state political campaigns and received almost $77 million in state funding; the state even imported prisoners from Arizona (Oklahoma Department of Corrections Annual Report 2009).

This chapter of the Oklahoma story is a reminder—as if one were needed—that engaged citizens face formidable enemies and need political reform to prevail. Nevertheless, community sentencing boards continue to handle nonviolent cases in most Oklahoma counties. The state's Department of Corrections argues that these boards save money and reduce incarceration (Lawmaster and Neumann 2009, 9–12).

Oklahoma's community boards resemble other widespread initiatives in which the justice system engages lay citizens. "Problem-solving courts" specialize in particular issues, such as drugs or domestic violence. The judges work with social workers and representatives of community groups to develop comprehensive solutions to local problems. In one impressive example, a housing court judge worked with a broad-based neighborhood group to fight urban blight and abandonment in Buffalo, New York. The judge used his power to fine landlords who violated the housing code, but he would also accept improvements satisfactory to the neighborhood activists. The activists would observe and report housing violations, and when the court seized properties, they would take them over and rehabilitate them. The court and the neighborhood group chose their targets selectively to redevelop the community block by block and were able to raise the value of privately owned homes tenfold, essentially creating wealth for long-term residents (Oakerson and Clifton 2011).[17]

In youth courts, panels of teenagers are empowered to sentence their peers for minor offences. In restorative justice programs, violators negotiate agreements with representatives of their community to repair the harms their actions have caused (National Association of Youth Courts n.d.; Wolf 2007). Modern restorative justice was first proposed by outsiders to the legal system (Mennonite activists and others), but it has grown thanks to the support of prosecutors and corrections officials who see substantial cost savings and much higher satisfaction among victims and other residents (Dzur 2012, 175–79). Like youth courts, restorative justice has shown promising effects on recidivism. These reforms also engage citizens in deliberations within the legal system.

By expanding such opportunities, we may be able to change the national conversation about crime and punishment (Dzur 2012, 205, 252). Restorative justice tends to satisfy both victims and offenders (O'Hear 2009, 128).[18] Jurors who successfully reach verdicts in conventional trials hold more favorable views of political institutions (including the jury trial itself), trust their fellow citizens more, and are more likely to vote in regular elections compared to citizens who are not randomly selected for jury service or whose trials end without verdicts (Gastil et al. 2010). That finding suggests that by making traditional juries (or modern alternatives such as restorative justice programs) more common and more prominent in the public discourse, we could raise public trust in courts and reduce the demand for Draconian sentencing. If alienation from institutions and from our fellow citizens is a root cause of the incarceration epidemic, these strategies offer the best hope for a solution.

CONCLUSION

This chapter began with an ethical framework that may seem idealistic and limited to exemplary groups of volunteers who work at small scales. I have ended by referring to two vast social problems. There is not room here to make the full case that civic engagement is the best path to addressing such problems, but I do argue that in the book *We Are the Ones We Have Been Waiting For*. The premise is not that all social problems under all circumstances respond to civic engagement, but that our particular condition—characterized by sclerotic institutions, corrupt government, weak political movements, a polarized public, and intractable issues—creates a particular need for citizens to deliberate, collaborate, and create horizontal relationships.

That means that you and I can contribute to addressing our worst crises by deliberating, collaborating, and forming civic relationships. But it is not enough for individuals to try to participate in these ways. Major institutions are set up to ignore and even frustrate civic engagement. Thus our task is not only to engage as citizens but also to work together to reform rules, incentives, and ways of thinking so that civic work becomes much more common and influential.

NOTES

1. I take a different perspective on citizenship from the state-centered view, which is exemplified by the first sentence of Saeed Khan's chapter in this volume: "Citizenship is based on the mutual exchange of rights and responsibilities between the state and the citizen." I see the relations among people as primary; the state is a tool that they may (or may not) decide to use for their purposes. Meanwhile, the state is actually a collection of people who are also citizens, in the sense that they ought to deliberate, collaborate, and form relationships with fellow members of their community.
2. Portions of this chapter are adopted from that book.
3. For evidence that people do learn when they deliberate, see, e.g., Fishkin 1995, 161–68.

4. Eliasoph 1998; Mutz 2006. I am using a framework here that derives (with important modifications) from Jürgen Habermas's threefold distinction: lifeworld, system, and public sphere. The "lifeworld," reflected in ordinary conversation among friends and family, is natural and authentic but does not necessarily connect to broad public issues. The "system" refers to strategic communications by organizations that have fixed interests and goals, especially corporations and government agencies. The "public sphere" is the metaphorical space in which citizens emerge from their diverse lifeworlds to discuss public issues, creating reasoned public opinion that is a counterforce to the system. I hold that this theory is too cognitive; the public sphere should not be understood primarily as a place for talking and forming public opinion because most people lack motivation for mere talk, and talk alone is not adequately informed by experience. The public sphere should rather be a place of talk and work. Compare a somewhat similar critique in Dzur 2008, 35–36.

5. I draw here on Briggs 2008.

6. Readers with some background in modern Anglophone moral philosophy may recognize John Rawls's concept of reflective equilibrium here. But I am expanding that idea dramatically. Rawls (1971, 18) envisions a binary dialogue between fundamental principles and concrete situations. I think there can be a reflective equilibrium between any two concrete or abstract moral ideas in a person's brain.

7. I address this issue in more technical detail in Levine 2009, 73–83.

8. From the introduction by Harry C. Boyte.

9. Initial results were published in a report by CIRCLE (2011).

10. By themselves, community service and service-learning programs enroll too few people to explain the link between social capital and employment at the state level, but they provide interesting cases for understanding causal mechanisms. National service participation has been found to boost "basic work skills, including gathering and analyzing information, motivating coworkers, and managing time" (Jastrzab et al. 2004).

11. Mark Granovetter's seminal 1973 article asserted that people find jobs through contacts, and especially through their "weak ties"—individuals whom they know but who are not especially important to them. See Granovetter 1973, 1360–80. More recent studies have confirmed that workers are more likely to find appropriate jobs quickly if they have large and diverse networks (Franzen and Hangartner 2006; Stone, Gray, and Hughes 2003; Grenier, Li, and Xue 2009).

12. See, for example, Irwin et al. 2004; Tolbert et al. 2002.

13. This section is indebted to Albert Dzur (2012).

14. Freiberg and Gelb (2008) provides an overview.

15. The seminal study is Kalven and Zeisel 1966, but confirmation comes from Eisenberg et al. 2004.

16. American National Election Studies data, analyzed by the author.

17. Manuscript under review, manuscript cited by permission. I recognize the significant danger of corruption (not reflected in this case), so oversight would be important.

18. O'Hear argues that problem-solving drug courts do not reduce racial disparities but that restorative justice would build "constructive citizen-police interactions," "stronger relationships among community members," and "the sort of social capital that permits communities to address their own problems more effectively (2009, 137).

WORKS CITED

Arendt, Hannah. 1963. *On Revolution*. London: Penguin.

Barabasi, Albert-Laszlo. 2003. *Linked: How Everything Is Connected to Everything Else and What It Means*. New York: Plume.

Berry, Jeffrey M., Kent E. Portney, and Kenneth Thomson. 1993. *The Rebirth of Urban Democracy*. Washington, DC: Brookings Institution.

Briggs, Xavier de Souza. 2008. *Democracy as Problem Solving: Civic Capacity in Communities across the Globe*. Cambridge, MA: MIT Press.

Campbell, Jim. 2011. "Oklahoma Prison Sentencing Reform Has Factious History." *Tulsa World*, February 14.

CIRCLE (Center for Information and Research on Civic Learning and Engagement). 2011. *Civic Health and Unemployment: Can Engagement Strengthen the Economy?* Medford, MA: CIRCLE.

———. 2012. *Pathways into Leadership: A Study of YouthBuild Graduates*. Medford, MA: CIRCLE.

Citizens' Research Council of Michigan. 2008. Growth in Michigan's Corrections System: Historical and Comparative Perspectives, Report 350 (June).

Coleman, James S. 1988. "Social Capital in the Creation of Human Capital." *American Journal of Sociology* 94, supplement: S98, S113.

Dávila, Alberto, and Marie T. Mora. 2007. "Civic Engagement and High School Academic Progress: An Analysis Using NELS Data." CIRCLE Working Paper 52.

Doble Research Associates. 2001. *Reframing "Accountability": The Public's Terms*. Report to the Kettering Foundation, Dayton, OH.

Dzur, Albert. 2008. *Democratic Professionalism: Citizen Participation and the Reconstruction of Professional Ethics, Identity, and Practice*. University Park: Pennsylvania State University Press.

———. 2012. *Punishment, Participatory Democracy, and the Jury*. New York: Oxford University Press.

Eisenberg, Theodore, Paula L. Hannaford-Agor, Valerie P. Hans, Nicole L. Mott, G. Thomas Munsterman, Stewart J. Schwab, and Martin T. Wells. 2004. "Judge-Jury Agreement in Criminal Cases: A Partial Replication of Kalven and Zeisel's *The American Jury*." Cornell Law School Research Paper No. 04-025.

Eliasoph, Nina S. 1998. *Avoiding Politics: How Americans Produce Apathy in Everyday Life*. Cambridge: Cambridge University Press.

Fishkin, James S. 1995. *The Voice of the People: Public Opinion and Democracy*. New Haven, CT: Yale University Press.

Franzen, A., and D. Hangartner. 2006. "Social Networks and Labour Market Outcomes: The Nonmonetary Benefits of Social Capital." *European Sociological Review* 22 (4): 353–68.

Freiberg, Arie, and Karen Gelb, eds. 2008. *Penal Populism, Sentencing Councils, and Sentencing Policy*. Sydney, Australia: Hawkins Press.

Fukuyama, Francis. 1995. *Trust: Social Virtues and the Creation of Prosperity*. New York: Free Press.

Gastil, John, E., Pierre Deess, Philip J. Weiser, Cindy Simmons, E. Pierre Deess, Philip J. Weiser, and Cindy Simmons. 2010. *The Jury and Democracy: How Jury Deliberation Promotes Civic Engagement and Political Participation*. New York: Oxford University Press.

Granovetter, Mark S. 1973. "The Strength of Weak Ties." *American Journal of Sociology* 78 (6): 1360–80.

Grenier, Gilles, Li Li, and Li Xue. 2009. "Duration of Access of Canadian Immigrants to the First Job in Intended Occupation." Working Paper 0908E. University of Ottawa, Department of Economics.

Grey, Amy. 2015. "'The Spectacle of a Farmer Bending Over a Washtub': Gendered Labor in the Preparation for American-Indian Citizenship in Nineteenth-Century Arizona." In *Generations: Rethinking Age and Citizenship*, edited by Richard Marback. Detroit: Wayne State University Press.

Irwin, M., T. Blanchard, C. Tolbert, A. Nucci, and T. Lyson. 2004. "Why People Stay: The Impact of Community Context on Nonmigration in the USA." *Population* 59 (5): 567–92.

Jastrzab, JoAnn, Leanne Giordono, Anne Chase, Jesse Valente, Anne Hazlett, Richard LaRock Jr., and Derrick James. 2004. "Serving Country and Community: A Longitudinal Study of Service in AmeriCorps." Corporation for National and Community Service Office of Research and Policy Development. Abt Associates, Cambridge, MA.

Jefferson, Thomas. 1816. Letter to Samuel Kercheval. June 12. http://teachingamericanhistory.org/library/document/letter-to-samuel-kercheval/.

Johnson, Jean, Jonathan Rochkind, and Samantha DuPont. 2011. "Don't Count Us Out: How an Overreliance on Accountability Could Undermine the Public's Confidence in Schools, Business, Government, and More." A Report from Public Agenda and the Kettering Foundation. http://publicagenda.org/dont-count-us-out.

Kalven, Harry, Jr., and Hans Zeisel. 1966. *The American Jury*. Boston: Little, Brown.

Knight Foundation and Gallup Survey. 2010. Soul of the Community survey. www.soulofthecommunity.org.

Lawmaster, Becky, and Sharon Neumann. 2009. "Community Sentencing: The Department's 'cents-able' Alternative to Incarceration." *Inside Corrections*, January: 9–12. www.doc.state.ok.us/.

Leighninger, Matt. 2006. *The Next Form of Democracy: How Expert Rule Is Giving Way to Shared Governance . . . and Why Politics Will Never Be the Same.* Nashville: Vanderbilt University Press.

Levine, Peter. 2009. *Reforming the Humanities: Literature and Ethics from Dante through Modern Times.* New York: Palgrave Macmillan, 73–83.

———. 2013. *We Are the Ones We Have Been Waiting For: The Promise of Civic Renewal in America.* Oxford: Oxford University Press.

Lichtenberg, Judith. 1994. "Moral Certainty." *Philosophy* 69 (268): 181–204.

Marback, Richard. 2015. "The Challenge of ANC Youth from the Soweto Uprising to Julius Malema." In *Generations: Rethinking Age and Citizenship*, edited by Richard Marback. Detroit: Wayne State University Press.

Missouri v. Freye. 2011. Supreme Court Syllabus. Supreme Court, no. 10-444.

Mutz, Diana. 2006. *Hearing the Other Side: Deliberative versus Participatory Democracy.* Cambridge: Cambridge University Press.

National Association of Youth Courts website. N.d. www.youthcourt.net.

Oakerson, Ronald J., and Jeremy D. W. Clifton. 2011. "Neighborhood Decline as a Tragedy of the Commons: Conditions of Neighborhood Turnaround on Buffalo's West Side." The Vincent and Elinor Ostrom Workshop in Political Theory and Policy Analysis Working Paper W11-26. Indiana University.

O'Hear, Michael. 2009. "Rethinking Drug Courts: Restorative Justice as Response to Racial Injustice." *Stanford Law and Policy Review* 20 (9): 128, 137.

Oklahoma Department of Corrections Annual Report. 2009. www.doc.state. ok.us; National Institute on Money in State Politics, table at www.followthemoney.org/database/IndustryTotals.phtml?f=0&s=OK&b[]=G7000.

Office of the Principal Deputy Assistant Attorney General for John A. Rizzo (CIA). 2005. May 10, p. 15. www.fas.org/irp/agency/doj/olc/techniques.pdf.

Oppel, Richard A., Jr. 2011. "Sentencing Shift Gives New Leverage to Prosecutors." *New York Times*, September 25. www.nytimes.com/2011/09/26/us/tough-sentences-help-prosecutors-push-for-plea-bargains.html?pagewanted=all.

Portney, Kent E., and Jeffrey M. Berry. 2010. "Participation and the Pursuit of Sustainability in U.S. Cities." *Urban Affairs Review* 46 (1): 119–39.

Putnam, Robert D. 1993. *Making Democracy Work: Civic Traditions in Modern Italy*. Princeton, NJ: Princeton University Press.

———. 2000. *Bowling Alone: The Collapse and Revival of American Community*. New York: Simon and Shuster, 19.

———. 2001. "Community-Based Social Capital and Educational Performance." In *Making Good Citizens: Education and Civil Society*, edited by Diane Ravitch and Joseph P. Viteritti, 58–95. New Haven, CT: Yale University Press.

Rawls, John. 1971. *A Theory of Justice*. Cambridge, MA: Belknap Press of Harvard University Press.

Sanders, Lynn M. 1997. "Against Deliberation." *Political Theory* 25 (3): 347–76.

Saunders, Harold H. 2005. *Politics Is about Relationships: A Blueprint for the Citizens' Century*. New York: Palgrave.

Sirianni, Carmen, and Lewis Friedland. 2001. *Civic Innovation in America: Community Empowerment, Public Policy, and the Movement for Civic Renewal*. Berkeley: University of California Press.

Sønderskov, K. M. 2010. "Does Generalized Social Trust Lead to Associational Membership? Unravelling a Bowl of Well-Tossed Spaghetti." *European Sociological Review* 27 (4): 419–34.

Stone, W., M. Gray, and J. Hughes. 2003. "Social Capital at Work: How Family, Friends, and Civic Ties Relate to Labour Market Outcomes." Australian Institute of Family Studies Research Paper No. 31.

Su, Celina. 2009. *Streetwise for Book Smarts: Grassroots Organizing and Education Reform in the Bronx*. Ithaca, NY: Cornell University Press.

Sweet-Cushman, Jennie, Mary Herring, Lisa J. Ficker, Cathy Lysack, Marc W. Kruman, and Peter A. Lichtenberg. 2015. "Is Participation Decline Inevitable as Generations Age? Insights from African American Elders." In *Generations: Rethinking Age and Citizenship*, edited by Richard Marback. Detroit: Wayne State University Press.

Szakos, Kristin Layng, and Joe Szakos, eds. 2007. *We Make Change: Community Organizers Talk about What They Do—And Why*. Nashville: Vanderbilt University Press.

Tolbert, C. M., M. D. Irwin, T. A. Lyson, and A. R. Nucci. 2002. "Civic Community in Small-Town America: How Civic Welfare Is Influenced by Local Capitalism and Civic Engagement." *Rural Sociology* 67 (1): 90–113.

Topa, Giorgio. 2001. "Social Interactions, Local Spillovers, and Unemployment." *Review of Economic Studies* 68 (2): 261–95.

Warren, Mark R. 2001. "Power and Conflict in Social Capital: Community Organizing and Urban Policy." In *Beyond Tocqueville: Civic Society and the Social Capital Debate in Comparative Perspective*, edited by Bob Edwards, Michael W. Foley, and Mario Diani, 169–82. Medford, MA: Tufts University Press.

Warren, Mark R., Karen L. Mapp, and the Community Engagement and School Reform Project. 2011. *A Match on Dry Grass: Community Organizing as a Catalyst for School Reform*. New York: Oxford University Press.

Wolf, Robert A. 2007. "Principles of Problem-Solving Justice." Bureau of Justice Assistance, Center for Court Innovation. www.courtinnovation.org/

2

"APPRECIATION AND ELEVATION OF LABOR"

· · · · · · · · · ·

Working-Class Youth and Middle-Class Citizenship

JANE FIEGEN GREEN

In July 1840, Orestes Brownson, the editor of the *Boston Quarterly Review*, published an attack on the factory labor system by decrying the degraded condition of the industry's female workforce. Bright, healthy young women came from the farms of New Hampshire, Vermont, and Maine, after which "few of them ever marry; fewer still ever return to their native places with reputations unimpaired." As a mark of disgrace upon factory managers and owners, Brownson claimed that working in a textile factory was "almost enough to damn to infamy the most worthy and virtuous girl" (Brownson 1840). Harriet Farley, a twenty-three-year-old textile worker who contributed to the community's literary magazine, took offense at the portrayal of women as victims of capitalism rather than autonomous economic agents. In an article in the *Lowell Offering*, she wrote that women worked "under restraints, but they are voluntarily assumed; and we are at liberty to withdraw from them, whenever they become galling or irksome." Young women came to Lowell because "the avails of factory labor are now greater than those of many domestics, seamstresses, and school-teachers." They made a rational choice "and strange would it be, if in money-loving New England, one of the most lucrative female employments should be rejected because it is toilsome, or because some people are prejudiced against it." Farley firmly stated: "Yankee girls have too much *independence* for *that*" (Farley 1840).

Inspired by the *Lowell Offering*, a group of young men in Boston started a similar literary magazine in 1845, called the *Mechanic Apprentice*, to uplift youth laborers. Urban apprentices needed to account for their age and subordinate position before asserting opinions about "the wrongs of Labor, and the means of its elevation." The *Apprentice* recognized that many political leaders considered labor relations a "subject in which persons of our time of life can have no immediate interest." However, because they lived in a democratic society that expanded suffrage to all white men, "the period will so soon arrive when we may be called upon to *act*." The apprentice writers claimed authority not on account of their current status, but based on their emerging autonomy and self-ownership. The publication claimed apprentices' right to express independent opinions as an aspect of their path toward full maturity and citizenship.[1]

As they struggled to come of age while making a living in early industrial New England, mill operatives and apprentices encountered the hegemonic script of American citizenship. Access to political rights and civic participation depended on fulfilling narrow, and closely guarded, ideals of whiteness, masculinity, and wealth. Like other essays in this section, this project demonstrates the fluid nature of citizenship through the experiences of young people who failed to meet dominant standards of American nationhood and found themselves relegated to an intergenerational cohort of second-class citizens. Amy Grey's analysis of American Indian education shows how reformers viewed training in gender-specific work as the best way to uplift the degraded economic and political status of an "uncivilized" and subordinate people. John Hink's account of transnational custody cases shows how American institutions promoted a hegemonic model of citizenship over children in order to gain leverage in a geopolitical conflict. This essay shows how occupation and class status pushed some young people outside of the dominant model of citizenship, and how they fought to get it back. The ideal of maturity—the social construction of individuals' competence and self-ownership in relation to their chronological age—masked the class-based hierarchy of civic participation behind an ideology of equality and merit. Like Grey, I show how young people challenged and adapted the dominant paradigm to meet their own needs. Although the rhetoric of maturity allowed New England's political and economic leaders to ignore growing economic inequality, it also gave working-class youth an avenue to circumvent the middle-class standards of citizenship by portraying themselves as responsible and respectable members of the community.

Many scholars of citizenship in the United States overlook age as a category of analysis because it is a temporary experience of subordination that rarely supersedes exclusions based on gender, race, or class.[2] However, maturity was the foundation for justifying many forms of hierarchy in postrevolutionary America (Brewer 2005, 338–67). Examining the legal and social progression to adulthood allows scholars to see the limits and opportunities of citizenship. Looking beyond formal practices such as property ownership, suffrage, and direct political engagement is especially important for understanding the lives of the legally disempowered because "other cultural sources of selfhood and belonging become especially important for those marginalized or subordinated . . . by law" (Welke 2010, 6). This chapter uses maturity to understand the criteria that qualified individuals for political influence because the terms that defined eligibility for citizenship—self-ownership, character, and respectability—were central elements in the coming-of-age process in the early republic. Although overshadowed by race, class, and gender, maturity helped set the boundaries of civic participation. A focus on age shifts the question from *whether* a person was considered a citizen to *how* he or she came to be regarded as worthy of participating in American society. This chapter reconceptualizes the criteria for citizenship as the ability to marshal cultural resources to exert *social authority*—the recognition of an individual's competence to contribute to the community.[3] Examining civic reputation through the experiences of young people reorients the study of citizenship from abstract legal categories and formal political rights toward a broader process of achieving adulthood.

Understanding citizenship as the capacity to exert authority through claims to maturity brings a valuable perspective to scholars across disciplines, covering contexts from active political engagement by the elderly to the ethics of deliberative democracy. Tamara Mann, Jennie Sweet-Cushman, and Jessica Robbins-Ruszkowski identify the issues of disability, dependence, and perceived "backwardness" that stand as barriers to participation by older citizens. When citizenship is understood as the epitome of responsible, active, and autonomous personhood, we recognize how age can resign older individuals to second-class status through beliefs about the "natural" decline of physical, cognitive, and social capacity. Participation in civic and political discourse throughout the life course requires a public reputation for dignity, self-ownership, and intellect. The seemingly egalitarian goals of deliberative democracy, described here by Peter Levine, depend on a shared understanding of the basic levels of competence, intelligence, and foresight required to participate in this deliberative process. We can improve access to citizenship if we understand not only the formal barriers to political rights but also the de facto qualifications that recode political exclusion through seemingly natural capacities related to maturity.

———

First published in October 1840, the *Lowell Offering* was designed as a "Repository of original articles on various subjects, written by Factory Operatives."[4] Articles came from the women's "Improvement Circle," a self-culture project where operatives shared written compositions. By creating a literary publication solely through the work of female operatives, the contributors hoped to achieve respectability in the face of public criticism through their efforts "to encourage the cultivation of talent . . . and to correct an erroneous idea which generally prevails in relation to the intelligence of persons employed in the Mills."[5] Although much of the *Offering* featured odes to pastoral life, familial love, or religious sentiment—subjects that associated the authors with the domestic sphere rather than the industrial environment—the publication also served as a platform for young operatives to participate in public debates about capitalist labor relations in antebellum New England.

The *Lowell Offering* was not the only publication by working-class youth in 1840s New England. In an environment that threatened their path to adulthood, a group of male apprentices in Boston formed their own magazine, the *Mechanic Apprentice*. The magazine, which published its first issue in May 1845, was organized for "the purpose of mutual improvement, for the purpose of acquiring knowledge" and "of cultivating the social and moral faculties."[6] The publication grew out of the Elocution Class offered by the Mechanic Apprentices' Library Association (MALA). Membership in the MALA was restricted to "minors only"—meaning young men under age twenty-one—which made the unique needs of youth central to the group's operations. The editors used literary contributions from apprentices to demonstrate the intellectual capacity of young mechanics. They took pride in being "written, edited, printed, and published, solely by apprentices, members of the Mechanic Apprentices' Library Association."[7] By highlighting their labor identity, the *Apprentice* authors, like those of the *Lowell Offering*, hoped to repair their reputations with the refinement of their literary productions.

Although targeting different audiences, the *Lowell Offering* and the *Mechanic Apprentice* shared a desire to promote the social authority of both men and women engaged in manual labor. A short story published in the *Offering* praised the literary compositions of young apprentices by having the young protagonist rejoice in being "a daughter of New England, where I may claim as countrymen, these noble-spirited youths."[8] The editors of the *Apprentice* referred to the *Offering* as "our worthy contemporary." Their discussions of the *Offering* and of the female editors avoided paternalism or expectations that young women should be working in the home. They saw female operatives as "laboring on in the same good cause . . . in the same sphere, and on the same footing."[9] Drawing together an intergenerational cohort based on occupation and class, these young authors called upon "all, then, who are engaged in a laborious calling, whether by the loom of the factory or the bench of the workshop, strive to this end, the proper appreciation and elevation of labor."[10] Although the young apprentices felt "sincere and heartfelt sympathy with" female workers, they also claimed to "value their good opinion."[11] Working-class youth faced obstacles to adulthood and citizenship as their labor failed to receive the markers of maturity and competence prized by the middle-class model of citizenship. The middle-class ideal of citizenship depended on fulfilling gender-based labor roles, but young people often redefined these roles to meet their own ends.

The *Lowell Offering* and the *Mechanic Apprentice* gave young workers a public voice at a time of dramatic change in the organization of labor and the process of coming of age. As young women's traditional productive tasks moved outside of the home, their need to find paid employment threatened their standing as respectable women. The young women who came to work in the textile factories of Lowell, Massachusetts, in the 1820s had assurances that they would preserve their middling status by earning comparatively high wages, living in the protected environment of the company boardinghouse, and receiving access to education and civic culture. Despite their manual labor, factory operatives aspired to fulfill the expectations of the "cult of domesticity," which uplifted women's social authority through their non-economic activities within the domestic sphere.[12] By the mid-1830s a combination of longer hours, lower wages, and a worsening physical environment convinced some workers that the mills blocked women's opportunity to take their place within the middle class as the community's moral guardians and protectors of hearth and home.[13]

The distance between middle-class civic roles and manual labor conditions also threatened the adulthood of young male laborers. Apprenticeship declined in the nineteenth century and was supplanted by wage labor based on an economic relationship between employer and worker rather than an educative relationship between master and child. Instead of training to become master craftsmen, young men performed increasingly mundane, specialized tasks with little connection to the larger manufacturing process. Due to this de-skilling, fewer young artisans had the knowledge or the capital to become masters on their own. Yet the North's celebration of "free labor ideology" promised every young man of virtue and talent economic independence through his ability to contract in the labor market (Foner 1970). The ideal of self-ownership was supposed to democratize men's political participation by basing male citizenship on the ownership of one's own labor—wage based or otherwise. Despite rhetoric that seemed to unite men into a civic body based on independence and individual labor, young men who remained in menial positions within the early industrial economy failed to achieve the public reputation and material foundation necessary for political standing.[14]

The *Lowell Offering* and the *Mechanic Apprentice* balanced their critiques of working conditions and labor exploitation with support for the ideal of domesticity and free labor. Their working-class authors reconciled the divergent paths to adulthood by confronting the pillars of middle-class identity and demonstrating that laboring youth could achieve the same standard of respectability and authority as their privileged peers. They presented their periodicals and other forms of mutual improvement as alternatives to the education colleges, seminaries, and academies offered. They developed an ideology of labor dignity that gave working-class youth a place within America's national development and portrayed working-class exploitation as a betrayal of the nation's promise of meritocracy, a core middle-class value. Both publications supported dominant narratives of gender roles while adapting the constructions of masculinity and femininity to fit working-class conditions. And both magazines participated in antislavery debates, demonstrating their ability to contribute to a middle-class moral crusade. Through their writings, authors in the *Lowell Offering* and *Mechanic Apprentice* correlated industrial labor with the gradual development of maturity on a path to appropriate adult authority, despite the growing perception that manual work by its nature lacked the traits of competence necessary for citizenship.

During the early nineteenth century, formal schooling started to define the emerging middle class (Sundue 2009; Beadie 2010). In a democratic society based conceptually on the rational consent and independence of its citizens, education was essential for civic participation. Education reformers in Massachusetts created the common-school system both to uplift the conditions of the lower classes and to inculcate the virtues of intelligence and self-control in the population (Kaestle 1983). Despite these efforts to extend the capacities for citizenship to manual as well as mental laborers, middle-class men and women monopolized the highest levels of civic influence through their reputation for respectability gained from an academy, seminary, or college. The daily responsibilities of laboring youth prohibited participation in formal schooling, especially at the more advanced levels. To counter the middle-class standard of education as formal schooling, working-class youth demonstrated their ability to pursue knowledge within their labor environment. Demonstrating liberal knowledge could prove to skeptical social critics that wage labor did not create a mass of second-class citizens.

The stated goal of both magazines was to improve the educational reputation of apprentices or operatives through the production of literary material. The *Offering* acknowledged, "It is in the intelligence of the mass, that the permanency of our republican institutions depends" (Robinson 1976, 105). Knowledge protected the population from threats to citizens' character: "Intelligence is the safe-guard of virtue; virtue is the promoter of intelligence." Workers' cultural literacy presumably distinguished the independent American laborer from the European drudge. With moral autonomy, the American working class would be able to contribute to the common good of the nation in its experiment with expanded citizenship. The *Offering* assisted in this endeavor, arguing that without the "intelligence and virtue of our population, there would be a downward tendency to the degradation, want and woe of the mill operatives of Great Britain."[15] On this account, "the Offering is *prima facie* evidence, not only of the American 'factory girls,' but of the intelligence of the mass of our country."[16]

The *Mechanic Apprentice* editors framed their periodical as part of the community's effort to uplift urban young men. Nineteenth-century Boston had no shortage of newspapers and magazines intended for apprentices, clerks, and other urban youth. These periodicals covered a range of issues, from religion, to science, to cheap amusement. The *Apprentice* editors "aim[ed] to render our magazine distinguishable by its devotion to the *instruction* as well as the amusement of our youthful readers." Positioning their monthly periodical as part of the effort to educate urban youth, the editors staked their claim to maturity. While other periodicals "teem[ed] with silly stories and senseless trash," the editors of the *Apprentice* "resolved to keep *ours* from the like degradation."[17] Because of the necessity of work for most young men in nineteenth-century Boston, MALA hoped to function as the primary educational institution for urban apprentices. But while Boston had many societies committed to the education of urban youth, MALA was unique in that it was an association of youths themselves.

The Mechanic Apprentices' Library Association made its goal to enhance the intelligence of urban apprentices in order to improve their claims to citizenship. The organization offered a variety of literary outlets to provide apprentices with the tools for civic engagement. The library provided a "fount of knowledge within the reach of every young man engaged in a mechanical employment, who would make himself an intelligent and respected citizen."[18] Knowledge achieved through the various offerings of the association, particularly of scientific principles foundational to artisan practices, provided "one of the best passports to future usefulness" (Alcott 1835, 290–91). The magazine was responsible for "upholding the character of the Apprentice, and proving his mental abilities . . . before the public."[19] Society needed to ensure that apprentices would become "*men*, rather than mere *machines*" by educating "the apprentice to assume and maintain a position in life which shall be his glory and his pride."[20]

As the divergence of class in the early nineteenth century separated men and women who worked with their hands from those who worked with their minds (or in the case of middle-class women, purported to avoid work altogether), the *Offering* and the *Apprentice* emphasized the importance of physical toil in the progress of civilization.[21] Labor uplifted humanity "wherever man has been himself a creature above the brutes around him, and aspiring to a higher dwelling-place than the earth which is their home."[22] In the act of proclaiming the dignity of labor, working-class youth also recognized when the fruits of toil were unjustly denied to them. An emerging class consciousness pitted the "poor"—honest working men—against the "rich"—men who did not need to work. The young editors asked, "Which of the two does the more good to society; the rich drone, that lives in his palace, or the poor hod-carrier that aided in its construction?" The author claimed that the social hierarchy should privilege "he who can from Nature's coarse materials produce the useful and the beautiful, to benefit himself and his race."[23] However, the author continued, the social, economic, and political order of the mid-nineteenth-century North kept the worker "physically, morally, and politically depressed and degraded." The nonproducing elite "seized upon the fruits of an industry of the burdens of which they have not partaken and appropriate it to their own personal aggrandizement and splendid ease." This violation was not only material, but it affected citizenship as well. The laboring classes were not only "robbed of their fair and just inheritance," but also "deprived of social importance and political equality."[24]

Appealing to middle-class ideals of meritocracy, factory operatives and urban apprentices envisioned citizenship based on social worth defined by physical contribution rather than status. They challenged the stigma toward manual labor that prevented working-class people from claiming full roles in moral, civic, and political leadership. As the industrial economy drove labor off the farm and into low-skilled jobs, many social commentators romanticized agricultural labor because of the worker's control of nature. Concerns about the dignity of manual labor threatened the nation's democratic project, as reformers worried that a class of degraded workers could never be free from conditions of economic dependence (Glickstein 1991).

In the *Lowell Offering* and the *Mechanic Apprentice*, working-class youth transformed the dignity of labor into a gendered vision of adulthood that embraced their labor conditions for the pursuit of middle-class ideals. With the rise of industrialization and the decline of household production, women were charged with making the home a sanctuary from the competitive public sphere. However, working women lost domestic status when the necessity of labor took them outside of circumscribed feminine roles. Authors in the *Offering* challenged the dichotomy between degraded operatives and virtuous homemakers by affirming the middle-class ideology that confined women's activities to the home because of their presumably natural role as nurturers. They recognized that a "woman might engage in noise and strife, but the overtasked heart would yearn for a humbler lot, and prematurely exhaust itself in the violence of self-contest."[25] Articles criticized women who wanted to leave the domestic sphere for public life. Given the "pleasant duties that await her at her own fireside," the author could not understand why any woman would pursue activities "which require the daring and bold spirit, and more enduring frame of man to execute." Because a woman was "fervent in her devotion to whatever is pure and good," her influence was better used in the domestic sphere.[26]

The *Offering* promoted an image of factory operatives as selfless young women who pursued the heartless world of wage labor in order to support aged parents and orphaned siblings. By publicly asserting their fidelity to familial concerns, Lowell workers connected domestic duty with civic duty. In a story following a common trope, Catherine comes to Lowell to help her parents. When her parents succumb to illness, Catherine faces the prospect of pulling her younger siblings out of school and putting them to work. In a display of her "self-sacrificing spirit," Catherine declares, "I will work till I die, before I will consent to such a course." As the oldest child, most capable of enduring "privation," she takes the burden on herself rather than let her siblings learn "that the cup of human existence is mixed with bitterness and sorrow." This image of domestic concern allowed operatives to preserve feminine claims to authority through duty within the private sphere, even while venturing into the masculine world of mechanized wage labor.[27]

Like the students in Amy Grey's study herein, Lowell mill workers adjusted the dominant gender narrative to serve their own ends. Articles in the *Offering* rejected marriage as women's only path to domestic duty. Authors wrote pieces that vindicated the social role of "old maids." Rather than being viewed as "unlucky, derided, and almost despised," the author claimed that society should view single women as "part of that wise design" for human happiness. Unmarried women contributed important resources to domestic harmony, stepping in whenever the family needed a capable and consoling female. When a couple's adult children had married and left home, the unmarried daughter would "be the light, life and joy of those who would otherwise be sad and solitary." In parents' declining health, the single daughter was ready "to repay their care of her early years, by the constant and much needed attentions." Married women, after an event of familial disruption, could find "help and consolation from the one of their number who remains free from such cares." Widowers "consigned their motherless children to the love and care of the trusty old maid." Whether through the natural life course, or from an unexpected accident, domestic life could be fractured, and single women were ready to repair the damage. *Offering* writers demonstrated how women actually improved their ability to fulfill domestic duties by earning money in nondomestic jobs.[28]

For young men in antebellum New England, the dignity of manual labor needed to serve as a foundation for economic and political autonomy. With the rise of industrialization, middle-class leaders promoted an ideology of the free laborer, which provided a narrative of adulthood alongside a formula for social authority. As an alliance between wageworkers and independent proprietors against the economic exploitation of slave labor, free labor ideology emerged in the early nineteenth century as a narrative of Northern nationalism. It allowed men across the economic spectrum to "rally to the defense of the superiority of their own system, even as [they] questioned whether the contrasts with slavery did not disguise the forms of compulsion within free labor" (Foner 1970, x). As the boundaries of political inclusion incorporated the masses of propertyless men, the rhetoric of free labor established a standard of political independence on self-mastery and the potential for economic ownership. Free labor ideology embraced the cult of the self-made man and judged individual success based on the ability to conform to middle-class values. However, the stigma faced by unskilled manual laborers, as well as the poor, degraded men who seemed to lack the ability to improve their economic station, presented a powerful obstacle to the civic role of workers.

In response, the *Mechanic Apprentice* embraced the image of the self-made man as a coming-of-age narrative that connected artisan apprentices to independent manhood. Proponents of nineteenth-century free labor ideology lauded individual freedom and self-reliance secured through the freedom of contract. The usefulness of the apprentice would be achieved through social mobility. The *Apprentice*'s narrative of adulthood portrayed the coming-of-age process as a parallel achievement of maturity in the economy and in society. A brief narrative told the story of a "youth who left his native village in 1820, to seek a livelihood in New York, by industry and honorable dealings with all men" and became "the possessor of one of the largest establishments in the city, and looked upon as one of the most influential persons in the state." The story, which shared common tropes with juvenile literature of the mid-nineteenth century, emphasized not the financial reward but the social respect gained through honest labor. The apprentice achieved adulthood by becoming "his own master," a status that gave him a claim to masculine conceptions of citizenship.[29]

This story of an apprentice's transition to adulthood demonstrated an idealized path for manual laborers to achieve citizenship. The editors invoked this image whenever they referenced "the honored and successful career in life" their former members achieved. In the magazine's self-narrative, the Library Association's opportunities for mutual improvement redeemed apprentices from vice and ignorance, setting them on that path to respectability and authority expected of their gender status. The editors praised former MALA members while taking credit for "those, who, having arrived at their majority, represent our association, not only in our own city, but in the 'uttermost parts' of the Union."[30] These articles invoked the rhetoric of free labor ideology through appeals to virtue, honor, and character. The goal of the association was to improve apprentices' conditions through education and moral uplift, consistent with free labor ideology's support for meritocracy and the self-made man. They pushed back against the class divergence that privileged managers, businessmen, and professionals when awarding civic leadership. The story showed other young mechanics, as well as the general public, that manual work provided the foundation for citizenship equal to any other type of work.

Alongside editorials that promoted the manual worker's ability to achieve independence, maturity, and authority, articles in the *Mechanic Apprentice* also challenged systemic obstacles to manual laborers' advancement endemic within the early industrial economy. Some authors articulated the ways economic structures, rather than individual maturity, stratified civic leadership. Despite the respectable and worthy character of New England's laborers, economic and political success remained elusive. The young mechanics interpreted the degradation of labor as a threat to the important tenets of manhood: economic independence and political influence. By critiquing the exploitation and political domination of laborers by the capitalist system, the *Mechanic Apprentice* recognized that the stratification of class centered on social authority. They also extended the dignity of labor beyond masculinity, offering the possibility of a cross-gender alliance among working-class youth.

In a three-part series on "The Redemption of Labor," an apprentice asserted his right to speak on one of the nation's most pressing issues. Instead of proposing a means of uplifting the character of Boston's apprentices through mutual improvement, the author, "A. L. M.," charged the political and economic system of capital with denying New England's working men their just claims to maturity and authority. The threats to mechanics' economic livelihood and political standing were "closely interwoven with each other," preventing laborers from achieving adult independence. A. L. M. listed the numerous obstacles manual laborers faced that violated America's promise as a land of equal opportunity for fulfilling human potential. "To be a workingman is to court poverty,—to stand as a sign of reproach,—to be a mark of general contempt. A man of that class is considered to be without mind, without soul, and entitled to none of the decencies of life—and when he attempts to rise above his condition, to assert the innate supremacy of humanity over all the accidents of birth or fortune, he is met by an opposition that seeks to crush him to the earth." The power of capital, harnessed by the "idle few," reduced workingmen to slaves by co-opting their productive capacity and silencing their political efforts.[31]

Instead of emphasizing the opportunities available for young men to rise to positions of economic authority, A. L. M.'s article portrayed an antagonistic relationship between workers and employers. Rather than depicting labors as potential owners—the heart of free labor ideology—he wrote that Labor and Capital represented two "conflicting interests" that needed equal representation in government "to preserve the proper balance, and prevent oppression and injustice." Because labor was "an interest of predominant importance, though shamefully insignificant influence," manual laborers needed to campaign for labor to "*represent itself*, in the halls of legislation." The political emancipation of labor would fulfill the civic ideals of masculinity. A. L. M. assured his readers that labor representation would appeal "to the plainest dictates of sacred duty, to the warmest love of liberty, to the best feelings of noble pride, to the most rigid regard for justice, to the innate promptings of humanity, and to every consideration of common defence [*sic*] and common safety."[32] Rather than articulating a robust critique of the distribution of capital and the inequality that sprang from ownership of the means of production, A. L. M., like much of the *Mechanic Apprentice*, focused on the divergence of public reputation and civic leadership between mental and manual workers and tried to prevent the traits of maturity from being monopolized by the middle class.

But the *Mechanic Apprentice* did not view its campaign for labor's dignity as a purely masculine endeavor. During a period in which women were legally and culturally separated from labor by the "cult of domesticity," the *Mechanic Apprentice*'s contributors' interest in maturity allowed them to

create an ideology of labor that celebrated the female wageworker. By praising "the bright array of youthful work-women that daily thread our narrow
thoroughfares in obedience to the never-ceasing promptings of the life-
task," male apprentices extended their own goals of maturity to their laboring sisters. Female workers had "independent feelings" as well as financial
autonomy because they "prefer[ed] their own burdens rather than should
their parents." Working women claimed the same work ethic because they
"deem[ed] reward more rightly due when bestowed for virtuous qualities
than for gay appearance." As a mark of their virtue and maturity, the working
girls of Boston were "not ashamed of honest industry." The gendered ideology of labor in the mid-nineteenth century portrayed women as nurturers,
sanctifying the home from economic corruption and ambition. The apprentices viewed urban workers as "girls, too, who deem propriety of conduct of
some avail in the estimation of personal character, and who feel that though
their calling is now to *toil*, toil daily, yet labor can be made honorable and
worthy."[33] By praising the diligence and industry of working women, the
author promoted young workers as an intergenerational cohort united in its
commitment to industry.

The young apprentices and factory workers also used the dignity of labor
to build solidarity across racial boundaries. New England's dominant labor
narratives sought to consolidate the moral superiority of the Northern labor
regime against the Southern practice of chattel slavery. Both the *Lowell
Offering* and the *Mechanic Apprentice* proclaimed antislavery sympathies in
order to bolster the opportunities that wage labor offered Northern youth.
By publicly supporting the antislavery cause, working-class authors showed
sympathy for the middle-class abolition movement, allowing them to assert
social authority and elevate their labor positions. Through their discussions
of abolition, working-class youth challenged the gender, class, and age barriers within the public sphere. Their critiques of slavery elevated the power of
free labor to confer maturity in contrast to the perpetual subordination of the
slave. For working-class youth, antislavery was not simply a moral position
but a way to show the civic responsibility and authority of manual laborers.

The *Lowell Offering* condemned slavery in order to defend female operatives from the criticism of conservatives who used the "wage slavery" of
Northern factories to justify the plantation's labor practices. Harriet Farley,
who became the magazine's principal editor in 1842, countered this attack
by simultaneously uplifting factory labor and leveling charges of inhumanity

against slaveholders. She defended mill labor by emphasizing operatives' control of time, their access to education, and their opportunities for marriage. Each of these characteristics represented a key feature of maturity claimed by Northern white women but denied to enslaved black women. In Lowell mills "the northern operative comes and goes at pleasure, and no one can prevent it." Rather than being "seduced" as the proslavery critic contended, another author insisted that operatives' "engagements are *voluntarily* entered into with our employers, with the understanding that they may be dissolved at our pleasure." Factory operatives were not kept in their positions by threat of being "branded, imprisoned and tortured." While operatives worked long hours, they were better off than the slave, for whom education and leisure time "must be considered *a favor* not a right." A factory worker was "encouraged . . . to improve her intellect." Most importantly, the Lowell worker was free to marry "at her own pleasure, the man of her choice" without fear of being separated from her children, unlike the slave who "marries at the choice of her master, and when her master chooses, the husband and wife are separated—the children scattered abroad." Although the polite nature of the *Offering* did not allow Farley to mention it, readers would have known that enslavement also made black women subject to sexual abuse and impregnation by their masters or other white men. By demonstrating the personal autonomy female workers enjoyed, Farley attacked both the oppression of slavery and Southern conservatives' attempt to deny women's labor.[34]

Farley's article used the Northern, middle-class ideology of domesticity to test the morality of factory labor and slave labor. Her critique assumed that black women deserved the same opportunities for education, marriage, and domestic security as white women in the North and the South. But Farley was unapologetic about the labor white factory workers performed. Ignoring the physicality of the work, Farley stressed the operatives' ability to enter and leave the factory at will, rather than the seduction portrayed by the proslavery author. In Farley's narrative, manual labor and domesticity coexisted as long as women had choices in both labor and love. Her defense of factory labor posited a reorganization of dichotomies of women's labor—away from the separation between toil and gentility toward a privileging of choice over coercion.

The *Mechanic Apprentice* also presented a vision of cross-racial sympathy. A short story published in 1845 displayed an encounter between a Southern "young man . . . of a strong nervous temperament, delicate constitution, and evidently a stranger to labor of any kind" and an apparent Northerner, "a strong, muscular man, several years his elder." The two start an argument about the charges of cruelty toward slaves levied by Northern abolitionists on plantation owners. The Southerner denies all allegations of violence against slaves, claiming that "it is only your low bred Northern nigger-drivers who are in the South, who ever act in that way." But the muscular man counters with a shocking revelation: "I was born a Southern slave; I have been house-servant, coach-driver, and field-hand. I have been through every grade in a slave's life; I have been beaten, branded, and sold." By revealing his true racial status, the former slave exposes the contradictions of labor degraded by assumed racial status. At first glance, the muscular man had the respectability of a white laborer, although his status as a slave would degrade his character in the eyes of many Americans. The story forces readers to see how the dignity of labor crossed racial boundaries.[35]

The story encouraged identification between Northern white laborers and enslaved African Americans by denigrating the character of the Southern son. The muscular man, now revealed as a slave, makes another revelation: "Your father is *my* father—*I am your brother!!* I am as white as you are, and you did not know me because I am a white man, among freemen." Both the nervous young man and the strong man came from the same line.[36] However, labor forged the older slave into a mature and confident man, while the favored son was protected from labor and was therefore denied a chance for autonomy. The "black" man tells his brother that his education was financed "by means of money that was received for me." The story not only demonstrated the dignity of the black male laborer but also connected the plight of black men and white apprentices who found the fruit of their labor appropriated by elites.[37]

Antislavery articles in the *Mechanic Apprentice* not only condemned the South's exploitative labor system but also challenged the acquiescence of Northerners that allowed slavery to continue. By addressing the political concerns surrounding the slavery debate, the authors of the *Mechanic Apprentice* represented the civic aspects of their manhood. They claimed the right to speak alongside the formally educated leaders of business and government. The *Apprentice's* political discourse tested the equal standing of able-bodied white men presumed by Northern conceptions of citizenship (Welke 2010).

The *Mechanic Apprentice* also addressed slavery as an issue of national character. It drew upon the rhetoric of maturity to criticize the nation's tolerance for the "abhorrent" practice. The continuation of the slave trade showed American's "moral turpitude." It revealed "men—christian men—men who by no other rule of action than that golden one laid down by our Saviour, and who in their national character have expressly declared that men are created free and equal" could succumb to hypocrisy. The lapse in values and resolve not only threatened the character of American leaders, but it threatened the United States' status "among nations the most civilized." The solution to the problem of this profound moral lapse was for "us as individuals and as a government, to take some decisive measures for the immediate suppression of this appalling traffic." For the nation and its leaders to claim autonomy and morality, they needed the fortitude to stand behind their principles.[38]

The *Mechanic Apprentice*'s antislavery position further modeled the mainstream movement by taking a definitive stance for preserving the Union. One author wrote, "A true patriot, one who cherishes a sincere regard for the honor and interests of his country, is continually pained while perusing the public journals of the day, at the frequent and continued allusion to the prospect of separation." The author appealed to "the duty of every American editor and every American citizen" as a member of the adult political community, calling upon people of influence "to frown indignantly upon any such manifestation, from whatever source it may come." The apprentice author portrayed the discussion of possible dissolution as the problem of adults who did not understand the full value of the Union.[39]

Opposition to slavery and fierce loyalty to the Union was the defining feature of the Republican Party that would become the standard-bearer for free labor ideology in the 1850s. When the party took the mantle of "Free Soil, Free Labor, Free *Men*" (emphasis mine), it signaled a status of maturity as much as gender. Although the free labor ideology of the Republican Party lauded Northern society for "the opportunity it offered wage earners to rise to property owning independence," the apprentices sought to tie adulthood to wage earning itself, and sought to carve out a place for working men within American civil society without the barrier of proprietorship (Foner 1970, ix). Even within the liminal position of apprenticeship, and with the specter of perpetual manual labor before them, the young mechanics addressed the civic debate about the evils of slavery, the importance of the Union, and the ability of wage labor to create maturity. Their efforts to portray manual labor within the narrative of middle-class respectability failed to overcome class prejudice but helped to solidify the relationship between self-ownership and citizenship that would continue through the nineteenth century.

———

The expansion of industrial manual labor challenged the idealized pattern of middle-class citizenship marked by women's domesticity and men's economic independence. Factory operatives and urban apprentices discovered that their conditions of work could not achieve the same status of civic competence as their privileged peers, which encouraged them to band together through an intergenerational ideal of citizenship. The *Lowell Offering* and the *Mechanic Apprentice* asserted their claims to respectability based on their working-class conditions. Because their age-based identity symbolized the economy's capacity to uplift or condemn manual laborers, operatives and apprentices offered a unique perspective on the labor debates of the period. They challenged popular perceptions of manual workers' ignorance and vice through their refined literary publications. Authors in both magazines claimed maturity by appealing to the traits of respectability that were becoming monopolized by middle-class New Englanders. They envisioned manual labor as a path to respectable adulthood in conformity with socially dominant gender roles.

However, these magazines were short-lived, as was the opportunity to bridge the class and gender divide in labor and citizenship. The *Offering* ended production in 1845, as Irish women replaced native-born mill workers. The *Mechanic Apprentice* ceased in 1846 as the term "apprentice" became more antiquated in the mid-nineteenth-century labor market. The prospect of a cross-gender ideology of labor, adulthood, and citizenship failed to extend beyond the fleeting labor movement of the 1840s. With the waves of immigration at midcentury, white, native-born New Englanders left the most degraded positions to newcomers whose maturity and civic participation could be denied because of their race and who would struggle for equality under a different set of circumstances.

The young people covered in this essay stood in a liminal space between working-class activities and middle-class aspirations. Alongside other essays in this collection, this chapter shows how young people expose citizenship as a site of agency, not as a passive status conferred by the state. Amy Grey, John Hink, Yuki Oda, and Saeed Kahn follow the experiences of young people in liminal positions regarding nationality or cultural identity. Children of foreign nationals or other subcultural parentage—whether American Indians, Armenian Americans, Mexican Americans, or Pakistani Britons—face ambiguities of legal status and as they grow up have a greater expectation of assimilating into a new culture while hanging on to their familial culture. Youth force legal and cultural institutions to recognize the fluidity of individual experience. Although it may be easy to place adults in categories of class, nationality, culture, or competence, childhood and youth represent the ability of individuals to determine their own destiny. Citizens are born, but full citizens—those who are welcomed as participants in the community's ongoing development—are made through the process of growing up.

NOTES

1. "Redemption of Labor, No. I," *Mechanic Apprentice*, November 1845.
2. For analysis of adulthood as less significant than manhood and womanhood, see Jordan 1976, 1–11. For discussions of citizenship in the early United States, see Sklar 1991; Sinopoli 1992; Smith 1997; Bradburn 2009; Welke 2010. These works focus on legal and political membership in the American polity based primarily on factors of race and gender. They particularly study the distribution of legal and political rights in order to challenge the triumphant narrative of American equality and democracy. Scholars of resistance and subcultural groups theorize alternative sites of political participation in a diffuse "civil society" or "public sphere." See Isenberg 1998; Rael 2002; Boylan 2002; Kelley 2006; Jones 2007.
3. My conception of *social authority* relies on Karen V. Hansen's analysis of the *social* as "that range of behaviors that mediates public and private activities, linking households to neighbors and individuals to institutions" and for the ways this conception "descriptively captures the everyday activities and communal relations" of early nineteenth-century New Englanders. The ability to exert influence and command respect in interactions defines *social authority*. See Hansen 1994, 8–9.
4. Title page, *Lowell Offering*, October 1840.
5. "Editor's Valedictory," *Lowell Offering*, August 1842.
6. "To Our Friends," *Mechanic Apprentice*, May 1845.
7. "Our Paper," *Mechanic Apprentice*, June 1845.
8. "Poems, Delivered on Various Occasions . . . ," *Lowell Offering*, May 1843.
9. "Editorial Notices," *Mechanic Apprentice*, July 1845.
10. "To Our Friends," *Mechanic Apprentice*, May 1845.
11. "Editorial Notices," *Mechanic Apprentice*, July 1845.

12. For the relationship between the "cult of domesticity" and the emerging middle class in the northern United States, see Welter 1966; Lerner 1969; Sklar 1973; Kerber 1980; Ryan 1982.

13. These deteriorating conditions provoked labor activism among Lowell operatives and their peers in other New England mill towns. Under the leadership of Sarah Bagley, the Lowell Female Labor Reform Association challenged the genteel portrayal by the *Lowell Offering* and campaigned for a ten-hour labor law in Massachusetts. See Foner 1977; Murphy 1992; Zonderman 1992.

14. The relationship between middle-class masculinity and self-made manhood has been theorized in Rotundo 1993, 3. Additional scholarship on this subject comes from August 2003; Opal 2008; Luskey 2010.

15. "Permanency of the Offering," *Lowell Offering*, March 1841.

16. "Editorial," *Lowell Offering*, November 1843.

17. "Our Paper," *Mechanic Apprentice*, June 1845.

18. "Our Library," *Mechanic Apprentice*, September 1845.

19. "Circular," *Mechanic Apprentice*, December 1845.

20. "Our Association," *Mechanic Apprentice*, October 1845.

21. This discourse challenged the hierarchy of mental labor over manual labor that developed alongside industrialization. See Glickstein 1991; Bromell 1993; Rice 2004.

22. "Aristocracy of Employment," *Lowell Offering*, November 1841.

23. "Poor but Respectable," *Mechanic Apprentice*, September 1845.

24. "Redemption of Labor, No. II," *Mechanic Apprentice*, December 1845.

25. "Woman," *Lowell Offering*, August 1841.

26. "Woman's Proper Sphere," *Lowell Offering*, October 1840.

27. "Tales of Factory Life, No. 2," *Lowell Offering*, November 1841. Thomas Dublin's analysis shows that most women used mill employment to fulfill their own goals of education, marriage, or a period of independence. Dublin 1979, 35.

28. "A Letter about Old Maids," *Lowell Offering*, October 1840.

29. "Life of an Apprentice," *Mechanic Apprentice*, May 1845.

30. "Our Past Members," *Mechanic Apprentice*, December 1845.

31. "Redemption of Labor, No. II," December 1845.

32. "Redemption of Labor, No. III," January 1846.

33. "Thought's Glimmerings—No. I," *Mechanic Apprentice*, September 1845.

34. Editorial, *Lowell Offering*, April 1844.

35. "Facts Are Stubborn Things," *Mechanic Apprentice*, August 1845.

36. Although not explicitly mentioned in the story, the fact that the white man and black man shared the same father was almost certainly a result of the white father's rape of one of his female slaves. This brutal, systemic practice offered abolitionists further evidence for the immorality of the South and its threat to idealized white, Northern domesticity. See Rothman 2003.

37. "Facts Are Stubborn Things," *Mechanic Apprentice*, August 1845.

38. "The Slave Trade," *Mechanic Apprentice*, May 1845. This article received a mixed review from William Lloyd Garrison's *Liberator*. Garrison praised the "commendable zeal of the "youthful writer," but faulted the author for not condemning Southern claims to chivalry, which might appear honorable, but was "nothing but mingled cowardice and ruffianism." *Liberator*, May 23, 1845.

39. "The Integrity of the Union," *Mechanic Apprentice*, August 1845.

WORKS CITED

Alcott, William Andrus. 1835. *The Moral Reformer and Teacher on the Human Constitution*. Published by Light and Horton.

Augst, Thomas. 2003. *The Clerk's Tale: Young Men and Moral Life in Nineteenth-Century America*. Chicago: University of Chicago Press.

Beadie, Nancy. 2010. *Education and the Creation of Capital in the Early American Republic*. New York: Cambridge University Press.

Boston Quarterly Review. 1838–42. Boston.

Boylan, Anne M. 2002. *The Origins of Women's Activism: New York and Boston, 1797–1840*. Chapel Hill: University of North Carolina Press.

Bradburn, Douglas. 2009. *The Citizenship Revolution: Politics and the Creation of the American Union, 1774–1804*. Charlottesville: University of Virginia Press.

Brewer, Holly. 2005. *By Birth or Consent: Children, Law, and the Anglo-American Revolution in Authority*. Chapel Hill: University of North Carolina Press.

Bromell, Nicholas Knowles. 1993. *By the Sweat of the Brow: Literature and Labor in Antebellum America*. Chicago: University of Chicago Press.

Brownson, Orestes. 1840. "The Laboring Classes." *Boston Quarterly Review* (July).

Dublin, Thomas. 1979. *Women at Work: The Transformation of Work and Community in Lowell, Massachusetts, 1826–1860*. New York: Columbia University Press.

Farley, Harriett. 1840. "Factory Girls." *Lowell Offering*, December.

Foner, Eric. 1970. *Free Soil, Free Labor, Free Men: The Ideology of the Republican Party before the Civil War*. New York: Oxford University Press.

Foner, Philip Sheldon, ed. 1977. *The Factory Girls: A Collection of Writings on Life and Struggles in the New England Factories of the 1840's*. Urbana: University of Illinois Press.

Glickstein, Jonathan A. 1991. *Concepts of Free Labor in Antebellum America*. New Haven, CT: Yale University Press.

Hansen, Karen V. 1994. *A Very Social Time: Crafting Community in Antebellum New England*. Berkeley: University of California Press.

Isenberg, Nancy. 1998. *Sex and Citizenship in Antebellum America*. Chapel Hill: University of North Carolina Press.

Jones, Martha S. 2007. *All Bound Up Together: The Woman Question in African American Public Culture, 1830–1900*. Chapel Hill: University of North Carolina Press.

Jordan, Winthrop D. 1976. "Searching for Adulthood in America." *Daedalus* 105 (4): 1–11.

Kaestle, Carl. 1983. *Pillars of the Republic: Common Schools and American Society, 1780–1860*. New York: Hill and Wang.

Kelley, Mary. 2006. *Learning to Stand and Speak: Women, Education, and Public Life in America's Republic*. Chapel Hill: University of North Carolina Press.

Kerber, Linda K. 1980. *Women of the Republic: Intellect and Ideology in Revolutionary America*. Chapel Hill: University of North Carolina Press.

Lerner, Gerda. 1969. "The Lady and the Mill Girl: Changes in the Status of Women in the Age of Jackson." *American Studies* 10 (1): 5–15.

Liberator. 1831–65. Boston.

Lowell Offering. 1840–45. Lowell, MA.

Luskey, Brian P. 2010. *On the Make: Clerks and the Quest for Capital in Nineteenth-Century America*. New York: New York University Press.

Mechanic Apprentice. 1845–46. Boston.

Murphy, Teresa Anne. 1992. *Ten Hours' Labor: Religion, Reform, and Gender in Early New England*. Ithaca, NY: Cornell University Press.

Opal, J. M. 2008. *Beyond the Farm: National Ambitions in Rural New England*. Philadelphia: University of Pennsylvania Press.

Rael, Patrick. 2002. *Black Identity and Black Protest in the Antebellum North*. Chapel Hill: University of North Carolina Press.

Rice, Stephen P. 2004. *Minding the Machine: Languages of Class in Early Industrial America*. Berkeley: University of California Press.

Robinson, Harriet Jane Hanson. 1976. *Loom and Spindle; or, Life among the Early Mill Girls: With a Sketch of "The Lowell Offering" and Some of Its Contributors*. Rev. ed. Kailua, HI: Press Pacifica.

Rothman, Joshua D. 2003. *Notorious in the Neighborhood: Sex and Families across the Color Line in Virginia, 1787–1861.* Chapel Hill: University of North Carolina Press.

Rotundo, E. Anthony. 1993. *American Manhood: Transformations in Masculinity from the Revolution to the Modern Era.* New York: BasicBooks.

Ryan, Mary P. 1982. *The Empire of the Mother: American Writing about Domesticity, 1830 to 1860.* New York: Copublished by the Institute for Research in History and the Haworth Press.

Sinopoli, Richard C. 1992. *The Foundations of American Citizenship: Liberalism, the Constitution, and Civic Virtue.* New York: Oxford University Press.

Sklar, Judith N. 1991. *American Citizenship: The Quest for Inclusion.* Cambridge, MA: Harvard University Press.

Sklar, Kathryn Kish. 1973. *Catharine Beecher: A Study in American Domesticity.* New Haven, CT: Yale University Press.

Smith, Rogers M. 1997. *Civic Ideals: Conflicting Visions of Citizenship in U.S. History.* New Haven, CT: Yale University Press.

Sundue, Sharon Braslaw. 2009. *Industrious in Their Stations: Young People at Work in Urban American, 1720–1810.* Charlottesville: University of Virginia Press.

Welke, Barbara Young. 2010. *Law and the Borders of Belonging in the Long Nineteenth Century United States.* New York: Cambridge University Press.

Welter, Barbara. 1966. "The Cult of True Womanhood: 1820-1860." *American Quarterly* 18 (2): 151–74.

Zonderman, David A. 1992. *Aspirations and Anxieties: New England Workers and the Mechanized Factory System, 1815–1850.* New York: Oxford University Press.

3

THE SPECTACLE OF A FARMER BENDING OVER A WASHTUB

· · · · · · · · · ·

Gendered Labor in the Preparation for
Native American Citizenship in Nineteenth-Century Arizona

AMY GREY

On January 15, 1889, the busy superintendent of the Tucson Indian Industrial Training School sat down to write a letter to his counterpart at the Albuquerque Indian School. The Reverend Howard Billman began his letter: "My dear Mrs. Walker," and went on to protest the practice of putting male Indian students to work doing laundry. Billman wrote: "As a farmer boy in my youthful days, I migrated from Ohio to Kansas and back again . . . and the spectacle of a farmer bending over a washtub is something that I never witnessed in all that time. Our Indian boys do not like to do such work. They will not do it when they go home. Why have them do it now?"[1] Billman went on to urge the Albuquerque superintendent to avoid training boys to learn "the female position of the family," because he feared it would not teach them to become good providers for their families. Over and over in much of his correspondence the Reverend Billman expressed the hope that "his boys" would learn to become good farmers and "his girls" good homemakers. Reverend Billman and other school personnel promoted this gendered labor pattern as the only course to American citizenship for the Tucson Indian Industrial School students. This ideal for American citizenship combined political philosophy, pragmatic considerations, and scholarly theories about race. For missionaries, citizenship training also incorporated a strong evangelical impetus. In contrast to the Anglo-American conceptions of citizenship, the first generations of Tucson Indian Industrial School students, by selectively adopting some of the school's philosophies and neglecting others, developed alternative visions of what it was to be an American citizen.

Between 1888 and 1895, the Reverend Howard Billman's letters simultaneously build a picture of the development of an industrial school and the growth of his thought process about the Americanization of Indians. Late each evening, the Presbyterian minister would sit at his desk and write letters to his Mission Society, to Sunday school teachers, to fellow missionaries, and to the superintendents of other Indian schools. Soon after the Billman family had arrived in October 1888, Reverend Billman wrote two letters to the director of the Presbyterian Board of Home Missions, one asking for three dozen eclectic first readers and another asking for a seed catalog and 1,400 pounds of "White Russian Oats of good quality seed."[2] These two requests reflect the dual educational emphasis of the school: half of the day was to be spent teaching Tohono O'odham, Akimel O'odham, and other Indian students how to read and write in English, while the other half was to be spent teaching the students the Anglo-American work ethic.[3]

The Tucson Indian Industrial School students in the 1880s and 1890s were the first generation among the desert Indians of the American Southwest to attempt to straddle both the Anglo-American and their own traditional worlds. This group of students negotiated not an assimilated Anglo-Americanism but a Native American citizenship for themselves and for the generations of Indians following their lead. They absorbed some of what the Reverend Billman and the other mission teachers had to offer, but they used only what seemed most useful to them and wove it into their lives in ways that made sense to them—rather than the full cultural assimilation Reverend Billman envisioned. Some students in this generation focused on the academic subjects or farming skills taught at the Indian School, and other students absorbed the evangelical religion, but all of the students interpreted their new knowledge in light of their own life experiences. In addition, it was Indian schools, like the Tucson school, that fostered a pan-Indian environment that allowed Indian students from different language groups to come together and begin to forge an identity that was not O'odham or Apache or Yaqui, but for the first time Native American (Ferguson 1997).

The mission teachers did not intentionally contribute to this new Native American citizenship but hoped for a full Anglo-American assimilation for their charges. In another of the Reverend Billman's letters to the superintendent of the Albuquerque Indian School he wrote: "In my judgment . . . the urgent need here is that our boys and girls should be taught to be productive of the necessities of life. The children know nothing at all in the line of self-support. Nor do their parents for that matter."[4] This quote reflects the initial ill-informed response of many Anglo-Americans to the quite sophisticated subsistence strategies of Arizona desert Indians, but as the Tucson Indian Industrial School grew from one small adobe building into a multibuilding campus, the Reverend Billman's assimilation ambitions for his students grew as well. Whereas in 1889 Billman expressed an urgency to teach Indians what he saw as the basic rudiments of subsistence farming, by 1891 he would write to a church group in Illinois that: "Here are the coming husbands and wives and fathers and mothers, and possible ministers and physicians and teachers, a company of responsive children: shall we leave them to the blanket and straw house, or give them an education, habits of industry, and the faith of our blessed Lord?"[5] If in the beginning Billman merely hoped for a more comfortable subsistence for his students, he quickly learned to hold greater ambitions for them in professional leadership positions.

The letters Billman wrote also reflected new US strategies for dealing with Indians. In 1869, President Ulysses S. Grant initiated his Peace Policy, which advocated assimilation and education over extermination. Education, in the minds of Anglo-American advocates of the Peace Policy, would teach Indians how to farm, to read and write, and to worship God in a Christian church—in short, education was expected to turn the Indian into an Anglo-American. Educational initiatives through the Peace Policy were responsible for the existence of the Tucson Indian Industrial School, and much of the school's funding came from the Bureau of Indian Affairs in Washington, DC. Reverend Billman sent quarterly claims to the Indian Bureau for $31.75 per student. This money, when combined with funds from the Presbyterian Board of Home Missions, allowed the school to serve from a hundred to two hundred students per year. The children learned to read and write from the eclectic reader series. They learned to add and subtract with special emphasis placed on teaching them the accounting necessary to run a farm and to do business with Anglo-Americans. As Billman wrote: "The Indian needs friends. He needs education. Otherwise he is at the mercy helplessly of unscrupulous whites."[6] School officials were very aware that while they were teaching the Indian students to become as much like Anglo-Americans as possible, they must also teach them how to avoid the corruption and deceitfulness of some whites. It was a specific kind of Anglo-American behavior the school would hope to instill in their students: honesty, hard work, and truthfulness were the qualities they emphasized.[7]

While the federal policy and the Protestant missionizing seemed to converge in the Peace Policy, the Grant administration and the Presbyterian missionaries were never in complete harmony. For the Grant administration, the turn to religious organizations to provide services to Indians was a pragmatic strategy to chip away at the widespread corruption in the Indian service. The Bureau of Indian Affairs had become notorious, with positions in the Indian service given out as political prizes and dishonest agents pocketing both money and resources meant for Indians confined to reservations. The assumption was that churchmen would be less tempted to fraudulence than other political office seekers. President Grant was also under increasing pressure from westward-moving whites to protect them from Indian attacks. When a Quaker group wanting federal funding to run Indian schools approached Grant, he agreed, saying, "If you can make Quakers out of the Indians it will take the fight out of them. Let us have peace."[8] In political venues other than the Bureau of Indian Affairs, President Grant was ordinarily a strong supporter of the separation of state and church and not personally a religious man. For the administration, promoting Christianity was of secondary importance to combating corruption or decreasing the violent, costly, and politically damaging Indian-white confrontations.[9]

For the Presbyterians the funding available through the federal government's Peace Policy was the answer to a long-term mission goal of converting Indians and saving souls. The Presbyterian Church had sent exploratory groups to the Southwest in the 1850s, as soon as the Arizona Territory was established, searching for locations to establish evangelical outposts and home missions. The Tucson Indian Industrial School was initially funded by money the Women's Board of Home Missions of the Presbyterian Church raised, but the availability of federal money allowed it to expand from thirty to seventy-seven students in its first year. This expansion was important because the Presbyterians strongly believed that incorporating the vast southwestern territories and the non-Christian southwestern populations into the American union could only happen if the people were properly evangelized. Although the Spanish had established Catholic missions to the O'odham over 150 years earlier, in the eyes of the Presbyterians, Catholic Indians were almost as alarmingly un-American as were Indians in their original condition.[10]

Presbyterian theology underlay every aspect of the day at Tucson Indian Industrial School. Each morning opened with a prayer, and the bible was used for reading, writing, and even geography lessons. The children were taught to memorize psalms and older students could become members of Christian Endeavor youth clubs. Every Sunday, the entire school would don their best clothes and walk several blocks to the Trinity Presbyterian Church for services. Most importantly, Reverend Billman noted that all of the children left the school as Christian ambassadors to their own people. To the Presbyterians, Christianity was a vital aspect in the development of Indians as eventual American citizens.[11]

Although the federal government and the Presbyterians diverged in their interpretation of the Peace Policy, not all federal officials saw Indian education as merely a pragmatic solution to corruption or frontier violence. Some of the Reverend Billman's letters to the government were agonizing pleas for more resources, an indication of the generally inadequate funding and support for both the new Peace Policy and the Bureau of Indian Affairs. The assimilation of Indians was simply not a high priority for the American government. In his second year at Tucson Indian Industrial School, Billman wrote to General Thomas Jefferson Morgan, the commissioner of Indian Affairs, about supplying necessary medical care on the nearby reservation: "I do wish our Government had an easy way of getting at this matter. Our Papago Indians lie out there in the desert and suffer and die, without one particle of relief."[12] Despite the failures of government agencies, Commissioner Morgan was also sympathetic to the goal of assimilation rather than extermination, reporting in 1889: "When we speak of the education of the Indians, we mean that comprehensive system of training and instruction which will convert them into American citizens, put within their reach the blessings which the rest of us enjoy, and enable them to compete successfully with the white man on his own ground and with his own methods."[13] Even if he did not share the evangelical aspirations of Reverend Billman, Commissioner Morgan believed as strongly as the Presbyterians in the power of education to change Indians into Americans.

Billman and Morgan were part of a generation of Anglo-American Progressives who shared many of the same concerns and enthusiasms. In the 1880s, American democracy was still an experiment unfolding, and many people worried that the additional 525,000 square miles Mexico ceded after the Treaty of Guadalupe Hidalgo would be enough to unbalance the fragile democracy. The Civil War had intensified the perception that a democratic population must have unified goals and values, and the vast western territories were far from unified or homogenous. Reformers, such as Billman and Morgan, saw education as the solution to cultural unification. In part, this passion for education came from the conviction that democratic political participation required knowledge about civil and political activities that literate men could best understand. In addition, they strongly believed that the attainment of political independence required economic independence. Small-scale farmers were understood to be the most independent members of the populace, since, in theory, they were free from the coercion of overseer or master. Reformers saw agricultural or industrial training as the ticket for creating a population of independent farmers. At the same time, newer ideas of social evolution contemporary anthropologists developed helped reformers, like Billman and Morgan, understand how Indians would take their place in the larger context of American political development. Although the Reverend Billman clearly embraced the necessity for Christian evangelism more than Commissioner Morgan, they both espoused many of the same Progressive ideas about democracy, independence, and social evolution.[14]

Only a year before the Reverend Billman and his family moved to Tucson, the US Congress had passed the Dawes Act, which was intended to create the conditions for Indian citizenship. The 1887 Dawes—or General Allotment—Act stipulated that each Indian family could choose 160 acres of reservation land on which to farm. The remaining Indian land would be sold to non-Indians, creating a fund for education and agricultural training. The idea was that allotment of land would provide motivation for families to pursue the Jeffersonian pattern of small-scale, independent farming. It was hoped that helping Indians to become farmers and farm wives would to lead to cultural and political independence from the tribal group and foster a direct relationship between the state and the head of each household—resulting in widespread Indian citizenship. In this scenario, educational programs, like the Tucson Indian Industrial School, were essential to turn seminomadic, hunter-gatherer groups, like the O'odham, into farmers. As historian Jane Fiegen Green's essay, in this volume, argues, earlier generations of Anglo-Americans had struggled to define manual labor occupations as particular sources for adulthood and self-ownership. As factories drew both men and women off of small farms and into the wage economy, many middle-class observers became nostalgic for what they imagined was the independent and more "natural" life of the farmer. Despite this middle-class nostalgia, the American economy had been irrevocably transformed by the market economy, and the wageworkers that Green discusses had been at least partially successful in redefining the source of political independence and self-ownership in honest wage labor. The Dawes Act was a product of the middle-class nostalgia for an American way of life that had disappeared forever (Sim 2008; McCool, Olson, and Robinson 2007; Green this volume, xx, xx).

The Dawes Act was intended to assimilate and homogenize all Indian groups in the Anglo-American mold. The Reverend Billman and the Indian agents on the O'odham reservation looked at the subsistence strategies of the Indians and did not see the richly varied diet of deer, peccary, quail, cactus fruit, tepary beans, squash, melon, mesquite pods, and wild herbs, but saw, instead, a starving people who grew no wheat and kept no livestock. Rather than seeing a fully functioning separation of labor in which women were responsible for the construction of homes and the planting and harvesting of crops, while men were responsible for group safety and for hunting, the missionaries saw a dangerously mixed-up gender pattern that emasculated men while making drudges out of Indian women. The industrial education for Tucson Indian students attempted to re-create Anglo-American Victorian gender roles. The girls kept the dormitories clean, served at table, and worked in the kitchen and laundry. The boys planted and harvested crops, cared for animals, and repaired farm machinery (McCool, Olson, and Robinson 2007, 6; for dietary information Dolores and Mathiot 1991; Celaya, Ezell, and Dobyns 2007).[15]

The Reverend Billman's gendered goals for his Indian students overlapped with the impetus behind the Grant Peace Policy and the later Dawes Act, specifically around the idea that individual farm owners were the ideal on which American democracy was built. The ideal of the independent farmer dates back to the early republic. In the election of 1800, the Jeffersonian Republican Party had positioned themselves as different from the Federalist Party in their confidence that "plain folk," working their own farms, could uphold a democracy. In fact, President Thomas Jefferson considered yeoman farmers the strong core of a democracy that could balance a self-interested upper class against a mass of degraded wageworkers. In his 1781 volume *Notes on the State of Virginia*, Jefferson wrote: "Those who labour in the earth are the chosen people of God, if ever he had a chosen people, whose breasts he has made his peculiar deposit for substantial and genuine virtue."[16] Virtue was vital in a democracy in which public honor and confidence resulted "not from birth, but from our actions."[17] The Jeffersonian notion of democracy as rooted in "those who labour in the earth" was still a foundational component of conceptions of American democracy by the late nineteenth century. The federal government supported this notion over and over in homestead acts between 1804 and the 1870s, which were intended to create a nation of independent farmers. As a former farmer himself, the Dawes Allotment Act would have had special resonance for Reverend Billman as a way to introduce Indians to the virtues of labor and the ideology of American democracy. Central to this project was ensuring that Indian men learned to take the primary role of farmer, while their wives learned to provide domestic comforts in the Anglo-American fashion.[18]

Although the federal government was still actively supporting a rural agricultural lifestyle in the late nineteenth century, the irony of the Dawes Act was its coincidence with a national shift toward urbanization over the nineteenth century. Urbanization was accompanied by the industrialization of the workforce and a move away from land ownership as the basis of citizenship rights such as voting. Throughout the century, suffrage was extended to wider and wider groups of American men. The vote was made available to non-property-owning white men in state after state during the antebellum and, after the Civil War, to all black men, until by the 1880s, political participation was open to a greater percentage of American males than ever before. Citizenship for white or black men was, at least constitutionally, not dependent on property ownership, farm productivity, or adherence to proper gender roles. Just by being born in America, white and black men gained at least the legal right to full citizenship. To open citizenship up to American Indian men, however, both the Presbyterian missionaries and the Bureau of Indian Affairs officials fell back on the Jeffersonian ideal of yeoman farmer and wife as the appropriate goal for Indians. The fact that this was an outdated model on which to base citizenship standards never seems to have bothered Billman, who continued to promote it during his tenure at the Tucson Indian Industrial Training School.[19]

Reverend Billman's support of farming and the agricultural training provided to male O'odham students at the Tucson Indian Industrial School ultimately failed to win citizenship rights for Arizona Indians. In fact, the Dawes Act, although it would strip land from Indian tribal groups in Arizona, did very little to bring full political and economic citizenship to the O'odham or other Arizona Indians. If voting rights alone are considered an indicator of political citizenship, Indians in Arizona were kept from full citizenship for many more years. While the federal Indian Citizenship Act of 1924 brought the legal right to those American Indians who had not already abandoned their tribal affiliations, Arizona officials continued to restrict Indian voting rights, maintaining that Arizona Indians who were tribal members or who received state or federal financial support of any kind should be considered wards of the state and therefore ineligible to vote. In 1948, through the action of an Arizona state Supreme Court decision, this practice was overturned. Into the 1970s, the state still managed to keep some Arizona Indians from voting by arguing that suffrage be withheld from nontaxpayers or by establishing literacy restrictions. The agricultural training provided to Tucson Indian students, while it may have given many valuable skills, was a relative failure in terms of its primary goal of readying Arizona Indians for citizenship, or, more accurately, readying Arizona for Indian citizens (McCool, Olson, and Robinson 2007).

If the Jeffersonian model of farmer-citizen was a primary impetus behind the Dawes Act and the agricultural training at Tucson Indian Industrial School, there were other ideas circulating that motivated reformers to create schools for Indians. Americans in the 1870s were embracing the ideas of the English theorist Herbert Spencer, who felt that cultures evolved toward a state of higher complexity and civilization. The American anthropologist Lewis Henry Morgan, in particular, had applied the ideas of sociocultural progress to American Indians. Morgan believed that cultures evolved from a savage state, through barbarism, ultimately progressing toward civilization. According to Morgan and his fellow anthropological enthusiasts, this evolution occurred through a specific sequencing of developments: the use of fire for savages, the domestication of animals for barbarians, and the development of a written alphabet for the civilized. Morgan originally published his major work, *Systems of Consanguinity and Affinity of the Human Family*, in 1871 (Morgan 1997). According to his biographer, Daniel Moses: "the publication of Systems catapulted Morgan into the middle of the transatlantic scholarly debates about the evolution of the family" (Moses 2008, 194). Not many lay people read the full six-hundred-page book, but the publicity these scholarly debates generated pushed Morgan's theories fairly quickly out to the general public (Moses 2008; Harmon 1990).

While Morgan was primarily interested in the scientific classification of cultural development, his ideas entered the popular imagination as a prescription for possible progression for living groups of people. Reform groups such as the Friends of the Indian, the Indian Rights Association, and the Women's National Indian Association celebrated the possibilities of Indian evolution in books, articles, and at conferences such as the annual Lake Mohonk conference. "We have learned," claimed one conference attendee, "that education and example, and, preeminently the force of Christian life and Christian faith in the heart, can do in one generation most of that which evolution takes centuries to do."[20] Because the members of these reform groups were primarily Anglo-Americans from mainline Protestant denominations, they interpreted Morgan's anthropological descriptions of evolution into an agenda for Christian charitable work. This belief in the possibilities of Indian progressive evolution marks a positive transformation from earlier convictions that "the only good Indian is a dead Indian," and it explains the urgency many reformers felt for launching educational projects. Reverend Billman and the other missionaries at the Tucson Indian Industrial Training School moved in circles where ideas like this freely circulated, and it is clear from their correspondence that they hoped to accelerate the social evolution of their Indian students through education and exposure to Christianity (Harmon 1990; Moses 2008, 249; Deloria 1998; Bederman 1995; Warren 2010).[21]

If the Bureau of Indian Affairs officials and the Presbyterian Board of Home Missions wanted to create civilized citizens from savage Indians, according to the precepts of sociocultural evolution, they must encourage their charges to move through the progressive stages of savage, barbarian, to civilized citizen. The industrial training at the Tucson Indian school was constructed to teach students the basic skills necessary to run a small farm or a farm household as the first step toward civilization. The use of the English language, the constant reinforcement of the Protestant work ethic, and the immersion into the Christian environment were considered essential for jump-starting an accelerated evolution. In addition, many of the descriptions of first-year children arriving at the Tucson Indian Industrial Training

School pay special attention to the new students' reactions to the material life of civilization: light switches, water taps, and staircases. For Anglo-Americans the Indian use of such markers of civilization was an indication of an evolutionary change within that child, which promised to transform all Indians, if not entirely in that generation, then surely in the next (Culnan 1930, 4).[22]

The intense focus on the evolutionary necessity to remove Indian children from their homes collided with the stated fundamental goal of the Tucson Indian Industrial School: assimilation. The very nature of the boarding school was designed to completely remove children from their home environment and drop them into a type of laboratory meant to propel their evolution from savage to civilized. School organizers were so busy creating an idealized Anglo-American home for Indian children that they ultimately created an environment that was also completely isolated from the rest of Tucson. By 1906, when the town grew up around the first school location north of the downtown area, the perennially cash-strapped Board of Home Missions somehow found the money to relocate the school three miles south of town. While the goal of Indian social evolution was to assimilate them into the Anglo-American way of life, the Presbyterian missionaries seemed remarkably reluctant to allow them to mingle with Anglo-Americans. This may have been due to a reluctance to expose Indian children to non-Presbyterians or a measure to protect the students from white racism, but it had the effect of segregating Indian children from all Tucson non-Indians. In the 1920s and 1930s, as day schools were established on nearby reservations, the Tucson boarding school was slowly transformed into a high school, which meant that Tucson Indians were never required to come into daily contact with Anglo-American students in local schools. The young people at the Tucson Indian Industrial School were among the most segregated students in Tucson. When the Women's Board of Home Missions noted in a pamphlet that, "We always keep in mind the desired fruit of all our labor, to send out a company of clean, thrifty, self-reliant, self-supporting men and women—Christian home-makers and home-keepers," it became clear that they only ever intended to send them "out" to the reservation.[23]

Although the school's assimilationist intentions were hampered by the segregation of the boarding school, the school organizers remained dedicated to the ideals of social evolution for Indians. Occasionally, impatience got the better of this urge to ensure that individual Indians and the tribal groups as a whole progressed through the appropriate stages. In 1891, Reverend Billman got tired of waiting for the children in his school to grow up before they could influence their nonschooled peers. That year, the Tucson Indian Industrial School created a special program for five adult men and their wives. Instead of living in the dorms, the families lived in a detached building and had separate lessons. Billman wrote to a mission society colleague: "The men are in school, learning to be teachers and evangelists for their own people, the women are being taught to be good housekeepers. This is just what we are hoping will result from our work in the case of many of our boys and girls; but we hope by this means to send out very shortly five Christian families to be leaders in so many [Indian] communities. The way is long, often wearing, and very perplexing; but Christian intelligence, Christian industry, and Christian love will certainly triumph."[24] This program for married adult students is one of the clearest signs that the citizenship goals for Tucson Indian Industrial School students were different from those for other Tucson area students. No other schools intentionally enrolled adult married students and carefully trained male students to be evangelists and their wives to be home keepers.

The Reverend Billman's impatience to train adult Indians to be Christian leaders reveals the passion behind the most important of his motivations to create the Tucson Indian Industrial School: evangelism. Nineteenth-century American Presbyterians had generally relaxed in their adherence to the Calvinist principals of innate human depravity and predestination, but they had grown stronger in their conviction of a direct link between Protestant Christianity and what they saw as the remarkable achievements of the United States. Protestant Christianity meant progress. Presbyterians had thrown themselves passionately into the revivalism of the Second Great Awakening in the early part of the century, and that exhilarating experience had convinced them that American religious activism would triumphantly evangelize the whole world. In fact, many American Presbyterian missionaries firmly believed that the evangelization of the world must occur before the second coming of Christ and the establishment of the Kingdom of God on earth. With so much at stake, it is no wonder that Billman tried to jump the gun by training older men and women to spread the gospel among their fellow O'odham. Indeed, understanding the Presbyterian evangelical motivations makes it clear that although they were willing to cooperate with the federal government on a mutual goal of Indian education, the Presbyterian missionaries had ulterior motivations that were not necessarily shared with the Bureau of Indian Affairs. The routing of corruption and the generation of new American citizens, while important, must have surely taken second place to the ultimate goal of attaining the millennium in Christ. This fact was ever present for Billman and for the other Anglo-American missionaries at the Tucson Indian Industrial School. While they might praise a student for learning quickly or working hard, they kept their highest praise for those students who professed a love for Christ (Banker 1993; Berkhofer 1965; Bowden 1981; Huber 1999; Prucha 1979; Robert 1996; Shenk 2004; Welter 1978; Yohn 1995).[25]

Anglo-American reformers interested in the "Indian question" shared enough assumptions about Indian assimilation to be able to work together relatively successfully, but ultimately they held several distinct visions of American citizenship. Most Progressive reformers agreed about cultural hierarchies, the necessity of unity and uniformity for American democracy, the virtuousness of independent farmers, and the possibilities of social evolution. People like President Ulysses S. Grant, commissioner of Indian Affairs Thomas Jefferson Morgan, members of Indian reforms groups, and missionaries like Reverend Howard Billman all believed that education was the key to creating American citizens out of Indians. They did not necessarily agree, however, on the specifics of that program. Political officials pragmatically looked to education to provide the necessary tools to generate an intelligent voting population, individuals who were civically involved, and capable workers who would contribute to the national economy. For most government officials, education was the means to transform a multicultural population into a cohesive and patriotic unit. The end goal was social stability and a unified American citizenry.

Presbyterian missionaries, on the other hand, were focused on a millennial future in the second coming of Christ; a unified American population was only a pleasant by-product of their labors. Presbyterian missionaries certainly did not approve of all of the educational efforts of the Bureau of Indian Affairs, for instance. The Tucson Indian Industrial School superintendents often worried about the educational curriculum and agendas of the nearby government-run Indian schools. Reverend Billman's letter to the superintendent of the Albuquerque Indian School was highly critical of their practice of having male students work in the school laundry. Billman was wedded to the idea of proper gender relations as essential to his particular vision of American manhood and, ultimately, citizenship. A later Tucson superintendent, Haddington Brown, worried about the lack of religious training in the nonsectarian government schools: "Are the religious denominations of our land going to permit all of this generation of Indians to receive a mental training without any thought to their spiritual welfare? Training them to be farmers, blacksmiths, and carpenters . . . and still permit them to go on in their pagan religions as in their former condition, or even worse make infidels of them?"[26] To superintendent Brown, the formation of a generation of Indians who shared Anglo-American habits of industry and who would contribute to the American economy was, by far, secondary to the goal of Christianizing the world. On the surface, the assimilation efforts of Anglo-American reformers seem uniform and well harmonized, but in their definitive goals for citizenship the distinctions become most visible.

Just as the Presbyterian missionaries and officials of the Bureau of Indian Affairs conceived of slightly different versions of American citizenship based on their own requirements and experiences, American Indians also developed their own perceptions of how they would become American. Like most students, the students at the Tucson Indian Industrial Training School—children and adults—had their own agenda for the education and training they received. Regardless of the best-laid plans of the Reverend Billman, the Bureau of Indian Affairs, or the Presbyterian Church Home Mission Society, Indian school graduates made use of their education in ways that met their personal needs. They also interpreted the prevailing discussions of Americanization, assimilation, and citizenship through the filter of their own experiences. Rather than striving to become as Anglo-American as reformers hoped they would, Indian students combined aspects of Indian and Anglo-American cultures to create their own perceptions of Indian-American citizenship.

One student who had no intention of being a Christian leader or independent farmer attended the school in the 1880s. Juan Dolores hated the Tucson Indian Industrial School and ran away several times. Dolores recalled that "they were not kind these Presbyterians. They were just clever. They were just waiting for the time when our parents had gone back home to teach us God's rules the hard way, by beating us with a stick, by making us work hard, by making us go hungry" (Dolores and Mathiot 1991, 307). Dolores certainly recounts being beaten many times, but to be fair, he also recounts playing practical tricks on students and teachers, organizing an unauthorized nighttime trip to the circus, and regularly inciting misbehavior among other students. Dolores continued on in school after attending the Tucson Indian School and graduated from the Hampton Institute in Virginia in 1898. In 1909, Dolores traveled to Berkeley, California, to meet anthropologist Alfred Kroeber, at which time he began to work with Kroeber on the study of O'odham linguistics. Dolores continued to work with Kroeber and other linguists until ultimately taking a permanent position as a preparator in the University of California–Berkeley Museum of Anthropology. Although Dolores was initially resentful of his experiences at Tucson Indian School he would make use of his education to establish a career as cultural mediator (Dolores and Mathiot 1991; Kroeber 1994; Mason 1950; Kroeber 1961, 156–62).[27]

The use that Juan Dolores made of his Tucson Indian Industrial School training was not assimilation, as the Reverend Billman understood it; instead, it was a type of adaptive integration. Dolores took what he needed from his Anglo-American education to honor and protect his O'odham knowledge and to establish outside respect for the O'odham culture. Dolores did not accept everything from his Tucson education comprehensively. He entirely ignored the Presbyterian religion and the agricultural training, but he did learn to appreciate the power of the written word and would go on to publish several academic articles discussing different aspects of O'odham linguistics. Neither did Dolores run away from the Anglo-American world and retreat to an entirely O'odham space in the far reaches of the reservation. Even though he remembered hating his first taste of education, Dolores continued to try to make a distinctive space for himself by pursuing his Anglo-American education and yet still honoring his O'odham knowledge. Rather than narrowly following the prescription for American citizenship as Reverend Billman and other Presbyterian missionaries laid out, Dolores, through the choices he made during his life, articulated an alternative American citizenship: an O'odham-American citizenship (Dolores and Mathiot 1991).

Many other former students of the Tucson Indian Industrial School managed to subvert the prescribed usage of their education by pursuing paid jobs. Rather than establishing yeoman farm households, these students engaged in wage work, integrating their paid labor into older patterns of migration for seasonal gathering or religious reasons. While Reverend Billman insisted that the only way for Indian students to become American citizens was to settle into an outdated model of independent farmer and farmer's wife, former students took their technical skills—both agricultural and domestic—and made use of them in the region's modern wage economy. Ironically, this allowed them the freedom to follow O'odham habits of seasonal movement and yet make use of those aspects of Anglo-American life that appealed to them. Juan Dolores, himself, is an example of this, as he worked as a teamster before he met Kroeber in 1909. Another former student, Anna Shaw, remembered traveling alternately between paid wage labor and work on the reservation farms of relatives: "Threshing was always a kind of holiday, even though it was hard, hot work. Here was our chance to exchange news and gossip with our friends . . . often romances developed under the summer moon" (Shaw 1974, 78). Another student, Alberto Celaya, described to anthropologists a long history stretching back to the middle of the nineteenth century of integrating wage work for non-Indians with the production of desert foods such as saguaro pitayas or mesquite bean pods. Nomadic travel was an aspect of Indian life that Presbyterian missionaries had specifically set out to eradicate, but ironically the agricultural training at the Tucson Indian School gave the students marketable skills usefully suited for occasional labor, which meshed nicely with seasonal migrations. Like Juan Dolores, these former students were expressing, with their life choices and their daily activities, a multicultural vision of a combined O'odham-American citizenship (Meeks 2003; Meeks 2007; Celaya, Ezell, and Dobyns, 2007).

Even students who ostensibly followed exactly the path that Reverend Billman had planned, as Christian evangelists, adapted Christianity to meet their own needs. Sallie Simms Lewis, a student who attended Tucson Indian School in the 1920s, did become the wife of an Indian minister and was active in Presbyterian evangelism. Lewis's interpretation of evangelism, however, involved a more multicultural Presbyterian church that drew together Anglos, Blacks, Mexican Americans, and Indians. Lewis recalls: "I was on the board a number of times, helping with programs for all the Presbyterian churches" (in Rothschild, Logan, and Hronek 1992, 95–95). While Reverend Billman had hoped his students would go back to the reservation to evangelize other Indians, Sallie Lewis saw herself, not as an Indian evangelist, but as a Presbyterian evangelist. The reverse situation occurred in the life of Reverend Joaquin Lopez. Lopez was the first ordained O'odham Presbyterian minister. Unlike Sallie Lewis, Reverend Lopez returned to the reservation, translating his evangelical message into O'odham. Lopez did not see the training at the Tucson Indian Industrial School as a complete and integrated package with the English language and Anglo-American farming. Instead, he took the message of Christianity and combined it with the O'odham language and integrated Indian notions of spirituality. Both Lewis and Lopez disregarded the Anglo-American's assumptions that the Tucson Indian Industrial School should completely transform their cultural allegiance. They both created adaptive fusions of O'odham and Anglo-American culture that suited their own needs. In doing so, Lewis and Lopez, just like Dolores and generations of other Tucson Indian Industrial School students, also generated new ways to be O'odham-American citizens (Lewis in Rothschild, Logan, and Hronek 1992, 37–39, 94–95; Ferguson 1997, 14, 119).

One ironic aspect of Anglo-American assimilation and the efforts of the Tucson Indian Industrial School mission teachers was that it created several outspoken generations of graduates who envisioned a tribal citizenship to balance their American citizenship. While the Anglo-American reformers of the late nineteenth and early twentieth centuries tried for forty years to remove individual Indians from the tribe, or, as the saying went, "remove the tribe from the Indian," by the late 1920s they ended up contributing to the official recognition of tribal sovereignty. In 1928 the US government shifted direction in response to the "Meriam Report" and began to allow Indian tribal self-government for groups that adopted federally approved constitutions and elected governments. The O'odham and other Arizona Indian people who were most prepared to act as cultural intermediaries and work within a formal tribal government structure were those who had attended programs like the Tucson Indian Industrial School and could work as cultural intermediaries to forward tribal demands. A later superintendent of the school, Joseph Poncel, wrote in the 1940s that "most of the important members of the Pima Tribal Council, including the council head, have attended the Tucson Indian School. Nurses, government workers, Sunday school teachers, Christian farmers and housewives have been trained here" (quoted in Ferguson 1997, 110). O'odham parents were telling school officials by the 1930s and 1940s that they were sending their children to the Tucson Indian School, not to learn how to become Christian farmers and housewives but to be tribal leaders. As another Tucson Indian School superintendent wrote: "We are also serving a group, many of whom are children of former students, who have very definite ideas that their children must be prepared with a higher education that will allow them to go far in the management of community and governmental affairs" (quoted in Ferguson 1997, 94). The Indian students had been patient and persistent in the pursuit of their alternative image of an O'odham-American citizen. This implacability in the face of decades of Anglo-American assimilation effort ultimately paid off as the Indian Reorganization Act of 1934 made it legally possible to be both a tribal citizen and an American citizen. Historian Saeed Khan, in this volume, finds a similar example of what he calls "functional multiculturalism" in British citizens who have Pakistani roots and cultural sensitivities. Khan's example of multiculturalism revolves around a generation of South Asian British citizens who live in communities that share common cultural foundations, who travel between Pakistan or India and their birth homes in Europe, and who actively attempt to forge a sense of belonging "despite being of two 'worlds.'" For the O'odham, Apache, and Yaqui students at the Tucson Indian Industrial School, the two worlds they lived in were laid one atop the other but required the same kinds of attempts to "reconcile multiple identity markers" (McCool, Olson, and Robinson 2007; Deloria and Lytle 1983; Khan this volume, xxx).

Native American students not only pictured themselves as Indian Americans, they also convinced Anglo-Americans to begin to think more multiculturally. From the beginning in 1889, O'odham families and the children referred to the "Escuela" when talking about the Tucson Indian Industrial School. Although one primary goal of the teachers was to teach the children English, and they imposed a stern English-only rule, all the school staff soon began to refer to the "Escuela" in their correspondence. Eventually, Escuela would become the semiofficial name for the school used by Anglo-American Tucsonans, Presbyterian Board of Home Missions officials, and the Bureau of Indian Affairs. Anglo-American reformers came to the Southwest intending to remake Indian students into their own image and, instead, often found themselves integrating Indian behavior into their daily lives. As one school publication put it: "One deals with Indian pupils most successfully by adopting to some degree their own silence and deliberation" (Culnan 1930, 9). This adaptive assimilation of Indian habits was aided by the increasing national popularity of traditional native life and customs. The Bureau of Indian Affairs tried to showcase their boarding schools at national fairs, such as the 1891 Columbian Exposition, the 1899 Greater American Exposition, the 1901 Pan-American Exposition, and the 1904 Louisiana Purchase Exposition, but the public ignored exhibits of well-mannered schoolchildren and flocked to see teepees and peace pipes, baskets and mock cliff dwellings, Wild West shows and feathered headdresses. Prominent Anglo-American writers and arts patrons, such as Mary Hunter Austin and Mabel Dodge Luhan, encouraged Indian artists to create salable works for the international art market. The Boy Scouts and the Campfire Girls adopted a romanticized version of Indian life, while adults adopted Indian symbolism in their fraternal lodges. The ever-increasing symbolic presence of Indians in commercial American culture made it ever more difficult for missionaries to remake their Indian students in the Anglo-American mold. Popular culture itself was moving further and further away from a unicultural, Anglo-American model (Burns 2010; Deloria 1998, 95–127; Trennart 1987; Banker 1993, 145; Dilworth 1996; Carr 1996; Bederman 1995; Jacobs 1999; Mullin 2001; Gifford and Higgins 1974).

The great irony of the Tucson Indian Industrial School was that while it set out to "remove the tribe from the Indian," it ended by providing the common ground for this first generation of students in the 1880s and 1890s to meet each other and begin to forge a multicultural identity. The school provided a way to access those aspects of Anglo-American culture that they could then incorporate into their own lives, and once they had done so they had the tools to begin to make demands for Indian self-government. Once the first few generations had successfully absorbed academic achievement, or knowledge of farming techniques, they incorporated and interpreted these ideas into their lives in ways that made the best economic or cultural sense to them individually. The strategic cultural adaption pursued by the first generations of Tucson Indian Industrial School students was passed down to their children, giving these subsequent generations the strength required to demand a multicultural citizenship from the American government that had so recently been intent on eradicating all American Indians.

While President Grant's Peace Policy and the educational aims of the Bureau of Indian Affairs were certainly more humane than the earlier US goal of Indian extermination, their expectations that Indians must assimilate fully before becoming citizens were never realized. Although the Tucson Indian Industrial Training School continued to work toward creating independent farmers out of their Indian charges, most students entered the wage economy while retaining ties to the reservation. The idea that Indian students would use the education they received at the Tucson Indian School to integrate useful aspects of Anglo and Indian life into a personally meaningful whole would not have occurred to early Bureau of Indian Affairs officials or to Reverend Billman. Anglo-American Bureau of Indian Affairs officials and missionaries, like Reverend Billman, were hampered by their Victorian conceptions of appropriately gendered families and popular ideas of sociocultural stages of evolution. They could not imagine the development of a multicultural society in which Anglo-American cultural values were only one choice among many. Luckily the first generation of graduates of the Tucson Indian Industrial Training School had more imagination. These students actively worked to become cultural mediators, to adapt aspects of the modern wage economy or of Christianity that met their needs, and saw themselves as both Indian and American. It was the Tucson school and others like it that gave this generation of Indian students the economic tools and the pan-Indian community that they needed to push for tribal recognition and self-government.

NOTES

1. Letter from Reverend Howard Billman to Mrs. Walker, superintendent of the Albuquerque Indian School, January 15, 1889. Tucson Indian Industrial Training School Records, Arizona Historical Society Library and Archives, Tucson, Arizona (hereafter referred to as AHSLA).

2. Letter from Reverend Howard Billman to Mr. Boyd, October 23, 1888 and November 28, 1888, AHSLA.

3. Billman and the other Presbyterian missionaries knew the Tohono O'odham (desert people) and Akimel O'odham (river people) by their Spanish names: Papago and Pima. The school also served small numbers of Apache, Mohave, Yaqui, Maricopa, and Yuma students in the 1880s and would later serve at least twelve different Indian groups by the 1930s, including Mono, Walapai, Hopi, Navajo, and Zuni students. See Ferguson 1997, 78; Franco 1989, 143–60; Hamilton 1948.

4. Letter from Reverend Howard Billman to Mrs. Walker, superintendent of Albuquerque Indian School, December 10, 1888, AHSLA.

5. Letter from Reverend Howard Billman to Mrs. Robinson, Ladies of the Synod of Illinois, January 2, 1891, AHSLA.

6. Letter from Reverend Howard Billman to Mrs. M. T. Scripps, October 14, 1889.

7. "Quarterly claim," Reverend Howard Billman to US Indian Bureau, October 1, 1889, AHSLA. For quarterly claims see letter books I–V, Tucson Indian Industrial Training School Records, AHSLA. See also Sim 2008.

8. T. C. Battery, introduction to Lawrie Tatum, *Our Red Brothers and the Peace Policy of President Ulysses S. Grant*, quoted in Sim 2008, 242.

9. David Sim notes that President Grant was not an atheist, nor was he a Christian. Grant's son, Fred, remembered that "he was not a praying man." Sim 2008, 266.

10. Reverend Howard Billman to "My Dear Brother Boyd," September 6, 1889, AHSLA; Hamilton 1948; Banker 1993; Coleman 1980; Coleman 1985; Salpointe 1898; Women's Board of Home Missions 1893; see also letter books I–V, Tucson Indian Industrial Training School Records, AHSLA.

11. See letter books I–V, Tucson Indian Industrial Training School Records, AHSLA; Ferguson 1997; Franco 1989.

12. Letter from Reverend Howard Billman to General T. J. Morgan, April 17, 1891, AHSLA.

13. Thomas Jefferson Morgan, commissioner of Indian Affairs, "Supplemental Report on Indian Education," *House Executive Document* no. 1, part 5, vol. 2, 51st Congress, 1st session, serial 2725, 1889.

14. Mexico, United States, El Tratado de Guadalupe Hidalgo, 1848 / Treaty of Guadalupe Hidalgo, 1848 (Sacramento, CA: Telefact Foundation, 1968); Griswold del Castillo 1998.

15. See also Reverend Isaac T. Whittemore, "The Pima Indians, Their Manners and Customs," in Women's Board of Home Missions 1893. Many historians have described the specific emphasis on assimilation of Anglo-American gender roles in Indian schools, important among them are: Lomawaima 1993; Trennert 1988; Trennert 1982; Mihesuah 1993; Paxton 2006; Wall 1997.

16. Thomas Jefferson, *Notes on the State of Virginia*, Query XIX. Electronic Text Center, University of Virginia Library. http://etext.lib.virginia.edu/toc/modeng/public/JefBvo21.html. Accessed on June 12, 2012.

17. Thomas Jefferson, "First Inaugural Address, March 4, 1801, quoted in Wilentz 2006, 96.

18. For an analysis of the Federalist-Republican clash, see especially Wilentz 2006; Bailyn 1967; Mayer 1994).

19. The federal support for small farm ownership is evident in the Land Act of 1804 for settlement along the Ohio and Mississippi River valleys; the Military Land Act of 1812; the Donation Land Claim Act of 1850 for Oregon; and the Homestead Act of 1862. Utley and Mackintosh 1989; Krabbendam, Roholl, and de Vries 2001; Keyssar 2000. This is not to say that Universal Manhood Suffrage, as legalized in the Fifteenth Amendment, was not discursively and violently contested across the country, but especially in the postwar South. Immediately

following the passage of the Fifteenth Amendment, many whites, North and South, began to construct gendered perceptions of blacks as inappropriately gendered for American citizenship. This Anglo-American anxiety about blacks was certainly a factor in the very similar anxiety about all nonwhites, including American Indians. Historian Hannah Rosen notes that "the legal scaffolding for a biracial democracy would remain in place, but it could no longer be sustained in practice," after the period of Southern Reconstruction ended in the 1870s (Rosen 2009, 16).

20. Lake Mohonk Conference Proceedings (1900), quoted in Harmon 1990, 14.

21. Warren (2010) notes that many of the same Anglo-American reformers also met at Lake Mohonk to discuss the "Negro Question" during the same periods.

22. See letter books I–IV, Tucson Indian School Records, AHSLA.

23. Reverend Arthur T. Pierson, "Industrial School for Indians . . . Tucson, Arizona" (New York: Women's Board of Home Missions of the Presbyterian Church in the U.S.A., 1902), 7, Elsie Prugh Herndon Records, AHSLA. Frederick Hoxie describes the efforts of Thomas Jefferson Morgan, the commissioner of Indian Affairs between 1889 and 1893, to integrate Indian children into public schools near reservations. Soon after Morgan's tenure as commissioner, the bureau abandoned that effort and returned to the practice of segregating Indian children, which has continued to this day in bureau-funded schools (Hoxie 1982).

24. Letter from Reverend Howard Billman to Miss Moore, March 26, 1891, AHSLA.

25. See also letter books I–V, Tucson Indian Industrial School Records, AHSLA.

26. Haddington Brown to Mrs. Rogers, November 30, 1908, AHSLA.

27. Theodora Kroeber described Juan Dolores as a close friend of Ishi, while they were both living on the campus of the University of California–Berkeley between 1908 and 1916, when Ishi died.

WORKS CITED

Bailyn, Bernard. 1967. *The Ideological Origins of the American Revolution*. Cambridge, MA: Belknap Press of Harvard University Press.

Banker, Mark T. 1993. *Presbyterian Missions and Cultural Interaction in the Far Southwest, 1850–1950*. Urbana: University of Illinois Press.

Bederman, Gail. 1995. *Manliness and Civilization: A Cultural History of Gender and Race in the United States, 1880–1917*. Chicago: University of Chicago Press.

Berkhofer, Robert. 1965. *Salvation and the Savage: An Analysis of Protestant Missions and American Indian Response, 1787–1862*. Lexington: University of Kentucky Press.

Bowden, Henry. 1981. *American Indians and Christian Missions: Studies in Cultural Conflict*. Chicago: University of Chicago Press.

Burns, William James. 2010. "We Must Grow Our Own Artists: Mary-Russell Ferrell Colton, Northern Arizona's Early Art Educator and Advocate." PhD. diss., Northern Arizona University.

Carr, Helen. 1996. *Inventing the American Primitive: Politics, Gender, and the Representation of Native American Literary Traditions, 1789–1936*. New York: New York University Press.

Celaya, Alberto, Paul H. Ezell, and Henry F. Dobyns. 2007. "An Interview with Alberto Celaya, 1952." *Journal of the Southwest* 49 (3): 433–87.

Coleman, Michael C. 1980. "Not Race, But Grace: Presbyterian Missionaries and American Indians." *Journal of American History* 67 (June): 41–60.

———. 1985. *Presbyterian Missionary Attitudes toward American Indians, 1837–1893*. Jackson: University Press of Mississippi.

Culnan, Catherine. 1930. *Indian Sketches*. New York: Board of National Missions of the Presbyterian Church in the U.S.A.

Deloria, Philip. 1998. *Playing Indian*. New Haven, CT: Yale University Press.

Deloria, Vine, and Clifford M. Lytle. 1983. *American Indians, American Justice*. Austin: University of Texas Press.

Dilworth, Leah. 1996. *Imagining Indians in the Southwest: Persistent Visions of Primitive Past*. Washington, DC: Smithsonian Institution Press.

Dolores, Juan, and Madeleine Mathiot. 1991. "The Reminiscences of Juan Dolores, an Early O'odham Linguist." *Anthropological Linguistics* 33 (3): 232–315.

Ferguson, Daniel Bruce. 1997. "The Escuela Experience: The Tucson Indian School In Perspective." Master's thesis, University of Arizona.

Franco, Jeré. 1989. "Howard Billman and the Tucson Indian School, 1888–1894." *Social Sciences Journal* 26 (2): 143–60.

Gifford, Wava, and Bill Higgins. 1974. *The Story of the Smoki People, Prescott, Arizona: Dedicated to the Preservation of Indian Ceremonial Dances and Artifacts*. Prescott, AZ: s.n.

Griswold del Castillo, Richard. 1998. "Manifest Destiny: The Mexican-American War and the Treaty of Guadalupe Hidalgo." *Southwestern Journal of Law and Trade in the Americas* 5: 31–43.

Hamilton, John. 1948. "A History of the Presbyterian Work Among the Pima and Papago Indians of Arizona." Master's thesis, University of Arizona.

Harmon, Alexandra. 1990. "When Is an Indian Not an Indian? 'The Friends of the Indian' and the Problems of Indian Identity." *Journal of Ethnic Studies* 18 (2): 95–123.

Hoxie, Frederick. 1982. "Redefining Indian Education: Thomas J. Morgan's Program in Disarray." *Journal of the Southwest* 24 (1): 5–18.

Huber, Mary. 1999. *Gendered Missions: Women and Men in Missionary Discourse and Practice*. Ann Arbor: University of Michigan Press.

Jacobs, Margaret D. 1999. *Engendered Encounters: Feminism and Pueblo Cultures, 1879–1934*. Lincoln: University of Nebraska Press.

Keyssar, Alexander. 2000. *The Right to Vote: The Contested History of Democracy in the United States*. New York: Basic Books.

Krabbendam, Hans, Marja Roholl, and Tity de Vries. 2001. *The American Metropolis: Image and Inspiration*. Amsterdam: VU University Press.

Kroeber, A. L. 1994. "Juan Dolores, 1880–1948." *American Anthropologist* 51 (1): 96–97.

Kroeber, Theodora. 1961. *Ishi in Two Worlds: A Biography of the Last Wild Indian in North America*. Berkeley: University of California Press.

Lomawaima, K. Tsianina. 1993. "Domesticity in the Federal Indian Schools: The Power of Authority over Mind and Body." *American Ethnologist* 20 (2): 227–40.

Mason, J. Alden. 1950. *The Language of the Papago of Arizona*. Philadelphia: University Museum, University of Pennsylvania.

Mayer, David N. 1994. *The Constitutional Thought of Thomas Jefferson*. Charlottesville: University of Virginia Press.

McCool, Daniel, Susan M. Olson, and Jennifer L. Robinson. 2007. *Native Vote: American Indians, the Voting Rights Act, and the Right to Vote*. New York: Cambridge University Press.

Meeks, Eric. 2003. "The Tohono O'odham, Wage Labor, and Resistant Adaptation, 1900–1930." *Western Historical Quarterly* 34 (4): 468–89.

———. 2007. *Border Citizens: The Making of Indians, Mexicans, and Anglos in Arizona*. Austin: University of Texas Press.

Mihesuah, Devon. 1993. *Cultivating the Rosebuds: The Education of Women at the Cherokee Female Seminary, 1851–1909*. Urbana: University of Illinois Press.

Morgan, Lewis Henry. 1997. *Systems of Consanguinity and Affinity of the Human Family*. Lincoln: University of Nebraska Press.

Moses, Daniel. 2008. *The Promise of Progress: The Life and Work of Lewis Henry Morgan*. Columbia: University of Missouri Press.

Mullin, Molly H. 2001. *Culture in the Marketplace: Gender, Art, and Value in the American Southwest*. Durham, NC: Duke University Press.

Paxton, Katrina A. 2006. "Learning Gender: Female Students at the Sherman Institute, 1907–1925." In *Boarding School Blues: Revisiting American Indian Educational Experiences*. Lincoln: University of Nebraska Press.

Prucha, Francis. 1979. *The Churches and the Indian Schools, 1888–1912*. Lincoln: University of Nebraska Press.

Robert, Dana. 1996. *American Women in Mission: A Social History of Their Thought and Practice*. Macon, GA: Mercer University Press.

Rosen, Hannah. 2009. *Terror in the Heart of Freedom: Citizenship, Sexual Violence, and the Meaning of Race in the Postemancipation South*. Chapel Hill: University of North Carolina Press.

Rothschild, Mary Logan, and Pamela Claire Hronek. 1992. *Doing What the Day Brought: An Oral History of Arizona Women*. Tucson: University of Arizona Press.

Salpointe, Jean Baptiste. 1898. *Soldiers of the Cross: Notes on the Ecclesiastical History of New-Mexico, Arizona, and Colorado*. Banning, CA: St. Boniface's Industrial School.

Shaw, Anna Moore. 1974. *A Pima Past*. Tucson: University of Arizona Press.

Shenk, Wilbert R., ed. 2004. *North American Foreign Missions, 1810–1914: Theology, Theory, and Policy*. Grand Rapids, MI: William B. Eerdmans.

Sim, David. 2008. "The Peace Policy of Ulysses S. Grant." *American Nineteenth Century History* 9 (3): 241–68.

Trafzer, Clifford E., ed. 2006. *Boarding School Blues: Revisiting American Indian Educational Experiences*. Lincoln: University of Nebraska Press.

Trennert, Robert A. 1982. "Educating Indian Girls at Non-Reservation Boarding Schools, 1878–1920." *Western Historical Quarterly* 13 (3): 271–90.

———. 1987. "Selling Indian Education at World's Fairs and Expositions, 1893–1904." *American Indian Quarterly* 11 (3): 203–20.

———. 1988. "Victorian Morality and the Supervision of Indian Women Working in Phoenix, 1906–1930." *Journal of Social History* 22 (1): 113–28.

Utley Robert M., and Barry Mackintosh. 1989. *The Department of Everything Else: Highlights of Interior History*. National Park Service. www.cr.nps.gov/history/online_books/utley-mackintosh/index.htm. Accessed June 13, 2012.

Wall, Wendy. 1997. "Gender and the 'Citizen Indian.'" In *Writing the Range: Race, Class, and Culture in the Women's West*, edited by Elizabeth Jameson and Susan Armitage. Norman: University of Oklahoma Press.

Warren, Kim Cary. 2010. *The Quest for Citizenship: African American and Native American Citizenship in Kansas, 1880–1935*. Chapel Hill: University of North Carolina Press.

Welter, Barbara. 1978. "'She Hath Done What She Could': Protestant Women's Missionary Careers in Nineteenth-Century America." *American Quarterly* 30 (5): 624–38.

Wilentz, Sean. 2006. *The Rise of American Democracy: Jefferson to Lincoln*. New York: Norton.

Women's Board of Home Missions. 1893. *Among the Pimas; or, Mission to the Pima and Maricopa Indians*. Albany, NY: Ladies' Union Mission School Association.

Yohn, Susan. 1995. *A Contest of Faiths: Missionary Women and Pluralism in the American Southwest*. Ithaca, NY: Cornell University Press.

4

HE WANTS TO TAKE
THEM TO RUSSIA!

· · · · · · · · · ·

American Courts and the Battle for Birth Citizens
during the Cold War

JOHN W. HINK JR.

Prior to the mid-twentieth century, the citizenship status of many American-born children remained unclear to the US government. Although the Supreme Court's decision in *United States v. Wong Kim Ark* (1898) had affirmed the Fourteenth Amendment's declaration that all children born in the United States and subject to its jurisdiction are American citizens, there was uncertainty over whether children born in the United States to alien parents retained their citizenship when taken abroad to live in their parents' ancestral homelands, or whether they in fact became denationalized. Finally, in the case of *Perkins v. Elg* (1939) the Supreme Court upheld a child's right to retain American birth citizenship, even if domiciled abroad, allowing such children to choose which country they would be a citizen of when they reached majority.[1] This was a profound development in the history of children's citizenship, declaring it to exist independent of their parents' actions or status.

International custody cases involving American children in the first decades of the Cold War signaled another shift in thinking, although one that would not carry as positive a result. As the United States and the Soviet Union stood in a perpetual standoff over borders and arms, even children became a contested commodity. Due to the sharp contrast between life in the United States and the Soviet Union, as well as the mutual suspicion that each country had for the other, the Cold War made the American courts and the American public more possessive of children who held birth citizenship. In fact, Cold War politics even shaped judicial rulings, at times preventing American-born children from being taken abroad by their parents to live in a communist country under the justification of protecting their right to American citizenship.

As the cases discussed below demonstrate, it was not enough for American-born, dual-citizen children to have the right to *possess* American citizenship. Rather, the Cold War forced many in the United States, often including the courts, to fight to ensure children would have the *benefits* of their American citizenship as well. These benefits, while varying from person to person, most commonly included the right to mobility, to practice one's religion, and an abstract right to a standard of living commensurate with that of ordinary Americans. Such thinking often resulted in court rulings that prevented children from moving with their parents to another country, a violation of the principle of family unity, and the spirit of the recognized right of expatriation, protected by statute since 1868.[2]

This increased interest in protecting American-born children from life under Soviet control was part of a much larger battle between the United States and the Soviet Union over refugees, prisoners of war, displaced persons, and other contested persons. Thus the US government created policies aimed at protecting those who did not wish to be repatriated behind the Iron Curtain and eventually encouraged those in Soviet territories to flee to the West. Within this context several cases arose from the late 1940s through the 1950s in which judges had to decide whether allowing American-born children to accompany their emigrating parents to Soviet-controlled nations would deprive the children of their rights as American citizens.

While scholars such as Susan L. Carruthers (2009) have addressed at least a few of these cases as part of greater Cold War tensions, the cases discussed here say a great deal about the shifting views of Americans regarding children's citizenship, and birthright citizenship in particular, in the wake of World War II. Similarly, these cases highlight the continued expansion of children's rights to citizenship that had been in the works for decades. Of course, the United States lacked the means to intervene in situations where individuals wished to exercise their right to legally expatriate and take their children with them. However, the cases examined here are exceptional in that they all, through one means or another, opened a legal window that allowed the courts to decide whether the children's interests were best served by remaining in the United States or by joining their parents abroad.

Such was the case with Armenian immigrant Hamportzoon Choolokian. Despite having lived in the United States for over thirty years, when the government of Soviet Armenia called for a return of the Armenian Diaspora in 1946, Choolokian became one of several hundred Armenians in the United States to answer. Choolokian's life in America had been difficult, at least in recent years. After his wife had given birth to their sixth child in 1942, she took ill and had to be committed to an asylum. A single parent with six young mouths to feed, Choolokian worked through the New York City Department of Welfare to place his children in orphanages. Due to the lack of a more appropriate institution, the Armenian Orthodox Choolokian agreed to have his five oldest children placed in a Roman Catholic institution, the Mission of the Immaculate Virgin, while his infant son went to the New York Foundling Hospital (Blinken 1949).

After he decided to take his family to Armenia, Choolokian began the process of regaining custody of his children. The Department of Welfare conducted an investigation into his fitness as a parent and gave him a glowing report, noting his devotion to his children, and released his three oldest into his custody. Believing that he would soon be able to regain custody of his younger children, Choolokian secured passage on a resettlement ship to Armenia set to depart November 1, 1947. Having quit his job and given up his apartment, Choolokian only needed to retrieve his wife and three youngest children before his journey. In the days before he was to travel, Choolokian spoke with officials at the Department of Mental Hygiene, where his wife had been institutionalized, who agreed to release her just before they were to board.

However, employees at the mission refused to release the children due to the fact that Choolokian planned to take them to Soviet Armenia. In response, Choolokian retained lawyer Samuel M. Blinken to push his cause. When Blinken confronted the employees about their actions, one exclaimed, "do you know what he wants to do with those children. . . . He wants to take them to Russia!" (Blinken 1949, 552). Unable to persuade the institutions to hand over the children, Blinken spoke with officials in the Department of Welfare. After a second investigation confirmed his fitness as a parent, the Department of Welfare overruled the Catholic institutions and ordered them to release the children.

However, when Choolokian went to retrieve his children a day before he was to sail, officials again refused to comply with his request, despite the Welfare Department's orders. When Blinken attempted to have the Welfare Department intervene once more, officials informed him that the only recourse available to Choolokian would be through the courts. Facing Choolokian's imminent departure, Blinken quickly drafted writs of habeas corpus, had them signed by a judge and served them by early morning on the two institutions holding the Choolokian children. On November 1, hours before his ship was to leave port, Choolokian found himself in the courtroom of New York Supreme Court justice J. Edward Lumbard Jr., fighting for the custody of his three youngest children.

Choolokian appeared to have the facts on his side. He had passed two prior investigations, and the US State Department supported Armenian repatriation. Yet signs quickly appeared that Choolokian would have a difficult time earning a favorable decision in Justice Lumbard's courtroom. Instead of ruling on the matter immediately and possibly allowing Choolokian to sail off with his family, Lumbard delayed the proceedings to allow the Catholic institutions time to prepare their defense. Lumbard's delays carried grave consequences for the Choolokian family's hope for reunification. With his ship set to depart, Choolokian had to decide whether to stay in the United States, jobless and homeless, to fight for his children, potentially losing his opportunity to return to Armenia, or leave his children behind in the hope that they could eventually join him. Ultimately, both parties agreed that Choolokian and his wife could depart without prejudice and continue their efforts from abroad.

When the trial began in early December of 1947, the Catholic institutions alleged that Choolokian was an unfit parent and noted their concern over what would happen to the children should Choolokian be unable to provide for them. However, it became apparent that the central issue behind the Catholic institutions' objection to releasing the children lay in the fact that they would be going to a Soviet state. The institutions stressed that Choolokian intended to take his children to a foreign land culturally distinct from the United States. When Blinken cross examined the director of the

Mission of the Immaculate Virgin, Monsignor John J. Corrigan, Corrigan asserted that "we considered the children American boys adapted to American ways of living and we consider it unfair to subject them to foreign influences contrary to our ideals and to our American way of life." Blinken later asked Corrigan whether he felt that he had the right to prevent the children from going with their father to Soviet Armenia. Corrigan responded, "as an American citizen I believe I have. Our contention is that we have a responsibility to the children reposed in our care." Blinken continued his line of questioning, asking Corrigan, "would you have the same objection if the father wanted to take these children to Spain?" When Corrigan stumbled to find an answer for this question, Blinken asked, "Isn't it a fact that it is a Communist system that you object to?" Here Corrigan clearly displayed the core objection from the Catholic institutions, replying, "I wouldn't hesitate to answer yes to that" ("Mission Here Opposes" 1947).

Signaling that the Choolokian case would have larger legal ramifications, the American Civil Liberties Union (ACLU) began to mobilize in support of the Armenian father, filing an amicus brief on his behalf. The ACLU based their argument around Choolokian's civil and parental rights, noting that "his right to live in Soviet Armenia under a different political and economic system and to have his children with him is an inalienable civil right with which our federal and state governments are prohibited from interfering by those portions of their respective constitutions known as the 'Bill of rights.'" Furthermore, the ACLU contended that unless Choolokian's actions violated American law, the state had no grounds to interfere (American Civil Liberties Union 1950, frame 388).

On December 30, 1947, Justice Lumbard issued a decision against the Choolokian parents.[3] Lumbard threw out the writs of habeas corpus Choolokian had filed on account of the fact that Choolokian had voluntarily given up his children. Lumbard noted that these would not prejudice Choolokian's parental rights to apply to have his children returned to him provided "that the rights of the children as American citizens would be protected and respected, that the interests of the children would be promoted by taking them to Soviet Armenia and that the father is fit, competent and able to duly maintain, support and educate the children in Soviet Armenia." Lumbard's opinion reveals that he saw the case through a Cold War lens, focusing on the question of whether the children would be able to retain the benefits of their American citizenship. Lumbard continued this theme by noting that due to the present conditions in Soviet Armenia, "the court should not permit this father to place his infant children in such an irretrievable position," as this would "dissipate beyond redemption the priceless rights of American citizenship of the children." Lumbard also cited recent diplomatic exchanges between the United States and the Soviet Union over the refusal of the Soviet government to allow American citizens living in the Soviet Union to return to the United States. Lumbard lamented that "probably at no other time in our history as a nation have we been confronted with a situation where our citizens have been treated virtually as prisoners by a foreign power with whom we are at peace."[4] According to Lumbard, then, "If the father were permitted . . . to take these three infant children to Soviet Armenia . . . their American citizenship might be forever lost."[5] Finally, Lumbard upheld the claims that Choolokian could not take care of his children, stating that "it is not in the best interests of the children to be cared for by their father in Soviet Armenia. He is not fit, competent or able to care for them."

In the span of a few pages, Justice Lumbard stripped from Choolokian the long-recognized right of a parent to leave the United States and settle in another country with their children. Similarly, this ruling cut against the principle of family reunification. While he constructed his ruling around multiple factors, clearly the issue that most unnerved Lumbard, as well as the officials of the Mission of the Immaculate Virgin and the New York Foundling Hospital, was the fact that the children were going to live in a communist country.

Lumbard's ruling drew immediate criticism from religious and legal circles. Protestant religious organizations, most notably the Armenian Orthodox church, slammed the ruling for violating Choolokian's right to raise his children according to his religious beliefs. Legal critics also questioned the merits of the ruling. One *Columbia Law Review* article criticized Judge Lumbard's about-face from legal precedent. The article noted that if, in fact, the parent was not fit to care for his child, then such a ruling remained justified in a legal sense. However, the author noted that mere "denial of custody on the ground of the child's possible loss of his citizenship confront the parent with a choice inconsistent with his right of expatriation, a right protected by federal statute." Furthermore, the review questioned whether the interest of the child would be served if courts blocked children from being taken to a communist country, as the alternative would be them living in an institution

("Denial of Custody" 1948). Even a *Virginia Law Review* article that supported state interference in such circumstances noted that the ruling could set a far-reaching precedent that might allow the United States to prevent children, even from stable households, from relocating to other countries if there was a belief that their rights as American citizens could be jeopardized ("Citizenship, Dual Allegiance" 1948).

Choolokian appealed the case unsuccessfully to the New York Appellate Court and the State Supreme Court.[6] Unfortunately for the Choolokian family, those with the power to decide the fate of the Choolokian children held firm to their anticommunist principles.[7] The Supreme Court, too, declined to hear the case during the 1950 term. As Susan L. Carruthers has noted, "few Americans leapt to defend a parent's right to remove an American-born child to the USSR, having for years received strong prompts from the judicial system that 'communists' had no business to be rearing children, let alone removing them from the United States" (Carruthers 2009, 93). However, while the court considered the case, the Soviet Union cited it as part of the reason for not allowing thirty-three American citizens to return to the United States. Thus the significance of the Choolokian case went beyond the custody of three children ("Child-Case" 1950).

Having failed to attain legal redress, Choolokian remained in Soviet Armenia with his wife and oldest children, separated from the rest of his family. Five years later, in January 1955, the Soviet Union offered to release two Americans who had been jailed in the Soviet Union since the 1940s. Although not explicitly delivered as a quid pro quo, at the same time that they made the offer to release the two Americans, Russian officials asked the United States to return twelve children "of purported Soviet origin" living in the United States and West Germany, a group that included the Choolokian children. The proposed exchange brought the now-older Choolokian children back into the spotlight. By 1955 the children had grown up. In fact, George, age twenty, and the oldest of the Choolokian children left in America, was a corporal in the US Marine Corps. Having not seen their parents since they left for Soviet Armenia in November 1947, the Choolokian children expressed little interest in being reunited with their family in a foreign land, nor was the United States looking to repatriate them. Faced with the theoretical prospect of being relocated from the country of his birth, George stated emphatically to the press that "he would definitely say no." When asked if his siblings would leave the United States behind in favor of life behind the Iron Curtain, George replied that "they had a chance to go in the first place and didn't. I doubt if they would change their minds." In the end, the Choolokian children remained in the United States, citizenship intact, family disjointed ("Wouldn't Go" 1955).

The *Choolokian* case offers significant insight into children and citizenship during the Cold War, highlighting the growing importance that the courts, and Americans in general, placed on the benefits of citizenship. The case also affirms the precarious situation that citizen children found themselves in under such circumstances. In acting to protect the Choolokian children's rights to American citizenship, the courts deprived them of the ability to live with their families, forcing them into welfare institutions. Finally, this case was also notable in that a religious institution, whose legal authority over the children came from the state of New York, held the power to decide whether the children would grow up as Americans or Armenians. Accordingly, these children became subject to the paternalism of both the Catholic Church and the courts. Thus while the Choolokian children retained the benefits of American citizenship, they enjoyed such benefits as wards of the state of New York.

A 1954 case obtained similar results, albeit through different legal reasoning. Yugoslavian national Slavoljub Djurovic came to New York with his wife, Zivka, and young son in 1950 as a temporary worker for Yugo metals. However, in January 1954, Slavoljub's employment with Yugo metals abruptly ended. Since he was on a work visa, he and his family would have to return to Yugoslavia. Employment, however, was the least of his problems. Slavoljub and his wife, they now had a second child, had become estranged, their relationship degrading so much as to compel Zivka to accuse him of having an affair. Slavoljub also was subjected to rumors that he was disloyal to Yugoslavia and that he rejected communism. Fearful of the consequences these accusations could bring to him should he return to Yugoslavia, Slavoljub told his wife that he wished to remain in the United States.[8] Zivka initially tried to convince her husband that he would not be harmed if he returned to Yugoslavia. When her efforts proved unsuccessful, she informed him that she would take the children and return on her own. Unable to resolve their differences, the couple placed their children in a boarding school with the understanding that they would take the next month to find a solution to their impasse. Two days later, Zivka arrived at the school escorted by two representatives of the Yugoslavian consulate and took the children into hiding with the intent of returning secretly to Yugoslavia. However, Slavoljub managed to find out about his wife's plot and whereabouts and hastily filed a writ of habeas corpus against her in an attempt to gain custody of his two young sons, now four and six.

The case went before the New York State Supreme Court on February 4, 1954. There Judge Thomas L. J. Corcoran found in favor of the father, Slavoljub, stating his belief that Slavoljub had a legitimate fear of returning to Yugoslavia. Corcoran also emphasized that Slavoljub wanted to "bring up his sons as Americans." Unlike Justice Lumbard in the Choolokian case, Corcoran embraced the legal precedent of family reunification, whereby courts made concerted efforts to keep families intact in immigration and custody cases. Yet Corcoran's reliance on this principle allowed him to circumvent another legal precedent in custody cases, that of giving custody to the mother. He noted that while the courts traditionally ruled in favor of the mother, based on the peculiar circumstances of Slavoljub's position, awarding custody to the mother would deprive the father of all contact with his children forever. However, if the court awarded the father custody, the mother could still visit the children.[9]

Finally, Judge Corcoran pointed out that the youngest Djurovic child had been born in the United States and thus was an American citizen. Citing the *Elg* case, where the Supreme Court ruled that a minor could not lose their birth citizenship even if taken and naturalized abroad, Corcoran stated that "the fact that Yugoslavia may also consider him a citizen of that country does not deprive him of his American citizenship," implying that a move to another country would infringe upon his rights as an American citizen. Furthermore, Corcoran noted that in the case of the Choolokian children, the parents were unable to care for their children, whereas in the *Djurovic* case the father "is willing and anxious to have him brought up as an American boy," suggesting that this case offered an even clearer justification to keep the children in the United States.

Like the *Choolokian* case, the *Djurovic* case shows the emphasis the courts placed on children's rights to the benefits of citizenship. However, *Djurovic* reveals that in order for the courts to keep children in the United States, thus protecting their citizenship, judges had to reevaluate the importance they placed on other factors they usually called upon in making their decisions. In contrast to the Choolokian ruling, which shunned parental rights, Judge Corcoran used Slavoljub's parental rights as the foundation of his ruling to uphold the children's right to citizenship. This, however, deprived the children's mother of custody, a departure from the legal norm. Taken together the rulings in *Choolokian* and *Djurovic* suggest that judges became so interested in protecting the children's rights to the benefits of their American birth citizenship that they looked past legal precedents such as parental rights and family unification.

A similar case that arose in the late 1950s resulted in a slightly different outcome. This case involved the four young boys of George and Madezhda Kozmin, former displaced persons who had survived Nazi labor camps. The couple came to the United States with their three young sons in 1950, settling in Chicago in 1952. George and Madezhda's hard lives eventually caught up with them, as they both suffered emotional breakdowns in 1953, resulting in their institutionalization and their children being placed in foster homes. In 1954 George was released, and his wife was released the year after. In 1956 the couple gave birth to a fourth son, Peter, a dual citizen by virtue of his birth in the United States and his Russian parentage. Peter, too, became a ward of the court, but lived with his parents due to his young age.

Having failed to attain emotional or financial stability in the United States, George and Madezhda decided to return to the Soviet Union and called upon the Russian embassy for assistance. In order to return to the Soviet Union as a family, however, George and Madezhda had to regain custody of their children, filing a case to get their children returned in Cook County Family Court in May of 1956. Due to the Cold War implications of the case, it drew front-page attention in the *Chicago Tribune*. The article placed the case firmly within its Cold War context, noting that the question before the court was essentially "whether the children of George and Madezhda Kozmin will have the chance of a life in the United States or be reared as young communists by the Kremlin rulers" (Thompson 1957d).

Judge John H. Clayton Jr. had the task of deciding whether allowing the children to join their parents was in their best interest. Clayton held several hearings on the issue to determine the well-being of the parents and whether the children's welfare in the Soviet Union could be ensured. Meanwhile, the media turned its attention to the children, depicting them as all-American boys and implying the boys should stay in the United States. One article noted that when Richard was told about the impending custody case and informed by the supervisor of the home that he would not have to go if he did not want to, he stated: "Of course, I don't want to, I want to stay here," a sentiment echoed by his younger brother George, who noted of Russia that

"I wasn't ever there." The article then noted that Richard could not find Russia on a map and spoke no Russian save for the phrase "I want some milk." Continuing to frame the children as being wholly American, the article recounted that Richard spoke unaccented English and watched the Mickey Mouse Club on television, activities that should have marked any American child as distinct from those in the rest of the world (Hutchinson 1957).

On April 10, 1957, Judge Clayton ruled consistent with the aforementioned cases, deciding not to award the Kozmin parents custody of their children. The parents had testified that morning that they would return to the Soviet Union with or without their children. After his ruling, Clayton informed them that if they remained in the United States, the court would work with them on getting their children back; however, they would have fewer guarantees of assistance should they choose to leave. The judge set a hearing for May 15 to hear from the Red Cross on what the Kozmin children would face in Russia, theoretically leaving the door open to their return (Thompson 1957d).

With custody of the children settled for the immediate future, newspapers turned their attention to the efforts of Soviet officials to lure the Kozmins back to the Soviet Union without their children. One article claimed that Russian officials attempted to woo the Kozmin parents through fancy dinners, forcing readers to ponder the real motives for the Kozmin's actions, especially in light of their precarious economic circumstances. The Kozmin case was thus being tried in the court of public opinion as much as the court of Judge Clayton (Thompson 1957c).

On May 15, Judge Clayton heard once more from Soviet officials who guaranteed that the children's well-being and education would be assured back in Russia. Stephen Love, the Kozmin parents' attorney, framed the case in terms of foreign policy, stating to the judge that "he would not like the Russians to be able to say that an American court had enforced a family separation" (Thompson 1957a). Despite Soviet assurances, Judge Clayton again refused to award George and Madezhda custody of their children. Clayton did, however, propose an arrangement should the parents remain in the United States, whereby the family would be reunited over the summer for a trial period to see whether it could function properly. However, George and Madezhda, without physical custody of three of their sons and without legal custody of all of them, decided that they would return to the Soviet Union without their children and pursue their case from there. Notably, at the time of the decision, Madezhda had found out that she was expecting another child. Were she to give birth on American soil, that child would also be an American citizen, an option Madezhda did not wish to entertain out of fear that the child could become a ward of the state as well (Thompson 1957f; "Kozmins Plan Plea" 1957).

One month later, on June 11, after Judge Clayton had refused a plea to allow Peter to return to the Soviet Union with his parents, deputy sheriffs stopped Mr. and Mrs. Kozmin in the LaSalle Street train station in Chicago. They were attempting to take their nine-month-old son, Peter, with them to New York City en route to the Soviet Union. Upon seeing the couple preparing to leave for New York, sheriff deputies had contacted the probation officer of the family court who issued a writ permitting them to seize the child. Despite having their child taken from them, George and Madezhda continued on their Soviet-financed journey to Russia. With the parents gone, Judge Clayton placed the youngest child in a foster home, spreading the four Kozmin children across three locations. After Peter's removal, attorney Stephen Love expressed dismay over the outcome of the Kozmin case, remarking that "this is the most illogical, silly, impractical decision I've ever heard of in any court. The result will be used by the Russians for the propaganda against us all over the world." His words proved quite prophetic (Thompson 1957b; "Boy Saved" 1957).

The Soviet press seized the opportunity to use the case to besmirch the United States. *Pravda* ran an article depicting the Kozmin's misfortune as typical of life in the United States. In the article, George Kozmin told a tale about working for a farmer in Arkansas who attempted to feed him canned dog food until Kozmin became the wiser. The article also implied that Russian repatriates had a good chance of being incarcerated in the United States and accused the United States of institutionalizing the Kozmins as a means of preventing them from returning to the Soviet Union. It then claimed that once the parents were released, the children were held hostage to prevent their departure. However, it noted that the Kozmin parents nobly "did not abandon their decision to return to Russia even tho threats had been made to take away their fourth child" ("Pravda Emphasizes" 1957; "Red and American" 1957). *Komsomol Pravda*, a Soviet youth publication, ran a similar article in which George Kozmin alleged that Judge Clayton and Benjamin Novoselsky, the assistant state's attorney, had offered him $5 million to stay in the United States. These claims lacked any factual basis. However, they played right into the hands of the Soviet propaganda machine. The Kozmins even appeared on Soviet television, where they shared their story and stated their desire to be in the Soviet Union rather than the United States ("Kozmin Says" 1957; "Chicago Couple" 1957).

American sentiment largely favored the Kozmin children remaining in the United States. One letter to the editor of the *Chicago Tribune* expressed distaste for the actions of the Kozmin parents, arguing, "No good mother leaves her children behind," and noting, "They should have appreciated this country more." Some, however, did find fault with the ruling. Yet even those who did not agree with the outcome of the case tended to frame their dissent in terms of American exceptionalism. One letter to the *Tribune* from "Anti-Communist Citizen" suggested that preventing the Kozmins from keeping Peter was "most unfortunate" and harkened back to early American history by asking, "How would a family of pilgrims have liked to have their children snatched from them had they been unhappy in this new land?" The writer continued by arguing that letting the child return with the parents "would have shown them and the world that the United States could be kind in its dealing." Thus while there may not have been total agreement about what should have happened to the Kozmin children, those commenting on the case agreed upon the superiority of life in the United States ("Voice" 1957; "Glad" 1957).

With the Kozmin parents back in Russia, the case appeared to be wrapped up, receiving no attention in the press for the remainder of 1957. However, in early 1958, the Kozmin case reemerged, becoming subject to high-level diplomatic negotiations between the United States and the Soviet Union. In March 1958, Soviet ambassador Mikhail Menshikov called upon the US secretary of state, John Foster Dulles, to discuss reuniting the Kozmin children with their parents. For the State Department, the Kozmin children had become part of much larger foreign policy concerns ("Soviet Envoy" 1958).

Despite the greater national interest in the case, Judge Clayton remained unmoved, rejecting a plea by the Russian embassy to release the boys by citing the children's best interest ("Court Rejects" 1958). Still, Soviet officials continued to pressure the United States to release the children ("Russia Prods" 1958). In September 1958, the *Chicago Tribune* reported that the State Department had begun an investigation into the living conditions in Russia and had discussed reopening the case with assistant Illinois attorney general Grenville Beardsley ("U.S. Expected to Aid" 1958). The article noted that the State Department's interest in the case stemmed from a fear that the Soviets would retaliate against the United States by not permitting the travel or emigration of relatives of Americans living in the Soviet Union.

As a means of preventing such threats, the United States would allow the children to leave in order to serve greater foreign policy interests. In March 1959, the Soviets again demanded that the four Kozmin children be sent to the Soviet Union to be with their parents ("Reds Ask U.S." 1959). Bowing to Soviet pressure, the US State Department sent a letter to Illinois governor William G. Stratton that June, asking the state to assist in reunifying the family. Heeding the wishes of the federal government, the Illinois attorney general's office reopened the case in July, placing it in the circuit court of Cook County before Chief Justice Thomas E. Kluczynski.

By this point the Kozmin parents had been out of the country for almost two years, and the children had been in state custody for six. The Kozmin's attorney and the Soviet officials acting on their behalf submitted considerable documentation to Judge Kluczynski aimed at demonstrating their ability to care for their children. Kluczynski was informed that George was working as a mechanic and Madezhda as a seamstress, and that they lived in a building that had a nursery where the children could have hot meals ("Joys of Russia" 1959). Judge Kluczynski also received a copy of the State Department's letter to Governor Stratton stating its wishes. Notably, Kluczynski decided to meet with the boys in person in order to ascertain their desires. Meanwhile, Vice President Richard Nixon and Soviet Premier Nikita Khrushchev carried out discussions over reuniting families divided between the East and West. In a letter to Khrushchev, Nixon intimated that the United States favored such family reunifications, whether in the United States or the Soviet Union, specifically citing the Kozmin case as one of interest.[10]

With the US government eagerly awaiting the court's decision, Judge Kluczynski ruled that the children should be reunited with their parents no later than October 1, 1959. Kluczynski cited the fact that the children wanted to be together and live as a family. Kluczynski also noted that the state had failed to convince him that the Kozmins were unfit parents, indicating that he believed the evidence Soviet officials furnished. Finally, Kluczynski asserted that the fact that the Kozmin parents do not hold beliefs in accordance with American principles should not affect the outcome of the case (Southerland 1959; "Soviet Couple" 1959).

While some in the United States who had followed the case were no doubt perplexed that a judge would send four children, one of whom was a US birth citizen, to the Soviet Union, others saw reasons to be optimistic about the Kozmin decision. In addition to the Kozmin parents, the decision also pleased Victor and Bedriska Lonsmin. The Lonsmins had left behind three daughters in Czechoslovakia when they came to the United States in 1948. Having tried unsuccessfully to get the government of Czechoslovakia to release their children, they saw the Kozmin case as a positive development in their quest for family unity. They had even written Judge Kluczynski to share their story in the hope that he would allow the Kozmin boys to follow their parents to Russia ("Joys of Russia" 1959). Following the Kozmin decision, the Lonsmins stated in a *Chicago Tribune* article, "now that America has given the Kozmin children to their parents, we hope the Communists will give our children back to us." Judge Kluczynski's decision thus had the potential to affect other international custody disputes ("New Hope" 1959).

On August 28, the Kozmin boys landed in Moscow, reunited with their parents at long last ("Kozmin Boys" 1959). By the end of 1959 the boys had slipped from the public eye as they began their new lives in Soviet Russia. Their case was not forgotten, however. Several years later Judge Kluczynski cited the Kozmin ruling as "probably the most difficult I ever had to make." Yet even in hindsight the judge believed he made the right call, noting that "we cannot force our way of life on others and we should not interfere with the natural rights of parents to their own children" (Browning 1961).

In 2000, while the Elian Gonzales case, which paralleled the story of the Kozmins, dominated American headlines, *Chicago Tribune* reporters tracked down the Kozmin brothers in Russia. The article explained that the children had struggled growing up "aliens, in a xenophobic country," caught between two worlds, a strange irony considering the fact that both countries had fought so hard for the children. Richard, now Rotislav, Kozmin remarked, "Since we came from America, our life is broken. . . . Everything has been ruined." Ironically, Peter, the only Kozmin child born in the United States, suffered the least of his siblings and claimed to understand his parents' decision to return. An artist by trade, Peter had been able to take advantage of his American citizenship and travel to the West with ease, offering him advantages unavailable to his brothers. Yet both Peter and Richard expressed regret at the way the Soviets dealt with their case, noting that "they used us as an advertisement" (Osnos and McMahon 2000).

The aforementioned cases highlight the precarious position that children's citizenship occupied within the context of the Cold War. The children who became embroiled in these custody disputes became unwitting victims in an international tug-of-war due to the disabilities and uncertainties placed upon their citizenship by virtue of their age, as minors who lacked standing before the law, and their generational status, as they were still subject to their parents' authority. Under the complicated circumstances the Cold War created, the children's parents, and the Soviet officials who frequently spoke on their behalf, could craft arguments in favor of the children's relocation based on a parent's right of expatriation, subordinating the importance of the child's citizenship. Meanwhile, those Americans who sought to protect the children from a life under communist rule could justify keeping these children in the United States and separating them from their families by claiming to act in defense of the children's American citizenship. Tragically, however, the wishes and concerns of the children themselves often became obscured by foreign policy objectives and Cold War thinking, a tragic development that called into question just what rights these children's citizenship afforded them. Even the Kozmin children, who were reunited with their parents, only attained family unity when it was in the interest of US foreign policy.

These custody cases also reveal significant shifts in American thought with regard to the value placed on children's birth citizenship, revealing how American courts and public opinion became possessive of birth citizens and assertive in their willingness to protect the benefits of American citizenship. Whereas Americans had once deemed dual nationals as less than American and as those they wished to purge from the rolls of citizenship, due to the political climate of the Cold War, Americans heartily supported children's "right" to grow up as Americans in the United States, if the alternative was life behind the Iron Curtain. Of course, such possession was tied explicitly to the context of the Cold War. At the same time that Americans were fighting to keep the Choolokian, Djurovic, and Kozmin children in the United States, Yuki Oda shows in his work in this collection that the US government was simultaneously seeking to limit the ability of American citizen children born to Mexican American repatriates from entering the United States and enjoying the rights of their citizenship.

For Cold War custody cases, protecting children's birth citizenship often required judges to reevaluate the criteria they used to adjudicate such cases in order to justify keeping children separate from their parents. Instead of adhering to the precedent that children with dual nationality would follow their parents physically to whatever country they wished to go, deciding at majority which country's citizenship they wished to retain, courts emphasized children's rights to the benefits of citizenship. This was largely a new development, but one that followed the expansion of children's rights to citizenship that had been underway since the *Elg* decision of 1939. Unfortunately, judicial efforts to protect children's citizenship did not necessarily benefit the children involved, as children often had to suffer being separated from their parents and institutionalization.

The fact that many of the parents involved in these cases had been institutionalized had a great impact on their ability to win a favorable outcome in court, as judges weighed not only the legal merits of the case but also sought to make determinations regarding their mental fitness. The institutionalization for mental health reasons of the Choolokian and Kozmin parents placed an even greater burden on them to prove to the state that they were fit and competent parents while tainting them in the eyes of the court and the public. Thus even when provided evidence that Hamportzoon Choolokian was a mentally fit and competent parent, Judge Lumbard could rule against him. Similarly, the Kozmin parents, who also had been institutionalized, lost their first legal attempt at having their children returned to their custody largely due to concerns about their mental health, yet they were still allowed to have physical custody of their newborn child. Thus institutionalization offered judges a window to rule against the interest of the parents.

Similarly, the fact that the children had been voluntarily placed under the care of the state offered further complications, as it created an opportunity for both the state and those who ran the various foster institutions that held the children to weigh in on what their best interest would be. Thus these cases show how discussions over citizenship were influenced and at times were co-opted by nongovernment entities. The Catholic Church, in particular, played an influential role in the Choolokian case by virtue of its anticommunist positions and the opportunities afforded them by these unique circumstances. Thus the Catholic institutions holding the Choolokian children refused to return them to their parents even when ordered to do so by the Department of Welfare. The church, no doubt, viewed its efforts as saving souls, ensuring the children's spiritual well-being at the expense of family unity. Of course, as Amy Grey reveals in her essay in this volume, religious institutions have a long history of involvement in citizenship issues in the United States.

Finally, global politics shaped these cases a great deal. The anticommunist climate of the day clearly shaped the way the courts and the American public perceived the Soviet world. Yet as the Kozmin case reveals, American foreign policy could also directly affect a case's outcome. The Kozmin children were only reunited with their parents when the State Department, concerned over Soviet refusals to allow American citizens living in the Soviet Union to return to America, pressured the state of Illinois to reopen the case. The children thus became pawns in a game between the two superpowers, largely unconcerned with the individual welfare of young children.

The political fears of the Cold War are long gone. Yet these cases still carry relevance for children's citizenship today. First, they speak broadly to the influence that global politics can have on American citizenship, shading the way in which the American people and their government socially construct the idea of American citizenship. As Yuki Oda's and Saeed A. Khan's articles in this collection attest, a legal right to citizenship is often distinct from social acceptance in society. Such questions were once again brought to the fore in the Elian Gonzales case of 2000. There the American people watched as a young child's relatives in America argued against returning him to his father in Cuba by employing anticommunist rhetoric eerily reminiscent of that used in the 1950s.

The recent debates over immigration reform in this country have similarly forced Americans to confront relationships between age, generation, and citizenship, raising the question of whether the rights of a child born in the United States are infringed upon if their undocumented parents are deported to their country of origin. Like the cases above, such questions force the courts to try to reconcile the letter of the law with the spirit of citizenship and force judges to weigh the importance of the legal status of the parent as an undocumented alien against the right of a child to not have to choose between the country of their birth and family unification. Although these questions are legal and political in nature, their solutions carry significant and at times catastrophic social consequences.

NOTES

1. *Perkins v. Elg*, 307 U.S. 325 (1939).
2. Act of July 27, 1868, ch. 249, 15 Stat. 223, 223 (1868) (the Expatriation Act).
3. *People ex. Rel. Choolokian v. Mission of Immaculate Virgin*, 192 Misc. 454, 76 N.Y.S. 2d 509, N.Y. Sup. 1947.
4. The communiqué asked the Soviet Union to facilitate the return of American nationals who had been forcibly removed to the Soviet Union and Soviet women married to US citizens. The Department of State to the Embassy of the Soviet Union, May 28, 1947. *Foreign Relations of the United States*. Vol. IV.

5. *People ex Rel. Choolokian v. Mission of Immaculate Virgin*, 192 Misc. 454, 76 N.Y.S. 2d 509, N.Y. Sup. 1947.

6. *People ex re. Choolokian v. Mission of Immaculate Virgin*, 300 N.Y. 43 (1949); *People ex re. Choolokian v. Mission of Immaculate Virgin*, 300 N.Y. 622 (1949).

7. Samuel M. Blinken to American Civil Liberties Union, June 13, 1949. In American Civil Liberties Union 1950–90.

8. *People Ex Rel. Djurovic v. Djurovic*, 205 Misc. 216 (1954).

9. Ibid.

10. Vice President Richard M. Nixon to Chairman Nikita Khrushchev, August 1, 1959, in *Foreign Relations of the United States*, 1958–60, vol. X, Part I, Eastern Europe Region, Soviet Union, Cyprus, Document 104.

WORKS CITED

American Civil Liberties Union. 1950–90. Series 4: Legal Case Files. "Choolokian, Hamportzoon," Child Custody Case 1950. Roll 90.

Blinken, Samuel M. 1949. "The Shoemaker's Children." *The Nation*, May 14, 551–54.

"Boy Saved from Soviets." 1957. *New York Times*, June 12.

Browning, Norma Lee. 1961. "Court Decisions Are Sometimes Criticized But—Could YOU Be the Judge?" *Chicago Daily Tribune*, June 11.

Carruthers, Susan L. 2009. *Cold War Captives: Imprisonment, Escape, and Brainwashing*. Berkeley: University of California Press.

"Chicago Couple on Moscow TV Show." 1957. *Chicago Daily Tribune*, June 21.

"Child-Case Review Refused Despite Plea of Russia." 1950. *Seattle Times*. March 13.

"Citizenship, Dual Allegiance: Repatriation of Minors to Soviet Armenia." 1948. *Virginia Law Review* 34 (5): 601–2.

"Court Rejects Russian Plea For 4 Children." 1958. *Chicago Daily Tribune*, March 20.

"Denial of Custody of Children to Parent Contemplating Expatriation." 1948. *Columbia Law Review* 48 (4): 643–45.

Foreign Relations of the United States, 1947. 1971–73. Washington, DC: US Government Printing Office.

Foreign Relations of the United States, 1958–60. 1992. Washington, DC: US Government Printing Office.

"Glad to Be Here." 1957. *Chicago Daily Tribune*, June 22.

Hutchinson, Louise. 1957. "Child Sought By Russians Prefers U.S." *Chicago Daily Tribune*, March 31.

"'Joys of Russia' Told Court in Kozmin Custody Battle." 1959. *Chicago Daily Tribune*, July 28.

"Kozmin Boys Share 2 Room Moscow Flat." 1959. *Chicago Daily Tribune*, August 31.

"Kozmin Says He Refused U.S. Million's." 1957. *Chicago Daily Tribune*, June 21.

"Kozmins Plan Plea to Take Baby to Russia." 1957. *Chicago Daily Tribune*. May 18.

"Mission Here Opposes Plan to Send 2 Boys to Join Their Parents in Soviet Armenia." 1947. *New York Times*, December 4.

"New Hope for 3 Girls Still in Red Land." 1959. *Chicago Daily Tribune*, August 21.

Osnos, Evan, and Colin McMahon. 2000. "Elian Case Echoes '50s Custody Fight. The 4 Kozmins Were Torn between Their Parents and Global Politics. *Chicago Tribune*, February 6.

"Pravda Emphasizes Soviet Repatriates." 1957. *New York Times*, June 15.

"Red and American Views on Kozmins." 1957. *Chicago Daily Tribune*, June 15.

"Reds Ask U.S. Again to Send 4 to Parents." 1959. *Chicago Daily Tribune*, March 13.

"Russia Prods for Return of Four Children." 1958. *Chicago Daily Tribune*, July 13.

Southerland, Jacquelin. 1959. "Judge Orders Four Boys, Court Wards, Sent to Parents in Russia." *Chicago Daily Tribune*, August 20.

"Soviet Couple Wins U.S. Custody Battle." 1959. *New York Times*, August 20.

"Soviet Envoy Seeks Return of 4 Boys." 1958. *New York Times*, March 19.

Thompson, John H. 1957a. "Bars Taking Four Boys to Russia." *Chicago Daily Tribune*, May 16.

———. 1957b. "Reds Depart; Baby Seized." *Chicago Daily Tribune*, June 12.

———. 1957c. "Reds Wine and Dine Dad of 4." *Chicago Daily Tribune*, April 18

———. 1957d. "Refuses to Return Four Children to Soviet Pair." *Chicago Daily Tribune*, April 11.

———. 1957e. "Russia Seeks 4 Boys Here." *Chicago Daily Tribune*, March 30.

———. 1957f. "Russian DP Couple to Go Home, Leave 3 Sons Here." *Chicago Daily Tribune*, May 17.

"U.S. Expected to Aid Russia in Kozmin Case." 1958. *Chicago Daily Tribune*, September 29.

"Voice of the People." 1957. *Chicago Daily Tribune*, June 18.

"'Wouldn't Go,' Says Marine Sought by Russ." 1955. Associated Press, January 5.

PART 2

....

Young Age, Globalization, Migration

5

THE NEGOTIATION OF CITIZENSHIP AMONG PAKISTANI YOUTH IN GREAT BRITAIN

· · · · · · · · · ·

Intersections, Interventions, and Interactions

SAEED A. KHAN

Citizenship is based on the mutual exchange of rights and responsibilities between the state and the citizen. It allows for both the passive and active membership of its individuals to engage within a specified and prescribed degree of equality (Janoski and Hicks 2009). At the same time, however, with the forces of globalization and transnationalism dismantling and then reconfiguring national boundaries and interpersonal relations within political, legal, social, cultural, and ideological spheres, traditional constructions of citizen-state discourse are increasingly in need of similar reformulation. The phenomenon of global citizenship is now emerging as an additional, sometimes competing, category of political engagement and identity construction. Like its more conventional, nation-based counterpart, global citizenship is based on social rights and a shared fate, yet it allows for the boundaries of the nation-state to be de-emphasized, even ignored, as a barrier to engagement (Arneil 2007).

If citizenship can assume a global character, especially given migrational and transnational realities, do one's rights and responsibilities require such exchange to occur reciprocally, that is, within a single nation-state? If the characteristics of global citizenship allow for a recognition and assertion of social rights and the realization of shared fate, then it is plausible to claim one's legal rights of citizenship within one space and discharge the responsibilities of citizenship in another, provided that it does not lead to a consistently asymmetrical relationship between citizen and nation from where those rights are derived.

This chapter examines the notion of citizenship as it relates to Pakistani Muslims in Great Britain, and specifically, British Pakistani youth, for whom Britain is their country of birth, domicile, and nationality. At the same time, however, cultural, emotional, and familial connections to Pakistan inform their perspectives on identity, belonging, and how their citizenship, as both an ontological category and a legally defined status, is contested, reconciled, and reified. Various factors inform the way these youth perceive their citizenship, their identity, and their sense of belonging; equally poignant are the factors that inform the way in which British society and the state perceive these individuals who possess British nationality and citizenship in the legal sense, but may be regarded nonetheless as culturally and ethnically foreign or alien. To examine the effects of citizenship on the consciousness of this subgroup of an ethnic minority community, this chapter will explore two case studies of Pakistani youth in Britain, one focused on the urban, cosmopolitan atmosphere in London, the other within the well-established and sustained ethnic enclave of Bradford in the country's north.

In 2008, Ibrahim Khalid was seemingly a typical eleven-year-old schoolboy hailing from the northern suburbs of London, England. Although born in Great Britain and having lived there his entire, albeit short, life, Ibrahim self-identified as a Pakistani. When asked why he did not consider himself to be British despite his nationality and upbringing, Ibrahim replied that it was because British society did not see him as being British and reminded him everyday that he was a "Paki." Given the experience of many South Asians in Britain over the past several decades, Ibrahim's account was unremarkable, as racism as a function of ethnic origin is a common, sustained phenomenon in Britain, particularly vis-à-vis those of Pakistani heritage. And yet the "push" factor of dominant society rejecting the legitimacy of Ibrahim's birthright British citizenship was accompanied by the "pull" factor of his Pakistani identification, an affiliation that was reinforced by the self-evidence of his physical appearance as much as by the prevailing perspective in his home. But how strong were his ties to a Pakistani identity beyond the obvious bonds informed by his parents, siblings, and the atmosphere in his family home? After all, Ibrahim spoke to his mother and father in English despite their primary use of Urdu. In addition, Ibrahim conceded that he had only visited Pakistan once in his life, "When I was a kid." Other forces clearly were reinforcing, even enhancing Ibrahim's sense of dislocated ethnic and national identity. The answer was satellite ethnic television, which dominated his window to the world at home, and the subject of Pakistan, which dominated the family conversations. Admitting that Pakistani channels like ARY and GEO monopolized television viewing in his living room, Ibrahim was the recipient of a steady wave of news from the "homeland," and especially the effects of US drone attacks along the Afghan-Pakistani border. Ibrahim witnessed hundreds of images of children of his age and countenance, women, and men killed and maimed by the aerial bombings. Intentionally provocative through the selection of ever increasingly graphic photos and video, these satellite channels exercised little restraint or warning of broadcasting shots of mutilated and bloodied bodies who for Ibrahim, "looked a lot like me" (Khan 2012a).

Deeply affected by the consistent consumption of such imagery, Ibrahim internalized the conflict occurring thousands of miles away in a distant land he had visited only once yet identified as being the birthplace of his identity. He also intensified his anger at those he perceived to be actively involved in killing his compatriots, and he sought to engage in what he regarded as his duties as a Pakistani *citizen*: fight the Americans in Pakistan. When informed that he was too young to fly unaccompanied to the war zone and conceding that his parents would disapprove of his intentions and travel plans, Ibrahim resigned himself to remain in London—and fight there. Although reminded that it was the Americans, not the British, who were conducting the drone assaults in Pakistan, Ibrahim seemed unaffected by the distinction, replying that for him, the British and the Americans were the same thing; after all, if the British could reject him as being Pakistani, not British, based on his appearance, then he was justified in perceiving Americans and Britons to be fungible as "they all look alike to me" (Khan 2012a).

With sufficient contrast to life in London, Bradford is a postindustrial town in the north of England. Situated roughly halfway between Leeds and Manchester, the city has endured an arduous period of readjustment after its main economic base, the wool industry, dwindled and departed for the new manufacturing countries. Over one-fourth of Bradford's population is Asian, primarily Pakistani Muslims from Mirpur. Having migrated from Pakistan in the 1960s and 1970s to work in the textile factories, members of this community are largely an unskilled labor force. With few qualifications and educational credentials, many older generation Pakistanis have been adversely affected by the city and region's economic changes or have simply retired and accepted to live off their benefits. For subsequent generations, however, economic prospects are bleak at best; poor employment opportunities from deindustrialization, the general absence of familial and communal emphasis on education, and institutional barriers impeding upward mobility all limit chances of success for the youth to advance academically, socially, financially. Of course, such conditions are not confined to the Pakistani youth population of Bradford; it is a dilemma facing many Britons, especially in recent years with successive recessions and government austerity measures exacerbating economic strain. However, the insular nature of the Bradford Pakistani community, heavily intermarried and interbred, and poorly integrated into broader British society, further complicates and impedes progress and simultaneously intensifies the torpor, alienation, and isolation of the youth.

During the long summer evenings of the British north, many young ethnic Pakistani men may be seen gathering in groups in the Bradford city center. With no meaningful work or prospects for employment, they simply sit around day after day, in gang-like groups. Yet beneath their passive appearance, these young people perceive a world to which they claim no sense of belonging and significant engagement. When asked what they felt about the 2005 "7/7" London bombings that had occurred the prior year, many proudly offered the statistic that three of the four perpetrators hailed from the industrial north, close to the Bradford region. But such approbation was not for the attack itself or its violent results; rather, it was because people from their locale had actually committed an act of notoriety, even celebrity, especially as the British north had finally struck the perceived arrogance of London and Londoners. But did they not feel a sense of outrage at a terrorist strike in Britain? Apparently, these young men harbored a very negative opinion of British society and state, arguing that dominant British culture rejected them, refused to accept them as British despite their birthplace, their residence and future all being resigned and confined to Britain and perhaps Bradford specifically. If British society in their estimation rejected them, and if they reciprocated such sentiment upon British society, was this an attitude reinforced in the mosque or Muslim discourse of Bradford? The answer was a shocking "no." These young men rejected the mosque as much as they rejected enfranchisement in British society because the religious community was culturally alien to them. The use of imported clerics with little to no cultural context or focus on the challenges facing the Pakistani youth of Bradford helped to create the chasm between the mosque and these youth, in a sense, dispelling any notions that these youth were jihadists or proto-jihadists, while at the same time informing the intensity of their feelings of alienation. Again, Pakistani satellite television was the primary, if not sole, currency of communications to the outside world within the households of all of the young people. That their parents were singularly focused on happenings in Pakistan to the almost categorical neglect and awareness of the Bradford or British landscape placed a further barrier for the youth, forcing them, in a sense, to seek a more realistic space, that is, their town's central square.

Alienation from society for the Bradford Pakistani youth is both a cause and a function of an inability and unwillingness to participate in any form of civic or political engagement. Consequently, they do not feel as though state authority applies to them. The religious and ethnocultural community to which they belong is inadequate to address the challenges they face as second- and third-generation Pakistanis, by compelling them to live pursuant to a code that is spatially and even temporally anachronistic. As a result, they reject their own ethnic community and refuse to consider developing stable relationships through marriage, partly due to a fear that they will not only be made to marry someone from Pakistan itself, but also, per Mirpuri cultural modalities, a cousin. Lines of communication are tenuous at best within the home, as parents are seen as conniving matchmakers, plotting with uncles and aunts for future wedding plans, or living in a virtual ghetto through their focus on events in Pakistan as refracted through GEO and ARY. Rejecting state, community, and family modes of authority, these young men have become serial nihilists, answering to the authority of their own conscience or to the collective conscience of their circle of friends (Khan 2012b).

In examining the theoretical constructs and narratives regarding multiculturalism and citizenship, Will Kymlicka's groundbreaking work on multicultural citizenship (1995) offers a helpful point of departure to assess the situation of British Pakistani youth and their relationship to citizenship. Kymlicka argues that there are multinational states, containing "national minorities," or national groups, that possess a distinct language, culture, and territory, and polyethnic states, which experience immigration and the presence of ethnic groups, having a culture and language but no defined territory or claim of ownership.[1] Ethnic groups usually integrate into larger society, whereas national groups tend to remain distinct.

Kymlicka's categories also address the degree and depth of integration efforts. As such, they seemingly would place the British Pakistani community firmly in the ethnic group. An immigrant community with its own cultural and linguistic identity markers, ethnic Pakistanis in Britain have allowed for the organic infusion of their cultural modalities, cuisine, apparel, and such to become part of broader society.[2]

Ethnic and national groups, according to Kymlicka, interact civically and politically with broader society in different ways, especially to assert what is perceived to be special treatment. Both groups may assert the claim of special representation within the central government, given their relatively small size. In addition, national groups strive for greater autonomy or even self-determination, even if it requires a federal structure to exist; this is political citizenship to protect political and cultural space. By contrast, ethnic groups may avail themselves of the political process but only to preserve and protect cultural space from dominant society, for example, use of ethnic languages, apparel, and such. One may contend that the Pakistani community exhibits inclinations toward being a national group by maintaining increasingly isolated and culturally distinct modalities. While it may certainly appear to be treated by these communities as their own and special territories in an implicit manner, there is no evidence that these cities or boroughs are seeking self-rule or engaging in the civic or political arenas to limit access for those outside their respective groups. Instead, and in accordance with ethnic group priorities, the British Pakistanis strive for the buoyancy of their cultural and linguistic space as a harmonious, not antagonistic, element of broader society.

The British Pakistani community, in seeking special accommodation for its cultural modalities, does so not to remain different and distinct; after all, it acknowledges and accepts dominant culture and resides and operates in large measure within its construct without denial or disdain. Rather, as Kymlicka maintains, it is an example of an ethnic community exercising its political citizenship optimally. Motivated by being full participants in the public sphere, the community seeks recognition of certain cultural markers to function within broader society to allow for the continued participation in that public space. These efforts are attempted despite efforts by dominant society to impose artificial and arbitrary barriers to group integration and the exercise of cultural citizenship. If, for example, cultural citizenship in Britain requires the pub to be the preferred or primary venue for such activity, it is reasonable for self-regulating communities to seek the expansion of such venues to allow for more inclusive and integrative relations to occur.

Citizenship is no longer the exclusive province of an intranational discourse. Migration and transnationalism, particularly in light of forces of increasing globalization, have spawned new analyses and inquiries. As conventional notions of citizenship, qua, nationality are proving to be incomplete explanations for ethnic communities leading diasporic or relocated lives, cosmopolitanism and global citizenship are new approaches being taken in scholarship. Seyla Benhabib (2006) contends that cosmopolitanism, a concern for the world as one's polis, is a more accurate paradigm in which ethnic minority groups operate.[3] Favoring cosmopolitanism over citizenship, a new, disaggregated citizenship may emerge that allows for multiple allegiances and networks across conventional nation-state boundaries (Benhabib 2006). This requires separating the traditional link between the resident alien, that is, demos, and its being subject to the legal authority of the recipient state, though not part of broader society's community of identification (Benhabib and Resnik 2009).

Does Benhabib's model apply to the British Pakistani youth? While cosmopolitanism certainly augurs optimism to allow the youth to maintain multiple, unconflicted modes of allegiance and identity, it appears as though the disaggregation of citizenship will be elusive. Benhabib assumes for her model that the demos is a resident alien. By contrast, the British Pakistani youth are full, legal citizens of Great Britain, thus bearing legal obligations to the state quite different in nature, scope, and scale from those borne by resident aliens. At the very least, access to political enfranchisement is a significant distinction between the two categories. Moreover, the severance of demos from ethnos is not a facile matter if the demos is a citizen; mutual rights and responsibilities fortify the covalent, legal, and political bond between them.

Beyond the conceptual challenges facing the application of Benhabib's advocacy of cosmopolitanism, its viability as a possible construct for British Pakistani youth is highly suspect as it doesn't address potential antagonistic relations caused by maintaining multiple allegiances. Although Britain and Pakistan have diplomatic relations, share a colonial era history, are in the Commonwealth of Nations and have moderately close diplomatic and commercial ties, it is a tenuous and brittle relationship at best. With some British Pakistani youth, alienated from British state authority and society, seeking potentially to fight on British soil because they fail to distinguish between British and American military action in Pakistan, it is difficult to assess whether cosmopolitanism can be the panacea required for the stabilization of ethnic identity construction and furtherance of productive civic participation. While cosmopolitanism allows for flexible citizenship and even encourages global citizenship, it appears as though applicability to this particular group will not achieve the desired objectives.

Assimilation is an oft-cited goal as well as a demand made of immigrants and minority ethnic groups by societies seeking to implement policies of multiculturalism and participatory citizenship. As part of his formula for how societies can include their "other," Jürgen Habermas contends that there are two levels to this assimilation; the first, more abstract, component involves political socialization. It requires the individual's assent to constitutional principles within a certain scope of interpretation that is both determined and prescribed by the citizens' ethical and political self-understanding and society's political culture. In addition, such assimilation expects a level of willingness by the minority individual to be acculturated and to be habituated to the local, qua, dominant culture's lifestyle, practices, and customs across their full range. Habermas is careful to qualify his argument by excluding fundamentalist immigrant cultures from his objective of political integration; he claims that they are both inherently unwilling to participate and, perhaps, even dangerous to the existing social order if they engage and then subvert the system from within. At the same time, however, he dissuades any effort to compel assimilation simply for the sake of self-affirmation of a society's dominant cultural form of life (Habermas 2000).

It is confusing to assess where Habermas would locate British Pakistani youth in his model for social engineering vis-à-vis assimilation. There is no evidence that they belong to a fundamentalist immigrant culture; they lack either an orthodox or orthopraxic perspective regarding their religious or cultural attitudes, with many eschewing mosque attendance, rigid religious observance, or even ethnic apparel. Additionally, Habermas's calls to avoid compulsory assimilation efforts merely to assert cultural dominance appear naive as British society and government policies have either actively or tacitly attempted to achieve precisely that objective. Furthermore, the Habermasian approach completely, though unsurprisingly, ignores the Foucauldian recognition and emphasis on power dynamics. While British policy may not explicitly force ethnic minorities to swear fealty to the British cultural zeitgeist, the subtle reminders and coercions are ubiquitous and unmistakable. While Habermas focuses on societal and government efforts to include the "other," his proffer does not dismantle the underlying cultural structure that only includes, but does not transform, the "other" into the "self." Moreover, his highly idealized view of social and state apparatuses neglects or purposely overlooks their paradoxical efforts to exclude ethnic minorities from any meaningful level of civic engagement or exercise of citizenship.

Multiculturalism has served as both a meme and an official government policy in Great Britain for at least two decades. The country's ethnic and cultural diversity had been a cause for celebration as well as concern with regard to how various minority groups could integrate and assimilate into broader society. Yet recently, the perceived lack of progress of some such groups to achieve this absorption to the satisfaction of the zeitgeist has led to public opinion questioning the very merits of the effort. When Prime Minister David Cameron conceded that multiculturalism was dead in Britain, he implied that the project, though well intended and well implemented, was unsuccessful because of the intransigence of certain minority groups, for example, Muslims, to be active participants. Of course, the very nature of multiculturalism and the metrics of such purported success are ambiguous, even arbitrary, thereby leaving in doubt for the target communities a coherent formula to follow. In addition, British policy vis-à-vis multiculturalism makes no distinction between the assimilation of immigrants and minority citizens, treating both groups as equally "alien," and ironically, impeding integration and eliciting critiques of systemic flaws.

Accusations abound that British citizenship policies are "increasingly designed for purposes of disenfranchisement and political dispossession." More pointedly, such programs are designed to fail particular groups and populations. Employing a Foucauldian notion of state racism in examining the 1981 Nationality Act, Tyler argues that British citizenship regulations create a sharp dichotomy between the lived realities of "national minorities" and the stated goals for greater "community cohesion, political participation, social responsibility rights and pride in national belonging" (Tyler 2010).

British multiculturalism efforts have been a matter of national policy for several decades, a priority irrespective of the majority ruling party. Prior to the Cameron government, New Labour embarked on a series of programs emphasizing national dialogue and mutual respect as part of its citizenship project, with professed, guaranteed political rights for minority groups. Labour cabinets sought to address the relationship between cultural rights and individual equality, between national boundaries and global belonging in promulgating multicultural and citizenship policies (Kim 2011). Yet by safeguarding minority political rights without distinction made for immigrants or citizens, British policies reinforced the division along ethnocultural and religious lines, facilitating the othering of peoples regardless of how long they had been in the country. By implementing policy solely with an ethnic/minority focus, the government placed newly arrived migrants in the same category of treatment with second-, third-, and fourth-generation minorities, defying any attempts to regard the latter as being indigenous or indigenized populations. Moreover, critical issues pertaining to class and socioeconomic marginalization remained unaddressed, as such policies neglected these categories.

New Labour policies did not focus solely on citizenship as a function of minority status. Many efforts placed their attention on the youth, a demographically large and growing segment of not only the minority communities but of society as a whole. Unfortunately, within this category of government engagement the most glaring flaws and counterproductive results are evident. Official policy that regarded minorities as immigrants regardless of nationality disregarded the fact that the vast majority of South Asian Muslim youth were born in Britain and were thus citizens. Educated in the British curriculum, these youth were already familiar with and acclimated to social and national modalities for civic engagement and participation. They were native English speakers and understood the British cultural landscape. But the government chose to treat them as part of the immigrant community and worse, framed them as a security threat, especially after the July 7, 2005, London bombings. Surveillance, counterterrorism, and intelligence measures all placed the youth community under the specter of collective suspicion and defined them as a threat to citizenship and democracy. More pernicious was how these policies positioned popular political and official government rhetoric toward the youth as being a suspect group. Such generalizations failed to account for anthropological and socioeconomic factors regarding youth alienation and attitudes toward the state, preferring instead to assume the more convenient, less complicated trope of violence and radicalism, enabled in large measure by existing perceptions of Muslims as being potential or actual terrorists (Hart 2009).

As evidenced by recent riots in Great Britain on issues of the economy and budget cuts to education, youth violence is hardly the exclusive province of South Asian Muslim youth; in fact, that particular community was scarcely a participant in those disturbances. Yet, again, government policy seemed to obsess over the potential for South Asian Muslims, as a determined "other," to be the primary threat to the country; despite being citizens vis-à-vis legal conventions, they were viewed as citizens from a political perspective. Defining citizenship narrowly as a political phenomenon fails to address and acknowledge how citizenship transcends its physical acts of engagement, such as voting or participating within the deliberative, discursive process that is a central feature of democratic societies, both of which by legal fiat exclude the youth. Rather, one must also view citizenship as an ontological category, where the individual sees him/herself as a citizen beyond political action and as an engaged and accepted member of the body politic. Such engagement may manifest itself through the employment of cultural citizenship, where the national ethos nurtures and encourages the involvement of its members as equal participants regardless of whether their particular cultural modalities mirror those of the dominant society.

Quandaries over identity and belonging are not necessarily insurmountable issues for minority communities. While many perceive their country of domicile and country of ethnic origin as espousing incompatible cultural values, travel between the two countries appears to enable the attainment of a cultural modus vivendi. British Muslim women of South Asian ethnicity contend that frequent visits to the Indian subcontinent during different phases of their lives have allowed them to dispel perceptions of each nation in discrete terms along religious and cultural dimensions (Bhimji 2008). Gauging Pakistan and Britain to have porous and permeable cultural spaces, these women are able to avoid perceptions that one needs to choose one cultural paradigm over the other. With a self-assurance that she can be a British citizen with Pakistani cultural sensitivities, this hybridized South Asian Muslim woman offers an example of functional multiculturalism.

Of course, the ability to reconcile multiple identity markers is a difficult process and one not always fated to succeed. Experiential opportunity, as Bhimji contends, plays a critical role in determining whether a minority individual can indeed achieve a sense of belonging despite being of two "worlds." The women in Bhimji's study had the opportunity to make frequent trips between Britain and Pakistan throughout their lives. Although access to the subcontinent from Britain is relatively easy, with several flight options available on a daily basis, it is still an expensive endeavor, particularly if conducted with any degree of frequency. It is therefore difficult, given the socioeconomic conditions of the community in Britain, to expect all South Asian Muslims to maintain a physical connection with the subcontinent. If such interaction, as argued, reduces the likelihood of cultural schizophrenia (Shayegan 1997), then, conversely, the inability to engage in such travel will adversely affect and impede efforts to reconcile competing identity markers, perpetuating feelings that they are in conflict with one another.

A significant amount of scholarship pertaining to citizenship, especially with regard to the British condition, examines ethnic minorities as either resident aliens or as dual citizens. Yet the vast majority of the British Pakistani youth possesses a single legal (British) nationality and citizenship. Still, efforts to furnish subcategories of citizenship may prove helpful in understanding the consciousness and perceptions of the subject group. Ronkainen studies multiple citizenship through a further taxonomical breakdown, describing individuals as mononationals, hyphennationals, or shadow nationals (Ronkainen 2011).

In the present cases, Ibrahim, despite legally being a British national, has the self-perception of either a resident or expatriate mononational, whose nationality is in fact transferred, that is, Pakistani. As such a construction is technically impossible per Ronkeinen's metrics, with Ibrahim having never possessed Pakistani legal nationality, he may be seen as a hyphennational, that is, "one foot in each country." Ibrahim does not identify with being British, partly because he does not feel as though British society recognizes him as such. His consciousness is very much located in Pakistan, shaped by images he witnesses on Pakistani satellite television, and it is in Pakistan where he seeks to participate as a citizen in some capacity. Yet absent the legal grounding of Pakistani citizenship, Ibrahim must contend with and concede to being a British citizen with his empathy and sympathy clearly overseas in Pakistan. Hyphennationality does not necessarily imply parity of consciousness or engagement, rather, the recognition of a multiple consciousness of citizenship.

By contrast, the young men of Bradford represent shadow nationals. They admit to bearing no consciousness of a Pakistani identity beyond what is unavoidable, that is, home life and physical appearance. In fact, they try to avoid any additional cultural markers such as mosques or social functions. At the same time, they possess a deep-rooted alienation from British society and even resent the state and its authority over them. As such, they reside beyond a consciousness of civic or political engagement that is a function of citizenship. As they don't necessarily expect or demand rights from Britain, they do not feel obligated to fulfill citizenship duties. They cannot escape their British citizenship as a legal construct, but they feel free to avoid seeing themselves as citizens in any ontological capacity.

While the lens through which British society and young British citizens of Pakistani heritage perceive and negotiate citizenship projects different images to each side, which don't necessarily align in focus, new approaches and modalities of defining and describing have emerged. With the emergence of global citizenship as one such approach, a myriad of promises and predicaments arise. From a position of cautious optimism, global citizenship allows for the young ethnically Pakistani Briton, alienated from his dominant society, to still be a political citizen by engaging with the country of his cultural heritage. It may even facilitate his/her efforts to reconcile two seemingly incompatible aspects of identity—British and Pakistani culture—by allowing for multiple allegiances and identities to coexist. At the same time, however, this reconstituted form of citizenship must be treated with caution, as it is fraught with uncertainty. The convenience by which traditional notions of citizenship, that is, the mutual exchange of rights and duties between citizen and a single nation-state, are promulgated will be challenged and viewed as a special category of opportunity for minority ethnic groups who can claim and demand such an alternative, thereby shirking expectations of primary allegiance to the country of domicile. Perhaps the point of reconciliation between conventional and global modes of citizenship lies in the essence of citizenship and the need to focus upon its ontological, rather than its legal, categorization. If citizenship is not a function of ethnocultural and legal criteria of the conventional, but the concern for social rights and recognition of shared fate of the global, then British citizens, regardless of ethnicity, country of origin, or culture, can have equal access to global citizenship without their loyalty, identity, or legitimacy being called into question.

NOTES

1. Examples of defined territories and claims of ownership would be Quebec, Canada, by the Quebecois. One may argue that ethnic enclaves, for example, Bradford or Birmingham, are similar models, but at best, these are de facto defined territories and lack the other element of ownership claim, as none of the ethnic communities in these enclaves asserts sovereignty, exclusivity, or demand for acceptance of their cultural modalities as being dominant and normative.

2. Pakistani food and the "Balti culture" of such cuisine have become a part of the British cultural lexicon and custom. Chicken tikka masala has surpassed fish 'n' chips to become the "national" dish.

3. Both Benhabib and Jürgen Habermas share the conceit that "we live in a post-national constellation" (Arneil 2007), thus requiring an expanded theory of transnational discursive democracy. Of course, age is a key limiting factor in the deliberative process of democracy and disenfranchises the youth from the very participation sought by the process.

WORKS CITED

Abbas, T. 2011. *Islamic Radicalism and Multicultural Politics*. London: Routledge.

Abbas, T., ed. 2005. *Muslim Britain*. London: Zed Books.

Ahmed, A. S., and H. Donnon. 1994. *Islam, Globalisation, and Identity*. London: Routledge.

Ahmed, I. 2007. *Unimagined*. London: Aurum Press.

Ali, M., V. S. Kalra, and S. Sayyid, S. 2008. *A Postcolonial People*. New York: Columbia University Press.

Alsayyad, N., and M. Castells, eds. 2002. *Muslim Europe or Euro-Islam*. Lanham, MD: Lexington Books.

Ameli, S. R. 2002. *Globalization, Americanization, and Muslim Identity*. London: Islamic College for Advanced Studies Press.

Anderson, B. 1983. *Imagined Communities*. London: Verso.

Ansari, H. 2004. *The Infidel Within*. London: Hurst.

Ansari, Z., and J. Esposito, eds. 2001. *Muslims and the West: Encounter and Dialogue*. Islamabad: Islamic Research Institute.

Anwar, M. 1998. *Between Cultures: Continuity and Change in the Lives of Young Asians*. London: Routledge.

Appiah, K. 2006. *Cosmopolitanism*. New York: Norton.

Arneil, B. 2007. "Global Citizenship and Empire." *Citizenship Studies* 11 (3): 301–28.

Baubock, R. 2009. "The Rights and Duties of External Citizenship." *Citizenship Studies* 13 (5): 475–99.

Baubock, R., and V. Guiraudon. 2009. "Introduction: Realignments of Citizenship: Reassessing Rights in the Age of Plural Memberships and Multi-Level Governance." *Citizenship Studies* 13 (5): 439–50.

Benhabib, S. 2006. *Another Cosmopolitanism*. New York: Oxford University Press.

Benhabib, S., and J. Resnik, eds. 2009. *Migrations and Mobilities: Gender, Borders, and Citizenship*. New York: New York Univesity Press, 1–44.

Benhabib, S., I. Shapiro, and D. Petranović. 2007. *Identities, Affiliations, and Allegiances*. Cambridge: Cambridge University Press.

Bennett, D. 1998. *Multicultural States*. London: Routledge.

Bhimji, F. 2008. "Cosmopolitan Belonging and Diaspora: Second-Generation British Muslim Women Traveling to South Asia." *Citizenship Studies* 12 (4): 413–27.

Bleich, E. 2003. *Race Politics in Britain and France: Ideas and Policymaking since the 1960s*. Cambridge: Cambridge University Press.

Brah, A. 1996. *Cartographies of Diaspora*. London: Routledge.

Breckenridge, C., H. Bhabha, S. Pollock, and D. Chakrabarty, eds. 2002. *Cosmopolitanism*. Durham, NC: Duke University Press.

Carens, J. 2000. *Culture, Citizenship, and Community*. Oxford: Oxford University Press.

Castles, S., and M. J. Miller, eds. 2003. *The Age of Migration*. 3rd ed. New York: Guilford Press.

Croucher, S. 2004. *Globalization and Belonging*. Lanham, MD: Rowman and Littlefield.

Dijkstra, S., K. Geuijen, and A. De Ruijter, A. 2001. "Multiculturalism and Social Integration in Europe." *International Political Science Review* 22 (1): 55–83.

Ebaugh, H., and J. Chafetz, eds. 2004. *Religion across Borders*. Walnut Creek, CA: Altamira Press.

Eder, K., and B. Giesen, eds. 2001. *European Citizenship*. Oxford: Oxford University Press.

Enjorlas, B. 2008. "Two Hypotheses about the Emergence of a Post-National European Model of Citizenship." *Citizenship Studies* 12 (5): 495–505.

Eriksen, T. 1993. *Ethnicity and Nationalism*. London: Pluto Press.

Favell, A., 1998. "Applied Political Philosophy at the Rubicon: Will Kymlicka's 'Multicultural Citizenship.'" *Ethical Theory and Moral Practice* 1 (2): 255–78.

Giannankos, S. 2002. *Ethnic Conflict: Religion, Identity and Politics.* Athens: Ohio University Press.

Gilliat-Ray, S. 2010. *Muslims in Britain.* Cambridge: Cambridge University Press.

Habermas, J. 2000. *The Inclusion of the Other.* Cambridge, MA: MIT Press.

Harris, D., ed. 1995. *Multiculturalism from the Margins.* Westport, CT: Bergin and Garvey.

Hart, S. 2009. "The 'Problem' with Youth: Young People, Citizenship and the Community." *Citizenship Studies* 13 (6): 641–57.

Hasan, R. 2010. *Multiculturalism: Some Inconvenient Truths.* London: Politico's Publishing.

Hellyer, H. 2009. *Muslims of Europe: The "Other" Europeans.* Edinburgh: Edinburgh University Press.

Hill, G. 1993. "Citizenship and Ontology in the Liberal State." *Review of Politics* 55 (1): 67–84.

Hopkins, P., and R. Gale, eds. 2009. *Muslims in Britain.* Edinburgh: Edinburgh University Press.

Janoski, T., and A. Hicks. 2009. "The Difference That Empire Makes: Institutions and Politics of Citizenship in Germany and Austria." *Citizenship Studies* 13 (4): 381–411.

Jenkins, P. 2007. *God's Continent.* New York: Oxford University Press.

Joppke, C. 2007. "Transformation of Citizenship: Status, Rights, Identity." *Citizenship Studies* 11 (1): 37–48.

Kabir, N. 2012. *Young British Muslims.* Edinburgh: Edinburgh University Press.

Kepel, G. 2004. *The War for Muslim Minds.* Cambridge, MA: Belknap Press of Harvard University Press.

Khan, S. 2012a. "Location Nowhere: Alienation, Nihilism and Radicalism among British Pakistani Muslim Youth." In *Defining and Re-Defining Diaspora*, edited by M. David and J. Muñoz-Basols. Oxford: Inter-Disciplinary Press.

———. 2012b. "The Phenomenon of Serial Nihilism among British Muslim Youth of Bradford, England." In *Muslim Youth*, edited by F. Ahmed, and F. Seddon. London: Continuum.

Kim, N-K. 2011. "Deliberative Multiculturalism in New Labour's Britain." *Citizenship Studies* 15 (1): 125–44.

Klausen, G. 2005. *The Islamic Challenge.* Oxford: Oxford University Press.

Kymlicka, W. 1989. *Liberalism, Community, and Culture.* Oxford: Oxford University Press.

———. 1995. *Multicultural Citizenship.* Oxford: Oxford University Press.

———. 2001. *Politics in the Vernacular.* New York: Oxford University Press.

———. 2007. *Multicultural Odysseys*. Oxford: Oxford University Press.

Kymlicka, W., and W. Norman. 2000. *Citizenship in Diverse Societies*. Oxford: Oxford University Press.

Lehning, P. 2001. "European Citizenship: Towards a European Identity?" *Law and Philosophy* 20 (3) 239–82.

Levey, G., and T. Modood. 2009. *Secularism, Religion, and Multicultural Citizenship*. Cambridge: Cambridge University Press.

Lewis, P. 2002. *Islamic Britain: Religion, Politics, and Identity among British Muslims*. London: I. B. Tauris.

———. 2008. *Young, British and Muslim*. London: Continuum.

Lewis, R. 1988. *Anti-Racism: A Mania Exposed*. London: Quartet Books.

Ley, D. 2004. "Transnational Spaces and Everyday Lives." *Transactions of the Institute of British Geographers* 29 (2): 151–64.

Malik, I. 2004. *Islam and Modernity*. London: Pluto Press.

Meer, N. 2010. *Citizenship, Identity, and the Politics of Multiculturalism*. Basingstoke: Palgrave Macmillan.

Modood, T. 2005. *Multicultural Politics*. Minneapolis: University of Minnesota Press.

Modood, T., A. Trianadafyllidou, and R. Zapata-Barrero, eds. 2006. *Multiculturalism, Muslims and Citizenship*. London: Routledge.

Modood, T., and P. Werbner, eds. 2005. *The Politics of Multiculturalism in the New Europe*. Minneapolis: University of Minnesota Press.

Nielsen, J. 2004. *Muslims in Western Europe*. 3rd ed. Edinburgh: Edinburgh University Press.

Parekh, B. 2006. *Rethinking Multiculturalism*. London: Palgrave Macmillan.

———. 2008. *A New Politics of Identity*. London: Palgrave Macmillan.

Paul, K. 1997 *Whitewashing Britain*. Ithaca, NY: Cornell University Press.

Peled, Y. 2007. "Towards a Post-Citizenship Society? A Report from the Front." *Citizenship Studies* 11 (1): 95–104.

Phillips, A. 2007. *Multiculturalism without Culture*. Princeton, NJ: Princeton University Press.

Phillips, M. 2006. *Londonistan*. London: Encounter Books.

Poole, E. 2002. *Reporting Islam: Media Representations and British Muslims*. London: I. B. Tauris.

Ramadan, T. 1999. *To Be a European Muslim*. Leicester: Islamic Foundation.

———. 2001. *Islam, the West, and the Challenges of Modernity*. Leicester: Islamic Foundation.

———. 2004. *Western Muslims and the Future of Islam*. New York: Oxford University Press.

Roche, M. 1987. "Citizenship, Social Theory, and Social Change." *Theory and Society* 16 (3): 363–99.

Ronkainen, J. K. 2011. "Mononationals, Hyphennationals, and Shadow-Nationals: Multiple Citizenship as Practice." *Citizenship Studies* 15 (2): 247–63.

Roy, O. 2004. *Globalized Islam*. New York: Columbia University Press.

Salvatore, A. 2007. *The Public Sphere*. New York: Palgrave Macmillan.

———, ed. 2001. *Muslim Traditions and Modern Techniques of Power*. Hamburg: Lit Verlag.

Samad, Y., and K. Sen. 2007. *Islam in the European Union: Transnationalism, Youth and the War on Terror*. Oxford: Oxford University Press.

Savage, M., G. Bagnall, and B. Longhurst. 2005. *Globalization and Belonging*. London: Sage.

Schmidtke, O., and S. Ozcurumez. 2008. *Of States, Rights, and Social Closure*. New York: Palgrave Macmillan.

Seddon, M. S., D. Hussain, and N. Malik, eds. 2004. *British Muslims between Assimilation and Segregation*. Leicester: Islamic Foundation.

Shaw, A. 1988. *A Pakistani Community in Britain*. Oxford: Basil Blackwell.

Shayegan, D. 1997. *Cultural Schizophrenia*. Syracuse, NY: Syracuse University Press.

Solomos, J. 1993. *Race and Racism in Britain*. 2nd ed. Hampshire: Macmillan.

Somers, M. 1995. "Narrating and Naturalizing Civil Society and Citizenship Theory: The Place of Political Culture and the Public Sphere." *Sociological Theory* 13 (3): 229–74.

Soysal, Y. 1994. *Limits of Citizenship*. Chicago: University of Chicago Press.

Taylor, C., and A. Gutmann, eds. 1994. *Multiculturalism*. Princeton, NJ: Princeton University Press.

Tibi, B. 2005. *Islam between Culture and Politics*. 2nd ed. Hampshire: Palgrave Macmillan.

Trianadafyllidou, A., T. Modood, and N. Meer, eds. 2012. *European Multiculturalisms*. Edinburgh: Edinburgh University Press.

Tyler, I. 2010. "Designed to Fail: A Biopolitics of British Citizenship." *Citizenship Studies* 14 (1): 61–74.

Van Oenen, G. 2010. "Three Cultural Turns: How Multiculturalism, Interactivity, and Interpassivity Affect Citizenship." *Citizenship Studies* 14 (3): 293–306.

Vertovec, S. 2009. *Transnationalism*. London: Routledge.

Werbner, P. 2002. *Imagined Diasporas among Manchester Muslims.* Oxford: James Currey.

Werbner, P., and T. Modood. 1997. *Debating Cultural Hybridity.* London: Zed Books.

Wikan, U. 2002. *Generous Betrayal.* Chicago: University of Chicago Press.

Yalcin-Heckmann, L. 2011. "Introduction: Claiming Social Citizenship." *Citizenship Studies* 15 (3–4): 433–39.

6

COMPLICATING CITIZENSHIP

· · · · · · · · · ·

How Children of Immigrants in Italy
Represent Belonging and Rights

ENZO COLOMBO

CHANGING CITIZENSHIP

In the last two decades much has been said about developing "new forms of citizenship." Innovative terms have been introduced to highlight the various directions of the transformations of citizenship and the implications they may produce in the regulation of public sovereignty, distribution of rights and duties, and social and political participation. Terms such as "postnational" (Soysal 1994; Jacobson 1996; Tambini 2001), "transnational" (Basch, Schiller, and Blanc 1994; Portes, Guarnizo, and Landolt. 1999; Bauböck and Guiraudon 2009), "cultural" (Stevenson 2001; Miller 2002; Pawley 2008), "multicultural" (Kymlicka 1995; Koopmans et al. 2005), "global" (Dower 2003; Schattle 2008), "cosmopolitan" (Delanty 2000; Smith 2007), or "active" (Isen and Nielsen 2008) citizenship have all been suggested as appropriate in order to understand the transformations. The proliferation of these new terms points out the current difficulty of our language to account for new social experiences in which new tensions between human rights and citizen rights, or between social, civic, and political rights, may arise. These new terms signal the necessity of reviewing our ideas of inclusion, exclusion, belonging, and participation that issued from the political thought in nineteenth- and twentieth-centuries Western societies. We need to face the new ways we experience being insiders and outsiders, marginal and mainstream, or citizens and foreigners.

The intensification of the speed and reach of the processes of globalization—in particular flows of people, ideas, and goods (Appadurai 1996), not to mention the planetary interconnections that increasingly seem to unite people and phenomena over great distances in complex systems of dependency and mutual influence (Tomlinson 1999)—contributes to the transformation of the idea of citizenship, highlighting the contradictory link that binds belonging to a political community to the protection of individual and collective rights.

The latest communication and transportation technology creates new social fields connecting spatially separated territories and groups as well as a new category of social actors who experience more complex, mobile, and differentiated forms of belonging. These processes contribute to blurring national boundaries and pose new questions about the principles of inclusion and exclusion that were used to allocate civic, political, and social rights during a large part of the previous century in Western societies. In particular, postwar globalization and new international migrations question the way in which Western societies have conceived of citizenship as the result of, on the one hand, a close relationship between loyalty to and recognition within the national community and, on the other hand, the endowment of rights.

"Transmigrants" (Levitt and Glick-Schiller 2004), "cosmopolitans" (Held and Archibugi 1995; Nussbaum 1997; Beck 2012), and Internet surfers, accustomed to living simultaneously *here* and *there*, may be—in reality as well as virtually—"residents" who actively participate in the community in which they are (temporally and partially) engaged, even though they may not be (completely) citizens. The presence of these new "global Argonauts" leads to the deconstruction of the apparent unity of citizenship, highlighting the fact that the recognition of rights (civil, political, and social), and of identity, and the willingness to participate in collective life, may constitute distinct elements that may also diverge from or compete with one another.

Belonging, participation, and the recognition of rights reveal themselves to be aspects that are partially autonomous, never completely traceable to the idea of national identity (Delanty 2000). Being a society no longer necessarily coincides with being a nation because, from certain standpoints, society exceeds the nation: people may wish to participate without the feeling of belonging "exclusively," "completely," and "definitively"; people may participate not because they identify with the nation, but because they feel involved (for personal interests, their sense of engagement in community life, or because in this way individuals can express their own particularity). As a result, the concept of citizenship as unique and exclusive membership needs to be revisited to account for the realities of the globalized world in which cultural and political units do not necessarily come together territorially. A revised conceptualization of citizenship as agency, showing different and mobile membership in order to assure contextual advantages, seems more appropriate in light of the fluidity of contemporary transcultural youth identities (Kapai 2012, 290).

GENERATION MATTERS

The necessity of a more fine-tuned idea of citizenship becomes even more evident when we look at the current experience of new generations. Young people—at least those who are attending high school, have good information and communications technology (ICT) skills, and have parents with high cultural capital—are developing specific forms of personal capacity (Melucci 1996): they mix different languages and manage different codes and rules, using them in the appropriate context. Moreover, they are able to change, switching from one context to another, and are committed to developing suitable forms of belonging to allow access without creating ties that are too strong to prevent consistent freedom of motion. As a result, they display a preference for the ability to fit a context rather than showing a coherence that makes compromise and mediation difficult.

All this configures the rise of a new *generation as actuality* (Mannheim 1952).[1] In fact, a significant number of today's youth—especially those with a higher cultural capital—are facing experiences and problems that were largely unknown to previous generations. They must be able to cope in an increasingly changing and globally interconnected world. They learn to face and manage cultural diversity, recognize it, and put it into viable schemas for interpretation and evaluation. They learn to contend with patterns of consumption, information, and identification circulating within the global networks with which they are connected (Noble 2009; Colombo 2010) rather than growing up rigorously embedded in their local environment. For them, it becomes important to develop the ability to adapt to different relational contexts, characterized by different rules, audiences, and interests, coping with the increasing difficulty of transferring what one learns or acquires in one sphere of life to other spheres (Melucci 1996). The ability to count on differentiated cultural references, a certain relativism in one's interpretation of the rules, the ability to adapt and be flexible and to manage different languages and codes fluently seem to be fundamental skills that every young person must acquire in order to succeed in an increasingly global world. For adolescents growing up in a global, changing, and interconnected world, managing this ambivalence may often be more important than being consistent; being able to cope with the context in order not to diminish personal opportunities may be more important than showing an integrity unaffected by the diversity of the situations (Colombo and Rebughini 2012).

Within this potential *generation as actuality* it is possible to identify a more specific *generation unit* (Mannheim 1952),[2] which feels more acutely the necessity to overcome an idea of citizenship that presupposes strong identification with the "nation" or the "autochthonous": the children of immigrants. Far from being the simple extension of their parents' "native soil," and indeed from embracing without regret or resistance the models of their "autochthonous" schoolmates, these young people highlight the distinction between national identity and citizenship (Hussain and Bagguley 2005), elaborating multiple and diverse individual and collective identities that demand recognition and participation according to criteria dissociated from—or not entirely reducible to—a single ethnic or national identity (Colombo, Leonini, and Rebughini 2009). They present claims for the recognition of citizenship that remain distinct from a full and total identification with a presumed community able to furnish models and meanings for every aspect of their experience.

PRESENTATION OF THE RESEARCH

The chapter explores how children of immigrants enrolled in high schools in Milan, northern Italy, conceive and speak about citizenship. The data are based on 115 narrative interviews with sixty-nine girls and forty-six boys (sixteen- to twenty-two-year-olds), part of qualitative research, conducted between 2007 and 2010, which aimed to analyze how a comparatively privileged section of immigrants' children—those with relatively high cultural capital who decided to invest in their education in Italy beyond the compulsory level—reelaborates the experiences of their parents, how they react to the perceived opening and closing of Italian society, and how they face the problem of inclusion and participation.

Among the interviewees, thirty-five attended a scientific college, fifty-three a technical institute, and the remaining twenty-seven a professional institute. The origins of their parents are fairly differentiated, reflecting the spectrum of the so-called Mediterranean model of immigration: thirty-one from Asia (seven from China), twenty-two from North Africa, seven from Sub-Saharan Africa, sixteen from Eastern Europe, seven from other European countries, and thirty-two from South America. Almost half had completed all their schooling in Italy (thirty-four were born in Italy, fifteen arrived before they were seven years old), and a third (forty-two) began attending primary or elementary school after beginning their schooling in their parents' native country, while the others (twenty-four) came to Italy as adolescents and began their Italian education at the high school level. Although their parents mainly do low-status jobs, they generally hold good educational qualifications.[3]

The decision to interview only students enrolled in high schools derives from a precise theoretical choice: these young people are certainly not "representative" of young children of immigrants in southern Europe; they constitute instead an "exemplary" selection with a high cultural capital, youth who experience globalization in an acute and pervasive manner and who may find themselves in a privileged social position in terms of their skills and mind-set. They may represent a specific new generational unit that can be understood as an "active minority" (Moscovici 1979) engaged in processing new codes and new languages in order to cope with specific historical experiences. It is not a question of encouraging an uncritical exaltation of what is produced, or of embracing a conciliatory vision that suppresses the dimensions of the conflict, but of proposing an analytical viewpoint that recognizes the identification processes activated by these young people as a significant and privileged place where new meanings and patterns of action are being produced (not necessarily better, democratic, or exponents of pacific cohabitation and without generating new forms of discrimination).

The second theoretical assumption informing this study is the importance of looking at citizenship not only from a normative and formal perspective but also from the point of view of people (especially young people) living in a globalized world.[4] This means looking at the *representations of citizenship* rather than at citizenship's formal realization. The focus in this research is on the experience and the narration of what being a citizen means for the children of immigrants, favoring the significance they give to belonging and feeling active parts of society, as well as how they articulate their rights and their responsibilities in specific situations.

This chapter explores the mapping of belonging and representations of identification among children of immigrants attending high, noncompulsory schools in Italy. It contributes to developing the implication of an analysis of citizenship "from below," stressing its active, contested, adjusted contents and showing how the meaning young people attach to it may vary according to variations in discourse and context.

In-depth analysis of this specific "active minority" in Milan could highlight not only how citizenship changes in the process of personal development "along a life course from birth to death" (Marback, introduction this volume, x) but also how contemporary globalization processes are deeply changing the way in which younger generations look at participation, national identification, and rights, constructing and reflecting historical continuities and ruptures in citizenship (Robbins-Ruszkowski this volume).

In line with French (Youcef this volume) and British (Khan this volume) experience, children of immigrants in Italy actively contribute to show the limits of a too narrow "pensée d'Etat" (Sayad 1999), which makes rights conditional on loyalty and identification with the nation.

Italian children of immigrants are nevertheless peculiar because, differently from the French and British cases, Italy is their country of birth and domicile but they do not have Italian citizenship,[5] or, if they have it, they are not recognized as "real" Italians in political and public discourses. Instead, they are engaged in claiming participation in Italian society while at the same time changing the very meaning of being Italian. In so doing, they are producing a complex and mobile idea of inclusion and exclusion. For all these reasons, how they conceive and speak about citizenship might be a good starting point from which to understand how citizenship is going to change in a globalized world.

THE COMPLEXITY OF BELONGING

When children of immigrants interviewed speak about belonging they differentiate three different aspects of feeling part of a community, which can be summarized by the terms *admittance*, *allegiance*, and *involvement*.

Admittance refers to the formal features of recognition. When the opportunity to participate is at stake, young people stress the universalistic claim to be equal, to not be excluded on the basis of prejudice or systematic and institutional discrimination. Facing the experience of being considered "foreign," "alien," and not legitimized to stay in the place they were born, they put the emphasis on equality and on recognition of equal respect and dignity for all human beings, regardless of physical, social, or cultural differences.

> Everybody should be treated the same way, and their nationality should not have anything to do with it, with the fact that we are foreigners or not . . . personal abilities count for more, not nationality . . . we are all equal and what distinguishes us from others are our personal abilities and not the group to which we belong. . . . I feel just like the other young people and I want others to see me that way, for what I can do, not as a Filipino or an Italian or any other (Titus, nineteen years old, born in the Philippines, in Italy since the age of eight).

Admittance concerns the need to be accepted on a par in different contexts, the possibility to have equal opportunities to participate and to play personal cards on the same terms as others in fair competition, transcending cultural differences and cultural bonds. Not being recognized as equal, not legitimately having the identical opportunities as all the other members of the same community, is perceived as an unjustifiable injustice.

> Even if I don't have citizenship yet, I already feel Italian, I mean, I don't know, to be honest, for me to be an Italian is to be as I am, as I am now, Italian, because I am what I am because I grew up in this place, with a specific point of view, with this kind of people; I live here, I obey the law, I have rights and duties like all the people who live here have. . . . I feel one hundred per cent Italian, so I don't understand why I cannot have the Italian citizenship right now . . . after all it is always the same story, yes, I am Italian, but I haven't got the citizenship . . . so you feel different because you only have an alien's residence permit to stay here in the country where you were born while all the other people can stay here without permits . . . you must have a permit, you don't have the freedom to live in the country where you were born, you have to ask for a permit, and if you are lucky, it's ok,

> otherwise you have to go back to a country where you have never lived
> and you barely know . . . it really makes you feel different, it makes
> you feel incomplete. . . . I know that citizenship is only a paper, noth-
> ing will change with it, maybe only greater freedom for traveling, but
> for me it is important, it has always been important. . . . I always feel
> the lack of it as an unequal and pointless discrimination. . . . I never
> understand why I cannot have it (Adian, eighteen years old, born in
> Italy, Eritrean parents).

When inclusion or exclusion is at stake, formal citizenship provides a useful
document that attests to the rights to stay in a country, to live there legally.
Here Adian expresses the idea that citizenship is regarded as fundamental
to being considered equal to others; it represents a minimal but necessary
qualification to be considered a full member of the community and to have
the opportunity to develop personal capabilities to their fullest. As Albena,
an eighteen-year-old Bulgarian girl, effectively points out, possessing formal
citizenship may constitute the minimum requirement for being recognized
as a human being and treated as a person:

> Having citizenship also means being treated in another way, I would
> like to have Italian citizenship. It would be great, if I had Italian citi-
> zenship then maybe at customs they would see the Italian passport
> and let us go, usually they stop us and check us, with Italian citizen-
> ship we would be like one of them . . . and then they look at you
> from a different viewpoint, they look at you like a person (Albena,
> eighteen years old, Bulgarian citizen, living in Italy since the age of
> nine).

The relevance of the formal dimension of citizenship for being considered as
human beings and being allowed to participate on a par in social life points
to how far the nation-state continues to play a central role in guaranteeing
adequate development of "personal capacities."

When claiming formal citizenship that guarantees against exclusion and
discrimination, children of immigrants mainly use universalistic grounds,
stressing equality over individual differences and cultural belonging. However, the relevance given to being accepted on an equal basis does not mean
complete dismissal of difference or the wish for full assimilation. If it is true

that citizenship seems to be a crucial device for claiming equality of opportunity beyond differences, it is not necessarily equivalent to a complete eclipse of differences, or a wish for full assimilation (Kymlicka 1995; Hart 2009; Yuval-Davis, Kannabiran, and Vieten 2006). There are certain situations in which the emotions attached to belonging require the recognition of specific differences along with the sentiments attached to being part of a specific community.

Allegiance stresses the importance of specific traits that are "unavoidably" acquired by birth; they require loyalty and cannot be dismissed without betraying the more personal and inner self. When identity issues are at stake, the classical rhetoric of roots may be useful for claiming respect and recognition of difference and cultural belonging. In this case, the children of immigrants interviewed use differentialist motives, and they stress the necessity of recognizing cultural particularism.

Roots are understood as a normative reference that summarizes an entire package of values and traditions coinciding with the national community (or, less often, the ethnic group) of a person, directly inserted into a nonnegotiable space according to the tautological procedure that grounds the concept of roots itself (Baumann 1999).

Citizenship has to do with the future you are going to construct, both for yourself and your children. If you want to have your future in Italy, you have to be a citizen, you cannot say "I live here" without thinking of citizenship. Holding citizenship means that you are part of that community, that you are engaged and committed with that community. Citizenship means that you have all the rights and all the duties to be a member of that community. After that, if you want to conserve your ties with the place where you were born, that is another question, in this case there is always a tie. . . . In my opinion, citizenship and identity are not strongly tied to each other, because if I take Italian citizenship I still remain what I am, I still hold all the ties with the country where I was born. I don't change as a person. To be a person is not connected with a document where it is written who I am. Citizenship is just bureaucratic stuff, which can help you both at the economic level and for a better integration with other people, but what you are is bound up with your family, the place where you were born, where you come from (Amed, twenty years old, born in Egypt, in Italy since the age of eight).

I think that we shouldn't forget our own culture, in the end that's you, you were born there, that is your culture; in the end there are things that you can disagree with, but it is your identity. . . . We shouldn't forget our own roots, then of course there are things in your culture that you don't agree with . . . that shows that you care about it, you want it to improve. . . . Even if I lived here [in Italy] for thirty, forty years, until I die, no . . . no, I wouldn't feel Italian, I was born in Egypt. No, I feel Egyptian (Christine, seventeen years old, born in Egypt, in Italy since the age of nine).

The insistence and the certainty with which this reference to "roots" is expressed clearly show not only how an essentialist conception of identity has far from vanished from the social scene but also highlight to what extent national borders continue to function as the main *frame of reference* to describe and justify one's social position. At the same time, they show how the alleged mandatory ties between identification with nation and recognition of rights (Miller 1995) are becoming problematic and contested. As many interviewees point out, in a truly democratic, global, and multicultural society it should not be necessary to fully identify with a unique majority culture in order to be a "good citizen" entitled to rights.

The claim for recognition of difference as an indispensable facet of full citizenship is also important when facing discrimination and racism. Italian citizenship is a means for reclaiming inclusion without homologation, for asking for the recognition of cultural and personal differences.

I've always had problems at school. My classmates are almost all right-wing, racists, I had a lot of problems because of my headscarf . . . they didn't accept me and . . . I mean . . . they saw me as a foreigner and said "go back to your country!" I mean, I was born here and I don't like people telling me those things. . . . I think of myself as more Italian than many others . . . but people think that being both Muslim and Italian is impossible. So I'd like Italian law to recognize me as Italian, also if I'm not only Italian, I mean, they have to respect me because I was born here and I'm part of this country, but they cannot expect me to become Italian. Citizenship ought to be a way to obtain respect. It ought to show that we are all the same but we still keep our differences (Asma, seventeen years old, born in Italy, Algerian parents).

When citizenship is seen as a form of allegiance toward one's specific community, being different is more important than being merely admitted. Citizenship ought to protect and preserve (individual and collective) difference, because an effective recognition of rights should allow people to freely manifest their diversity. Self-recognition and external recognition of difference are both perceived as the crucial condition for creating a space of protection and solidarity that permits personal fulfillment, autonomy, dignity, and respect. Considering citizenship as a form of allegiance can also be sustained by the necessity to react and resist forms of external aggression or discrimination. In both cases, the reification of culture and traditions is emphasized and young people claim recognition and respect for their alleged differences.

In any case, children of immigrants in Italy rarely transform ethnic difference into an insurmountable boundary—showing on this point many similarities as well as important differences with the experience of the young ethnic Pakistani men in Great Britain described in this book by Saeed Kahn. Although they are not recognized as citizens and are not formally recognized as part of the society in which they were born and raised, and in which they are planning their future, the children of immigrants interviewed do not totally reject Italian society. Like the young Pakistanis in Bradford and London, children of immigrants in Italy acknowledge and accept the dominant culture and reside and operate within its construct without denial or disdain. Differently from the British Pakistanis, they seldom seek recognition of certain cultural markers to function within broader society to allow for the continued participation in that public space (Khan this volume) and prefer a tactical and contextual use of difference. They claim the recognition of their difference but avoid transforming special cultural markers—language, religion, physical appearance—into fixed and unchangeable substances. They seem engaged in managing the continuous fluctuation between identification and differentiation, combining equality and difference. Ethnic difference is used in a tactical way: on the one hand, it is emphasized when it proves to be a resource, when it arouses curiosity and allows distinctions, when it assists in the activation of relationships; on the other hand, it is left in the background or contested when it risks hindering fruitful opportunities, or when it is rigidly imposed from without and becomes a vehicle for discrimination or an excuse for exclusion.

Using ethnicity tactically, they contest that membership has to be seen as an inescapable fate, and they challenge any perfect equivalence between belonging and citizenship. Their use of ethnicity and belonging supports Floya Anthias's consideration: "it is important not to confuse ethnicity with community. You can have ethnicity, in the sense of a conscious political assertion of ethnic boundaries, without feeling that you fully belong to such a community (e.g., second-generation migrants). You can also treat ethnicity as purely a matter of fact, as something you can't avoid being purely because of background and family, without necessarily according it a central place in your sense of belonging" (Anthias 2010, 239).

Differences should not be lost, nor should they be imposed. A proper use of equality and difference is guided by a pragmatic need: never be out of place, stay in tune with the situation to avoid being excluded.

> Culture is important. It defines who you are, how you are . . . you cannot break away from family ties, from the things you have learned . . . in some way those things are you, it is your way of being . . . but you should never be too attached to your own culture. I mean, you have to know how to adapt—like me—adapt a little to the culture that is in Italy instead of importing your own culture and setting it down right here. . . . I mean, if someone has a tradition, he doesn't necessarily have to lose it, but if someone imposes his culture, then I don't think that's right . . . that's a mistake, because he doesn't understand that he has to live with the others . . . he will always find himself out of place (David, twenty years old, born in Peru, in Italy since the age of three).

Admittance and allegiance are able to coexist. Citizenship ought to recognize both the formal equal access to rights and the recognition of the existence of different experiences and individual and collective histories that constitute part of the inner self—an inner self that cannot be ignored without negatively affecting individual agency. In the effort to bring together these two facets of citizenship, claiming respect for the equal opportunity of all human beings, without distinctions based on ascribed characteristics, does not exclude also claiming recognition of difference and refusing complete homologation. They both represent two different, and often complementary, rhetorical resources for claiming participation and manifesting agency. This is evident when the opportunity to actively participate in communal life, expressing personal preferences and interests, is at stake.

Involvement concerns this more articulated level of belonging. Citizenship, in this case, is a guarantee that people have the right to take an active part in public social life and to intervene directly in order to manifest a personal point of view, pursue personal goals, and defend private interests.

Neither can citizenship be reduced to assimilation—a form of participation that means giving up any recognition of personal distinctiveness—nor can it be reduced to recognition of an ineliminable and unchangeable difference—a form of acknowledgment that implies separation and isolation. Instead, it is defined in terms of claiming autonomy and participation by cultivating (personal and collective) difference (cf. Marback this volume). Difference allows autonomy, and autonomy is expressed through difference.

Where a sense of involvement is concerned, some perceive citizenship as an important resource that allows people to actively, effectively, and efficiently participate in collective decisions. Citizenship ensures the opportunity to take part in shaping one's future, to influence the definition of the contexts in which one acts; it allows a person to make opinions and preferences heard, to fully exercise *voice* (Hirschman 1970). Citizenship is seen as an effective opportunity to influence social reality, to be a protagonist, to be in control.

> Look, if I decide to live here, it's because I like it here, I feel that this place has now become a part of my life.... I am the one who decides ... then if I decide to live here it is right that I have my say, that I am accepted and can contribute to making things go well here ... if I have some good ideas that can help, they must not tell me: "you can't talk because you are a foreigner!" I want to have my thoughts heard and I don't even want them to say: "First become an Italian and then you can talk," no, I want to live here and therefore I want to say what I think but I also remain a Kosovar (Marcus, twenty-one years old, born in Kosovo, in Italy since age thirteen).

Citizenship represents, in this case, a resource for participation; it enables agency and self-determination. Citizenship sustains personal will and supports individuals in achieving their goals, assuring, protecting, or hiding—in relation to constraints imposed by context and personal interests—equality and difference.

Involvement emphasizes autonomy, agency, and the possibility to intervene directly to shape one's future, it refers to the capacity to act as a citizen, that is, to engage actively in civic and political life with the possibility of making a difference (Schugurensky 2010). Citizenship constitutes the necessary precondition needed to participate on a par with all others in the social arena. Participation requires plural involvements, which may change or become more or less accentuated when people move from one context to another. There are clear generational skills involved here: the ability to be flexible and changeable depending on the situation as well as the ability to manage different languages and codes in order to fit the circumstances.

Involvement means recognizing that people are more complex than can be synthesized into one unique belonging (local, ethnic, national, religious) because belonging is more complex than a single choice, it involves ambivalence and multiple loyalties.

> I'm Russian, but I don't know anymore. . . . I lost a lot of the Russian culture I had before. . . . If I go to Russia now everyone will think I'm a foreigner . . . because I don't dress like them anymore, they don't recognize me as Russian. . . . You surely lose something, obviously I have breathed so much Italian air that I recognize myself in a lot of Italian things, I have Italian citizenship, I'm Italian . . . but that doesn't mean I'm less Russian . . . it's more complex than a single choice (Kristina, eighteen years old, born in Russia, in Italy since age five).

Kristina then goes on to proudly claim being *both* Italian and Russian; in so doing she highlights new specific generational skills: the capacity to embrace a both/and logic, rather than being compelled to accept an either/or one. Recognizing the importance of the contexts, and relativizing rules, values, and codes, young people may construct a more complex and layered representation of citizenship that better fits their everyday experience of living enmeshed in multiple bonds of belonging created by the proliferation of social positions, relational networks, and reference groups:

I feel indeterminate, a perfect pastry dough, a perfect pie, well done, I mean I stored pieces from both sides, I took the best parts of both cultures and I mixed them in order to create my unique personality, so I have some facets which are more Russian and others which are more Italian, and I think that each part helps me to be more complete, more interesting. I'm very proud of my Russian side, also if I'm no longer really Russian, I mean, I've mixed everything together in order to give more flavor to my personality. However, people cannot be linearly defined by a single culture, each person is unique, and people who change contexts, who don't always live in the same place have more ingredients, so to speak, to create their original pie (Kristina, eighteen years old, born in Russia, in Italy since the age of five).

For the children of immigrants interviewed, citizenship might coherently reflect the fact that people belong to many different contexts, none of which summarize the complexity of personal experience. In order to participate in a globalized world, exploiting contextual opportunities and personal skills to the best of their ability, people need to be entitled to choose and modulate equality and difference. Citizenship ought to testify to such an entitlement.

COMPLICATING CITIZENSHIP

The image of citizenship the children of immigrants interviewed portrayed is multivalent and mobile. Rights and duties, roots and personal choices, inclusion and exclusion appear more as discursive registers to be used in different ways depending on contexts and personal purposes than as absolute criteria in rigid opposition to each other and from which young people should choose.

Citizenship is still seen as essential to ensure the rights to fully develop an autonomous personality and participate fully in social life. It is conceived as a fundamental part of the tool kit necessary to fully develop personal capacity and to act in an independent, self-directed way. Being excluded from citizenship means not being recognized as a human being, being prevented from developing the "personal capacity" that allows for the expression of agency and self-fulfillment. At the same time, as I have argued on the basis of interviews with immigrant youth, simple formal citizenship is not enough if it does not go together with the recognition of the place of the difference and the passions in the exercise of citizenship: the possibility to express likes and dislikes, "anger and antagonism, as well as frailty and suffering, and hope and joy in life lived with others" (Marback this volume). To be included without having the possibility of manifesting individual difference and of defending personal interests prevents effective participation and forces adaptation to the dominant point of view. To effectively sustain the development of personal capacity, citizenship rights must support difference as well as equality. Citizenship rights must recognize the importance of cultural difference and family roots.

It is evident that the children of immigrants interviewed hold a complex and multidimensional idea of citizenship. Depending on the situation, it may—and should—include: (1) a formal status that allows full recognition, on an equal and universalistic basis, of membership to a particular political community; (2) the recognition of specific identities that relate to the feeling of belonging and to loyalty to specific groups and traditions, that are not seen as in opposition and incompatible with the political community, but that constitute part of it; (3) the recognition of personal agency, the capacity to express personal opinion, to act as a citizen, to defend and promote specific interests, the possibility to engage actively in civic and political life with the chance of making a difference. The complexity of citizenship suitable for a globalized and mobile experience becomes evident when autonomy, agency, and the opportunity to master one's future are emphasized. In this case, a clear generational attitude surfaces. Citizenship ought to support the necessity/skill to be flexible and changeable according to the situation.

In this dimension the classical construct of identification, nationality, and citizenship is most criticized. Having rights, an interest in active participation in community life and the feeling of involvement, does not mean absolute loyalty to and complete identification with a single group. On the contrary, the fundamental rights citizenship ought to assure include the chance to be flexible, to be mobile, and to modulate equality and difference in order to prevent an excess of each of them becoming a cause for discrimination or the reduction of personal opportunities. A citizenship unable to recognize difference and excessively conditioned by national or ethnic identification turns out to be a constraint because it does not recognize the plurality and complexity of belonging in a globalized world.

Therefore, citizenship cannot be represented in a too-fixed way. If it is to support mobility and change, it must be mobile and changeable; it must be a situated resource rather than a static and formal entitlement.

The following table summarizes the different facets of complex citizenship as the children of immigrants interviewed represent them:

Facets of Citizenship		
	Admittance	Allegiance	Involvement
Keywords	Rights, nondiscrimination	Origins, tradition, essence	Practices, experiences, relations, personal opportunities
Frame of Reference	State	Nation/Community	Everyday life processes and contexts
Moral Orientation	Universalistic	Particularistic	Contextual
Feeling Part of	Humanity	Communitarian life, warm relationships	Political arena, public sphere
Priority	Inclusion / Not to be excluded	Cohesion, group solidarity and support. Reacting external negative labeling	Relations, not to miss opportunities, to have a say and to be listened to
Recognition of	Equality	Difference	Agency, autonomy
Scope of Citizenship	Recognition of human rights	Recognition of privileges, defence against discrimination	Recognition of personal capacities
Type of Citizenship	Formal	Multicultural	Plural

Source: Fig. 1: Articulation of the idea of belonging and how it relates to citizenship (Colombo, Domaneschi, and Marchetti 2011).

It is important to stress the fact that admittance, allegiance, and involvement are three aspects of the same figure. They are rhetorical resources used in different contexts to pursue different goals rather than incompatible or incoherent languages. Young people use all three rhetorical resources and highlight or minimize one or more of them depending on context, audience, and personal opportunities. The rhetoric justifying the claim for recognition of citizenship is based on equality and difference, and young people are able to use a "dual competence" (Baumann 1996) that allows them to manage the reified aspect of culture as well as the relative instrumental trait of personal choice.

The capacity to use different justifications and to move from one to another in relation to constraints and opportunities of the different contexts represents one of the most striking features of a potential new generational location, and children of immigrants may constitute a specific generational unit that is about to develop its unique way of facing new experiences of ongoing mobility, flexibility, and change. For this specific generational unit, flexibility and the ability to fit into different situations are more important than finding a coherence that reduces opportunities. It becomes important to relativize, translate, and mediate, to privilege complexity and change over coherence and fixity. All this requires a more complex—sometimes complicated and confused—idea of citizenship. The young people interviewed are engaged in trying to manage and make sense of their complex experience. They are elaborating a new idea of citizenship that mixes admittance, allegiance, and involvement. These three facets of a more complex citizenship, in the experience of the children of immigrants, create a meaningful picture that does not necessarily privilege coherence but does show how numerous resources are needed to move quickly and competently among the three different dimensions without feeling obliged to abandon any. They show that ambivalence does not necessarily mean contradiction, disorientation, or confusion; managing ambivalence may become an indispensable skill instead.

The capacity to manage ambivalence in a fruitful way does not totally depend on individual skills; structural constraints matter and define the space for individual agency. Race, gender, class, age, and other social differences provide the opportunity to switch codes and to tactically use equality and difference. The ways in which these social differences interact are complex and cannot be understood by a simple addition of their distinct effects. To be a middle-class, young, black woman makes some identification rhetoric more plausible, effective, and justifiable than others in ways that are specific to this social position. In changing the intersection of these social differences, the space for oscillation and ambivalence also change.

In general, the high social status of not being considered a bearer of a discriminatory racial marker and not showing behaviors or cultural attitudes that are interpreted as a threat to the majority way of life creates the favorable conditions for the emergence of a fluid and dynamic identification. It results more difficult when cultural and material resources are limited and when discrimination and racism affect heavily on people's lives.

Finally, we cannot help considering—as Richard Marback highlights in the introduction—the inevitable conflicts that arise when the interests and priorities of one generation are brought into contact with the interests and priorities of another. Children of immigrants in Italy are challenging both the idea of Italianness of older generations of Italians and the one of their 'autochthonous' peers. These different ideas of what being Italians means clash and it is uncertain whether and how they can find a new synthesis. Nevertheless, in the confrontation the idea of citizenship may find new grounds for strengthening and expanding its meanings. As modern history tells us, citizenship has always been an open concept and it has always enlarged and reinforced itself through conflicts in which the marginalized and excluded challenged the rights of the powerful. Conflicts and changes are part of a vital and effective citizenship because, over time, rights which are not constantly discussed, contested and enlarged to others often tend to become privileges: special advantages limited to particular persons or groups.

NOTES

1. "Generation" is employed here in its sociological meaning. It is not used as a mere synonym for "cohort," as a collection of people who are born at the same time and thus share the same condition that characterized them at a given point in history. Instead, it refers to a cohort of individuals that, sharing some important historical events that shape their lives and personalities, *potentially* develop the feeling of being part of *the common destiny*—in this case the transformations introduced by the processes of globalization (Mannheim 1952, 303)—and create a concrete bond that permits them to intervene significantly in social change (Edmund and Turner 2002).

2. "The *generation* unit represents a much more concrete bond than the actual generation as such. *Youth experiencing the same concrete historical problems may be said to be part of the same actual generation; while those groups within the same actual generation which work up the material of their common experiences in different specific ways, constitute separate generation units*" (Mannheim 1952, 304; emphasis in original).

3. Fifty-six percent of fathers and 47 percent of mothers do unskilled jobs. In particular, 21 percent of mothers do full-time assistance of elderly persons, and 22 percent are housewives. Concerning educational qualifications, 15 percent

of parents hold a degree and 35 percent have completed their high school program.

4. For research showing the importance of this perspective, see Lister et al. 2003; Hussain and Bagguley 2005; Miller-Idriss 2006; Benedicto and Morán 2007; Hart 2009).

5. Italian citizenship law is mainly based on *jus sanguinis*. Children of foreign parents who are born in Italy are not automatically recognized as Italian, let alone entitled to stay in the country. On the contrary, they need to fulfill a series of tricky requirements in order to apply for Italian citizenship. In fact, they have just one year to submit their application (they must be between eighteen and nineteen); they must prove they have been living in Italy without interruption; moreover, their parents had to be legally recognized at the moment of the child's birth and have remained so for the entire period until the coming of age of the son or the daughter. This latter requirement is particularly penalizing for the children who end up paying for the "faults" of their parents. Around half of the foreigners who currently hold a regular permit to stay have previous experience of irregular migration. Moreover, it is quite common that parents decide to raise their children in the country of origin, at least for a short period of time, due to the long hours and harsh working conditions in Italy that do not allow them to take care of their children adequately, or because, by entrusting their children to relatives in their country of origin, they want their kids to learn their native language and traditions. Although they were born in Italy and spent much of their life there, children of immigrants who fail to obtain Italian citizenship when they come of age have to apply for a regular permit to stay, without which they may be expelled from Italy to the country of their parents that they barely know and are not interested in living in.

WORKS CITED

Anthias, F. 2010. "Nation and Post-Nation: Nationalism, Transnationalism, and Intersections of Belonging." In *The Sage Handbook of Race and Ethnic Studies*, edited by P. Hill Collins and J. Solomos. London: Sage.

Appadurai, A. 1996. *Modernity at Large: Cultural Dimension of Globalization.* Minneapolis: University of Minnesota Press.

Basch, L. G., N. G. Schiller, and C. Szanton Blanc. 1994. *Nations Unbound: Transnational Projects, Postcolonial Predicaments, and Deterritorialized Nation-States.* Langhorne, PA: Gordon and Breach.

Bauböck, R., and V. Guiraudon. 2009. "Introduction: Realignments of Citizenship: Reassessing Rights in the Age of Plural Membership and Multi-Level Governance." *Citizenship Studies* 13 (5): 439–50.

Baumann, G. 1996. *Contesting Culture*. Cambridge: Cambridge University Press.

———. 1999. *The Multicultural Riddle*. New York: Routledge.

Beck, U. 2012. "Redefining the Sociological Project: The Cosmopolitan Challenge." *Sociology* 46 (1): 7–12.

Benedicto, J., and M. L. Morán. 2007. "Becoming a Citizen." *European Societies* 9 (4): 601–22.

Colombo, E. 2010. "Crossing Differences: How Young Children of Immigrants Keep Everyday Multiculturalism Alive." *Journal of Intercultural Studies* 31 (5): 455–70.

Colombo, E., L. Domaneschi, and C. Marchetti. 2011. "Citizenship and Multiple Belonging: Representations of Inclusion, Identification, and Participation among Children of Immigrants in Italy." *Journal of Modern Italian Studies* 16 (3): 334–47.

Colombo, E., L. Leonini, and P. Rebughini. 2009. "Different but Not Stranger: Everyday Collective Identification among Adolescent Children of Immigrants in Italy." *Journal of Ethnic and Migration Studies* 35 (1): 37–9.

Colombo, E., and P. Rebughini. 2012. *Children of Immigrants in a Globalized World: A Generational Experience*. Basingstoke: Palgrave Macmillan.

Delanty, G. 2000. *Citizenship in a Global Age*. Buckingham: Open University Press.

Dower, N. 2003. *An Introduction to Global Citizenship*. Edinburgh: Edinburgh University Press.

Edmund, J., and B. S. Turner. 2002. *Generations, Culture, and Society*. Buckingham: Open University Press.

Hart, S. 2009. "The 'Problem' with Youth: Young People, Citizenship, and the Community." *Citizenship Studies* 13 (6): 641–57.

Held, D., and D. Archibugi. 1995. *Cosmopolitan Democracy*. Cambridge: Polity Press.

Hirschman, A. O. 1970. *Exit, Voice, and Loyalty*. Cambridge, MA: Harvard University Press.

Hussain, Y., and P. Bagguley. 2005. "Citizenship, Ethnicity, and Identity: British Pakistanis after the 2001 'Riots.'" *Sociology* 39 (3): 407–25.

Isen, E. F., and G. M. Nielsen, eds. 2008. *Acts of Citizenship*. London: Zed Books.

Jacobson, D. 1996. *Rights across Borders: Immigration and the Decline of Citizenship*. Baltimore: Johns Hopkins University Press.

Kapai, P. 2012. "Developing Capacities for Inclusive Citizenship in Multicultural Societies: The Role of Deliberative Theory and Citizenship Education." *Public Organization Review* 12 (3): 277–98.

Koopmans, R., P. Statham, M. Giugni, and F. Passy. 2005. *Contested Citizenship: Immigration and Cultural Diversity in Europe.* Minneapolis: University of Minnesota Press.

Kymlicka, W. 1995. *Multicultural Citizenship.* Oxford: Oxford University Press.

Levitt, P., and N. Glick-Schiller. 2004. "Conceptualizing Simultaneity: A Transnational Social Field Perspective on Society." *International Migration Review* 38 (3): 1002–39.

Lister, R., N. Smith, S. Middleton, and L. Cox. 2003. "Young People Talk about Citizenship: Empirical Perspectives on Theoretical and Political Debate." *Citizenship Studies* 7 (2): 235–53.

Mannheim, K. 1952. "The Problem of Generation." In *Essays on the Sociology of Knowledge.* London: Routledge (original 1928).

Melucci, A. 1996. *The Playing Self.* Cambridge: Cambridge University Press.

Miller, D. 1995. "Reflections on British National Identity." *Journal of Ethnic and Migration Studies* 21 (2): 153–66.

Miller, T. 2002. "Cultural Citizenship." In *Handbook of Citizenship Studies,* edited by E. F. Isin and B. S. Turner. London: Sage.

Miller-Idriss, C. 2006. "Everyday Understanding of Citizenship in Germany." *Citizenship Studies* 10 (5): 541–70.

Moscovici, S. 1979. *Psychologie des minorités actives.* Paris: PUF.

Noble, G. 2009. "Everyday Cosmopolitanism and the Labour of Intercultural Community." In *Everyday Multiculturalism,* edited by A. Wise and S. Velayutham. Basingstoke: Palgrave Macmillan.

Nussbaum, M. 1997. *Cultivating Humanity.* Cambridge, MA: Harvard University Press.

Pawley, L. 2008. "Cultural Citizenship." *Sociological Compass* 2 (2): 594–608.

Portes, A., L. E. Guarnizo, and P. Landolt. 1999. "The Study of Transnationalism: Pitfalls and Promise of an Emergent Research Field." *Ethnic and Racial Studies* 22 (2): 217–37.

Sayad, A. 1999. *La double absence.* Paris: Editions du Seuil.

Schattle, H. 2008. *The Practices of Global Citizenship.* Lanham, MD: Rowman and Littlefield.

Schugurensky, D. 2010. "Citizenship and Immigrant Education." In *International Encyclopedia of Education,* 3rd ed., edited by E. Baker, P. Peterson, and P. McGaw, 113–19. Oxford: Elsevier.

Smith, W. 2007. "Cosmopolitan Citizenship: Virtue, Irony and Worldliness." *European Journal of Social Theory* 10 (1): 37–52.

Soysal, Y. 1994. *Limits of Citizenship*. Chicago: University of Chicago Press.

Stevenson, N., ed. 2001. *Culture and Citizenship*. London: Sage.

Tambini, D. 2001. "Post-National Citizenship." *Ethnic and Racial Studies* 24 (2): 195–217.

Tomlinson, J. 1999. *Globalization and Culture*. Chicago: University of Chicago Press.

Yuval-Davis, N., K. Kannabiran, and U. Vieten, eds. 2006. *Situated Politics of Belonging*. London: Sage.

7

CHILDREN, POSTCONFLICT PROCESSES, AND SITUATED COSMOPOLITANISM

· · · · · · · · · ·

PAULINE STOLTZ

INTRODUCTION

Views of children's citizenship, and birthright citizenship in particular, have shifted a great deal in the wake of World War II. This is the case in the United States (see Hink this volume) and also in other parts of the world. At the same time children's global rights to citizenship have continuously expanded. When families migrate after military conflicts (or after natural disasters or following a financial crisis) children's citizenship and senses of belonging and the ways in which these are related to their respective parents and different states become quite complex (see also Hink, Oda, and Khan this volume).

From a *global* perspective, researchers as well as practitioners with an interest in the political processes that follow military conflicts rarely concern themselves with children. In the following I argue that including children in our thinking about these processes is vital for the accomplishment of equality and justice after conflict. I use the rarely discussed case of the citizenship of Indo-European migrant children in the Netherlands to illustrate my argument. These mixed-race children migrated from Indonesia to the Netherlands during and after the late 1940s in the aftermath of the Japanese occupation of the Dutch Indies during the Second World War and the Indonesian war for independence from Dutch colonial rule that immediately followed. The political processes that followed these events influenced the lifelong experiences of citizenship and senses of belonging of a first generation of Indo-European children and young people in the Netherlands (and elsewhere) and also the lives of their children and grandchildren (see Vries 2009; Agt et al. 2007; Meijer 2005).

This case raises the question of how researchers should address the citizenship of children after conflict, notably as this concerns the citizenship of first and subsequent generations of migrant children in liberal democracies. Notions of cosmopolitanism and global citizenship are increasingly being used to take issue with the responsibilities we have toward strangers (see also Khan this volume, on perceptions of citizenship, identity, and belonging of British Pakistani youth). Cosmopolitanism is important for our understanding of the political processes that follow conflicts, including the position of children in these processes.

Professor in political science and philosophy Seyla Benhabib has long been engaged in discussing the rights of aliens, residents, and citizens in the context of ethical concepts of justice and equality in the global era (see Benhabib 2002; 2004). Context and situatedness have always been important to her ethical thinking (see Benhabib 1992). Here I argue that the situated cosmopolitan thought as expressed in her recent work (2008; 2011) can be used to analyze the citizenship of migrant children in postconflict processes.

Notions of childhood, age, and generation are temporal in character, as are postconflict processes. Unfortunately, since Benhabib, with her focus on multilevel governance, hardly mentions the impact of time upon her analysis, it seems that her cosmopolitanism prioritizes issues of space over those of time, where I would argue both time and space are needed in an analysis of postconflict processes. I turn to postcolonial, feminist, and childhood research to compensate for this.

After an introduction to the case and to the thought of Seyla Benhabib I introduce the notions of childhood, age, and generation. I then analyze key elements of Benhabib's thought in relation to my case. Finally, I use postcolonial, feminist, and childhood research about unequal power relations to address assumptions of time in the political analysis of world politics, citizenship, and generation. I conclude that cosmopolitan thought, postcolonial feminist thought, and childhood research all have a lot to contribute to our thinking on the citizenship of migrant children after conflict in liberal democracies. Regrettably, these theorists/theories are not often in conversation with each other. This perpetuates the invisibility of migrant children in postconflict processes.

THE BACKGROUND: INDO-EUROPEANS IN THE NETHERLANDS

In this section I introduce the case of the citizenship of Indo-European migrant children and subsequent generations in the Netherlands. This provides the background to the arguments that follow.

Colonialism and World War II

Dutch colonial presence in Indonesia lasted many centuries. The Dutch trade companies that arrived after 1596 started doing business on a small scale, but their influence in the Indonesian archipelago and the Indian Ocean rapidly increased in 1602 with the merging of some of these in the Verenigde Oostindische Compagnie (VOC) or the Dutch East India Company. This influence continued until 1796 when the company went bankrupt and the Dutch government established the Dutch East Indies as a nationalized colony (Bosma, Raben, and Willems 2008, 25–47).

Colonization was, in the Dutch East Indies, primarily a male activity; more men than women were moving from the Netherlands to the Indonesian archipelago. The marriage regulations of the Dutch companies that had started up in the Dutch East Indies, such as the VOC, played a crucial role. The planters and the companies allowed relationships between European male planters and Asian women. Such relationships usually took the form of a concubinage and not of a marriage, leaving both the women and the children in legally vulnerable positions (Gelman Taylor 1986, 10–33; Lucas 1986, 78–97; Pollmann 1986, 98–125).

During the Second World War, in 1942, the Japanese occupied the Dutch East Indies, in effect ending Dutch colonial rule. Only days after the surrender of the Japanese on August 15, 1945, Indonesian nationalists declared the country independent and appointed Sukarno as president. The Dutch disapproved of these events and attempted to reestablish their control, but this only led to a revolution (the so-called bersiap), which lasted for over four years. The conflict ended in the Dutch acknowledgment of Indonesian independence in December 1949 and their subsequent final withdrawal from the country (Bosma, Raben, and Willems 2008, 25–47).

About 330,000 Europeans migrated from Indonesia to the Netherlands between 1945 and 1968. The Dutch government constantly underestimated this figure and had to regularly adjust their policies for recognition of citizenship and for the related claims for financial support several groups made (Bosma, Raben, and Willems 2008, 47–48). The migration from Indonesia included individuals and families from the different "racially" constructed categories that were prevalent at that time and place. These groups had lived through the Japanese occupation and the bersiap under diverse conditions, but issues of gender, "race," and generation all played a role in their experiences in Indonesia and after migration to the Netherlands.

Citizenship, Gender, and Race

The politics of inclusion and exclusion under Dutch colonial rule in the Dutch East Indies were contingent on constructing categories: legal and social classifications like "Indo's" or Indo-Europeans, designating who was "white," who was "native," who could become a citizen, which children were legitimate progeny and which were not. What mattered were not only a person's physical properties but also whether the person counted as "European" and by what measure (Stoler 1997, 374). During their more than 350 years in the country, the Dutch replaced the existing state, which was characterized by several principalities, with a society based on "race" (Pattynama 1994, 30–45).

The terminology around "European" centered on the racist idea of purity of "race" and to the amount of "blood mixture" that determined the distance between social groups in this society. Totoks, or "full-blooded" Europeans, were found at the top of the hierarchy. Indo's or Indo-Europeans, who were thought of as having "mixed blood" and were sometimes called "half-blooded," were, at times, legally "equated" to totoks, but socially separated. They were the result of the previously mentioned relations between European men and Asian women. In a social sense it did not matter which generation a person belonged to since physical appearance was of greater importance. Inlanders, or "full-blooded" Asians were found at the bottom of the hierarchy (Pattynama 1994, 30–45; Stoltz 2000, 9–14). As the authors of a book on the history of "indische nederlanders" point out, a recurring problem is terminology (Bosma, Raben, and Willems 2008, 47–48). Neutral names are not available. A precise boundary between groups is neither possible nor really necessary, since the groups have always been fluid and subject to change. Patterns of movement and a focus on (legal and social) inclusionary and exclusionary mechanisms are also of greater importance, and these mechanisms continued to play a role in the Netherlands.

Political and Legal Processes after Colonialism and War

The inclusionary and exclusionary mechanisms that played a role in the citizenship of Indo-Europeans in the Netherlands were related to the events of the 1940s. Much of the violence that Indonesian nationalists used during this period was directed toward Indo-Europeans, since this group provided a political alternative in the Indonesian republic (Cribb 2007). This violence made children and youth both victims and perpetrators. During the Indonesian revolution and war for independence, many Indo-European children felt more in danger outside than inside the internment camps in which many white Dutch people remained for a period after Japanese surrender. This was due, in part, to the violent activities of another category of young people, the so-called pemudas, or young Indonesian freedom fighters. These freedom fighters would rape, kidnap, torture, and murder Indo-European children and youths, as well as adults (Agt 2007; Vries 2009). An example is the infamous bloodbaths by the hands of Indonesian nationalists during the Indonesian revolution in Surabaya in late 1945 (Hollander 2008, esp. chaps. 14 and 15). Also, the Dutch committed what today would be called "crimes against humanity" or war crimes. The Dutch military, for example, executed 431 men and boys in the village of Rawagede in Indonesia in December 1947. In December of 2011 (finally), the Dutch government offered a late apology and war damage compensation for these events, but only after a legal process that nine descendants of victims won.[1]

Researchers of postconflict processes, policy makers, and those who are victims of a conflict agree that a lack of public debate and of political and legal non-decision-making after war or colonialism is a bad option, since silence leaves societies open to new conflicts and acts of terrorism (See Blumenthal and McCormack 2008; Rotberg and Thompson 2000; Celermajer 2009). During the second half of the twentieth century, the Netherlands was silent about, and failed to make political decisions about, the traumatic experiences of the Japanese occupation of the Dutch East Indies during World War II and of the colonization of present-day Indonesia. This silence has not only influenced the experience of citizenship and senses of belonging of a first generation of Indo-European children and young people who lived in Indonesia during the 1940s and who since then migrated to the Netherlands but also the lives of their children and grandchildren (See Oostindie 2011; Vries 2009; Agt et al. 2007; Meijer 2005).

Nira Yuval-Davis argues that citizenship should not be seen as limited to only state citizenship but should be understood as the participatory dimension of membership in all political communities. Thus state citizenship should include an analysis of the citizenships of sub-, cross-, and suprastate political communities (Yuval-Davis 2011a; 2011b). In this case, migration is also a particular concern. The agency of Indo-European children (as well as adults) in the Netherlands can be viewed from the perspective of their legal status as citizens and also of their identities and senses of belonging. The question as to who was and who was not a citizen was politically sensitive both in the Netherlands and in Indonesia during the decades following Indonesian independence (Bosma, Raben, and Willems 2008).

"Back Pay" and Delegation Debts

Today, over sixty years after the repatriation of a first generation of Indo-Europeans to the Netherlands, complaints about a lack of recognition and unfair treatment can be identified within the Indo-European community. These voices are not new, since protests have prevailed and include the voices of subsequent generations (see, e.g., Oostindie 2011; Bosma, Raben, and Willems 2008; Meijer 2005). Given the above remark about the politics of silence in the Netherlands, it might come as a surprise that the mixed-race group of Indo-Europeans—as a group—was and still is considered to be well integrated, at least in comparison to other groups in Dutch society (Oostindie 2011; Lucassen and Penninx 1994; Vries 2009).

It may come as an even bigger surprise that this public silence from Dutch politicians was recently, around the turn of the century, broken by means of war damage compensation and other reconciliation projects (see Ridder 2007; Agt et al. 2007). The reaction to these initiatives among the Indo-European community was not undividedly positive.

This was due, for example, to the racial divide between those who were and those who were not eligible to receive war damage compensation, once it was granted, but also to other issues of gender, age, and generation that play a role in the ongoing controversy. The internment experience influenced, for example, the possibilities of public recognition. The experiences of those who had not been in camps were not recognized, regardless of other claims they might have, such as for so-called back pay or unpaid wages of employees in the Dutch East Indies during the Second World War (Meijer 2005). Back pay is the big politically and morally sensitive issue within the Indo-European community, which has engaged not only a first but also subsequent generations. Back pay also included so-called delegation debts. These concern the part of the wages that public and private employers in the Dutch Indies "delegated" to children and other relatives who for shorter or longer periods resided in the Netherlands, for example, for educational purposes. These delegation debts have only partly been settled, and within Indo-European activism they eventually ended up in the background (Meijer 2005; 2007).

An early refusal to settle war damage compensation was related to the poor economic situation of the state. It was not until the early 1980s that war damage compensation was rewarded, and then it covered few categories of people. New generations took over the struggle, which led to some results in the 1990s in ways that did not satisfy many people. Then, in March 2000, the Dutch government made a public apology for the legalistic and bureaucratic way in which Indo-Europeans were treated after the war, and the government decided it wanted to make "a gesture." This "gesture" (het "Indische" Gebaar) involved, in part, funding for historical research and collective aims in education, welfare, and culture. For many Indo-Europeans, this gesture was too small and came too late (Meijer 2005, esp. chap. 10).

In addition to the issues of violence, issues over war damage compensation have had an influence on the life chances of the involved children. Both issues should in my opinion be taken into account in an analysis of the citizenship of these children, but before I return to our case, I would like to briefly introduce the cosmopolitan thought of Seyla Benhabib and explain her relevance to postconflict processes. Also, I would like to introduce some key notions in relation to citizenship, children, and generation.

INTRODUCTION TO THE COSMOPOLITANISM
OF SEYLA BENHABIB

Postconflict processes are related to cosmopolitan claims that humanity is to be treated as one single moral community with moral priority over national communities. This includes attempts to define the moral responsibilities we have toward others and the way in which these responsibilities should govern the universal community legally and politically. The recent establishment of the International Criminal Court and its role in the punishment of individuals who have committed crimes against humanity can be seen as an example of how this could be implemented in practice.

The situated cosmopolitanism of Seyla Benhabib is in my opinion of special interest in relation to the citizenship of migrant children in postconflict processes, since she has been particularly concerned with the political agency of migrants in Europe in light of the relationship between law and politics from local and global perspectives (Benhabib 2004; 2008; 2011; see also Khan on Benhabib in this volume). Here, we can think of the previously mentioned political and moral claims for war damage compensation Indo-Europeans made in the Netherlands.

In her book *Another Cosmopolitanism* from 2008, Benhabib poses the following questions: "How can the will of democratic majorities be reconciled with norms of cosmopolitan justice? How can legal norms and standards, which originate outside the will of democratic legislations, become binding on them?" (Benhabib 2008, 17). That is, she questions how legal norms and standards can become binding locally if they derive from outside democratic political communities (for example, if they are formulated globally, morally, or according to customary law). This is also why she addresses the local, the national, and the global levels of law and politics and the way in which these interact.

In reply to the questions she has posed, Benhabib introduces the notion of a "jurisgenerative politics." These politics imply that a democratic people consider themselves bound by certain guiding norms and principles. Because they do so, they engage in repetitive acts of using these norms and principles in their relation to the law. Benhabib calls these acts "democratic iterations." That is, by using these norms, a democratic people are not only the subject of the law but they are also authors of the law (Benhabib 2008, 49). Jurisgenerative politics mediate between universal norms and the will of democratic majorities. Democratic iterations change democratic law so that this reflects principles of ethical universalism, and they alter the boundaries that define democratic states. All democracies require borders of inclusion and exclusion, but since law fixes these borders, they can be changed in democracies. They are therefore subject to the force of democratic repetitions—by democratic iterations. Below I will exemplify and discuss these notions more thoroughly.

Benhabib is also concerned with moral learning. She argues: "We have to learn to live with the otherness of others, whose ways of life may be deeply threatening to our own. How else can moral and political learning take place, except through such encounters in civil society?" (Benhabib 2008, 61). To her, the law provides the framework within which the work of politics and culture takes place. Politics leads to the breaking down of, or at least to assuring, the permeability of the barriers the laws provide.

This is also why she is interested in the struggle of marginalized people such as migrants. Benhabib wants to "signal forms of popular empowerment and political struggle through which the people themselves would appropriate the universalist promise of cosmopolitan norms in order to bind forms of political and economic power that seek to escape democratic control, accountability and transparency." To her this means that cosmopolitanism is never fixed in values, time, or place. It rather "anticipate(s) another cosmopolitanism—a cosmopolitanism to come" (Benhabib 2008, 177).

I find the notions of "democratic iterations" and "jurisgenerative politics" useful, since these enable me to highlight the moral and political agency of Indo-Europeans in relation to the local, national, and global levels of law and politics and the way in which these interact. These notions echo the previously mentioned Nira Yuval-Davis, who said that state citizenship should include an analysis of the citizenships of sub-, cross-, and suprastate political communities. Also, I agree with Benhabib's final remark that it is good to understand cosmopolitanism, not as something that is, but rather as something to come. On the other hand, neither Yuval-Davis nor Benhabib focuses on issues of children, age, or generation, which are of key concern here.

CHILDHOOD, AGE, AND GENERATION IN POSTCONFLICT PROCESSES

We will now turn to the notions of childhood, age, and generation, before returning to the relevance of Benhabib's notions in relation to postconflict processes.

Childhood

Childhood is a phase in the life course of all people everywhere. This implies that the biological base of childhood is a cultural universal. Also, eventually children grow up and in so doing leave their "childhood" behind. However, although all of today's adults have been children and will have some experiences in common, the "childhood" of the current generation of children will undoubtedly be different from that their parents remember (James and James 2004, 19–20; Qvortrup 1994, 5–6). Thus although childhood as a social space remains and is both a constant and a universal, as James and James argue, "its temporal location in generational history means that its character, nonetheless, changes over time, shaped by changes in the laws, policies, discourses and social practices through which childhood is defined" (James and James 2004, 20).

This observation could be especially pertinent when we compare the childhood of a first generation of migrant children with experiences from war or colonialism in one society with the childhood of their children and grandchildren and their childhood experiences from other and, hopefully, more peaceful societies later in history. Not only space but also time plays a role in how we socially construct and thus think of certain children and certain childhoods.

Age and Generation

Age is also important in our understanding of childhood, but even age is a relative concept. Since I am concerned with international law, we can take the United Nations Convention on the Rights of the Child (UNCRC) from 1989 as an example. Article 1 of the UNCRC states: "For the purposes of the present Convention, a child means every human being below the age of eighteen years *unless, under the law applicable to the child*, majority is attained earlier" (my italics). This definition of a child not only shows us when the more powerful and relational concept of "adult" should be used as opposed to "child," it also locates the age of the child in different cultural and social settings and is sensitive to legal changes over time.

Children are thus that which adults are not, but what this means in detail can differ both between and within societies. According to James and James, such exclusions are defined by the adult world, so in order to understand children and childhood, the notion of "generation" becomes of key concern in that it forces consideration of the *power relations* between adults and children (James and James 2004, 21–23). This happens similarly to that in which the notion of gender emphasizes the relations between genders and ethnicity between different ethnic groups. Mutual hierarchies develop between generations, genders, and ethnic groups, creating dominating and dominated categories (Eilard 2011, 37). Postcolonial feminists and other feminists discuss how tensions between the local and the global indicate that the formulation of the intersections of gender, generation, "race," and ethnicity in citizenship and human rights discourses are worthy of investigation (Stoltz et al. 2010; Yuval-Davis and Werbner 1999; John 1996).

Time and the Citizenship of Children

Childhood research uses two related perspectives: a child perspective and a child's perspective, respectively. A *child perspective* implies ideas about the best interest of a child as adults formulate them. Following Trondman, I would like to describe this as the way in which adults take responsibility for future life opportunities that children do not yet understand the meaning of, in order to assure every child's moral right to an open future. The above-mentioned UNCRC is a good example of a document that was written from this perspective (Trondman 2011, 68–69).

A *child's perspective*, on the other hand, concerns the moral right of every child to freedom of thought and to having a voice of his or her own. Every child has the right to have a version of its experiences, judgments, and will. The first perspective points to an adult responsibility to keep the future of children open, the second emphasizes children's rights to have their voices respected and to be taken seriously. The first concerns investments in future rights, the second the right to speak and to a sense of well-being. Both perspectives are important for our understanding of children and childhood (Trondman 2011). According to Trondman, a child is a "being" with present citizenship rights, but a child is also a "becoming" as a future adult citizen.

Generational aspects of childhood can also be related to how societies deal with time (the past, the present, and the future) in the analysis of postconflict processes. Whereas a first generation of migrant children can be among those most directly affected by conflict, generational aspects highlight traumas that have been dealt with for an extended period of time in such places as the Netherlands, Indonesia, and Japan. Generational aspects of childhood help us understand the frustrations second- and third-generation children feel toward those directly involved in the traumas of war and colonialism. In this regard justice is related to time and to intergenerational aspects of postconflict processes.

Bohman argues that interaction between past and future generations seems unavoidably mediated by the present. In fact, the past often has political claims upon the present, which are usually related to past injustices and harm. Such claims are intergenerational; they refer to the future as well as to the past. Intergenerational democracy, he argues, requires that the past is not closed, at least in the sense that those living in the present can make legitimate claims on the basis of ongoing domination. This means that dealing with claims of past generations can change the polity in the present (Bohman 2011, 138).

SITUATING COSMOPOLITANISM

Here I discuss the earlier introduced notions of democratic iterations and jurisgenerative politics in the analysis of postconflict processes. I illustrate this with examples from our case. Finally, I argue that children receive too little attention in political and legal processes after conflicts.

Democratic Iterations and Children

In *Another Cosmopolitanism* Benhabib uses the case of the so-called scarf affair, or "l'affaire du foulard," as one example of the use of democratic iterations. Interestingly enough, this affair concerns girls. It occupied French public opinion and politics throughout the 1990s and still continues to do so (see, e.g., Open Society Foundations 2011). French authorities banned the wearing of the veil in schools; this intervention cascaded into a series of democratic iterations, ranging from an intense public debate about the meaning of the wearing of the scarf, to the self-defense of the girls involved and the rearticulation of their actions, the encouragement of other immigrant women to wear their headscarves in the workplace, and to the public act of resignifying the face of "Marianne" by having immigrant women from Arab countries and Africa represent her (Benhabib 2008, 51–61). The girls themselves also performed democratic iterations. Benhabib writes: "The girls' voices are not heard in this heated debate" (Benhabib 2008, 56). Unfortunately, she does not follow up on this, since she is just concerned with the effect of the total amount of iterations. Overall, she considers this case to be an example of successful democratic iterations and argues that "it is clear that all future struggles with respect to the rights of Muslim and other immigrants will be fought within the framework created by the universalistic principles of Europe's commitment to human rights, on the one hand, and the exigencies of democratic self-determination, on the other" (Benhabib 2008, 61).

Much more can be said about this case and about Benhabib's conclusion, but because of what I mentioned earlier about a child's perspective and the moral right of every child to have a voice of its own and to have its own version of its experiences, judgments, and will, I want to emphasize her observation about the girls who were not heard. Of course, there can be several reasons as to why they were not heard, but I suggest that one of these is that they are children. The assumptions adults have of the agency of children often differ (for better and for worse) from those of the agency of adults. The first point I make is that in general, political thinkers such as Benhabib often ignore, or ignore to develop, an analysis of the agency of children in their thinking. I elaborate on this below.

Popular Empowerment and Inequalities in Power

Another point I would like to make brings me back to my case. The Indo-Europeans who came to the Netherlands as children fought for recognition. Subsequent generations joined in and took over this struggle. But, as explained above, no political results—no war damage compensation or public apologies—were obtained until the turn of the century. That is, half a century later. Despite repeated democratic iterations by Indo activists, Dutch politicians did not listen, and when results were eventually seen, we were able to speculate on the reasons why these came at that particular point in time. By the turn of the century a formidable explosion of policy options, including truth commissions, public apologies, and the introduction of the International Criminal Court, could be observed. When elites became involved in postconflict processes at a global level, something also happened in the Netherlands. That is, other developments and other actors than these activists were presumably also involved in the decisions Dutch politicians made at the time. This observation raises the issue of how to deal with the unequal power relations between marginalized groups and elites in public debate.

My second point is that the popular empowerment in struggles for justice and equality in the context of global democracy Benhabib focuses on needs further investigation. Critics of cosmopolitanism have argued that cosmopolitanism has been a project of empires, born out of privileges: economic, political, cultural, linguistic, and perhaps especially citizenship privileges in certain states. This criticism focuses on the ways in which cosmopolitanism, at its worst, concerns a naive, elitist, and/or Western-oriented project that advances neoliberal global capitalism. At the same time, many of these critics do not want to dismiss the notion entirely (see, e.g., Calhoun 2003, 113; Kapoor 2008, 33–37; for an overview of the critique, see also Held 2010).

Postcolonial thought is concerned with the historical relations between colonial powers and colonized states and takes its starting point in the lives and experiences of colonized people, rather than those of colonial powers. Many postcolonial theorists also argue that the colonial hierarchies of race, class, and gender that prevailed during the colonial period can still be recognized today (Sylvester 2011); this is also the case in the Netherlands. Postcolonial critique, including postcolonial feminist critique, emphasizes the inadequate attention paid to the relationships between what sometimes are called political elites and subalterns (or marginalized people), for example in democratic theories. Kapoor suggests that both ends of the elite-subaltern relationship need to work on improving communication (Kapoor 2008). Following his suggestion and recognizing that Benhabib focuses on individuals as bearers of cosmopolitan rights who can challenge the limits of their own nations, I would like to argue that Benhabib's suggestion of popular empowerment needs further investigation in the case of Indo-European children in the Netherlands.[2]

The Outcome of Democratic Iterations

A third point concerns whether iterations, even if these are democratic, lead to a desirable result. This question is inspired by postcolonial thinker Dipesh Chakrabarty, who points at the ways in which the previously, and in many ways still oppressed, lower castes of India have, on the one hand, challenged traditional hierarchy and authority by using Indian electoral democracy, and how, on the other hand, this has not necessarily produced forms of governance that he, as an academic, would recognize as good or just (Chakrabarty 2004).

Benhabib does not include any particular outcome of democratic iterations since, as I understand her, she seems to be more concerned with procedural democracy and political representation. In her previously mentioned argument about the scarf affair, for example, she does not underestimate the possibility that democratic iterations can lead to processes of public self-reflection. She also does not underestimate the generation of public defensiveness, such as the mobilization of right-wing parties throughout Europe whose members hold significant xenophobic resentment toward Muslim populations (Benhabib 2008, 61). The democratic problem in postconflict processes probably starts when resentments and inequalities in power lead to the use of violence as a result of unsolved past injustices.

By comparison we can think of another category of youth, a group that actually succeeded in their struggle. The previously mentioned pemudas, or young Indonesian nationalist freedom fighters, obtained independence and used violence in their struggle. As much as I agree with the just cause of their fight for independence and the injustice of colonialism, acts of violence are neither democratic nor just. Also, both individual and collective Indonesian and Dutch actors used violence in ways that today, under contemporary conditions of international law, would be (and are) considered unacceptable.

This raises not only the issue of the democratic character of iterations but also the question as to whether the use of violence is morally, politically, and legally defensible, and of how to deal with these questions over time and space. This issue abandons the prioritization of the present moment (which could be claimed is what Benhabib is doing) and links the present to both the past and the future. Also, since Benhabib is not concerned with war, her thought reflects a presumption of peace and democracy, which appears to be problematic in the case of postconflict processes.

Jurisgenerative Politics, Multilevel Governance, and Postconflict Processes

This brings us to the ethics of war and to the responsibilities that people living in the present have toward those in other states as a result of historic injustices. Let us focus on Benhabib's notion of jurisgenerative politics as the result of democratic iterations in relation to postconflict processes.

The ethics of war gained much interest around the turn of the century, especially in relation to cosmopolitan thought about our responsibilities toward others. The global political and legal developments concerning postconflict processes have been dramatic since the Second World War and the period of the bersiap. This has influenced national and regional politics around the world, involving, for example, the establishment of the European Union, the European Court of Justice, the advancement of human rights (also for children), the related introduction of institutions like the United Nations and the European Court of Human Rights, and also the development of new ideas concerning policy options such as truth commissions and public apologies after conflicts and, in 2002, the establishment of the International Criminal Court in The Hague.

These developments involve a dramatic increase in and experimentation in the methods that can be used to obtain justice and equality in postconflict societies. Many of these policy options have not been properly evaluated yet, simply because it is too early to be able to do so. At the same time it can be observed that silence, at least at this point in history, is almost considered to be a taboo as a consequence of the expansion and normalization of these developments. Nowadays the issue is not whether something should be done but rather how it should be done (Teitel 2003, 71–72 and 89; Miller 2008).

This concerns the Netherlands, given the establishment of the International Criminal Court in The Hague two years after the previously described public apology to Indo-Europeans in 2000. The answer to the question, "Why did Dutch authorities break the silence after such a long time?" might thus, at least speculatively, just as well be related to the interplay between different national and global political actors and events as to the recurrent political pressure of different generations of Indo-European activists. One point that can be made here is that Benhabib is right in including different political levels in her analysis, including transnational processes.

Children, International Law, and Politics

We now turn our attention to children in the multilevel politics of postconflict processes and emphasize that until recently children have been overlooked. The first international attempt to formulate children's rights was made in 1924 in the Geneva Declaration of the Rights of the Child, proclaimed by the Save the Children International Union and endorsed by the Assembly of the League of Nations. At present, the UN Convention on the Rights of the Child from 1989 is the primary international legal source, but also the Security Council's creation of a Monitoring and Reporting Mechanism on Children and Armed Conflicts in 2005 provides a way to implement an effective system for the protection of children's rights at the international level.

Although these changes in the legal landscape sound good, the main point is that progress in this area is very slow. Girls are, for example, targeted in armed conflict and subjected to rape, mutilation, forced pregnancy, forced combat, death, and systematic abduction and used for forced labor and sexual slavery. Although nowadays international courts can prosecute these crimes—which are a global phenomenon—as war crimes, crimes against humanity, and genocide, prosecution has only taken place in a few instances (Machel 2010, xii).

Also, the ways in which international law and politics view gendered and racialized aspects of children's experiences in postconflict policy processes have changed over time, but much remains to be done. We can return to our case to emphasize this. Internment was a policy trend during the 1940s and included Dutch, Japanese, and Indonesian camps. Gendered and racialized hierarchies played an important role in relation to these different camps. Indo-European women and children often remained outside of the camps, whereas men more often ended up within them. Indo-European boys were often the target of Japanese education campaigns and demands for loyalty to a Japanese and Asian identity. Women and girls did not receive this kind of attention (Bosma, Rabens, and Willems 2008, 180–85). As we noted earlier, there was a racial, and also gender, divide between those who were and those who were not eligible to receive war damage compensation in the Netherlands, which included experiences in and outside of internment camps.

Siegrist points out that today, acts of sexual violence committed against boys and men are often underreported. In situations where systematic or widespread rape and other sexual violence have taken place, children are often reluctant to speak out because they fear for their safety or because of social stigma (Siegrist 2010, 9). Also children born as the result of war receive only little attention (for an exception see Carpenter 2010). Additionally, crimes against girls and women are important in postconflict processes, but unfortunately the focus is primarily on sexual crimes. This limits attention to other violations, such as the loss of education, forced labor, slavery, and trafficking. The focus on sexual violence can limit the understanding of the totality of the experiences of girls in conflict and leave them marginalized in postconflict processes and in the structure and relevance of postconflict institutional reform (Machel 2010).

In regard to Indo-European children, the previously mentioned back pay is a central concern. This brings material compensation into focus and also the wider economic, social, and emotional effects of this compensation for a second generation of Indo-European children. Miller points out that issues of development and inequality and notably the economic and political-distributional consequences of transitional justice have hardly been on the agenda. Tribunals and truth commissions emphasize, for example, civil and political rights rather than socioeconomic rights (Miller 2008, 271–75).

Concluding Remarks

The situated cosmopolitan thought of Seyla Benhabib can be used in the analysis of the citizenship of first and subsequent generations' migrant children in postconflict processes since she is concerned with multilevel governance and is sensitive to the citizenship rights and agency of migrants, although not of children. As we saw, children are often overlooked in postconflict processes and in the analysis of these processes. This applies not only to children in general, but as illustrated by our case, also to specific issues of concern to first and subsequent generations' migrant children (particular versions of violence and war damage compensation).

Inequalities in power between marginalized groups and elites in global public debate therefore require our special attention. Children, notably migrant children, can be seen as such a marginalized group, not only in relation to adults but in the case of migrant children also to majorities in a society.

Given the above and my earlier discussion of notions of childhood and generation, what or who is and/or should be a source of agency and change in political and legal postconflict processes concerning children and generation? Also, what or who is this in the cosmopolitan thought of Benhabib? In the next section I will discuss these questions in relation to assumptions on time and space in the analysis of global politics, citizenship, and generation.

GLOBAL POLITICS, CITIZENSHIP, AND GENERATION

Migration, diaspora, and transnationalism—all with a relevance to our focus on citizenship—play a role in postconflict processes. That is, in case a conflict has taken place in another part of the world, this will give a special dynamic to the analysis of the subsequent political and legal processes in relation to states and to individuals. The complexity of the analysis increases with the number of voices and (meta)narratives that describe the same events and with the moral, political, and legal consequences of this observation.

I will start this section by discussing the importance of analyzing power relations between marginalized groups and elites in relation to space and time and conclude by returning to issues of citizenship and generation.

Time and Global Politics

A research overview of the case of Indo-Europeans in the Netherlands suggests that regardless of how well integrated Indo-European children and adults are, the adaptation in the Netherlands to cultural traumas of colonialism and war cannot be described as a successful process for the Indo-European community or for Dutch society. Without having looked into this, intuitively I would like to suggest that neither can the claim necessarily be made that these traumas were or are adapted to in any better way in related processes in Indonesia or Japan. This would clearly need further investigation, but my point is that despite the common history and the continued and sometimes strained relationships between these states, and despite the movement of people between them, there has been, over the years, little question of a common process of adaptation to trauma, involving the different societies. We can only speculate as to what would have happened in case World War II had ended today or if Indonesia had become independent now. Indeed, due to recent changes in the legal and political landscape around postconflict processes, some very belated reactions on the part of the Dutch state can be observed, involving apologies and some war damage compensation (see above).

This suggests that today the Dutch state feels bounded by the legal norms and standards that prevail at present, and that what Benhabib might call moral learning in relation to postconflict norms of cosmopolitan justice has taken place. As I mentioned in the beginning, Benhabib's cosmopolitan thought started with the question: "How can the will of democratic majorities be reconciled with norms of cosmopolitan justice? How can legal norms and standards, which originate outside the will of democratic legislations, become binding on them?" (Benhabib 2008, 17). Her suggestion is that this occurs when a democratic people repeatedly performs acts in which they use guiding norms and principles in their relation to the law.

For Benhabib, the key to her argument lies in the repetition of the acts. The effect of these repetitions is that cosmopolitanism is never fixed in values, time, or place. It rather "anticipate(s) . . . a cosmopolitanism to come" (Benhabib 2008, 177). She does not suggest what is to come in detail, and, as we saw, this can be somewhat of a problem, but Benhabib is indeed optimistic about the cosmopolitan form the future will take and sees moral learning by democratic people as the source. At the same time, this raises the question as to what we know about the past and the present and how we deal with the uncertainty of the future.

Heterotemporality

Chakrabarty argues that dominant European thought on imaginations of socially just futures usually takes the idea of single, homogeneous, and secular historical time for granted. So he works from the assumption that historical time is not integral but out of joint with itself (Chakrabarty 2000, introduction). In other words, the dominant political theories that most social scientists in the world work with, such as liberalism and Marxism, are temporal metanarratives grounded in the experiences of dominant groups in society, and which provide theories, norms, and ideas that are universalized. Instead, Chakrabarty encourages us to become more sensitive to a multiplicity of times and temporalities.

Postcolonials argue that the only way in which non-Western people are brought into the story of world politics is as latecomers, as forced to join the party, or as outsiders of politics altogether. Similarly, feminists argue that women are placed outside of political time in European political thought. The point is not simply to demand recognition as part of the story, but to insist that there is no "story," only "stories," alternative temporalities. Instead of these temporal metanarratives, Hutchings draws attention to the plurality of temporalities relevant to theorizing world politics and suggests we look for ways of thinking world-political time as "heterotemporality" (Hutchings 2008, 160–76). This includes "the way in which theorist's own complex temporal structure is implicated in and with that which he or she seeks to describe, explain and judge" (Hutchings 2008, 176).

That is, when researchers with an interest in the Netherlands analyze World War II, they should not assume that this war was only fought in Europe and lost by the Germans, as is the metanarrative in the Netherlands. The focus should not be only on the acts of the Japanese, the Dutch, and the Indonesians on behalf of their states but should include the Indo-European or Chinese men and women, boys and girls who were also present in Indonesia during the 1940s. Also, children, issues of age, generation, and migration are of major importance.

At the same time, this does not necessarily mean that we need to reject or discard European thought. Chakrabarty suggests we "provincialize" Europe in order to remove European thought from and to the margins. Since the margins are as plural and as diverse as the centers, it is important to write narratives and analyses, he argues, that produce translucence in the relation between non-Western histories and European thought and its analytical categories (Chakrabarty 2000, introduction). Heterotemporality does not give us any universal, normative horizons by which to judge different narratives, as Chakrabarty points out. This is why he suggests a critical analysis of global and heterogeneous imaginations of democracy (Chakrabarty 2004, 458–62).

Benhabib also becomes interesting again. There were reasons to question unequal power relations between marginalized groups and elites in her cosmopolitanism, not least in relation to first and subsequent generations' migrant children. In this aspect lies the importance of what Hutchings and Chakrabarty say would involve being critical about the ways in which we think about heterotemporality and the present (Hutchings 2008, last chapter; Chakrabarty 2000). Also, Benhabib does not preclude undesired outcomes of democratic iterations and is in that sense very careful about the future. But her open-ended "cosmopolitanism to come" still indicates a normative horizon, which is what I think is needed in an analysis of postconflict processes.

Consequently, I argue that the presence of the Indo-European diaspora in the Netherlands emphasizes that postcolonial hierarchies of "race," gender, and class can still be recognized today. The narratives of war, colonialism, and migration by Indo-European activists challenge European notions of citizenship, belonging, and democracy. This includes challenges to ideas of benefit, entitlement, and responsibility in relation to historical injustices, including that those living in the present are members of a political community that bears collective responsibility for an ongoing failure to rectify historic injustice (for this last point see Butt 2008).

The Citizenship of Migrant Children in Postconflict Processes

Benhabib's way of addressing the future of world politics reminds me of what I wrote earlier about every child's moral right to an open future and the moral right of every child to freedom of thought and to having a voice of his or her own. As mentioned, the first concerns investments in future rights, the second the right to speak and to having a sense of well-being today. A child is a "being" with present citizenship rights, but also a "becoming" as a future adult citizen. As adults—in relation to children and to politics and law from local and global perspectives—we can and should work toward well-being today and toward the possibility of an open future for all. The importance of the past should not be forgotten here.

Time is also of concern in the citizenship of migrant children in postconflict processes in that citizenship has an internal boundary that children are expected to pass through in time. This is related to the external boundary that noncitizens provide. These internal and external boundaries overlap in the case of migrant children, or children of noncitizen residents whose rights are contingent upon their parents (Lister 2007).

The citizenship status of migrant children and their contingency upon their parents are not only important in general, but notably after war. As Van Bueren points out, citizenship rights are, as a matter of law, lost in situations of armed conflict. Although it is often the case that de facto citizenship rights are lost in situations of conflict, this is very different from accepting a de jure loss of citizenship (Van Bueren 2011). In times of transition, this can also lead to problems for particular communities in a society. In our case, the Dutch state encouraged, for example, Indo-Europeans with Dutch citizenship and residing in Indonesia to opt for Indonesian citizenship in connection with the independence of the new state. Eventually, most of these would opt for Dutch citizenship, which did not necessarily make their lives easier (Meijer 2005, 125–26).

Returning to what I wrote in the beginning of this chapter, the substantive citizenship of children involves more than legal rights and status. It is more of a total relationship involving senses of belonging, membership and participation, rights, responsibilities, equality of status, respect, and recognition (Lister 2007; Yuval-Davis 2011a and 2011b). Lister argues that the significance of rights-talk to lived citizenship is likely to vary according to political and cultural context, between groups and over time. This dynamic is more salient when rights are under threat or for groups who are denied full citizenship rights (Lister 2007). This emphasis on the importance of lived citizenship is highly relevant when we consider the special experiences of children during and after times of war and conflict. The ways in which capacities evolve is of specific concern here.

An example is when children who have committed crimes against their families and communities return home. Think of the previously mentioned example of the pemudas. We may wonder whether international law and victims would demand criminal prosecution in case the violence of the pemudas had happened today, or if traditional measures in Indonesia could be claimed to be sufficient.

Here, the question becomes, what processes of truth seeking or justice can enable them to reestablish meaningful relationships as members of their families and communities? Also, who is responsible for deciding upon measures of accountability in order to help restore normalcy? What measures should be taken to reaffirm children's self-esteem and agency after the conflict that has violated their childhood? (see Carlson, Mazurana, and Acirokop 2010).

An analysis of the lived experiences of these young people should be combined here with a discussion of legal rights and responsibilities in an analysis of who should be doing what for whom, where, how, and why. These questions are highly controversial in contemporary postconflict discourses and are a huge challenge for children's rights activists.

CONCLUSION

Today, the universalism of citizenship is supposed to cover women, as least in theory, and migrants are increasingly often included in mainstream accounts of citizenship, but usually these accounts do not make any claims to include children (see Lister 2007). In this chapter I have argued that it is important to include the citizenship of children in our thinking, especially about postconflict processes. Notably, the citizenship of first and subsequent generations' migrant children is often forgotten, both by practitioners and researchers (for a discussion of the impact of gender and age for the citizenship of children, see also Oda this volume).

It was not until December 2011 that the UN General Assembly adopted a new Optional Protocol to the UNCRC, establishing a complaints procedure for violations of children's rights. This new treaty will enable children, or their representatives, to claim that their rights have been violated, to bring a complaint to an international committee of children's rights experts. That is, if they have not been able to get remedies for these violations in their countries. Typically, until this protocol was adopted, the CRC was the only UN treaty body that was denied the power to examine individual cases.[3] Despite progress in terms of this Optional Protocol, and in relation to our case, the recent halfhearted change of mind of the Dutch state concerning their responsibilities toward the Indo-European community in the country, the citizenship and human rights of children are only very slowly being taken seriously. This also puts pressure on politicians and activists to ensure the implementation of documents such as the UNCRC.

The cosmopolitan thought of Benhabib, the postcolonial and feminist thought of Chakrabarty and Hutchings, and the childhood research of Trondman and Lister all have much to contribute to our thinking about the citizenship of migrant children after conflict. These theorists are not often in conversation with each other. This is unfortunate since this is presumably perpetuating the invisibility of first and subsequent generations' migrant children, not least in terms of issues of space and time in the multilevel governance of postconflict processes.

NOTES

1. *NRC Next*, "Excuses én 180.000 euro voor 431 doden," December 9, 2011.
2. See, for example, the results of the following questionnaire on "postcolonial Dutch people in the Netherlands": G. Oostindie and H. Steijlen, *Enquête*

postkoloniale Nederlanders in Nederland. KITLV maart 2009, www.kitlv.nl/pdf_documents/Enquete_en_artikel_postkoloniale_Nederlanders_1_.pdf, accessed June 28, 2012.

3. http://crin.org/resources/infodetail.asp?id=26980, accessed June 26, 2012.

WORKS CITED

Agt, B. van, et al. 2007. *Het Verborgen Verhaal: Indische Nederlanders in de oorlog-stijd, 1942–1949.* Den Haag: Stichting Tong Tong.

Benhabib, S. 1992. *Situating the Self: Gender, Community, and Postmodernism in Contemporary Ethics.* Cambridge: Polity Press.

———. 2002. *The Claims of Culture: Equality and Diversity in the Global Era.* Princeton, NJ: Princeton University Press.

———. 2004. *The Rights of Others: Aliens, Residents, and Citizens.* Cambridge: Cambridge University Press.

———. 2008. *Another Cosmopolitanism.* Oxford: Oxford University Press.

———. 2011. *Dignity in Adversity: Human Rights in Troubled Times.* Cambridge: Polity Press.

Blumenthal, D., and T. McCormack, eds. 2008. *The Legacy of Nuremberg: Civilising Influence or Institutionalised Vengeance?* Leiden: Martinus Nijhoff.

Bohman, J. 2011. "Children and the Rights of Citizens: Nondomination and Intergenerational Justice." *ANNALS of the American Academy of Political and Social Science* 633: 128.

Bosma, U., R. Raben, and W. Willems. 2008. *De geschiedenis van Indische Nederlanders.* Amsterdam: Bert Bakker.

Butt, D. 2008. *Rectifying International Injustice: Principles of Compensation and Restitution between Nations.* Oxford: Oxford University Press.

Calhoun, C. 2003. "The Class Consciousness of Frequent Travellers: Towards a Critique of Actually Existing Cosmopolitanism." In *Debating Cosmopolitcs,* edited by D. Archibugi. London: Verso.

Carlson, K., D. Mazurana, and P. Acirokop. 2010. "Accountability and Reconciliation in Northern Uganda." In *Children and Transitional Justice: Truth-Telling, Accountability, and Reconciliation,* edited by S. Parmer et al. Cambridge, MA: Harvard University Press.

Carpenter, C. 2010. *Forgetting Children Born of War.* New York: Columbia University Press.

Celermajer, D. 2009. *The Sins of the Nation and the Ritual of Apologies.* Cambridge: Cambridge University Press.

Chakrabarty, D. 2000. *Provincializing Europe: Postcolonial Thought and Historical Difference*. Princeton, NJ: Princeton University Press.

———. 2004. "Where Is the Now?" *Critical Inquiry* 30 (2): 458–62.

Cribb, R. 2007. "Misdaad, geweld en uitsluiting in Indonesië." In *Van Indië tot Indonesië*, edited by E. Bogaerts and R. Raben. Amsterdam: Boom.

Eilard, A. 2011. "Barndom under ett halvsekel i grundskolans läseböcker—generation och andra relationer i förändring." In *Skola och barndom: Normering, demokratisering och individualisering*, edited by I. Tallberg Broman. Malmö, Sweden: Gleerups.

Gelman Taylor, J. 1986. "Europese en Euraziatische vrouwen in Nederlands-Indië in de VOC-tijd." In *Vrouwen in de Nederlandse koloniën: Zevende jaarboek voor vrouwengeschiedenis*, edited by J. Reijs et al. Nijmegen, Netherlands: SUN.

Held, D. 2010. *Cosmopolitanism*. Cambridge: Polity Press.

Hollander, I. 2008. *Silenced Voices: Uncovering a Family's Colonial History in Indonesia*. Athens: Ohio University Press.

Hutchings, K. 2008. *Time and World Politics: Thinking the Present*. Manchester: Manchester University Press.

James, A., and A. James. 2004. *Constructing Childhood*. New York: Palgrave Macmillan.

John, M. 1996. *Discrepant Dislocations: Feminism, Theory, and Postcolonial History*. Berkeley: University of California Press.

Kapoor, I. 2008. *The Postcolonial Politics of Development*. London: Routledge.

Lister, R. 2007. "Why Citizenship: Where, When and How Children?" *Theoretical Inquiries in Law* 8 (2): 693–718.

Lucas, N. 1986. "Trouwverbod, inlandse huishoudsters en Europese vrouwen: Het concubinaat in de planterswereld aan Sumatra's Oostkust." In *Vrouwen in de Nederlandse koloniën: Zevende jaarboek voor vrouwengeschiedenis*, edited by J. Reijs et al. Nijmegen, Netherlands: SUN.

Lucassen J., and R. Penninx 1994. *Nieuwkomers, nakomelingen, Nederlanders*. Amsterdam: het Spinhuis.

Machel, G. 2010. Foreword to *Children and Transitional Justice: Truth-Telling, Accountability, and Reconciliation*, edited by S. Parmar et al. Cambridge, MA: Harvard University Press.

Meijer, H. 2005. *Indische rekening: Indië, Nederland en de backpay-kwestie, 1945–2005*. Amsterdam: Boom.

———. 2007. "Backpay: De oneindige strijd om een koloniale erfenis." In *Van Indië tot Indonesië*, edited by E. Bogaerts and R. Raben. Amsterdam: Boom.

Miller, Z. 2008. "Effects of Invisibility: In Search of the 'Economic' in Transitional Justice." *International Journal of Transitional Justice* 2: 266–91.

Oostindie, G. 2011. *Postcolonial Netherlands: Sixty-Five Years of Forgetting, Commemorating, Silencing.* Amsterdam: Amsterdam University Press.

Open Society Foundations. 2011. *Unveiling the Truth: Why 32 Muslim Women Wear the Full-Face Veil in France.* New York: Open Society Foundations.

Pattynama, P. 1994. "Oorden en woorden: Over rassenvermenging, interetniciteit, en een Indisch meisje." *Tijdschrift voor vrouwenstudies* 57 (15, no. 1): 30–45.

Pollmann, T. 1986. "Bruidstraantjes: De koloniale roman, de njai en de apartheid." In *Vrouwen in de Nederlandse koloniën: Zevende jaarboek voor vrouwengeschiedenis,* edited by J. Reijs et al. Nijmegen, Netherlands: SUN.

Qvortrup, J. 1994. "Childhood Matters: An Introduction." In *Childhood Matters,* edited by J. Qvortrup et al. Aldershot: Avebury.

Ridder, I., de. 2007. *Eindelijk erkenning? Het Gebaar: De tegemoetkoming aan de Indische gemeenschap.* Den Haag: Stichting het Gebaar.

Rotberg R., and D. Thompson, eds. 2000. *Truth v. Justice: The Morality of Truth Commissions.* Princeton, NJ: Princeton University Press.

Siegrist, S. 2010. "Child Rights and Transitional Justice." In *Children and Transitional Justice: Truth-Telling, Accountability, and Reconciliation,* edited by S. Parmar et al. Cambridge, MA: Harvard University Press.

Stoler, A. L. 1997. "Making Empire Respectable: The Politics of Race and Sexual Morality in Twentieth-Century Colonial Cultures." In *Situated Lives: Gender and Culture in Everyday Life,* edited by L. Lamphere, H. Ragoné, and P. Zavella. London: Routledge.

Stoltz, P. 2000. "About Being (T)Here and Making a Difference: Black Women and the Paradox of Visibility." PhD diss., Lund University, Sweden.

Stoltz, P., M. Svensson, Z. Sun, and Q. Wang, eds. 2010. *Gender Equality, Citizenship, and Human Rights: Controversies and Challenges in China and the Nordic Countries.* London: Routledge.

Sylvester, C. 2011. "Post-Colonialism." In *The Globalization of World Politics,* edited by J. Baylis, S. Smith, and P. Owens. 5th ed. Oxford: Oxford University Press.

Teitel, R. 2003. "Transitional Justice Genealogy." *Harvard Human Rights Journal* 16.

Trondman, M. 2011. "Snälla fröknar—om barns perspektiv och barnperspektiv." In *Skola och barndom: Normering, demokratisering och individualisering,* edited by I. Tallberg Broman. Malmö, Sweden: Gleerups.

Van Bueren, G. 2011. "Multigenerational Citizenship: The Importance of Recognizing Children as National and International Citizens." *ANNALS of the American Academy of Political and Social Science* 633: 30–51.

Vries, M., de. 2009. *"Indisch is een gevoel": De tweede en derde generatie Indische Nederlanders.* Amsterdam: Amsterdam University Press.

Yuval-Davis, N. 2011a. *The Politics of Belonging: Intersectional Contestations.* London: Sage.

———. 2011b. *Power, Intersectionality, and the Politics of Belonging.* Aalborg: FREIA working paper series no. 75.

Yuval-Davis N., and P. Werbner, eds. 1999. *Women, Citizenship, and Difference.* London: Zed.

PART 3

· ·

Generational Disparities
and the Clash of Cultures

8

(RE)CLAIMING US CITIZENSHIP

· · · · · · · · · ·

Mexican American Repatriation in the 1930s
and Mexican-Born Children

YUKI ODA

INTRODUCTION

In 1946, Cleofas Calleros, director of the El Paso office of the National Catholic Welfare Conference's Bureau of Immigration, reported that the organization was "literally swamped with the problems of our citizens of Mexican ancestry, who had returned to Mexico either forcibly or by their own choice" during the Great Depression. In 1957 he reported that the organization was "still faced with problems of citizenship that involve hundreds of our clients and which dates back to the wholesale repatriation to Mexico during the 1930 depression period, when American citizen families of Mexican descent were removed mainly from the Southwest."[1]

During the Great Depression, when approximately a half to one million Mexicans and Mexican Americans repatriated to Mexico,[2] the National Catholic Welfare Conference (NCWC), which had maintained an immigration office in El Paso/Juárez since 1923, protested against "repatriating people just to get rid of them in that it might be cheaper to advance two or three months budget money to pay transportation to the border."[3] The organization also estimated that "more than 80%" of the "over 700,000 Mexican descent persons" who were invited to "depart from the United States as 'Mexican Nationals'" were actually US citizens and that "sooner or later they and their children . . . would return to the United States."[4] Based on the organization's records as well as immigration rulings from the same period, this chapter discusses the struggles of repatriates and their families to return to the United States.

Sharing interests with the chapters by Pauline Stoltz and John W. Hink Jr., this chapter pays particular attention to children who were taken out of the United States during childhood, and to recognition or nonrecognition of their claims to citizenship. As Stoltz stresses, we must also examine the issue from a multigenerational perspective that not only concerns the generation that experienced repatriation but also concerns the lives of their children (Stoltz this volume; Hink this volume). In speaking of "our citizens of Mexican ancestry," the NCWC referred to two groups of US citizens. First were US-born citizens who went to or were taken to Mexico during the Great Depression. Many left the United States at a young age with their parents, while others of an older age accompanied their spouse. The other group of citizens included the generation born in Mexico. As the NCWC explained, "Mexican descent U.S. citizen[s] remained in Mexico, many were married and those that were married naturally had children born in Mexico, and since the majority of the couples were either citizens of the United Sates or one of the spouse was a U.S. citizen, their children became citizens of the United States on [a] derivative basis."[5] The two groups were not separate, and families often included both.

The age that the repatriates left the United States was significant on several levels. At one level was the issue of to what extent the US government recognized the interests of the children, with children's domicile assumed to follow that of their parents. At another level, as the repatriation generation aged and formed families, citizenship status of the family would also come to be sharply divided by the age of repatriation, as age became a crucial factor under US nationality law that governed citizenship derivation and acquisition of citizen families living abroad.

Citizenship cases of the repatriate families that the NCWC assisted fell into three general categories: First: both spouses were Mexican nationals but some or all of the children were born in the United States. Second: both spouses were US citizens, with children born in Mexico. Third: only one spouse was a US citizen, with some children born in the United States and others in Mexico. The latter two groups included spouses who were already married when they went to Mexico and those who were still young or were single when they went to Mexico and later married. In what follows, I pay particular attention to the last case, especially to those born of a US citizen and a Mexican national, where the question of citizenship was most complicated. I will first look at the transformation of US nationality laws in the 1930s, when age became a controlling factor of citizenship of foreign-born children, considering the transformation of US nationality law and its additional restrictions on derivative citizenship in relation to the racial exclusion of Chinese and Mexican American repatriates. I then look at the 1940s to the 1950s to discuss how the nationality laws enforced after the peak of repatriation to Mexico in 1931 crucially affected the citizenship status of the repatriates and their families, and their return to the United States.

"SAFEGUARDING" CITIZENSHIP: THE NATIONALITY ACT OF 1934 AND THE NATIONALITY ACT OF 1940

For children of the repatriates, the Nationality Act of 1934 and the Nationality Act of 1940 were the two key nationality laws that divided their citizenship status. Whether they were born prior to or after May 24, 1934, the effective date of the Nationality Act of 1934, or after January 13, 1941, under the Nationality Act of 1940 was critical. In the 1930s, "age" instead of "gender" became a controlling factor of citizenship *jure sanguinis*, especially for children born to a family in which only one of the parents was a US citizen. Age was a nonfactor before 1934, but by 1940 residence in the United States for a certain number of years at a specific age—both on the part of the parent and on the part of the child—became the two key requirements of acquisition and retention of derivative US citizenship by foreign-born children of US citizens. Taken together, gender of the parent came to have less relevance to the citizenship of the child, but instead, age of the parent and the child became important.

With regard to gender discrimination, US nationality law went through a significant liberalization in the 1930s. For the first time, the Nationality Act of 1934 enabled both fathers and mothers to pass on their US citizenship to their foreign-born children. Previously, a child born abroad acquired US citizenship at birth only if both of the parents or the father held US citizenship. If the father was a foreign national, the child could not derive US citizenship from a US citizen mother.[6]

As the historian Candice Lewis Bredbenner has shown, campaigns by women's organizations such as the National Women's Party were instrumental in bringing this change. Prior to 1922, the foremost issue regarding women's nationality was marital expatriation. The Expatriation Act of 1907 deprived women who married a noncitizen of US citizenship, forcing them to take on the nationality of their husband regardless of their will.[7] Following the enfranchisement of women in 1920, women's organizations first succeeded in abolishing marital expatriation in the Cable Act of 1922 and then tackled other nationality-related issues such as repatriation of US-born women who had lost their US citizenship under the Expatriation Act. Among such issues was the nationality of children born abroad. Although women's nationality was no longer determined by their husbands', children's nationality continued to be decided solely by their fathers' and not by their mothers'. Women's organizations demanded equal treatment of fathers and mothers and insisted that both fathers and mothers should be able to transfer their US citizenship to their foreign-born children.[8]

However, at the same time these changes were making it easier for children abroad to acquire US citizenship, Congress, speaking of the need to safeguard US citizenship, added entirely new conditions on acquisition and retention of US citizenship by children born abroad. While gender of the parent came to have less relevance, age of the child and the parent acquired increasing significance.

The Nationality Act of 1934 mandated foreign-born citizens to reside in the United States for a specific length of time at a specific age in order to retain their citizenship. Specifically, it required of children born abroad five-year continuous residence in the United States between the ages of thirteen and eighteen. In other words, failure to immigrate to the United States before one's thirteenth birthday at the latest, which essentially depended on the parents, resulted in automatic loss of US citizenship. While the maximum age to move to the United States was raised several times thereafter, this retention requirement remained as part of nationality law until 1978.[9]

Among the reasons Congress raised in the 1930s in speaking of the need to safeguard derivative citizenship and "putting teeth" into nationality law was the racial context of Asian exclusion and repatriation of Mexican Americans. The issue was discussed as an immigration problem as well as a citizenship problem. Chinese immigration was a centerpiece of debate on derivative citizenship. Since the late nineteenth century, the Chinese

Exclusion Act had excluded virtually all Chinese immigration, with a exception of certain nonimmigrants such as merchants and wives and children of
US citizens. When Congress banned immigration of all "aliens ineligible
to citizenship" by the Immigration Act of 1924, Congress further closed the
racial gate by excluding wives of US citizens. Two groups of people that the
racial exclusion did not apply were nonimmigrants admitted for temporary
residence and foreign-born children of US citizens. The latter were legally
neither "immigrants" nor "aliens" because they were US citizens themselves,
who derived US citizenship at birth from their citizen fathers. And with
regard to Chinese immigration, well before 1924, the dominant pattern was
for the US citizen children to come to the United States, while the wives
remained in China.[10] Exclusionists insisted that because children of Asian
Americans were not subject to restriction under "immigration" law, it was
necessary to amend the nationality law in order to reduce or ban them from
coming to the United States.[11]

Repatriation of Mexican Americans was another racial issue raised
against liberalizing nationality law and for restricting foreign-born children from acquiring US citizenship. Although lawmakers and government
officials spoke of "repatriation" to Mexico, they were more than aware that
a large number of repatriates were US citizens, and that as the repatriates
formed families in Mexico, their children would derive US citizenship from
the parents. Indeed, during the debates about the 1934 Nationality Act, congressmen from states such as California and Texas called attention to the fact
that "repatriation" to Mexico would include a large number of US citizens.
For example, a congressman from California insisted that Congress must not
forget that "we have sent as many as 12,000 back to Mexico in one month,"
calling attention to the fact that many were US citizens "born on the soil of
the United States or under its jurisdiction."[12]

The point of this argument was not to underline the injustice of sending
away US-born citizens. Instead, the purpose was to emphasize that when
Mexican Americans now living in Mexico formed families and eventually
sought return to the United States, derivative citizenship would make it difficult for the US government to prevent their return. They "will remain in
Mexico until there is some way of getting back into the United States. Sup-
pose the female of the family remains in Mexico long enough to raise her
own family. Then she is entitled to bring all of those back to the United
States when they return."[13] Unlike immigration from Europe that was

subjected to an annual ceiling, until the 1960s immigration from Mexico was instead regulated administratively by visa refusals. US citizens, however, were not obviously subject to visa restrictions, and having "repatriated" Mexican Americans, restrictionists in Congress spoke of the need of "the states that are on the border, California and Texas" to protect against the "danger of having to let in every child that is born of aliens," despite the fact that they were not "aliens" but US citizens.[14]

In 1940, six years after the retention requirement was introduced, Congress added another condition on derivative US citizenship of foreign-born children. At one level, the Nationality Act of 1940 somewhat relaxed the retention deadline from the thirteenth birthday to the sixteenth birthday.[15] However, more notable was the restriction on acquisition of citizenship at birth in the first place, which had to do with the residency requirement on the part of the parent. Prior to 1940, the only requirement for a foreign-born child to acquire US citizenship was for the US citizen parent (father before 1934) to have US residence of any length at any point before the child's birth. But the 1940 act required the parent to have resided in the United States for at least a specific number of years and at a specific age.[16]

The 1940 act was a mixed product, which on one hand reflected how the court came to provide more protection to US-born children and on the other hand was a more conservative response to citizens living and forming families abroad. As the essay by John W. Hink Jr. in this volume discusses, in 1939 the Supreme Court upheld the right of US-born children, who were taken abroad by their parents as minors, to retain their birthright citizenship and to choose a nationality after reaching majority.[17] The court decided that parents' decision to expatriate themselves did not deprive the children of their US citizenship, unless the children chose to relinquish citizenship. A judicial step toward protection of US-born citizens, however, was also countered by a Congress that sought to limit the rights that citizens living abroad could exercise, among which was the right to transfer their citizenship to their children. Moreover, the ongoing war in Europe added to the suspicion about both foreigners within the United States and citizens living abroad (Hink this volume).[18]

First, the 1940 act mandated that the US citizen parent must have a minimum of a ten-year residence in the United States before the child's birth in order for the child to acquire US citizenship at birth. Second, it provided that five of the ten years must be after one's sixteenth birthday. In other words, the 1940 act practically made it impossible for two groups of US citizens to transfer their US citizenship to their foreign-born children. One group included those who left or were taken out of the United States before reaching twenty-one years of age. Another group included citizens under twenty-one, for whom it was mathematically impossible to have five years residence in the United States after a sixteenth birthday.[19] As I will discuss in further detail, for Mexican American repatriates who left the United States with their parents as minors, as they formed families in Mexico, this residency requirement became a critical bar for their children to hurdle to acquire US citizenship. Unlike the retention requirement that was abolished in 1978, this is part of US nationality policy today.[20]

To summarize, by 1940 three nationality laws governed the citizenship status of the Mexican-born children of repatriates. For those born before the 1934 Nationality Act went into effect on May 24, 1934, they could only acquire US citizenship if the father was a US citizen. Those born between May 24, 1934, and January 13, 1941, could derive US citizenship from either parent. But in order to retain US citizenship, a child born to a US citizen and a Mexican national had to move to the United States before his or her sixteenth birthday and maintain continuous residence for at least five years. And for those born after January 13, 1941, in addition to the retention requirement, their conditions for acquiring US citizenship at birth was for the parent to have more than a ten-year residence in the United States, including five years after reaching sixteen years of age. Thus while gender of the parent came to have less importance, age of both the parent and the child became crucial for acquisition and retention of citizenship on *jus sanguinis* rule.

(RE)CLAIMING US CITIZENSHIP

From the 1940s to the mid-1960s, assisting former repatriates was one of the principal concerns of the National Catholic Welfare Conference's El Paso/Juárez office. In the 1930s, the organization condemned of the "serious mistake" of sending off "American citizens by simply giving them a ticket to go back to their former home in Mexico (a home which never existed)" as well as "many alien fathers and mothers who had several United States born children."[21] Providing assistance through the complex web of immigration and nationality laws was of particular concern to the organization as the former repatriates sought to return to the United States. For families struggling to establish their member's citizenship status, in addition to legal counsel, the NCWC through its extensive connections to Catholic parishes provided assistance in obtaining necessary documents such as birth certificates and baptismal certificates. As Cleofas Calleros, the El Paso/Juárez office director, reported in 1946, "securing the necessary identifications, with proof of citizenship and repatriation of the parents back to Mexico was a difficult and time consuming operation."[22] The agency sometimes had to urge parishes to locate baptismal records as soon as possible, emphasizing the urgent importance of the documents for their clients, because they were often making requests "on behalf of a person who is detained in jail by the Immigration authorities; other times the person is detained in Juarez."[23]

POST-1934 GENERATION AND LOSS OF US CITIZENSHIP

The years between 1950 and 1957 were of particular importance for Mexican-born children of US citizens. The members of the first post-1934 Nationality Act generation reached their sixteenth birthday in 1950, forcing those born after May 24, 1934, to apply to retain their US citizenship before the deadline. As a result of the looming deadline, in 1949, for instance, the NCWC's El Paso/Juárez office secured more than three thousand birth certificates and baptismal certificates of former repatriates so that they and their families could obtain US passports to come to the United States.[24]

Not all those interested in repatriation could meet the deadline. After May 1950, those who could not come to the United States before their sixteenth birthday lost their US citizenship. But in the mid-1950s, those who could not come to the United States before their sixteenth birthday sought to recover their US citizenship. They relied on the Immigration and Nationality Act of 1952, which was enacted two years after the first generation of post-1934-act foreign-born children began to lose their US citizenship. One of the changes the Immigration and Nationality Act of 1952 made in its comprehensive revision of both immigration and nationality laws was that the retention deadline for foreign-born children born to a US citizen and a non-US citizen was raised from the sixteenth birthday to the twenty-third birthday.[25]

The issue after 1952 was whether the new deadline applied retroactively to those who had already passed the old deadline. This question did not arise when the 1940 Nationality Act raised the deadline of the 1934 act, because nobody had passed his or her thirteenth birthday under the 1934 act. Although foreign-born children of US citizens appealed that they should be recognized as US citizens as long as they came to the United States before their twenty-third birthday, the US government, including consulates, the Immigration and Naturalization Service, and the Board of Immigration Appeals, maintained that the new deadline did not apply retroactively to those who had failed to meet the previous deadline and that it only applied to those who were under sixteen years of age when the 1952 act took effect.[26]

It was in 1957, five years after the 1952 act was enforced, that the Department of Justice changed their interpretation of the new nationality law. This was a result of a federal court case, *Lee You Fee v. Dulles*. Lee You Fee was born in China in July 1935, and had been raised in Hong Kong since 1936. His father, Lee Q. Pon, was a US citizen also born in China, who derived his citizenship from his US-born father. Lee Q. Pon moved to the United States in 1926, and during his visit to China a decade later married Lee You Fee's mother. In 1936, Lee Q. Pon returned to the United States and took up residence in Wisconsin, while Lee You Fee and the mother remained in China. Thus Lee You Fee was born as a US citizen. But when he reached sixteen in 1951, he was still in Hong Kong and lost his US citizenship under the Nationality Act of 1940. The family brought the case to the federal court, arguing that Lee You Fee should be able to recover his citizenship as long as he came to the United States before the new deadline. Both in the district court and the court of appeals, Lee You Fee lost his case. However, after the court of appeals ruling, the Department of Justice granted an error and the Supreme Court decided that Lee You Fee could retain his US citizenship as long as he came to the United States before his twenty-third birthday.[27]

The 1957 ruling provided an opportunity for those in a similar situation to recover their citizenship. Such was the case for Jose Martínez (pseudonym), who was born in Mexico in April 1935 to a father born in the United States in 1915 and to a Mexican mother. When he first moved to the United States in early 1952, he was admitted as a citizen and not as a Mexican national. In 1956, however, the Immigration and Naturalization Service discovered that Jose Martínez was already seventeen when he first came to the United States and ordered him to leave because he had failed to retain his US citizenship and because he did not hold a valid immigration visa. After obtaining a visa, Jose Martínez once again returned to the United States. Unlike the first time, his second entry was not as a US citizen but as an immigrant from Mexico. It was a year after he started living in the United States as a Mexican national that the Supreme Court decided on *Lee You*

Fee v. Dulles. Having learned of the decision, in order to recover his US citizenship, Jose Martínez appealed to the Department of Justice, maintaining that he should not have lost his US citizenship. The Board of Immigration Appeals acknowledged his claim, and since Jose Martínez had already lived in the United States for more than five years, he was finally able to obtain a certificate of US citizenship. Thus within six years, Jose Martínez lived in the United States first as a US citizen, then as a Mexican national, before he was finally able to claim his US citizenship in 1958.[28]

After the reinterpretation of the 1952 act, the NCWC's El Paso/Juárez office also saw renewed attempts by those who were not able to meet the old deadline to retain US citizenship before the new deadline. For some, *Lee You Fee v. Dulles* came too late. By the time of the ruling, some of the post-1934-act generation had already passed their twenty-third birthday. And those who were living outside the United States, unlike in the case of Jose Martínez, even under the new extended deadline could no longer recover their citizenship.

POST-1940 GENERATION AND ACQUISITION OF CITIZENSHIP AT BIRTH

For repatriates and their families, the Nationality Act of 1940 was a seemingly insurmountable barrier to US citizenship. For those born after January 13, 1941, the retention deadline did not become a pressing issue until the mid-1960s. Since the maximum age to come to the United States was raised to twenty-three by the Immigration and Nationality Act of 1952, the first retention deadline for the post-1940-act generation did not arrive until 1964. But the more fundamental issue was whether they had acquired US citizenship at birth to begin with.

Unlike the pre-1940-act generation,[29] the post-1940-act generation could acquire US citizenship only if the parent had lived in the United States for a certain number of years at a specific age—twenty-one. For Mexican Americans who were taken to Mexico as minors, even if they fulfilled the ten-year minimum residency, the other requirement that they must have resided in the United States for five years after age sixteen was a critical line that often divided the citizenship status of their families.

Depending on when a child was born and at which age the parent had left the United States, citizenship was divided among siblings within the same family, or among children of repatriates who went to Mexico in the same year, or among children born in Mexico in the same year.

For example, repatriates who left the United States as teens found that their children may not necessarily have the same citizenship status. Among such cases were the García family and the Hernandez family (pseudonym), which sought the assistance of the NCWC in the late 1940s. In the García family, the Colorado-born mother went to Mexico with her parents at the age of fifteen. In the Hernandez family, the Texas-born father went to Mexico at the age of twelve. They both left the United States in the same year, 1931, the peak of Mexican and Mexican American repatriation. After marrying Mexican nationals, both sought to return to the United States with their spouses and Mexican-born children.[30]

Although the parents were taken out of the United States in 1931 as teens, the citizenship status of their Mexican-born children was critically different, because the children were born under distinct nationality laws. The three Mexican-born children of the García family were all US citizens. They were all born in the 1930s when the citizen parent was still not required to have lived in the United States at a specific age in order for the children to derive citizenship. By contrast, none of the Hernandez children acquired US citizenship, because they were all born after the 1940 Nationality Act was enforced. Having been taken out of the United States as a teen, the father did not fulfill the requirement that he must have resided in the United States for at least five years after his sixteenth birthday in order to pass on his US citizenship.[31]

Whereas the dividing line between the García family and the Hernandez family lay in the year the children were born in Mexico, children born in the same year could also hold different citizenship status depending on how long their parents had lived in the United States. Among such cases were the González family and López family (pseudonym), who sought the NCWC's assistance in 1948. In both families, the mother was a US citizen, while the father was a Mexican national. Another commonality between the two families was that the elder siblings were born in Mexico in the 1930s and the youngest child was born in 1943. Yet whereas all the González children held US citizenship, the López children did not. In the López family, the elder siblings born in the 1930s held US citizenship, but the youngest child did not acquire US citizenship at birth.[32]

The difference between the two families had to do with the age the US citizen mother had left the United States. In the González family, the mother born in Arizona in 1908 had already reached twenty-one when she went to Mexico during the Depression. In the López family, however, the mother had left the United States while she was a teenager, and the 1940 Nationality Act did not allow her to transfer her US citizenship to her child born in 1943.[33] Thus a few years' difference in age either of the parent or the child divided citizenship status of families. And as in the case of the López family, citizenship status was often divided within the same family.

CITIZENSHIP IN SUSPICION

A series of difficulties started with proving US citizenship either by birth or by derivation before US officials such as consulates and the Immigration and Naturalization Service. Securing proof of birth in the United States could be a difficult task in itself, but when the family included children born after the 1940 Nationality Act, it was not only necessary to prove that the parent was a US citizen but also to establish how long they had lived in the United States and at what age they left the United States.

Above all, birth registration was not completely carried out in the 1920s in the 1930s, and this was especially true in the Southwest. As Adena Miller Rich of the Immigrant's Protective League of Chicago observed in 1940, even more than immigrants it was "the American-born man or woman . . . who may have the greatest difficulty in proving his or her United States citizenship." For naturalized US citizens, there was a crucial document to prove US citizenship: certificate of naturalization. "In fact, the American-born adult usually does not have such a certificate," because birth registration and birth certificates were a relatively recent system. It was not unusual for US-born people to be unable to secure any documentary evidence, even if they had not left the United States for an entire lifetime, and much more so if they lived abroad (Rich 1940, 20).

A Board of Immigration Appeals (BIA) case from 1956 illustrates the difficulties the repatriates encountered in establishing their citizenship status. The case also shows how the hurdle was much higher for those claiming US citizenship by derivation or for the generation born in Mexico than it was for those claiming citizenship by birth in the United States. In September 1956, the BIA ruled that twenty-year-old Alberto Martínez (pseudonym) should be deported to Mexico for having entered the United States without inspection and an immigration visa. Born in Huanuzco, Zacatecas, in 1935, Alberto Martínez first came to the United States with his parents in 1946 at the age of eleven. Six years later, in 1952, he was deported to Mexico. He reentered the United States the following day and lived in the United States for another four years until he was apprehended again. The question raised in 1956 was whether he was a Mexican national or whether he was in fact a US citizen. There was no question as to his birth in Mexico, but the issue was the birthplace of his parent. Although his father was a Mexican national, there was a possibility that his mother was a US-born citizen. If this was the case, Alberto Martínez was also a US citizen at birth not subject to deportation.[34]

The citizenship status of Laura Martínez (pseudonym), the mother of Alberto Martínez, had come into question two years earlier in her own deportation proceeding. She was one of the Great Depression repatriates who had gone to Mexico with their parents in 1931. Her parents had come to the United States around 1919 or 1920 and had lived in several states, such as Colorado, Montana, Kansas, and Minnesota, before going to Mexico. By the 1950s, her parents were already deceased, and Laura Martínez was the eldest of the six surviving siblings. What was at stake in the 1950s was whether Laura Martínez had been brought to the United States as a baby born in the United States or whether she had been born in Mexico. She testified that she knew that the family had lived in the United States for eleven or twelve years before going to Mexico, but that she did not know exactly "where she was born." Frequent migration between several states further added to her difficulty. Her younger siblings were all proven to have been born in the United States: one was born in Montana, and the other four in Minnesota. But with the parents deceased, her siblings could offer little information since they were all born after Laura, and her relatives offered contradictory testimonies as to her birthplace. With regard to documentary evidence, the only available papers in the United States were her school records and census records, which stated that she was a US-born citizen. The only document in Mexico was her marriage certificate, which did not indicate her place of birth. Neither the family nor the US government could locate her birth record or baptismal record either in the United States or in Mexico.[35]

Both Laura Martínez's and Alberto Martínez's citizenship and immigration status depended on whether Laura Martínez was born in the United States, yet conflicting evidences and testimonies divided the fate of the two. The INS could not prove that Laura Martínez was not a US citizen. At the same time, however, neither could the family positively prove that Laura Martínez was born in the United States. With both sides unable to provide affirmative evidence to prove their case, the Department of Justice concluded that Laura was "not an alien."[36] But the decision that she was "not an alien" had different consequences for Laura Martínez and Alberto Martínez.

The Board of Immigration Appeals ruled that the evidence that the family provided was sufficient for Laura Martínez to continue to reside in the United States but not for Alberto Martínez. The BIA decided that in the two cases the burden of proof lay with different parties. As for Laura Martínez, who claimed to have been born on US soil, the BIA maintained that the burden of proof was on the US government to prove that she did not hold US citizenship. And the evidence that the US government provided was not strong enough to overturn the evidence the family provided. However, the case was different with regard to Alberto Martínez. The BIA maintained that in order to establish derivative US citizenship of foreign-born citizens, the burden of proof was on the claimant to establish one's parent's birth in the United States, because a foreign-born person was *prima facie* an alien." The BIA held that in order to deport Alberto Martínez, the US government did not have to prove that Laura Martínez was not a US citizen. Unable to establish his mother's birth in the United States, Alberto Martínez's claim that he was a Mexican-born US citizen was denied and he was deported as a Mexican national.[37]

Although claims to citizenship were not the most common method of unauthorized immigration at the US-Mexico border, the rising concern since the late 1940s about unauthorized immigration added to the suspicion government officials such as the INS and consulates cast about citizenship claims. The INS estimated that when one individual established his or her birth in the United States an average of four dependents would derive US citizenship as a result. Because claims to US citizenship involved the citizenship and immigration status of not only one individual but also of their families and descendants, government officials doubted citizenship claims. The INS deepened its suspicion of citizenship claims especially after INS commissioner Joseph M. Swing, a former army general, launched Operation Wetback in July 1954. The quasi-military operation to apprehend unauthorized immigrants was highly publicized in order to scare off workers. In 1954 and 1955, approximately 34,500 persons were formally deported to Mexico by the INS, over one million were recorded to have voluntarily departed after apprehension, and an unknown number left the United States for fear of apprehension. The INS boasted that the program was an enormous success. At the same time, the agency now believed that because undocumented entry or stay became more difficult, more immigrants were induced to obtain fraudulent documents in order to enter and reside more safely in the United States (Niebuhr 1960, 1; Hernández 2010, 203–4).

As the National Catholic Welfare Conference's El Paso/Juárez office assisted their clients in establishing their citizenship or their family's immigration status, they found it was not uncommon to encounter cases like the Martínez family, where a contemporaneous birth record could not be located. For one, while states and localities had laws of some kind to record births and deaths, standardization of the practice did not begin until the early twentieth century. It was only in 1915 that the federal government began the practice of collecting birth data from states. States that met the federal standard of registering at least 90 percent of each year's birth was called "birth registration area." As of 1918, only nineteen states and the District of Columbia were included in the area, but western states such as California, Arizona, New Mexico, Arizona, and Texas had not met the standard. In fact, Texas was the last state in the country to meet this standard, in 1933 ("Progress" 1918; Dunn 1936). Especially in such cases where contemporaneous birth records could not be secured, a baptismal record was one of the most critical documents a claimant could use in order to establish the family's citizenship and immigration status. In addition to families, the organization also received requests from government agencies to secure a record. Based on baptismal records, the NCWC assisted their clients in applying for a delayed birth certificate, a birth certificate obtained sometime after birth. Filing for a delayed birth certificate was a cumbersome process that could take months if not more than a year.

Application for a delayed birth certificate was by no means uncommon, but the INS cast suspicions on citizenship claims involving "delayed birth certificates." In Texas, between 1940 and 1960, around 190,000 delayed birth certificates were issued to citizens of Mexican descent. But the immigration officials maintained that delayed birth certificates were "doubtfully reliable" proof of one's birth in the United States (Farb 1963). For instance, between April 1953 and May 1954, in a Texas county, the agency investigated 170 persons of Mexican descent who obtained a delayed birth certificate in order to determine whether they were born in the United States.[38] The INS only deepened their suspicion after Operation Wetback, and sometimes the simple act of applying for a birth certificate could lead to an investigation by the INS. In Cameron County, Texas, which included Brownsville, for instance, the INS and the county judge made an arrangement in 1959 that an INS officer should interview all applicants for a delayed birth certificate. Because the INS believed that one of the most effective ways to investigate a citizenship question was to call in the claimant's family, investigation of citizenship often involved interviewing the whole family.[39]

The NCWC reported in 1961 that the issue of citizenship of repatriated families seemed to "get more complicated as the 1929–1939 generation gets older," and passage of time since the Great Depression and enforcement of the US-Mexico border thereafter only added to the difficulties the repatriated families encountered in establishing their citizenship status.

CONCLUSION

Mexican American repatriation and post-1934 US nationality laws have often been discussed in isolation from one another, partly because the latter was enacted after the peak of repatriation in 1931, and also because more attention has been paid to the generation that was repatriated from the United States than to the generation born in Mexico after the repatriation.

This chapter has shown that nationality legislation regarding foreign-born children during the 1930s was an "immigration problem" associated with exclusion of Asian immigrants and Mexican American repatriation. Far from being isolated issues, the two were clearly tied together in the nativism of the time and the view of Mexican Americans as "aliens."

For the Mexican and Mexican American repatriates and their families, the issue of citizenship not only involved the question of the generation that directly experienced repatriation. Whether their children would be recognized as US citizens was a question that loomed for several decades thereafter, having a critical impact on how or whether the repatriates and families would be able to return to the United States, legacies of racial policy that they continued to struggle against.

NOTES

1. National Catholic Welfare Conference, Bureau of Immigration, *Annual Report 1946–1947*, 40, folder 4626, box 148; National Catholic Welfare Conference, Department of Immigration, *Annual Report 1957–1958*, 15, folder 4767, box 151,

Records of the National Catholic Welfare Conference, Center for Migration Studies, Staten Island, New York (hereafter NCWC Records, CMS).

2. For book-length studies of Mexican and Mexican American repatriation, Hoffman 1974; Guerin-Gonzales 1996; Balderrama and Rodriguez [1995] 2006.

3. Cleofas Calleros, to Mrs. Val M. Keating, Social Service Consultant, Texas Relief Commission, July 18, 1934, folder 2, box 14, Cleofas Calleros Papers, C. L. Sonnichsen Special Collections, University of Texas at El Paso (hereafter cited as Calleros Papers, UTEP).

4. National Catholic Welfare Conference, Mexican Border Office, *Annual Report 1958–1959*, 15; folder 3, box 9, Calleros Papers, UTEP. Based on consular records, historians Francisco E. Balderrama and Raymond Rodriguez estimate that as many as 60 percent were US citizens (Balderrama and Rodriguez [1995] 2006, 265–66).

5. National Catholic Welfare Conference, Mexican Border Office, *Annual Report 1959–1960*, 19, folder 3, box 9, Calleros Papers, UTEP.

6. The exception to this rule was when the US citizen mother and the noncitizen father were not formally married. In this case, the child derived US citizenship from the mother. At the same time, a US citizen father could not pass on his citizenship to his child if he was not married to the child's noncitizen mother.

7. Marital expatriation of citizen wives was coupled with marital naturalization of noncitizen wives because of the notion that women should hold the same nationality their husbands held. Before 1922, a foreign wife automatically gained US citizenship when her husband became a naturalized US citizen. The Cable Act abolished both marital expatriation and marital naturalization.

8. For women's organizations' movements to realize equal nationality rights, Bredbenner 1998, especially chapter 6 for the Nationality Act of 1934. The Nationality Act of 1934 was not applied retroactively, and children born prior to May 24, 1934, to US citizen mothers and non-US-citizen fathers were not accorded US citizenship (*Montana v. Kennedy* 366 U.S. 308 (1961)).

9. Sec. 1, Nationality Act of 1934, P.L. 73-250. The act of October 10, 1978 (P.L. 95-432) repealed this requirement.

10. In *Chang Chan et al. v. Nagle*, 268 US 336 (1925), the Supreme Court ruled that the 1924 act banned immigration of US citizens' wives that were "aliens ineligible to citizenship." After campaigns by Chinese American organizations, in 1932, Congress agreed to allow Chinese wives of US citizens to immigrate to the United States only if the marriage had taken place before

1924. Japanese wives, among wives of other nationalities, continued to be excluded under the 1924 Act, regardless of when they were married (Lee 2007, chap. 3).

11. As the House Committee on Immigration and Naturalization reported, the 1934 Nationality Act bill specifically provided that a child of a US citizen and an "alien ineligible to citizenship" did not acquire US citizenship at birth. This provision was removed on the floor (78 Cong. Rec. 7329–7350 [1934]). Those arguing for abolition of gender discrimination also raised the issue of Chinese immigration. For instance, Business Women's Legislative Council of California argued in specifically racial terms that "white American [female] citizens" were being denied the right accorded to "yellow United States [male] citizens," who were able to pass on their US citizenship to their Chinese-born children. Although most women's organizations avoided this argument, it was more prominent among congressmen. *Relating to Naturalization and Citizenship Status of Children Whose Mothers Are Citizens of the United States: Hearing before the House Committee on Immigration and Naturalization*, 73rd Cong. 50 (1933) (Statement of Business Women's Legislative Council of California).

12. *Relating to Naturalization and Citizenship Status of Children Whose Mothers Are Citizens of the United States: Hearing before the House Committee on Immigration and Naturalization*, 73rd Cong. 41 (1933) (Statement of Representative William Traeger, R-CA); Gardner 2005, 173–74.

13. *Relating to Naturalization and Citizenship Status of Children Whose Mothers Are Citizens of the United States: Hearing before the House Committee on Immigration and Naturalization*, 73rd Cong. 41 (1933) (Statement of Representative William Traeger, R-CA).

14. *Relating to Naturalization and Citizenship Status of Children Whose Mothers Are Citizens of the United States: Hearing before the House Committee on Immigration and Naturalization*, 73rd Cong. 42 (1933) (Statement of Representative Martin Dies, D-TX).

15. After the 1940 act, children born abroad had to fulfill the five-year residence between thirteen and twenty-one, instead of between thirteen and eighteen as under the 1934 act. In order to fulfill this five-year residence requirement by twenty-one, they had to come to the United States before reaching their sixteenth birthday. Sec. 201 (g), Nationality Act of October 14, 1940, P.L.76-853.

16. The Nationality Act of 1907 provided that derivative US citizenship "shall not descend to children whose fathers never resided in the United States." In 1927, the Supreme Court ruled that in order for the foreign-born child to

acquire US citizenship, the citizen father must have resided in the United States previous to and not after the child's birth (*Weedin v. Chin Bow* 274 U.S. 657 [1927]). To clarify the legislative intent, the Nationality Act of 1934 provided that the citizen father or citizen mother must have "resided in the United State *previous to* the birth of such child" (emphasis added). Still, the 1934 act did not require residence either at a specific age or for a specific length of time.

17. *Perkins v. Elg*, 307 U.S. 325 (1939).

18. Ibid.

19. In 1944, the Board of Immigration Appeals denied US citizenship to children born to a twenty-year-old mother and to an eighteen-year-old mother; both mothers had virtually spent their entire life in the United States. The denial was handed down simply because they were under twenty-one. S. F. was born in Texas in 1923 and went to Mexico with her parents in 1936 at the age of thirteen. After her marriage in 1939, she returned to the United States with her Mexican national husband. She gave birth during her one-month visit to Mexico in 1944, and upon returning to the United States her one-month-old baby was excluded for not having an immigrant visa. Although she lived in the United States for eighteen years, except for the three years during the Depression, it was decided that she did not meet the five-year residence requirement after sixteen, and therefore her child was not a US citizen. *Matter of S-F-, Matter of M-* 2 I&N Dec. 182 (BIA 1944); "Transmission" 1944.

20. Sec. 201 (g), Nationality Act of 1940. Since 1986, the citizen parent is required to have five-year physical presence prior to the child's birth, at least two years of which must be after reaching fourteen (8 U.S.C. 1401 [g] amended by Act of November 14, 1986, P.L. 99-653).

21. Cleofas Calleros, to Miss Maria Dresden, Director of Texas Relief Commission, May 13, 1934, folder 2, box 14, Calleros Papers, UTEP.

22. National Catholic Welfare Conference, Bureau of Immigration, *Annual Report 1946–1947*, 40, folder 4626, box 148, NCWC Records, CMS.

23. Cleofas Calleros, to Our Lady of Guadalupe Church, Fabens, Texas, June 26, 1948, folder 9, box 61, Calleros Papers, UTEP.

24. National Catholic Welfare Conference, Bureau of Immigration, *Annual Report 1948–1949*, 42, folder 4628, box 148; *Annual Report 1949–1950*, 37, folder 4629, box 148, NCWC Records, CMS.

25. Sec. 301 (a) (7) Immigration and Nationality Act of 1952 (P.L. 82–414).

26. In an early 1953 case regarding a man born in the Cayman Islands in 1935, the Board of Immigration Appeals ruled that foreign-born citizens who lost their US citizenship by failing to come to the United States before reaching sixteen could not recover their citizenship under the Immigration and Nationality Act of 1952 (*Matter of B-*, 5 I&N Dec. 291 [BIA 1953]).

27. *Lee You Fee v. Dulles*, 236 F. (2d) 885, 355 U.S. 61 (1957). The Department of Justice acknowledged that although members of the first 1934 act generation had passed the deadline when the Immigration and Nationality Act went into effect, they had not when congressional committees first proposed to raise the maximum age, and that the original intent of the Congress was to raise the deadline before those affected by the 1934 act reached their sixteenth birthday.

28. *Matter of M-*, 7 I&N Dec. 646 (BIA 1958). The Board of Immigration Appeals records do not show individual names, and this essay uses a pseudonym.

29. For those born before the Nationality Act of 1940, a few days in the United States sufficed to fulfill the residency requirement of the parent. An example is a 1953 exclusion case regarding two children of a woman born in Mexico to a US citizen father and a Mexican national mother. Her husband was a Mexican citizen, and prior to giving birth in 1935 and 1937, she had visited the United States twice (two days for the first time and a few hours for the second time). When the family sought permanent admission to the United States, the Immigration and Naturalization Service excluded the two children for lack of immigration visas. The INS maintained that the mother had not resided in the United States prior to giving birth and that the children did not acquire US citizenship at birth. But the Board of Immigration Appeals ruled that the mother's two visits to the United States satisfied the requirement and that her children were US citizens. *Matter of V-*, 6 I&N Dec. 9 (BIA 1954).

30. Case file, NCWC El Paso/Juárez Office, 1950, box 13, Calleros Papers, UTEP; Case file, NCWC El Paso/Juárez Office, 1949, box 26, NCWC Case Records, UTEP. This essay withholds individual names and folder level citation for privacy, and all the names in this essay are pseudonyms.

31. Case file, NCWC El Paso/Juárez Office, 1950, box 13, Calleros Papers, UTEP.

32. Case file, NCWC El Paso/Juárez Office, 1948, box 51, NCWC Case Records, UTEP; Case file, NCWC El Paso/Juárez Office, 1948, box 21, NCWC Case Records, UTEP.

33. Ibid.
34. *Matter of A-M-,* 7 I&N Dec. 332 (1956).
35. Ibid.
36. Ibid.
37. Ibid.
38. Seven were found to have falsely acquired the document (Niebuhr 1960, 1).
39. Investigation of the family was a method the INS implemented through the "Chinese-Confession Program" that began in 1956 (Niebuhr 1960). After the Chinese Revolution in 1949, a large number of persons in Hong Kong applied for US passports. They claimed derivative US citizenship as foreign-born children of Chinese Americans. In 1950 the US consulate in Hong Kong received around 117,000 such applications. In order to discover whose claims were fraudulent and to stem off immigration of paper families in the future, the Immigration and Naturalization Service turned to Chinese Americans living in the United States. In urging them to disclose their "true" and "paper" family history, the Department of Justice offered those who "confessed" legal permanent residence instead of deportation. Between 1956 and 1965, around 30,000 people of Chinese descent in the United States were discovered to be paper families. For the Chinese Confession Program, see Ngai 2004, chap. 6.

WORKS CITED

Balderrama, Francisco E., and Raymond Rodriguez. [1995] 2006. *Decade of Betrayal: Mexican Repatriation in the 1930s.* Rev. ed. Albuquerque: University of New Mexico Press.

Bredbenner, Candice Lewis. 1998. *Nationality of Her Own: Women, Marriage, and the Law of Citizenship.* Berkeley: University of California Press.

Dunn, Halbert L. 1936. "Vital Statistics Collected by the Government." *Annals of the American Academy of Political and Social Science* 188 (November): 340–50.

Farb, Ralph. 1963. "S.I.O. Hearings in the Southwest." *I & N Reporter* 12 (2): 17–20.

García, Juan Ramon. 1980. *Operation Wetback: The Mass Deportation of Mexican Undocumented Workers in 1954.* Westport, CT: Greenwood.

Gardner, Martha. 2005. *The Qualities of a Citizen: Women, Immigration, and Citizenship, 1870–1965.* Princeton, NJ, Princeton University Press.

Guerin-Gonzales, Camille. 1996. *Mexican Workers and American Dreams: Immigration, Repatriation, and California Farm Labor, 1900–1939.* New Brunswick, NJ: Rutgers University Press.

Hernández, Kelly Lytle. 2010. *Migra!: A History of the U.S. Border Patrol.* Berkeley: University of California Press.

Hoffman, Abraham. 1974. *Unwanted Mexican Americans in the Great Depression: Repatriation Pressures, 1929–1939.* Tucson: University of Arizona Press.

Lau, Estelle. 2007. *Paper Families: Identity, Immigration Administration, and Chinese Exclusion.* Durham, NC: Duke University Press.

Lee, Erika. 2003. *At America's Gates: Chinese Immigration during the Exclusion Era, 1882–1943.* Chapel Hill: University of North Carolina Press.

Ngai, Mae. 2004. *Impossible Subjects: Illegal Aliens and the Making of Modern America.* Princeton, NJ: Princeton University Press.

Niebuhr, Edgar. 1960. "False Claims to United States Citizenship by Mexican Aliens." *I & N Reporter* 9 (1): 1–3.

"The Progress of Birth and Death Registration in the United States." 1918. *Science* 47 (1224): 581–82.

Rich, Adena M. 1940. "Naturalization and Family Welfare: When Is a Client a Citizen?" *Social Service Review* 14 (1): 10–35.

"Transmission of American Citizenship to Children Born Abroad." 1944. *INS Monthly Review* 2 (6): 63–65.

United States Department of Justice. N.d. *Annual Report of the Immigration and Naturalization Service.* Washington, DC: Government Printing Office.

9

THE CHALLENGE OF ANC YOUTH FROM THE SOWETO UPRISING TO JULIUS MALEMA

· · · · · · · · · ·

RICHARD MARBACK

In his autobiography Nelson Mandela describes the unbridled rage and lack of discipline of the youth sentenced to imprisonment on Robben Island after the 1976 Soweto uprising that involved more than 20,000 student protesters and resulted in the deaths of 176 people. It is worth recalling here that the Soweto uprising was a student-led protest against the policies of the South African government regarding the education of black South Africans, especially the policy established in 1953, but not strictly enforced until 1974, of providing instruction in English and Afrikaans exclusively. What little education black students received at the hands of the apartheid government was intended to prepare those students for their lives as laborers, not as citizens, for citizenship belonged to the white descendants of South Africa's British and Dutch settlers. Relegation to one of the ten separate tribal homelands the government organized and administered counted as citizenship for black South Africans. And black South Africans experienced Bantu education, even as an education for a life of labor, as woefully inadequate (South African industry also criticized it).[1] Politicized by anger, despair, and frustration with their circumstances, and driven by the emerging black consciousness movement of Steve Biko and the South African Students' Organisation

(SASO), the Soweto youth were emboldened to protest their meager education. While Bantu education was the target of their protest, more was at stake for the Soweto youth than the quality of their schooling. They were also impatient with the lack of progress made in the liberation struggle over the course of their lives and were highly critical of what they perceived as the defeat of an older generation of freedom fighters. Biko summarizes it well: "The history of it starts off after 1963–4. If you remember, there were many arrests in this country which stemmed from underground activities by PAC (Pan Africanist Congress) and ANC (African National Congress); this led to some kind of political emasculation of the black population especially, with the result that there was no participation by blacks in the articulation of their own aspirations. . . . So we argued that any changes which are to come can only come as a result of a programme worked out by black people" (Biko 1978, 143–44).

The lack of progress in the struggle against apartheid that motivated black consciousness and in part alienated the Soweto youth from an older generation of black South Africans was, as Biko observes, the product of the government's imprisoning and forcing into exile during the early 1960s the majority of the leaders of the liberation struggle, including Mandela, who by 1976 had already spent thirteen years isolated in the prison on Robben Island.[2] In a very real sense the period from the Sharpeville massacre in 1960 to the Soweto uprising in 1976 was a period during which the apartheid government enjoyed relative stability. It was also a period during which two generations of freedom fighters—the older generation of Mandela and the younger generation of Biko—formed disparate senses of the kind of citizenship they imagined for themselves as the culmination of their struggle. The younger generation, coming of age in townships such as Soweto, learned from their experiences of life under the apartheid regime that liberation was less a matter of participating in an organized struggle for democratization and more a matter of overcoming the fears that kept them docile. That sense of pervasive fear is captured by Neo Lekgotla laga Ramoupi in his description of the apartheid government's power to imprison and isolate the older generation: "From a very, very early age, growing up in the 1970s, I was frightened to mention the place Robben Island. Because it was narrated to us as this mysterious location, so far away from us, in the middle of the sea, where Robert Sobukwe and Nelson Mandela were imprisoned for life. At that time to us in the townships of South Africa Robben Island was a myth."

The myth of Robben Island instilled in black South Africans a fear that fueled the apartheid government's power. As Naledi Tsiki explains, "we grew up in the '70s. . . . And we began to read, or to even here whispers, and the whispers were Nelson Mandela, the man on Robben Island. What is Robben Island? Robben Island is a jail where they keep people who don't like to be pushed around by white people" (quoted in Buntman 1997, 240).

An older generation, isolated from the youth of South Africa, imprisoned together on Robben Island, learned from their experiences a different lesson, a lesson in the decorum of deliberation. Mandela explains, "In the struggle, Robben Island was known as the University. This is not only because of what we learned from books. . . . Robben Island was known as the University because of what we learned from each other" (Mandela 1995, 467). Motivation to characterize the prison as a university and experience imprisonment as an education came from a number of sources. One of the first things motivating the imprisoned freedom fighters was the demoralizing effect of prison life. D. W. Zwelonke recalls in his memoir of imprisonment on Robben Island, "When your soul is low, sunk to the level of brainwashing through dejection, depression, frustration and despair, that is when the white man gets you. Soon you become a stooge, a pimp, a traitor to your cause" (Zwelonke 1973, 69). To counter the brainwashing of their long imprisonment, political prisoners decided together to carry on their struggle against apartheid in the only way they could, as a struggle against the conditions they faced inside apartheid prisons.

The decision to carry on the struggle against apartheid through the struggle of prisoners against the conditions of the prison system was more than a decision among the prisoners to maintain their resolve. The prison system in apartheid South Africa—and the prison on Robben Island in particular—represented the depredations of colonialism and apartheid not just to the youth in the townships, but in the international community as well. In a speech he gave in 1980 on behalf of Nelson Mandela, who was being awarded the Jawaharlal Nehru Award for International Understanding, ANC president Oliver Tambo explained, "The tragedy of Africa, in racial and political terms, is concentrated in the southern tip of the continent—in South Africa, Namibia, and, in a special sense, Robben Island" (Tambo 1997, 199).

Despite the larger political ramifications, Mandela, like Zwelonke, describes the initial hope behind the decision to protest prison conditions in more modest terms: "Our survival depended on understanding what the authorities were attempting to do to us, and sharing that understanding with each other.... We supported each other and gained strength from each other. Whatever we learned, we shared, and by sharing we multiplied whatever courage we had individually" (Mandela 1995, 390). Over the years the prisoners shared their insights and organized complaints against the conditions of the cells, the food, the labor. In her book-length study of political resistance on Robben Island, Fran Buntman summarizes the historical trajectory through which complaints against prison conditions were galvanized into struggle against apartheid: "Resisting the basic conditions of life in prison in most of the 1960s as well as in the early 1970s, was a necessary precursor to any more far-reaching resistance, such as using one's imprisonment to acquire an academic qualification or developing structures that created, organized, and gave meaning to the prisoner community. In turn, these various forms of resistance, which worked to protect the health of the social body as well as the minds and bodies of the individual prisoners, helped prisoners develop transformational strategies that sought not only to resist apartheid in and outside the prison but also to fundamentally transform South African politics" (Buntman 1997, 34–35).

What matters here for the generational conflict between Mandela's generation and the generation of the Soweto youth is that the strategy of organized prisoner complaint that galvanized the older generation was carried on behind prison walls, well outside the awareness of the youth growing up in the townships. As Biko put it, with the leaders of Mandela's generation living behind bars or in exile, the black youth in South Africa were "politically emasculated" and felt the need to discover on their own and assert for themselves their political autonomy. Unlike the Robben Islanders organizing to foster systematic change, the Soweto youth fomented revolutionary change.

By the time the Soweto youth arrived on Robben Island the sharing of information and orchestrating of complaints had evolved to include a more formal curriculum of lectures and discussions on the history of the ANC, political economy, and racial injustice. Mandela is worth quoting at length on the evolution of the curriculum:

> Our university grew up partly out of necessity. As young men came to the island, we realized that they knew very little about the history of the ANC. Walter [Sisulu], perhaps the greatest living historian of

the ANC, began to tell them about the genesis of the organization and its early days. His teaching was wise and full of understanding. Gradually, this informal history grew into a course of study, constructed by the High Organ, which became known as Syllabus A, involving two years of lectures on the ANC and the liberation struggle. Syllabus A included a course taught by Kathy [Ahmed Kathrada], "A History of the Indian Struggle." Another comrade added a history of the Coloured people. Mac [Maharaj], who had studied in the German Democratic Republic, taught a course in Marxism. (Mandela 1995, 467)

From this description of the curriculum and pedagogy political prisoners on Robben Island developed for the purposes of carrying on the struggle against apartheid we can begin to see the outlines of notions of citizenship and participation different from those of the Soweto youth.

Both generations, in isolation from each other, were compelled by their treatment at the hands of the apartheid government to challenge the respective institutions that dominated their lives. For the Soweto youth the challenge involved taking to the streets and abandoning school. For Robben Islanders, who could not simply leave prison, the challenge was to find ways of working to change the institution itself. For the prisoners such work was deliberate and organized. Their struggle against the conditions in the prison, as their struggle against the conditions of apartheid, was informed by a historical understanding of the political economics of racial injustice in South Africa. The contrast between a younger generation emboldened by black consciousness to rise up against apartheid schooling and an older generation steeped in Marxist thought fashioning a school in prison is a matter involving more than the physical isolation of each generation from the other. The differences in philosophy that grew out of the isolation of each generation from the other has consequences beyond the immediate conflict between the two generations when they first contacted each other on Robben Island.

The differences between the two generations persist in the respective legacies of Robben Island and the Soweto uprising. Buntman's quote above only alludes to the prominence of the figure of Robben Island as "University of Struggle" in postapartheid South Africa.[3] At the same time, for a younger generation, the Soweto uprising remains iconic as well, even though it has less resonance in a postapartheid government still dominated by Mandela's generation.[4] In what follows I discuss the conflict between these generations as Mandela presents it in his autobiography, *Long Walk to Freedom*. As I hope to make clear, my reasons for choosing to focus on Mandela's autobiography have to do with what such focus can reveal to us about the persistence in democratic South Africa of apartheid-era intergenerational conflicts over citizenship.

I begin in contrast to the Soweto youth by focusing first on Mandela and the other long-time members of the African National Congress (ANC) who prided themselves on their unwavering commitment to the protocols and pronouncements of the ANC. The deliberative decision-making process of the ANC followed more traditional African decision-making processes that depended on the judgment of a council of older, presumably wiser, individuals aspiring in their deliberations to reach total agreement. The inclusiveness and deliberateness of ANC decision making was motivated in part by the need to maintain at all levels an adequate level of organization, communication, and control even after the ANC was banned and its activities were driven underground during the early 1960s (Mandela 1995, 145). A not-unintended consequence of this organizational structure was careful consideration of the violent consequences of any actions. The years of deliberation and the final all-night meeting that led the ANC executive committee to finally authorize the use of violence by members of the offshoot organization, Umkhonto we Sizwe, is a case in point. However, more relevant for the purposes of contrasting the Robben Island generation to the generation of the Soweto uprising is Mandela's account of the ANC's response to the Sharpeville massacre.

On March 21, 1960, as several thousand people gathered at the Sharpeville police station to protest the pass laws, police opened fire, killing sixty-seven and wounding 186. The protest was organized by Robert Sobukwe, a former leader of the ANC youth who had broken ranks with the ANC to become the first president of the Pan Africanist Congress (PAC). While the Sharpeville massacre drew international attention to the cause of the liberation struggle and to Sobukwe's leadership, it gave rise within South Africa to increasing protests and a widespread crackdown on those protests by the government. Despite Sobukwe's success at organizing hundreds of thousands of Africans to protest the pass laws, Mandela, in his autobiography, accused the leadership of PAC of "amateurishness and opportunism" (1995, 238). Instead of acknowledging any virtue in what Sobukwe and PAC had accomplished, Mandela celebrates instead the response of the ANC to the massacre, describing how, as the result of an all-night meeting of a small group of ANC leaders, ANC president Chief Luthuli was provided with a plan to "give the people an outlet for their anger and grief" (239). According to this plan Chief Luthuli publicly burned his pass book on March 26, at the same time announcing a national day of mourning for March 28. On that day, Mandela recalls, "the country responded magnificently as several hundred thousand Africans observed the chief's call. Only a truly mass organization could coordinate such activities, and the ANC did so" (239). Through these passages from Mandela's autobiography we glimpse the deliberateness as well as the commitment to an appearance of unanimity within the ANC. We also get a strong sense of Mandela's view that the ANC was the representative organization in the liberation struggle. The point I want to make here though is that taking to the streets in protest of the apartheid government—whether at Sharpeville in 1960 or Soweto in 1976—is not an act entered into lightly. All such acts had to do more than tap into discontent or unleash rage. Just as the protests of the prisoners on Robben Island aimed at more than lodging complaints against prison authorities, demonstrations against either the pass laws or Bantu education, in order to be successful, had to do more to secure the hope of the people for the larger goal of liberation. At least for Mandela, the ANC provided that hope because its policies and procedures did what he thought PAC and the Soweto youth did not: align actions with a well-defined purpose.

With some sense of the culture of an older generation of Robben Island prisoners in mind—their deliberateness, their discipline, their conviction— it is easier to appreciate Mandela's understated contrast of his generation with the younger generation of prisoners who arrived on the island after the Soweto uprising. For the older prisoners, he writes, "These young men were a different breed. . . . They were brave, hostile, and aggressive" (Mandela 1995, 484). The younger prisoners, on the other hand, were "almost as skeptical of us as they were of the authorities. They chose to ignore our calls for discipline and thought our advice feeble and unassertive" (484). The contrast—between aggressive, impatient, skeptical youth and a disciplined, patient older generation—on the surface, draws on terms of maturation widely used to distinguish one generation from the next. If we look closer, however, it is a contrast that runs much deeper, expressing more than a natural process of maturation. Echoing Biko's account of the rise of black consciousness in South Africa, Mandela explains how in the vacuum created in the liberation struggle by the long-term imprisonment of senior ANC leaders, the youth were motivated by "the idea that blacks must first liberate themselves from the sense of psychological inferiority bred by three centuries of white rule." Diverging from Biko—who is nowhere mentioned in the autobiography—Mandela asserts, "I thought that their philosophy, in its concentration on blackness, was exclusionary, and represented an intermediate view that was not fully mature. I saw my role as an elder statesman who might help them move on to the more inclusive ideas of the Congress Movement. I knew also that these young men would eventually become frustrated because Black Consciousness offered no program of action, no outlet for their protest" (486).

While Mandela is clearly characterizing the politics of the Soweto youth as immature, it is a claim of immaturity that valorizes the position of the ANC. In *Long Walk to Freedom* Mandela consistently portrays the ANC as infallible and inviolable, no matter the subject being treated. The passage I just quoted is no exception. Mandela does not disagree with the view that black Africans must liberate themselves. He even admits black consciousness is a view he held in his youth, albeit a view he outgrew as his aging led him into the upper echelon of the ANC.

One implication of Mandela's joining in this way of conventional ideas about the process of maturation to specific political views is that any reasonable person, over the course of a life, cannot but come to share the views of the ANC. Most interesting in Mandela's appeal to a generational continuum is his joining of counterproductive anger, skepticism, and self-assertion to a youthfulness that precedes the maturity of calm cooperation, discipline, inclusivity, and commitment to a collective purpose. Oppositions of impetuous youth to deliberate maturity are nothing new. In this instance though the continuum is interesting for the notions of citizenship it delineates. Mandela's characterization of his citizenship ideal opposes youth who are more emotional, less deliberative, and more intent on personal autonomy to the mature ANC cadre who are less emotional, more thoughtful, and primarily concerned with promoting conditions for democratic inclusion as these are defined in the ANC's 1955 Freedom Charter and its nonracialist call that "The people shall rule." At issue then in Mandela's dismissal of the impetuousness of youth is the matter of what is required of people in order for them to participate in their own rule.

During the drafting of the Freedom Charter a variety of answers were offered to the question of what is required for the people to rule. The variation in answers among those who contributed to the charter is apparent in the document itself. While the charter begins with the statement "that South Africa belongs to all who live in it, black and white, and that no government can justly claim authority unless it is based on the will of all the people," it continues with statements about the rights of racially identified groups, "There shall be equal status in the bodies of state, in the courts and in the schools for all national groups and races," as well as redistribution of economic resources, "The mineral wealth beneath the soil, the Banks and monopoly industry shall be transferred to the ownership of the people." Issues of balancing individual rights, group rights, property rights, and commerce rights were left unresolved in 1955. That lack of resolution is in large part what drove ANC youth leaders such as Sobukwe to abandon the organization for PAC. For PAC, in anticipation of the emerging black consciousness of the Soweto youth, advocacy of African nationalism aimed at appealing to and unleashing an oppressed populace. In their reading of it, the Freedom Charter does not go far enough in the direction of acknowledging the importance of racial consciousness in the struggle for liberation from a minority white population that controlled the nation's wealth and resources.

With this brief sketch of political background I return to Mandela's autobiography. I do not take him to be saying he disparages the youth arrested after Soweto. He is clear about being encouraged by the energy and enthusiasm of the youthful protesters. The point is instead that his representation of the contrast between the Soweto youth and the older Robben Islanders is about the appropriate means of participation. Consistent with his dismissal of PAC's pass law demonstration, Mandela chides the youth for their lack of foresight. Protesting is not ruling. Ruling, as Mandela presents it, is a matter of participating in the ANC, an organization through which people are guided to strategically choose actions consistent with collective interests as these interests are defined by a more Marxist ideology. Recall Mandela's description of the Sharpeville massacre. Whatever else Sobukwe and PAC may have done in organizing the pass law demonstrations, their "amateurishness and opportunism" endangered lives. However much the people were willing to risk their lives to protest the pass laws, whether such willingness is motivated by despair or by some sense of justice, such willingness is futile when it is not made consistent with the larger purposes of a struggle organized around a nonracialist reading of the Freedom Charter. Ruling, according to Mandela's autobiography, thus involves self-discipline, a relegation of one's individual interests to the interests of the whole. The people rule when they organize themselves according to rules that define, and so delimit, the terms of their inclusion, not when they try to assert their autonomy by laying claim to such things as the nation's material resources. At odds here, then, are two versions of rule: one political and bounded by the rule of law, the other psychological and propelled by the autonomy of self-will.

So it is around questions of the terms of participation that generational differences in perceptions of citizenship turn. For the Soweto youth participation was defined not in terms of self-discipline but in terms of claiming autonomy by cultivating black consciousness. It was a claim they made against, but not from within, the apartheid institution of schooling. A number of factors influenced the youth revolt against Bantu education. Among these influences was the rapid expansion of schooling that required an influx of young teachers who had been exposed to the black consciousness movement at black universities such as the University of Fort Hare and the University of Zululand. These teachers encouraged psychological liberation, an assertion of black self-worth and independence that rejected apartheid institutions as well as white involvement in the liberation struggle. Student receptiveness to the young teachers was facilitated by the urbanization of the youth in the townships during the late 1960s and early 1970s. Where their parents lived in the townships in order to work in the cities, all the while retaining close ties to their designated homelands, the youth of the early 1970s generally rejected the futility of their parents' plight. They were aware of greater economic opportunities that remained, nonetheless, too meager. Underserved by their educations, alienated from their parents, frustrated by their prospects, and emboldened by their teachers, the Soweto youth had no patience for the deliberateness of the ANC.

Again, if we read his autobiography carefully we can see that Mandela captures the tension, this time in his account of the refusal of Soweto youth to follow prison regulations. One of the youth, Mandela recalls, refused to take off his cap in the presence of a senior prison official, asking instead why he should do it. Mandela makes clear his response, "I could hardly believe what I had just heard. It was a revolutionary question." Exasperated, the official walked away, asking Mandela to explain the regulation to the youth.

"But," Mandela writes, "I would not intervene on his behalf, and simply bowed in the direction of the prisoner to let him know that I was on his side" (Mandela 1995, 485).

Without reading too much into the cap incident, I think it is fair to say Mandela is hedging. I think it is also fair to characterize the incident, and Mandela's response to it, as betraying a larger question of deciding which rules enable self-rule when the inequality of a situation overwhelms the limits and focus of attitudinal resources. Mandela's incredulity at the youth's challenge to the prison dress code does seem a bit disingenuous. It is worth recalling that Mandela, early on in his Robben Island years, also took pride in challenging petty prison regulations, less the removing of caps and more the wearing of shorts year round or the inadequacy of the prisoner diet. As just one example, he writes, "From the first day, I had protested about being forced to wear short trousers" (387). As described above, such challenges became the foundation for an older generation of Robben Islanders to shape their struggle against apartheid. Yet the contrast between Mandela's presentation of his challenge against wearing shorts and the Soweto youth's challenge against donning his cap suggests differences between the two acts.

Concluding that such passages prove to be an inconsistency would be to miss the larger point of Mandela's narrative. He had asked the revolutionary questions when he too was young. But by the late 1970s his views had become more mature. In his maturity Mandela seems to see that challenging authority over each and every arbitrary rule is not necessarily an assertion of self-rule. Refusing the authority of apartheid rule is not in and of itself acquisition of self-rule. Self-rule not only involves deciding when and where and how to resist the arbitrary constraints of apartheid. Genuine self-rule involves as well deciding when and where it is appropriate to acquiesce to reasoned principles, and reasoned principles are necessary because they enable us to recognize the role of immediate actions in the realization of deliberately defined long-term goals. In this case, the measure of any act challenging prison authorities on Robben Island is made in terms of when and where and how that challenge best advances the cause of the ANC. These are not things one decides alone. As Mandela points out in his account of his refusal to wear shorts, when he was given trousers to wear he asked immediately if the other prisoners were also provided with trousers. When he was told they were not, he refused to wear them until the other prisoners could have them as well. Here, as in other prisoner protests recounted in the autobiography, the individual act is subsumed to the collective goal.

Self-rule is not absolute autonomy, a point—according to Mandela—that the Soweto youth miss. Black consciousness does not provide terms for self-rule because—according to Mandela's reading of it—black consciousness does not provide anything like guidance on questions of deliberation or decision making, which are questions of how best to cooperate with others. Autonomy, understood as a kind of personal freedom to resist imposition of (in this case) apartheid rule, does not rise to the level of self-rule because it lacks attention to important issues regarding our relatedness to each other.[5] The difference between the Soweto youth and Mandela is that the youth who refused to don his cap did not follow through on the revolutionary implications of his question, he treated it as a question of individual autonomy rather than as a question of collective liberation.

The view I am constructing here involves more than recognizing that people must have at least enough autonomy that each can participate in making decisions about matters that concern them all. Such autonomy can never be sovereign, where sovereignty is understood as a capacity for unimpeded exercise of self-will. The exercise of self-will by itself does not adequately characterize what is involved in participation. It is obvious enough that participation in a democracy is a matter of interactions with others, interactions through which people make claims on each other, claims that are necessarily limited and limiting. In such circumstances, whatever people end up deciding together is more often than not more than an aggregation of what each individual wanted alone. Citizens of a democracy, people who rule themselves, are bound to decide together, and so they are bound to attempt to influence each other if they are to fashion just decisions from their deliberations. The important point here, which often gets overlooked, is that if people are bound to attempt to persuade each other, then people are also bound to be open to persuasion. What this means is that self-rule is a matter of deciding when and where and how to accept the persuasive influence of others.

To be clear, the persuasive influence over others that I have in mind is far different from the coercive constraints on freedom institutionalized in the apartheid state. The very idea of apartheid was isolation of groups of people from each other, an isolation based on racial identification. The apartheid ideal of racial isolation as autonomy creates only an illusion of self-rule.

Self-rule requires acknowledging that people cannot and should not be isolated, that they are bound to interact with and be open to each other. We cannot, of course, make ourselves equally available to the persuasive influence of each and every person. There are limits, and these limits require from us explanations of individual perceptions of openness. One way these accounts of vulnerability to the impositions of influence function is by making sense of any potential influence as either an arbitrary constraint to be resisted or a reasoned principle to be accepted. In the view I am constructing out of Mandela's autobiography, it is only okay to be vulnerable to the influence of another when the experience of that influence is understood in terms that make submission to collective rule into a capacity for self-rule.

Using the example of the cap incident, Mandela does not get involved in either advocating for the youth or for the prison official because the question of removing a cap does not make sense in terms of the reasoned principles of the ANC. However much he may agree or disagree with the youth, his own self-rule is measured less in terms of emotional investment in such minor slights and more in terms of commitment to principled action. In Mandela's view of it, weighing the influence on self-rule of the rule about not wearing caps requires the taking of a dispassionate stance. Taking a dispassionate stance is a way of asking whether the experience of another's influence is emotional—a matter of pride—or rational—a matter of principle. I think it is the matter of this dispassionate stance that is most at issue in the generational differences on Robben Island, it is the matter of as yet unexamined and unresolved disagreements over the place of the passions in the exercise of citizenship, the question of whether dispassionate openness is preferable to passionate openness, an openness to anger and antagonism, as well frailty and suffering, and hope and joy in life lived with others.

Struggles between being passionate and being dispassionate were on violent display in South Africa during the late 1980s and early 1990s while the ANC and the apartheid government negotiated the transition to democracy. Thousands were killed each year by South African security forces, forces loyal to the ANC repeatedly clashed with forces loyal to Chief Buthelezi and the Inkatha Freedom Party, while youth in the townships took to the streets in protests that easily turned violent. In the end the transition from apartheid to democracy in South Africa was won in large part through cultivation of the kind of dispassionate stance Mandela advocated. And despite the miracle of democracy in South Africa, the violence of the transition also makes it easy to see that passions are not so readily tamed, to see that the kind of deliberate, mature, reasonable participation Mandela exemplifies and advocates is perhaps not the most viable option for promoting citizenship.

To better clarify my point I skip ahead in time about thirty years to suspended ANC youth leader Julius Malema, who in 2009 launched a campaign calling for the nationalization of South Africa's mines. Because of his prior antagonism with former South African president Thabo Mbeki and his antagonism with current South African president Jacob Zuma, Malema was suspended from the ANC for sowing seeds of divisiveness in the ruling party. Here, in the reason given for Malema's suspension— divisiveness—we see the priority accorded the rule of the party over the self-rule of the individual. Despite his standing within the ANC, or per- haps because of it, Malema remains popular among youth impatient with South Africa's burgeoning neoliberalism and the slow pace of restitution for apartheid-era policies.

Describing Malema's influence, executive director of Friends of the Congo Maurice Carney observed in an August 20, 2011, interview on Afro- Beat Radio, "So, this is something to look out for in the coming years, where young people, you know, we see it . . . in North Africa it's reflected in Tunisia and Egypt, but in Southern Africa we already see the South Afri- can youth calling for a greater ownership of their own wealth which they're not benefitting from" (Carney 2011).

Carney's admiration for Malema as a leader of the next generation is consistent with Carney's disdain for the South African government's post- apartheid economic policies, which he characterizes as a continuation of apartheid policies. He invokes Melanie Klein's *The Shock Doctrine*—and her view that capitalism is spread through the exploitation of peoples stunned by large-scale disasters—to explain dissatisfaction with the rise of a black elite in South Africa despite the persistent poverty of the majority of black South Africans. Drawing on Klein, Carney explains that Mbeki affirmed the ANC's neoliberalism, "because he was primarily responsible for nego- tiating some of the economic dynamics at the time, that there wouldn't be any radical change. For example, the ANC wouldn't hold to the tenets of its charter, which called for resource sovereignty." He continues, "Even after Mandela and after Mbeki, when Jacob Zuma, who was supposed to be more of a populist . . . was going to come to power, he had talks with companies at the time like Merrill Lynch and reassured the financial markets that under his leadership there wouldn't be any radical changes in the economic order" (Carney 2011).

Here Carney has appealed to resource sovereignty—the idea of people controlling the wealth of their nation—to remedy the vulnerabilities of disease, poverty, and unemployment wrought by capitalism. Carney's appeal turns on pitting self-rule understood in terms of individual access to and control over material resources against the traditional ANC understanding of self-rule in terms of individual acquiescence to the deliberative resources of the party.

Where on Robben Island the generational disagreement regarding self-rule turned on control of limited personal resources, here the debate turns on whether or not direct command of wealth determines the capacity for self-realization. With one side focused on the role of material resources and the other side focused on the role of principles in self-rule, the debate founders. This point is made evident by furor over the South African government's delay in granting a tourist visa to the Dalai Lama so that he could travel to Cape Town to celebrate Archbishop Desmond Tutu's eightieth birthday. The government's delay—which led the Dalai Lama to cancel his visit—appears to many to reflect an interest in nurturing improved trade relations with China at the expense of freedoms won through the struggle against apartheid. As University of Witwatersrand vice chancellor Loyiso Nongxa observed, "The state's deliberate indecision ridicules the values pertaining to freedom of speech, expression and movement enshrined in our Constitution and the freedoms for which so many South Africans have lived, and indeed died" (Makoni 2011). Similarly, the Congress of South African Trade Unions (COSATU) issued a statement concluding that "even though China is our biggest trading partner, we should have not exchanged our morality for dollars or yuan" (Polgreen 2011). For his part, Tutu publicly admonished the Zuma government: "You represent your own interest and I am warning you, I am really warning you—out of love—I am warning you like I warned the nationalists, one day we will start praying for the defeat of the ANC government" (Smith 2011). Whether or not the government's delay was intentional, the incident shows us how easily perceptions of economic interest can come to dominate an issue. The trouble with a debate that so easily opposes competing interests in terms of a command of economic resources is that it occludes the extent to which the issue at hand is not simply economic. Freedom and morality are not measured solely in terms of who controls what percentage of the wealth. This is not to say the distribution of wealth does not matter in questions of what is good and just. No doubt it does. Rather, it is to say that productive deliberation regarding competing corporate and individual as well as private and public interests are not had when people on all sides are unable to acknowledge their dependence on others as well as their relationships to the vulnerability of others.

I think though we would be mistaken to conclude from the current situation in South Africa that the rhetoric developed by Sobukwe and Mandela and Tutu and the countless others who struggled against apartheid coalesced in an appeal bound to a discrete time and place. Yet it is not difficult to lose sight of their larger ambition for a better means of managing lives lived with others. Issues and contentions that preoccupy South African politicians today—issues that include but are not limited to AIDS, freedom of the press and of movement, government transparency, and wealth redistribution—serve as prescient reminders of vulnerabilities to the dehumanizing effects of intractable material inequality. Witnessing the inequalities that persist despite the South African transition to democracy, we could easily resign ourselves to accept that irreconcilable differences are inextricably intertwined with the unfairness of circumstances—not only in South Africa, but anywhere people must decide their fates together. Disappointment with Mbeki or Zuma or Malema can motivate resignation that our appeals to each other are more often than not weighted with anxiety over our own self-rule.

If we are to be citizens and take part in our collective self-rule, we must at least accept the prospects of acquiescence, compromise, and defeat. Accepting this measure of vulnerability involves more than resigning ourselves to the limits of our capacities. While everyone at one time or another will experience disappointment, we constrain our participation if we cynically conclude that the inevitability of disappointment is something we must resign ourselves to accepting as the price paid for hope in a common good. My view is that the refusal to risk disappointment costs more. The greater loss is not acquiescence, compromise, or defeat, it is the loss of opportunities to elaborate shared public lives.

As my argument suggests, for people to successfully come together across their differences in order to create out of their interactions a common good they all share requires they do more than engage in dispassionately persuading each other to accept the normative expression of the common good that they all can share. The more that is required for citizens to find among themselves a common good they can come to share with each other is the product of sharing vulnerabilities about what is feared and what is hoped for. The South African experience in the years since the end of apartheid certainly cautions us about the challenges of such vulnerability. More than this, of the many things the South African experience has to teach us, one of the most important is a greater appreciation for the virtues of our vulnerabilities.

NOTES

1. Student resistance to apartheid education policy and the decline of South African industry due in part to a lack of semiskilled labor combined in the late 1970s and early 1980s with domestic corruption and mismanagement as well as increasing international sanctions to signal the imminent collapse of the apartheid state. For a useful background on the Soweto uprising in the larger context of South African history, see especially Brooks and Brickhill 1980. See also Hyslop 1999; Marx 1992; and Thompson 2001. For personal accounts of the Soweto uprising, see Brink et al. 2001.

2. Robben Island is located in Table Bay, approximately twelve kilometers from Cape Town. While the Dutch had used it as a prison as early as the seventeenth century, it was not until 1960 that the apartheid government transformed it into a political prison. Today it is a South African National Heritage Site and a UNESCO World Heritage Site. For general background on the island's history, see Smith 1997. For a history of Robben Island as political prison, see Buntman 2003. In his autobiography Nelson Mandela discusses much of this material. For memoirs of other Robben Islanders, see Dlamini 1984; Kathrada 1999; and Naidoo 1983.

3. The significance of identifying Robben Island as the "University of Struggle" cannot be underestimated for the transition from apartheid to democracy or for an understanding of what democracy means in postapartheid South Africa. The memoirs of all former Robben Islanders are replete with references. See also Mbeki 1991. For a film documentary, see *Robben Island: Our University*, 1988. For a sense of the broad use of references to Robben Island as the "University of Struggle," see Rickard 1990.

4. For a sense of the continued relevance of the Soweto uprising to a younger generation of South Africans, refer to the twenty-fifth anniversary commemoration in 2001. See especially the program for the South African celebration, available online at www.info.gov.za/speeches/2001/010614945a1004.htm.

5. I argue in *Managing Vulnerability* (2012) that the success of the struggle against apartheid turned on figuring out means of relating that are motivated less by the ambition for autonomy and more by the ambition for interrelatedness. Desmond Tutu provides a general sense of the importance of an ambition for interrelatedness in the transition to democracy in *No Future without Forgiveness* (2002). The theme of interrelatedness was expressed in a number of key legal documents, including the interim Constitution of South Africa, through the word *ubuntu*, which signifies the view that we achieve our humanity through our interactions with others. For a brief overview of uses of ubuntu in South African legal documents, see Cornell and Muvangua (2012).

WORKS CITED

Biko, Steve. 1978. *I Write What I Like: A Selection of His Writings*, edited by Aelred Stubbs, preface by Archbishop Desmond Tutu, introduction by Malusi and Thoko Mpumlwana. Chicago: University of Chicago Press.

Brink, Elsabe, Gandhi Malungane, Steve Lebelo, Dumisane Ntshangase, and Sue Krige. 2001. *Soweto 16 June 1976*. Cape Town: Kwela Books.

Brooks, Alan, and Jeremy Brickhill. 1980. *Whirlwind before the Storm: The Origins and Development of the Uprising in Soweto and the Rest of South Africa from June to December 1976*. London: International Defence and Aid Fund for Southern Africa.

Buntman, Fran. 1997. "The Politics of Conviction: Political Prisoner Resistance on Robben Island, 1962–1991, and Its Implications for South African Politics and Resistance Theory." PhD diss., University of Texas at Austin.

———. 2003. *Robben Island and Prisoner Resistance to Apartheid*. New York: Cambridge University Press.

Carney, Maurice. 2011. Interview with Ann Garrison, "Resource Sovereignty: Congo, Africa, and the Global South," AfroBeat Radio, August 20.

Cornell, Drucilla, and Nyoko Muvangua. 2012. *Ubuntu and the Law: African Ideals and Postapartheid Jurisprudence*. New York: Fordham University Press.

Dlamini, Moses. 1984. *Hell-Hole, Robben Island: Reminiscences of a Political Prisoner*. Nottingham: Spokesman.

Hyslop, Jonathan. 1999. *The Classroom Struggle: Policy and Resistance in South Africa 1940–1990*. Pietermaritzburg, South Africa: University of Natal Press.

Kathrada, Ahmad. 1999. *Letters from Robben Island*. Cape Town: Mayibuye Books in association with Robben Island Museum; East Lansing: Michigan State University Press.

Makoni, Munyaradzi. 2011. "South Africa: Uproar over Dalai Lama Visa Mess." University World News, October 7. http://www.universityworldnews.com/article.php?story=20111007120330030.

Mandela, Nelson. 1995. *Long Walk to Freedom: The Autobiography of Nelson Mandela*. New York: Back Bay Books.

Marback, Richard. 2012. *Managing Vulnerability: South Africa's Struggle for a Democratic Rhetoric*. Columbia: University of South Carolina Press.

Marx, Anthony. 1992. *Lessons of Struggle: South African Internal Opposition, 1960–1990*. New York: Oxford University Press.

Mbeki, Govan. 1991. *Learning from Robben Island: The Prison Writings of Govan Mbeki*. Cape Town: David Philip.

Naidoo, Indres. 1983. *Robben Island: Ten Years as a Political Prisoner in South Africa's Most Notorious Penitentiary*. New York: Vintage.

Polgreen, Lydia. 2011. "Dalai Lama's Visa Request Is Denied by South Africa." *New York Times*, October 4. http://www.nytimes.com/2011/10/05/world/asia/dalai-lama-cancels-south-africa-visit.html?_r=0.

Rickard, Carmel. 1990. "The Island Graduates Dominate Natal ANC." *Weekly Mail* (South Africa), November 23, 16.

Robben Island: Our University. 1988. Directed by Linda Wilson. Videocassette.

Smith, Charlene. 1997. *Robben Island*. Mayibuye History and Literature Series 76. Cape Town: Mayibuye Books and Struik Publishers.

Smith, David. 2011. "Desmond Tutu Attacks South African Government over Dalai Lama Ban." *The Guardian*, October 4. http://www.theguardian.com/world/2011/oct/04/tutu-attacks-anc-dalai-lama-visa.

Tambo, Oliver. 1987. *Preparing for Power: Oliver Tambo Speaks*. Prepared by Adelaide Tambo. London: Heinemann.

Thompson, Leonard. 2001. *A History of South Africa*. New Haven, CT: Yale University Press.

Tutu, Desmond. 2000. *No Future without Forgiveness*. New York: Image Books.

Zwelonke, D. W. 1973. *Robben Island*. London: Heinemann.

10

OLD BEURS, NEW BEURS, AND FRENCH CITIZENSHIP

· · · · · · · · · ·

ABDELDJALIL LARBI YOUCEF

INTRODUCTION

In 2005, while visiting a Paris suburb, former president Nicolas Sarkozy (then interior minister) made this notorious remark: "I will rid you of these riffraff." By riffraff, he meant the youth (most of whom hold French citizenship) from North and sub-Saharan Africa. Their parents, whose contribution to French economic prosperity is unquestionable, were retired, exhausted, and helpless. They had no hold on their children, either the *Old Beurs*[1] who through marches in the 1980s had dreamed of becoming citizens, or those born between 1980 and 1990, the New Beurs, who, having lost hope of ever becoming full citizens, were determined not to identify with their forebears, let alone with France. Today, the New Beurs prefer to challenge the established authority by jeering the flag during soccer matches, by jeering the national anthem, and by burning cars to show their discontent.

In truth, it seems no one generation of French-born Africans has succeeded in acquiring full citizenship. The reason is simple in that deeply entrenched stereotypes impact moves toward implementation of political and social equality. This could be perceived during colonization. Its advocates, convinced that humankind was divided into races that were uneven, came to conclude that the principles for which many died during the revolution—liberty, equality, and fraternity—should not be enjoyed by the inferior peoples. In this light, George Orwell's slogan in *Animal Farm*, "all people [animals] are equal, but there are those that are more equal than others," would not be exaggerated since it might well apply to the status given to the segments that composed the society.

Distinction between races implied for colonial jurisprudence distinction between citizenship and nationality. The superior, old-family, Germans, and Swiss, were de facto citizens. Arabs, Kabyles, Jews, and foreigners (Spanish, Italians) had to be nationals. When it appeared that French individuals and families were not prone to migrate, citizenship was imposed on Jews, Spanish, and Italians; only Arabs remained nationals. As such, they had to submit themselves to a segregationist piece of legislation, the Native Code. Sixty years after independence, stereotypes are aloof in the background. This is why for most beurs, to be a citizen means nothing but to live in another country.

INVADING ALGERIA

The French Revolution spelled doom for the European monarchs. Fear of seeing their respective countries turned into republics induced the monarchs of Austria, Prussia, Russia, and England to form a coalition. Fear was further aroused when a French general, Napoleon Bonaparte, became first consul of France thanks to the military coup of 18 Brumaire (November 9, 1799) by which he overthrew the established Directory and replaced it with the Consulate. The famine that hit the French population was the far-reaching consequence of isolation the European coalition of monarchs set up. Bonaparte's armies were not much better off. The alternative was to ask the Dey of Algiers for help, who, in turn, instructed two Algerian Jews, Jacob Bacri and Naphtali Busnach (Ben Moses) to deliver wheat.

His choice was grounded in the fact they were no ordinary people. Unlike many other coreligionists, they belonged to the privileged class and would swiftly reach the top of the social ladder. Busnach even succeeded in becoming the Dey's banker, controller of the Treasury, and monopolist of the prevailing trade thanks to a prosperous firm, Bacri & Busnach. His fame led to a nickname, "the viceroy of Algiers," but cost him his life. In fact, for the janissaries, if any one person had to shoulder the guilt for the shortage of wheat, it was Busnach; they killed him.

The exports of wheat lasted from 1792 until 1798. According to reliable estimates, the debt, interest included, totaled 24 million francs discharged, in part, to Bacri-Busnach and their heirs. The Dey, as creditor of the firm, was neither paid nor informed by Bacri-Busnach that they had obtained some payment. Dey Hussein III, infuriated by the refusal of France to reimburse the Algerians, and by the fact a commercial warehouse in La Calle (today El Kala, a small town close to the Tunisian border) was being built without his permission, summoned on April 30, 1827, the consul, Pierre Deval, whom he expected would provide explanations. After a stormy discussion, the Dey slapped the consul with his flyswatter.

Humiliated, Deval reported the event to his superiors. Diplomatic relations were cut; troops were ordered to disembark at Sidi Ferruch, twenty-seven kilometers west of the capital, Algiers, on June 14, 1830. The invasion was the answer to so-called lack of good manners. In actuality, "The Flyswatter Affair," the name given to the incident, constituted the pretext for an already planned invasion. Now, since a two-million-square-kilometer territory had, presumably become France's property, there was urgent need to devise a "particular" temporary legislation to administer it and its inhabitants until the devising of a special one in conformity with the Constitution of the Second Republic (1848–52). The temporary legislature gave way to a perennial, highly discriminative legislation, whose conspicuous feature could be perceived in the field of citizenship.

SEPARATE AND UNEQUAL

Insofar as citizenship was concerned, the legislator in France, no more a monarchy, came to bridge nationality and citizenship; men and women were henceforth citizens. That had not to be the case in the colony. The reason lay in that such bridging appeared antagonistic to the very foundation of colonialism. Besides, it was assumed that both religion and beliefs of the colonized precluded any attempt to that intent. Under this head, Arabs for instance, "be they viewed as savages or barbarians; their customs, their culture and their religion [were] so many obstacles that prevent[ed] them from understanding the full implications of the principles stemming from the Revolution" (Le Cour Grandmaison 2010, 132). Those principles of liberty, equality, and fraternity for which many died were deemed devoid of meaning and subsequently of inclusion in colonial jurisprudence.

Practically, one would see Arab conscripts, ready to give their lives during the Great Wars, denied the same treatment their French counterparts enjoyed. This discrimination has been subject of a film, *Days of Glory*, 2006, made by the Algerian-French moviemaker Rachid Bouchareb. Moved, President Jacques Chirac resolved to raise the pensions of African veterans and to point out that much was owed to these men. In sum, a seemingly "unprincipled" policy actually "obeyed a principle" (Harmand 1910, 170), to ensure durability of a system thanks to categorization. It went without saying, as one general, Paul Azan (1874–1951), pointed out, that proponents of equality were assuredly "wrongheaded" because

> the native is not like the French; he has neither his physical fitness nor his qualities, his education or traditions, his customs or his civilization. . . . The mistake is a very generous one and a very French one: it has already been made by those who drafted the "Declaration of the Rights of Man and of the Citizen," rather than more modestly drafting a "Declaration of the rights of the French citizen." It is not possible to mould humanity thanks to a single formula, even an excellent one, because the races do not change with the sound of few phrases, but take many centuries to evolve. (Azan 1925, 39)

A dogma was born. In his book *Le véloce; ou, Tanger, Alger et Tunis* (published in four volumes between 1848 and 1851), Alexandre Dumas set the tone. In 1846, upon a request from the ministry of public instruction, he toured North Africa. It was in Morocco that he encountered the first Arab. He challenged him on his cleverness to shoot with precision at game. Having lost, the Arab moved off. Dumas wrote: "it was obvious that he [the Arab] was moving off, crushed by his inferiority, and at that moment had doubts about everything, even the prophet. . . . All Morocco was humiliated by its representative" (Dumas 2006, 34). In much the same vein, the prefect of Algiers, M. Helot, could not comprehend the assimilation of Jews. He made clear in 1874, almost half a century after troops had disembarked, that "these people are not civilized enough to be treated differently from the way we treat them, conquered subjects; we must not assimilate them" (Blévis 2001, 557–80). That was not the opinion of Prime Minister Jules Ferry (1832–1893), who raised the necessity of a civilizing mission. Barely a decade later, addressing the representatives, he explained that "the superior races ha[d] a right because they ha[d] a duty to civilize the inferior races" (Speech, July 28, Ferry 1885).

In fact, society underwent division into superior and inferior races. Old-family (*de souche*), Germans, and Swiss belonged to the former; "the Other,"

Arabs, Kabyles, Jews, and foreigners (Spanish, Italians), belonged to the latter. After categorization, all that remained was to breathe subjectivity into the law by making a sharply cut legal distinction between *nationality* and *citizenship*, more precisely, civil rights, since *citizenship* had no room in colonial jurisprudence. The superior were de facto citizens with the same rights granted to fellows of the metropolis; the inferior were made nationals, a status rooted in the necessity "to affirm the sovereign power of the conquering country" toward other empires and in the necessity "to subject the Indigenous, to ensure the prerogatives of the colonists; in last analysis, to guarantee an all-out domination of the second over the first" (Runner 1927, 29–42).

Noteworthy, at the age of twenty-one and upon personal demand to the heads of their respective communities, the colonial administration could, after processing, grant "citizenship." But Arabs, Jews, Spanish, and Italians showed reluctance to undertake steps to gain citizenship. For the first two it meant nothing but giving up laws that drew from the Koran and the Torah and submitting to French law. For the last two, pride and sentimental ties to their respective countries made that "citizenship" unappealing. In so doing, they posed a rather peculiar problem. The dream to see the colony become French did not come true since individuals and families were not prone to emigrate. Eventually, the Spanish and the Italian element remained, by far, greater than the French one.

A census conducted in 1906 shows the disparity, as three out of five people were not French. The figures suggested that France was losing ground. The conquest, which cost blood and money, seemed to benefit the Spanish and the Italians who, given their high birth rate, were swiftly outnumbering the French in the eastern and western part of the country. There was talk of an "Italian peril" since they were on the verge of taking a strong hold of Tunisia. The authorities subsequently resolved "not to hack a Spanish egg in Algeria and an Italian one in Tunisia" (Bernard 1905, 167).

But to see exclusively Arabs beside old-family French was not without shortcomings. The totally different cultures and religions, it was contended, rendered assimilation impossible. On the contrary, the assimilation of Spanish and Italian migrants, notwithstanding their being of "a somehow inferior type," as Paul-Leroy Baulieu depicted them in his book *Algérie et Tunisie* (1887), appeared within reach given their European heritage. Consequently, France had to regard the Arab peoples no more as second classes but as citizens. On June 26, 1889, and July 22, 1893, "citizenship" was automatically imposed on the second generation of Spanish and Italians. Likewise, Jews were made citizens "en masse" by Napoleon III, Senatus-Consult in 1870, and by the Crémieux Executive Order (1871). Part of the old-family and the army resented the order; it was repealed in 1940 by the Vichy government that started a hunt for people of Jewish descent.

Of all categories, only Arabs remained nationals. Given that status, they had to submit themselves to a peculiar body of law, the Native Code (Code de l'Indigénat, 1874). Its harshness led them to call it "the Truncheon Code"; critics of colonization, "a Judicial Monster." The code consisted at the outset of twenty-seven offenses, which, though not illegal under the common law of France, were nevertheless held illegal and punishable to those who committed them. Among the offenses, one found, traveling without a permit, begging outside one's tribe, shooting in the air at a celebration, refusing to pay taxes, gatherings of more than twenty persons without prior permission, giving shelter to tramps, and refusing to salute an officer, civil or military, even when off duty. It was also customary to see an individual's offense lead to collective punishment. Capital punishment itself underwent changes. When administered, families were prevented from reuniting head to the body. In the meantime, "citizenship" was granted to some with a prerequisite: to understand it was "not a right but a function or a privilege" because they constituted no part of the French nation and subsequently had no right to intervene "in any manner whatsoever in the exercise of national sovereignty" (Runner 1927, 29–42).

FRENCH RULE INTO QUESTION

Uprisings against colonization in general, and the Native Code, in particular, led by tribal leaders like Emir Abd el Kader, a native of Mascara, today a twin city with Elkader, Iowa, bred a feeling of invincibility. It was not until the Great War (1914–18) that the belief was broken. The French could lose battles; they could be killed by the hundreds. The Indigenous, the name given to Arabs, were promised independence twice in case they accepted to fight the Germans that used to boast Deutschland "über alles" (above all). But 1918 and 1945 were years of broken promises. The survivors of the Great Wars and those who awaited them at home soon realized that freedom necessitated preparation for extreme events. At the heart of a seven-year-long bloody and stained war that broke out in 1954, the world was informed that Algeria was no longer part of France. That was much to the dislike of officials further exasperated by the speech of a young American senator, chairman of the Foreign Relations Sub-Committee on United Nations Affairs, John Fitzgerald Kennedy. In "Imperialism: The Enemy of Freedom," delivered on July 2, 1957, he dared say, in essence,

> The most powerful single force in the world today is neither communism nor capitalism, neither the H-bomb nor the guided missile, it is man's eternal desire to be free and independent. The great enemy of that tremendous force of freedom is called, for want of a more precise term, imperialism—and today that means Soviet imperialism and, whether we like it or not, and though they are not to be equated, Western imperialism . . . the war in Algeria confronts the United States with its most critical diplomatic impasse since the crisis in Indochina—and yet we have not only failed to meet the problem forthrightly and effectively, we have refused to even recognize that it is our problem at all. . . . American and French diplomats, it must be noted at the outset, have joined in saying for several years that Algeria is not even a proper subject for American foreign policy debates or world consideration—that it is wholly a matter of internal French concern, a provincial uprising, a crisis which will respond satisfactorily to local anesthesia. But whatever the original truth of these clichés may have been, the blunt facts of the matter today are that the changing face of African nationalism, and the ever-widening byproducts of the growing crisis, have made Algeria a matter of international, and consequently American, concern . . . the United States, a product of political revolution, must redouble its efforts to earn the respect and friendship of nationalist leaders. (Speech, July 2, Kennedy 1957)

In 1958, President Charles de Gaulle would launch his enigmatic sentence: "I have understood you" (Speech, June 5, De Gaulle 1958). His sentence divided opinions. The natives claimed he had understood their wish to be independent, and the descendants of colonists, known as blackfeet,[2] their wish to see him keep Algeria. Ultimately, President de Gaulle yielded to resistance and international pressure and agreed to Algerian independence. Blackfeet and military officials, in turn, founded the OAS (Secret Army Organization) in 1961. Their slogan was, "Algeria is and will remain French." There was no ambiguity in the message; any party to any deal that saw salvation in independence would find no rest. They also spray-painted another slogan on walls and doors, "The OAS hits wherever it wants, whenever it wants!" However, the fallacy and hopelessness of their struggle were becoming all too clear. Most members of the OAS were either killed or arrested. In 1962 a forced departure began for 690,000 blackfeet joined by 60,000 Loyalists, commonly known as harkis, meaning traitors; France abandoned 150,000 harkis.

BIDDING FAREWELL TO ALGERIA

Revenge flying high, the blackfeets' choice was rather limited; it was either "the suitcase or the coffin."[3] They had no right to cry over "their" country, over wealth left behind, fertile lands, vineyards, and big farms. It was up to them to decide whether to leave with a suitcase containing a few belongings, a few clothes, a few photographs yellowed by time of those cherished resting in cemeteries, or to leave dead inside a coffin. Although deeply affected, they resigned themselves to leave. With the traitors, they undertook a forced journey to the metropolis. Degraded people retreating to indiscernible horizons ended 132 years of presence. The French saw in blackfeet the once boisterous landed and moneyed aristocrats. This is why their uprootedness and longing turned up in a song by one of their famous singers, Enrico Macias, a native of Constantine (East), "J'ai quitté mon pays" (I left my country, I left my home, and here's my life, my sad life dragging out aimlessly, 1962).

Unlike blackfeet, traitors did not have the "either-or" choice. Algerians regarded them as cowards and double traitors. The hood-wearers—they used to hide their faces—were accused of having helped French soldiers; worse, when it became clear France would withdraw, of having joined the much-despised OAS. Among their most wanted figures was Saïd Boualam. In 1962 he escaped; had he stayed, his throat would have been cut. In his book *Mon pays, la France!* (*France, My Country*, 1962), he gave his explanation as to the motive that impelled him to join the OAS:

> Even at the moment, when everything seemed lost, there still was in the heart of a number of Moslems hope to see the prestigious military leaders, who were at the head of the French army and who took the lead of the OAS, become victorious. . . . It is my duty to point out that if Moslems, whose number is higher than avowed, embarked on such enterprise, it's because they saw in the OAS their

last hope, their last chance before they came to realize they were vanquished, before they came to declare definitely: We have been betrayed." (Boualam 1962, 246)

Both the French population and the authorities rejected the traitors. Untrustworthy to the former, chains for the latter, confinement in transit camps, was the solution. The repatriated, as they were called and called themselves, enjoyed "an amputated nationality" (Pitti 2011) since they were neither "repatriated like the others, blackfeet, [n]or French like the others (of the metropolis, author)" (Pitti 2011). They had to wait to see the blackfeet delivered housing and jobs before they could expect the same; political and civil rights were untimely. Their plight induced some critics to point out that France was carrying on its old racist and colonial attitude because if the Algerian combatants have the right to despise the harkis and to hold them traitors, the French government does not. Recently, on March 19, 2012, a bill was submitted to the French Senate, to be considered as law, aiming at punishing libel and insults against them. Georges Frêche, president of the Languedoc-Roussillon region, had called two of them "subhumans."

OLD BEURS: REQUESTING CITIZENSHIP

Blackfeet and harkis were not the only ones to leave. Well before independence, driven out of their land, Algerians headed for the cities to look for a nonexistent job then to France, where a booming economy necessitated cheap labor. The Algerian emigrants (Old Beurs) contributed to the Glorious Thirty (1945–73). It was, as its name implies, a thirty-year period of economic prosperity. They worked in companies like Renault and Peugeot; they built houses, roads, bridges, buildings, but they lived in slums. Illiteracy prevented the majority from specializing; they remained unskilled until they retired in the 1970s, when the economy started ailing. They always saw their going as a temporary enterprise. In the course of time, they brought their wives and children to France thanks to an enterprise known as family grouping. The illiterate wives, at once countrysiders, having tasted liberalism and consumer society, did not envisage return. But social exclusion, cohesion in society, and difficulty to integrate plagued their lives and their prosperity.

The Old Beurs' hopes and expectations to become citizens became heightened when the left-wing party came to power in 1981. They might become teachers, engineers, mayors, representatives, and senators, not just destined to be skilled workers. This is why they undertook in 1983 the March for Equality and against Racism. Political and social invisibility was denounced; citizenship was requested. Soon an ailing economy overshadowed the request, leaving room for the rise of Jean-Marie Le Pen's far-right party, the National Front. Fearing to alienate the French voter, the left chose leniency. In the meantime, a new generation came to light, the New Beurs.

NEW BEURS: CHALLENGING
THE CONSTITUTED AUTHORITY

The New Beurs were brought up in sensitive urban areas, the ZUS (Zones Urbaines Sensibles), a multiethnic space with closed gates to the outside world. Although granted citizenship thanks to the Jus Soli (right of soil), they are still trying to figure out what it means to be a French citizen. Ghettoization, failure at school, and difficulties in obtaining a job pushes this new urban underclass to reject their parents since they did not succeed. In short, they reject any authority, be it paternal or extrapaternal. But wrath bred the same.

In 2005, while visiting the Paris suburb La Courneuve, Sarkozy pledged, "Starting tomorrow, we are going to clean the Cite des 4000 with a Kärcher" (Kärcher is German pressure-cleaning equipment). Accusing the criminal youth, most of whom hold French citizenship, of being riffraff and thugs, he promised, "I will rid you of these riffraff." This led the Beurs, old and new, to understand, once for all, who they are. The Algerians claim that they are French, while those with French heritage see them as sons of emigrants, or worse, "On Paper Citizens," which suggests they do not deserve citizenship. Neither here nor there and in overbearing isolation, the pledge confirmed the idea that for those of Algerian descent, citizenship meant to live in a foreign country decidedly unwilling to part with a colonial past. Who are they then? They are Beurs, a new identity born and raised in sensitive banlieues that they are determined to control, a no man's land, where policemen are met with stones, and any incident involving one of them turns into the spark that ignites the fire.

As in 1981, there is now a new president from the Socialist Party, François Hollande.[4] The New Beurs, like their elders, have great expectations and great hopes. What will the future hold? The recent events in Trappes have a smell of history repeating itself. For two days, July 19 and 20, 2013, the New Beurs went to the streets of that very poor suburb, where they staged riots and burned cars. The cause was, presumably, the behavior of the police during an interrogation of a woman wearing a burqa. The bill to ban the veil and burqa was introduced by the Sarkozy administration in 2010. Implemented on April 11, 2011, the law imposes a €150 fine or mandatory "citizenship training" on those who do not comply. After scrutiny, one may assume that the law played the role of catalyst; the interrogation being the pretext that the youth seized upon to challenge what they perceived as continuous discriminative legislation of the constituted authority. Far beyond, there is, in progress, questioning of citizenship that appears synonymous of more duties and fewer rights and rooted in unshakable beliefs like the one formulated by the former interior minister Claude Guéant, "not all civilizations are of equal value."

NOTES

1. *Beur* is an informal word coined by reversing the syllables of the word *Arab*; a female is a *beurette*.
2. Blackfeet or *pieds-noirs*: French, Spanish, and Jewish colonial residents in an independent Algeria.
3. After the Oran Massacre of July 1962, where estimates of up to 3,500 French civilians were killed in the fight for Algerian independence, a referendum and the subsequent Evian Accords were instituted. The accords began the process of transfer of power from the French to the Algerians. The Evian Accords intended to guarantee the rights and safety of the blackfeet. However, rumor spread that the only choice they had was "the suitcase or the coffin."
4. Hollande was elected president of France on May 6, 2012.

WORKS CITED

Augustin, B. 1905. "Le peuplement italien en Tunisie et en Algérie." *Annales de Géographie* 14 (74).

Azan, P. 1925. *L'armée indigène nord-Africaine*. Paris: Charles Lavauzelle.

Bernard, A. 1905. "Le peuplement italien en Tunisie et en Algérie." *Annales de Géographie* 14 (74).

Blévis, L. 2001. *Les avatars de la citoyenneté en Algérie coloniale ou les paradoxes d'une catégorisation*. Archives nationales, C/2905. Droits et sociétés, no. 48, Paris.

Boualam, S. 1962. *Mon pays, la France!* Paris: France-Empire.

De Gaulle, C. 1958. Journal télévisé du 5 juin. Institut National de l'audiovisuel.

Dumas, A. (1848–51) 2006. *Le véloce; ou, Tanger, Alger et Tunis*. Paris: Cadot, 4 vols.; Montreal: Le Joyeux Roger.

Ferry, J. 1885. "Les races supérieures ont un droit sur les races inférieures." 28 juillet. France, Journal Officiel du 29 juillet.

Harmand, F. J. 1910. *Domination et colonisation*. Paris: Flammarion.

Kennedy. J. F. 1957. "Imperialism: The Enemy of Freedom." Congressional Record CIII. Part 8. July.

Le Cour Grandmaison, O. 2010. *De l'indigénat: Anatomie d'un monstre juridique: Le droit colonial en Algérie et dans l'Empire français* Paris: Zones.

Pitti, L. 2011. "De l'histoire coloniale à l'immigration post-coloniale: Le cas des harkis." Les deux rives de la Méditerranée. *Les harkis: Ni rapatriés comme les autres, ni français comme les autres*. Lundi 24 octobre.

Runner, J. 1927. *Les Droits politiques des indigènes des colonies*. Paris: LaRose.

Vidal-Naquet, P. 1962. "La guerre révolutionnaire et la tragédie des harkis." *Le Monde*, 11–12 novembre.

PART 4

....

Later Life, Civic Engagement,
Disenfranchisement

II

IS PARTICIPATION DECLINE
INEVITABLE AS GENERATIONS AGE?

· · · · · · · · · ·

Insights from African American Elders

JENNIE SWEET-CUSHMAN,
MARY HERRING, LISA J. FICKER,
CATHY LYSACK, MARC W. KRUMAN,
PETER A. LICHTENBERG

Journalist Tom Brokaw famously termed the generation of Americans who came of age around the time of the Great Depression and World War II the "Greatest Generation." Part of what made this generation great, Brokaw argued, was their unprecedented level of commitment to American society in the war effort and beyond. This cohort participated in the economy, in their communities, and in the political process in unprecedented numbers. However, scholars have noted that this generation, like the one prior to it, experienced a drop in participation as they moved into old age. If this phenomenon has applied to this "greatest" of generations, it is curious to consider the impact of a similar type of decline in the participation of their successors, the "Baby Boomers," who have consistently participated at lower rates than their predecessors.

Because the generation is so large, the aging of the baby boomers poses serious civic considerations. Will this cohort experience this traditional drop-off in participation? If so, what factors will encourage and discourage this decline? Questions of participation are critical to the understanding of any democracy in part because the health of a democracy is inextricably tied to the level of civic engagement found among its people. Thus participation—both political and civic—has been studied by a diverse set of academic disciplines. Extensive evaluation of participation in the United States has provided a complex picture of the factors contributing to engagement levels, particularly individual characteristics.

Despite the breadth of this research, the civic participation of this particularly important voting bloc remains understudied. This is primarily the result of the elderly typically comprising too small a subset of general population survey samples. Here we make use of data from a unique survey of African American elders in order to examine the influence of traditional predictors of participation, such as socioeconomic status and political efficacy, as well as to appraise several underexamined factors that are more prevalent among the elderly—namely, health-related factors and mobility. By considering these factors we can paint a clearer picture of what serves to encourage or depress political participation as individuals age.

WHO PARTICIPATES?

Although there are few legal barriers to taking part in politics and government affairs in the United States, many citizens choose not to participate. Why? Analysts have long known that voting and other means of political engagement are strongly associated with socioeconomic status, especially one's level of education. The linkage is so strong and consistent that since 1972 it has been part of the "standard model" of participation whereby social status reflects the acquisition of resources and attitudes that promote participation (Verba and Nie 1972; Milbrath and Goel 1977; Wolfinger and Rosenstone 1980; Teixeira 1992; and see Leighley 1995 for reviews).

Extensive research has yielded a variety of formulations of the linkages with political engagement, but Brady, Verba, and Schlozman (1995) offer the most concise summary of the reasons for participation: people participate because they *can*, because they *want to*, and because they *are asked*. Critically, all of these three conditions become more likely among those with higher socioeconomic status.

People participate because they can. That is, they have the resources, such as time, to participate, money to contribute, and the requisite civic skills, such as political knowledge, communication skills, and organizational abilities. Civic skills can be developed in all sorts of environments, including schools, workplaces, and religious and voluntary organizations, but in general the likelihood of acquiring them tends to be class stratified. An important exception is for skills developed through religious institutions. Because church attendance does not vary much by economic status, acquisition of civic skills in religious organizations is more equally distributed across social classes.

People participate because they want to. Certain attitudes are highly predictive of political participation. Political efficacy—the belief that one's efforts can influence political decisions—is especially influential (Abramson and Aldrich 1982; Shaffer 1981; Finkel 1985; Verba, Schlozman, and Brady 1995), as is interest in politics, belief that participation is a responsibility of citizenship (Gerber and Green 2000; Knack 1994; Rosenstone and Hansen 1993; Kam 2007), and partisan identification (Campbell et al. 1960; Bartels 2000; Finkel and Opp 1991).

People participate because they are asked. Citizens are more likely to be engaged—especially in the more demanding types of participation—when they are invited to do so. The potential for being asked improves when individuals are embedded in networks where recruitment occurs. These tend to be the same places where individuals develop civic skills: the workplace, volunteer organizations, churches, and informal groups (Verba, Schlozman, and Brady 1995; Rosenstone and Hansen 1993). Moreover, recruiters are more likely to ask those whom they know to have the resources that will enable them to participate (Rosenstone and Hansen 1993). Thus in mobilization models, as in models that focus on individual attributes, the opportunity for participation increases at the upper rungs of the socioeconomic ladder.

Again, places of worship are often exceptions. Unlike recruitment networks that occur through other voluntary organizations and workplaces, church attendance, and thus recruitment through churches, tends to be fairly uniform across social classes. Churches not only serve as prime centers for political recruitment (Djupe, Sokhey, and Gilbert 2007), but also serve as venues for the acquisition of civic skills (Verba, Schlozman, and Brady 1995), and as channels for dissemination of political information (Huckfeldt and Sprague 1995; Wald, Owen, and Hill 1988). This condition is particularly important for African Americans, for whom church often assumes a much larger role in social life. Thus church offers an opportunity to learn civic skills when opportunities in other environments have historically been more limited (Verba, Schlozman, and Brady 1995; Djupe and Gilbert 2006). Additionally, blacks are more likely to hear religious messages about political issues and messages that stimulate group consciousness and racial identity, which may also facilitate participation (Reese and Brown 1995; Tate 1994; Verba, Schlozman, and Brady 1995; Dawson, Brown, and Allen 1990a and 1990b).

While the casual processes leading to participation are the focus of much scholarly attention, demographic differences in engagement continue to be important, particularly with regard to race, gender, and age, where there are well-documented gaps in participation. For instance, black voter turnout is lower than white turnout, although when the historically lower socioeconomic status of blacks is controlled, the participation rates of blacks and whites are striking similar; once African Americans are engaged in the political process, blacks and whites participate at virtually the same rates (Verba, Schlozman, and Brady 1995). There also is a gender gap in participation, although the direction and nature of the gap has been changing since the 1960s. Women are now more likely to vote than are men, but men are more engaged in other forms of political activity. Differences in socialization, job experiences, and family responsibilities, as well as embeddedness in recruitment networks, are likely causes (Burns, Schlozman, and Verba 2001; Lawless and Fox 2010). To varying degrees, both race and gender have become less relevant as predictors of political participation as scholars become better at controlling for the various ways that socialization, wealth, work experiences, and other variables have differential impacts by race and gender.

Age differences in political engagement are also apparent. Most studies of participation over the lifespan find a curvilinear distribution: participation is fairly low among the young, increases as individuals approach middle age, peaks in the early to mid-sixties, and then declines (Jennings 1979; Jennings and Markus 1988; Wolfinger and Rosenstone 1980; but also see Rosenstone and Hansen 1993 who find no evidence of a decline in later life). When other major influences, including social class, are considered, the distribution flattens out some, but the atrophy of involvement for seniors typically remains significant (Schlozman, Verba, and Brady 2013).

Here, too, the variable of interest can be thought of as a surrogate for a variety of psychological, biological, and social developments over the course of a lifetime (Glenn 1974; Jennings and Markus 1988). Strate, Parrish, Elder, and Ford (1989), for instance, argue that everyday political experiences accrue over time such that, ceteris paribus, older people are more politically knowledgeable than the young, and thus more likely to participate in politics. Wolfinger and Rosenstone (1980) come to a like conclusion. They find that young adults with the highest levels of education vote at a rate of about 80 percent, while the least educated turn out at a rate of about 20 percent. Yet from early adulthood to old age, voting among the least educated increases by about thirty percentage points; among the most educated, it increases by only ten points. Thus, they conclude that "life experience is a substitute for school" (Wolfinger and Rosenstone 1980, 60).

In a similar vein, others argue that participation is self-reinforcing, and the participation habit strengthens over the lifespan (Plutzer 2002; Gerber and Green 2000; Gerber, Green, and Shachar 2003). Likewise, partisan attachments tend to intensify the longer they are held (Strate et al. 1989; Campbell et al. 1960; Sears and Levy 2003).

Finally, aging may also reflect the strengthening of ties to community as individuals becomes less mobile and more integrated into communities after they marry and have children. Community ties may change in old age, though, especially with changes in residence upon retirement. Given contemporary arguments about the importance of social capital and community context in encouraging participation (Putnam 2000; Huckfeldt and Sprague 1995), a loss of embeddedness in social networks may be a particularly negative influence on the participation of the elderly (Granovetter 1985).

While there are many studies of participation that incorporate age into their models, studies of participation among the elderly are few. Consequently, little is understood regarding the factors that influence the level of civic engagement among the elderly, despite a body of literature that demonstrates the tangible benefits of engagement later in life (Musick and Wilson 2003; Chappell 1999). The reason is that most data sources do not have a sufficient number of seniors to enable finely tuned analysis of this group.

One exception is Jennings and Markus's (1988) panel study of the parents of high school seniors—first interviewed in 1969 and reinterviewed in 1973 and 1982. In the final wave of interviews, 340 of the 898 parent-respondents were considered "old" (over sixty-five), the great majority between sixty-five and seventy-four. They find entering old age is associated with some decline in the more demanding kinds of participation, such as working to solve a community problem, but little change in less-demanding activities such as contacting public officials to communicate an opinion, or in attention to politics and government. Because few of the respondents were older than seventy-five, little could be said about participation rates among the "old-old."[1] Nor did survey items specifically inquire as to the reasons for falloff in participation.

Thus while it would seem evident that declining health and mobility in old age necessarily affect civic involvement, data sources with both sufficient numbers of elderly in the sample and specific questions for assessing the effects of physical change in old age have been absent. In this study we draw on a survey of elderly African Americans that includes various indicators of physical decline thought to affect participation.

DATA AND METHODS

The analysis is based on data collected from the Lifespan Investigation of Family, Health, and Environment (LIFHE) survey administered by the Healthier Black Elders Center—a joint collaboration between Wayne State University's Institute of Gerontology and the University of Michigan's Institute of Social Research. The goal of the Healthier Black Elders Center is to encourage older African American adults to consider participating in research projects. The center hosts community outreach educational events available to seniors at no cost. Attendees are invited to join the center's participant research pool, which signals the individual's openness to participate in research, but does not imply a commitment to do so.

Participants were included in the sample if they were of African American ethnicity and over the age of fifty-five; they were excluded if they did not speak English, had hearing difficulties that prevented clear communication over the telephone, or were unable to understand the survey due to cognitive difficulties. Participants who completed an interview received a $15 gift card for a national drug store chain.

The resulting sample consists of 501 community-dwelling respondents in independent living situations. Many of them lived in senior apartments, but none resided in nursing homes. The majority of the sample (82.6 percent) live in the city of Detroit, and the remainder reside in the larger metropolitan area. By way of comparison, 11.5 percent of Detroit residents are sixty-five years of age or older and 82.7 percent are African American (US Census 2010). Our data, as a nonprobability sample, offer limited generalizability to either the general population of elders or the population of African

American seniors. Thus we approach this work as a demonstration study with an eye toward understanding the relationships between civic participation and a set of variables that gauge the influence of standard predictors such as social class, civic attitudes, and embeddedness in community, as well as several indicators of physical and mobility limitations.

Our measure of civic participation is based on a battery of questions that asks about a diverse set of civic activities—from voting in an election to working on a community project to volunteering for a political campaign. The complete series is listed in appendix A. The items scale well, with a reliability coefficient of 0.82, and thus we begin by constructing an index of these items as an indicator of political participation broadly considered.

However, we know that some types of participation are more demanding than others. Verba and Nie (1972) distinguish four "modes" of conventional political participation: voting, campaigning, communal or cooperative activities, and personalized contacts. Verba, Nie, and Kim (1971) demonstrate that these modes are common across many nations, and Jankowski and Strate (1995) confirm that the voting and campaign modes are invariant across age groups. Principle components analysis of our participation items also suggests the existence of three separate dimensions of participation similar to the modes discerned by Verba and Nie. The results are displayed in table 1.

The first dimension consists of working on community projects, going to clubs or community meetings, attending public meetings in which there was discussion of community affairs, and working with others to solve a community problem. Keeping with the Verba and Nie terminology, we label this *communal* participation. A second component consists of the partisan political activities of wearing campaign buttons and displaying political yard signs, trying to persuade others to vote for or against a candidate, doing volunteer work for a political campaign, voting in an election, and making monetary contributions to political candidates, parties, or organizations, and we call this the *campaigning* dimension.[2]

Two of the three items that load on a third factor—contacting public officials about issues and submitting a letter or article for publication—are in the vein of Verba and Nie's *contacting* mode. The third item—trying to change local policies in a place like a school, workplace, or neighborhood—seems on its face to be more a communal activity, but we keep it in this dimension because of the empirical evidence, and we label this factor *contacting* participation. The Chronbach's reliability coefficients for these dimensions are 0.82 for the four-item communal dimension, 0.68 for the five-item campaigning factor, and 0.53 for the three-item contacting component. Thus our dependent variables include three index variables that tap traditional categories of political participation (Verba and Nie 1972)—communal, campaigning, and contacting—and one that captures overall political participation more comprehensively. The distribution of these variables is displayed in table 3.

Table 1. Rotated component matrix for participation items

	COMPONENT		
	Communal Participation	*Electoral Participation*	*Contacting Participation*
Wore political campaign button, put campaign sticker on car, or campaign sign in window or in front of house	0.153	0.741*	-0.039
Tried to change local policies in a place like a school, workplace, or neighborhood	0.455	0.113	0.545*
Worked on a community project	0.767*	0.132	0.259
Have you gone to a club or community meeting	0.857*	0.111	-0.048
Attended any public meetings in which there was discussion of community affairs	0.804*	0.204	-0.001
Submitted a letter or article for a magazine, newspaper, or online publication	0.024	0.020	0.753*
Contacted a public official about an issue of concern to you	0.215	0.447	0.472*
Worked with other people in your neighborhood to try to solve a community problem	0.651*	0.130	0.360
Tried to talk to at least one person to explain why they should vote for or against a political party or candidate	0.058	0.634*	0.210
Did volunteer work for a political campaign	0.259	0.549*	0.366
Voted in an election	0.066	0.550*	-0.255
Made a monetary donation to a political candidate, party or organization	0.125	0.610*	0.261

Principal component analysis with varimax rotation (Kaiser normalization, rotation converged in five iterations).
* indicates factor on which item loads most strongly.

Because the survey was designed primarily for the purpose of assessing the physical and mental health of participants, it has the virtue of including many indicators of the health and lifestyle of the elderly, and we explore those factors in detail. The drawback of the survey is that it does not include questions tapping attitudes known to be related to political participation, most notably, strength of partisanship and interest in politics. Although this is a limitation that will diminish the explanatory power of our models, the inclusion of indicators of physical well-being and community integration offer the possibility of additional insight into the civic participation of the elderly.

Table 2. Distribution of participation scores

	N	Minimum	Maximum	Mean	Standard Deviation
Global participation	501	0.00	12.00	6.43	3.15
Communal mode	501	0.00	4.00	2.40	1.55
Contacting mode	501	0.00	3.00	0.97	0.96
Campaign mode	501	0.00	6.00	3.56	1.72
Age	501	55.00	95.00	70.73	8.62
Gender	501	1.00	2.00	1.14	0.35
Education	500	1.00	5.00	3.92	0.89
Efficacy	499	0.00	12.00	9.63	2.76
Religiosity	501	0.00	3.00	2.28	0.79
Community integration	501	19.00	50.00	43.88	6.01
Pain level	500	0.00	3.00	1.24	1.16
Disability	501	0.00	1.00	0.48	0.50
Cognitive decline	501	0.00	1.00	0.30	0.46
Drive sat	501	0.00	10.00	7.21	4.09

Our explanatory variables can be classified as to whether they are customarily used in analyses of political participation. Among the variables ordinarily seen as predictive of participation is *age*, which is measured to the nearest year. Our primary indicator of socioeconomic status is level of *education*, measured in steps from 1 to 5: less than eighth grade, some high school, high school graduate or GED holder, some college or technical schools, college graduate.

Political efficacy is an indexed variable that uses the traditional, three-item measure: (1) "I don't have any say about what the government does," (2) "Sometimes politics and government seem so complicated that I can't really understand what's going on," and (3) "I don't think public officials care much about what I think." Scores vary from 0 (for those who completely lack efficacious responses) to 12 (for those who give the most efficacious response on all three questions). Although the American National Election Study now uses separate measures to tap internal and external efficacy, Craig, Niemi, and Silver (1990) find that the older measure is adequate in that it captures elements of both types of efficacy.

Our measure of *religiosity* is derived from the question, "How often do you go to church?" where response categories are: never, sometimes, often, or always. Because there was a high number of missing values for this item, we imputed the series mean to avoid dropping cases from analysis. Our measure of community ties is based on a ten-item instrument that was originally developed to assess the sense of belonging and social participation of individuals with disabilities such as traumatic brain injury (McColl et al. 1998). In responding to statements such as "I feel like part of this community, like I belong here" and "I have something to do in this community during the main part of my day that is useful and productive," individuals choose from five response categories that range from "strongly agree" to "strongly disagree." The entire series is listed in appendix B. The measure has been validated as psychometrically sound (Griffen, Hanks, and Meachen 2010; McColl et al. 2001), and the instrument measures integration with the general population as well as with a rehabilitation population (McColl et al. 2001). Although the *community integration* measure has not been used in studies of civic participation, it appears to tap into the broad concept of social connectedness, which Putnam (2000) and others argue has important implications for social capital (Uslaner 1999; Fuchs, Shapiro, and Minnite 2005).

The analysis includes a second set of variables that have not, to our knowledge, been previously used as predictors of participation. Three are indicators of physical and mental changes that uniquely affect the aging population. Respondents were asked whether they were often troubled with pain during the past year and, if so, to rate the severity of the pain. The resulting *pain* variable is coded as 0 for no pain, 1 for mild pain, 2 for moderate pain, and 3 for severe pain. We also calculate a *disability* dummy variable based on their answers to the question, "Are you currently disabled?" (0 = no, 1 = yes). *Cognitive decline* is also a dummy, constructed on answers to the question, "Are your memory, thinking skills, or ability to reason worse than a year ago?" with "no" coded as 0 and "yes" as 1.

A final question asks whether respondents currently drive and, if so, how satisfied they are with their ability to drive where and when they need. Answers are coded into a *drive* variable with values ranging from 0, if respondents do not currently drive, to 10, if they are very satisfied with their ability to drive where and when they want.

The distribution of these variables in the sample is illustrated in table 3. Respondents were between the ages of fifty-five and ninety-five with a mean age of 70.73 years (SD = 8.6 years). The sample is 86.2 percent female, which reflects a somewhat greater proportion of females than in the Detroit older adult cohort of 70 percent (Chapleski 2002) but is not inconsistent with other studies of older, African American adults (e.g., Dennis and Neese 2000; Manly et al. 2004). Respondents are well educated, with the mean indicating that the typical respondent has some college or technical school education. In addition to gender, the distributions of two other variables are highly skewed.

Frequency of church attendance exhibits a strong negative skew, with 84 percent indicating that they often or always attend. We could not locate studies of religious participation rates among the African American elderly, but the Pew Research Center (2009) reports that 79 percent of blacks say that religion is very important to them, whereas only 56 percent of the general population do so. Among African Americans of all ages, 53 percent say they attend religious services at least once a week, compared to 39 percent of the total population. There is also a tendency for churchgoing to be more frequent among the elderly (Pew Research Center 2009). Thus while our figures are skewed, we suspect they are reflective of the general population of black elderly.

The sample scores well on community integration, with a mean score of 45 out of a possible high score of 50, higher than the mean of 34 that McColl finds among a sample of community college students who volunteered to participate in her study. We suspect that this is a product of the method in which individuals were recruited into the participant resource pool,

Table 3. Bivariate correlations of predictor variables with participation scores

	Age	Male	Education	Efficacy	Religiosity	Com. Integration	Pain Level	Disability	Cognitive Decline	Drive Sat
GLOBAL										
Pearson's r	-0.001	0.038	0.275**	0.230**	0.078	0.216**	-0.104*	-0.079	-0.127**	0.132**
Significance	0.985	0.400	0.000	0.000	0.083	0.000	0.020	0.079	0.004	0.003
N	501	501	500	499	501	501	500	501	501	501
COMMUNAL										
Pearson's r	0.027	0.057	0.229**	0.166**	0.062	0.240**	-0.120**	-0.066	-0.126**	0.099*
Significance	0.553	0.206	0.000	0.000	0.167	0.000	0.007	0.140	0.005	0.027
N	501	501	500	499	501	501	500	501	501	501
CONTACTING										
Pearson's r	-0.013	0.041	0.228**	0.193**	0.038	0.076	-0.110*	-0.070	-0.124**	0.100*
Significance	0.772	0.359	0.000	0.000	0.402	0.087	0.014	0.115	0.006	0.026
N	501	501	500	499	501	501	500	501	501	501
CAMPAIGN										
Pearson's r	0.045	0.006	0.287**	0.248**	0.079	0.152**	-0.080	-0.108*	-0.081	0.181**
Significance	0.313	0.897	0.000	0.000	0.078	0.001	0.073	0.016	0.069	0.000
N	501	501	500	499	501	501	500	501	501	501

$*$ p < 0.05, $**$ p < 0.01

which resulted into the self-selection of those with already high levels of community involvement.[3]

Our expectations begin with the assumption that the processes that lead to participation in the general population also apply to the elderly population. Verba and Nie (1972) find that regardless of the mode of participation, socioeconomic status affects participation, as does one's sense of political efficacy. Similarly, although community integration has not to our knowledge been tested across modes of participation, the fact is that it clearly taps into the respondent's sense of embeddedness, and there is strong evidence that such networks are strongly related to political participation, which suggests that it will consistently exert a positive influence across the four modes.

Indicators of health have not been directly tested in political participation studies, and in the absence of previous research findings to draw upon, we begin by hypothesizing that pain, disability, and cognitive decline depress participation. Similarly, to our knowledge there is no research on the relationship between access to transportation and political participation. However, several studies demonstrate that the accessibility of polling places results in higher voter turnout (Gimpel and Schuknecht 2003), and the General Accounting Office (2008) has recently documented the importance of transportation as a potential barrier to voting for the elderly and handicapped. Driving mobility would seem to be connected to types of participation that require transportation, such as group-based, communal, and campaigning participation, but unrelated to participation that can largely be done from one's home, such as contacting.

FINDINGS

We begin by examination of the bivariate correlations of all independent variables with the four modes of participation, which are displayed in table 3. While most variables exhibit a significant relationship with at least one of the modes of participation, gender, age, and religiosity all fail to attain statistical significance with any of our participation measures. The small and statistically insignificant relationship of these variables with participation is illustrated in figure 1. There we bifurcate the sample, first by gender, then by age (fifty-five to sixty-four and sixty-five to ninety-five), and church attendance (those reporting they never or sometimes attend are compared to those reporting they often or always attend). In each of these cases, the height of the bars indicating mean participation levels is virtually the same for the two contrasted categories.

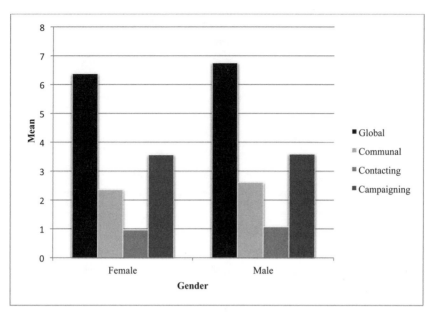

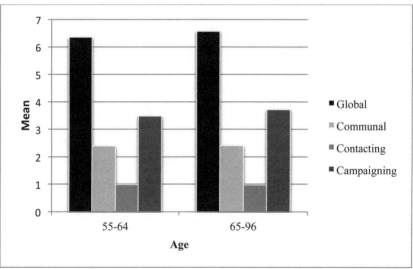

If the sample had been drawn from the general population, this would be a surprising finding, given the strong relationships found in previous research. With a sample of African American seniors, this is less troubling. For instance, given the preponderance of women in the sample and the small gender gaps in participation rates found in general population surveys, the failure of gender to achieve standard significance levels is unremarkable.

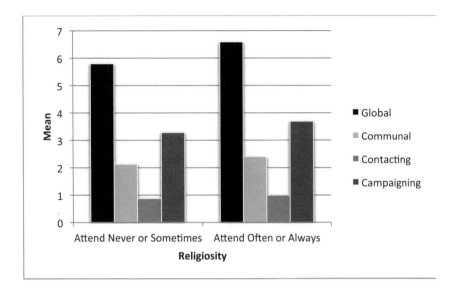

At first glance, the failure of age to attain significance is more surprising. General population studies find a strong curvilinear relationship between age and political engagement, with participation rates rising from early adulthood through late middle age and then declining in retirement years. Our sample, though, is drawn from the age range where the curve begins to flatten as the relationship diminishes and perhaps reverses. Additionally, the nonrandom nature of our sample leaves open the possibility that we may have selected respondents who are more active than the general population of African American seniors.

However, it may be that participation decline in old age has been exaggerated. Table 4 lists the percentage of respondents who engage in specific activities by age group for three different data sources. In the first section are the figures from the LIFHE study. The percentage of those aged sixty-five to ninety-five engaging in a specific activity is lower than the younger group on four of the activities and higher on eight activities. Only once, on monetary contributions to campaigns, is the difference in participation statistically significant. The second section illustrates differences for African American respondents by age groups for similar items asked in the 2008 American National Election Study. Again the differences are modest and inconsistent. In this survey older respondents were significantly less likely to engage in an activity only for displaying political signs and buttons.

In the third section we have reproduced the findings with similar survey items reported by Jennings and Markus (1988). These data are from a

Table 4. Political activity by age group

Percentage who . . .	Age 55–64	Age 65–95
Tried to change local policies in a place like a school, workplace, or neighborhood	35	29
Worked on a community project	52	56
Attended a club or community meeting	72	69
Attended a public meeting in which there was discussion of community affairs	65	67
Submitted a letter or article for a magazine, newspaper, or online publication	13	16
Contacted a public official about an issue of concern	50	51
Worked with other people in neighborhood to solve community problem	50	49
Wore campaign button, campaign sticker on car, placed campaign sign at house	58	65
Did volunteer work for a political campaign	34	36
Voted in an election	95	97
Made a monetary donation to a political candidate, party, or organization	42	55**
Talked to at least one person to explain why they should vote for or against a political party or candidate	70	67

Source: LIFHE

Percentage who . . .	Age 55–64	Age 65–95
Wore a campaign button or posted a sign or bumper sticker	37	28*
Did volunteer work for a political campaign	10	4
Voted in presidential election (2004)	69	78
Made a monetary donation to a political candidate, party, or organization	13	11
Talked to at least one person to explain why they should vote for or against a political party or candidate	50	49

Source: 2008 American National Election Study

| Percentage who . . . | Mean Age | | |
	53	61	70
Displayed slogans	25	19	15b, c
Donated to campaigns	24	23	21
Tried to influence others	41	30a	23 b, c
Attended political meetings	26	21	19c
Engaged in other political acts	13	9	9

Source: Youth Panel Socialization Study (Jennings and Markus 1988)

** p < 0.01; * p < 0.05 (two-tailed); a p < 0.05 for difference between the 1965 and 1973; b p < 0.05 for 1973 and 1985 percentages; c p < 0.05 for 1965 and 1982 percentages (two-tailed)

Table 5. Models of civic participation without religion, age, financial status.

	PARTICIPATION MODE			
	Global Participation	*Communal Mode*	*Contacting Mode*	*Campaign Mode*
Constant	-2.35	-1.47	-0.44	-0.51
Education	0.76***	0.28***	0.18***	0.36***
	(0.15)	(0.08)	(0.05)	(0.09)
	0.17	*0.16*	*0.17*	*0.19*
Efficacy	0.19***	0.05*	0.05**	0.12***
	(0.05)	(0.03)	(0.02)	(0.03)
	0.17	*0.09*	*0.14*	*0.19*
Community Integration	0.09***	0.05***	0.01	0.03*
	(0.02)	(0.01)	(0.01)	(0.01)
	0.17	*0.21*	*0.04*	*0.10*
Pain	-0.21+	-0.13*	-0.07	-0.03
	(0.12)	(0.06)	(0.04)	(0.07)
	-0.08	*-0.09*	*-0.08*	*-0.02*
Disability	0.09	0.12	0.12	-0.07
	(0.30)	(0.15)	(0.11)	(0.16)
	0.01	*0.04*	*0.07*	*-0.03*
Cognitive Decline	-0.54+	-0.31*	-0.19*	-0.13
	(0.29)	(0.15)	(0.09)	(0.16)
	-0.08	*-0.09*	*-0.09*	*-0.03*
Drive	0.07*	0.02	0.01	0.06**
	(0.03)	(0.02)	(0.01)	(0.02)
	0.09	*0.04*	*0.05*	*0.13*
R2 Adj.	0.17	0.11	0.08	0.13

Entries indicate unstandardized regression coefficients, standard errors (in parentheses), and standardized coefficients (in italics).

*** p < 0.001; ** p < 0.01; * p < 0.05; + p < 0.10 (two-tailed)

panel study in which the same individuals were interviewed three times over a seventeen-year interval. The table indicates the participation rate in the initial 1965 interviews, when the average age of respondents was fifty-three, again for the 1973 wave when the mean age was sixty-one, and finally for the 1982 interviews when the average age of respondents was seventy. Unlike the figures in the previous two groups, these are not exclusive to black respondents. Comparing the mean age of fifty-three to the mean of sixty-one, we see a general decline in participation rates, although only the activity of trying to influence another's vote is significant. From sixty-one to seventy, too, we note a general decline, but here none of the differences is statistically significant. Even comparison of the difference from the earliest wave to the latest wave finds significant declines only for trying to influence others and displaying slogans.

Another unexpected finding is the nonsignificant association between religiosity and participation. General population surveys typically find this relationship to be a strong one, but in this sample there is little variation in religiosity. Only 4.6 percent report never attending church while over 84 percent attend frequently or always. In addition, the measure taps only one aspect of religiosity and omits other indicators such as affiliation with a religion, participation in other church-related activities, and hearing politicized talks at places of worship. More importantly, it is not clear that the behavior of going to religious services has the same outcomes in the elderly population as in the general population. The effects of a lifetime of attendance may have accrued such that in old age it matters less whether one currently goes every week, and more whether one has in the past been a regular churchgoer.

It is possible that with more refined measures and a probability sample, the effects of age and religiosity could be more readily discerned. For now, though, we excluded these variables from our multivariate analysis, where participation is modeled as a function of a set of factors known to affect engagement in the general population, as well as a set of health and mobility variables thought to be more prevalent among the elderly. Table 5 presents the results, first for the summary participation score, and then for each of the three modes of participation.

Education exhibits the predicted positive impact. The standardized coefficient is virtually identical across the four models, indicating that the effect is approximately the same regardless of the type of participation being measured. Efficacy, too, consistently exerts a positive influence, although the magnitude varies with the type of participation examined. It is larger and more highly significant for campaigning and for the summary measure, more modest for the communal and contacting modes. Community integration has a nonsignificant impact on the more individualized activities of contacting participation, but positive and significant effects on the other measures. Its largest impact is on the communal mode where community ties are likely to both motivate individuals to participate and embed citizens in networks of recruitment.

The results for health indicators are more mixed. For two of our health indicators, the effect on participation depends on the mode. Pain produces the expected negative coefficients for all types of participation, but it attains standard significance levels only for communal participation and the summary score. Cognitive decline also yields negative coefficients, although it is not significant for campaign activities.

The effect of disability, however, is not consistent with our expectations. Although the zero-order correlation of disability with each mode of participation is negative, on three of the four dimensions, respondents who think of themselves has having a disability are more likely to participate than those who do not. Coefficients are not significant, but the positive signs for all four models suggest further investigation.

Finally, satisfaction with one's access to a car and the ability to use it is significant only for campaigning and global participation. Since this mode includes voting, the finding supports those studies that point to the role of accessibility of polling places in affecting turnout rates.

In sum, the effect of the standard predictors is fairly consistent across modes. The one clear exception is the lack of effect of community integration on contacting, and this difference can logically be pinned to the more solitary nature of contacting activities relative to other modes of participation. The effect of health and mobility variables is more uneven. Communal participation is affected by pain and cognitive decline, contacting by cognitive decline alone, and campaigning by the ability to access a car.

DISCUSSION

Although the nature of our sample does not provide conclusive generalization to elderly Americans, we believe it does offer valuable insights into factors that both encourage and discourage participation in old age. First, we do not find the same serious drop-off in participation after age sixty-five as has been documented elsewhere (Schlozman, Verba, and Brady 2013). While this may be reflective of our sample, or of African American participation differing in important ways from the general population, it is consistent with our analysis of black elderly from the American National Election Study and with the panel study Jennings and Markus (1988) reported. Rather, it suggests that declining participation in old age is not inevitable.

Second, we find that many traditional predictors of participation affect the elderly population in much the same way that they would be expected to affect the general population. For example, in general, higher levels of socioeconomic status (level of education in our analysis), political efficacy, and ties to the community (as measured by community integration levels) are each important and positive influences on levels of participation.

Third, our analysis explores a number of elderly specific considerations that have been previously underexamined. The findings are mixed. While pain and cognitive decline are negative influences, we find that these effects are significant for only some types of participation. Disability, which has been well documented as depressing participation, tended to affect participation positively if not significantly. Both of these findings would suggest that health considerations in the elderly population—a very obvious consideration for declining participation—might not be the depressant they may have been thought to be. Further study of these factors is warranted.

Our final finding indicates that studies that have evaluated overall (global participation in our analysis) may be clouding important features of elderly participation. Specifically, modes that are less physically demanding (such as our *contacting* mode) do not seem to experience a decline as individuals age. Different types of participation are affected in different ways or not at all by the factors considered in this analysis. In other words, even in the context of the new dynamics of old age, the elderly still *can* participate, *want* to participate, and are in social environments where they are *asked* to participate. With the largest single generation of Americans retiring, understanding these effects can be important in offering practical solutions to facilitating their continued participation.

APPENDIX A
LIFHE CIVIC ENGAGEMENT SURVEY ITEMS
I. Civic Participation Items

I will read you a list of activities that you may or may not have engaged in. For each activity, please tell me whether you have participated in that activity in the past twelve months.

(a) Have you gone to a club or community meeting?
(b) Worked on a community project?
(c) Attended any public meetings in which there was discussion of community affairs?
(d) Worked with other people in your neighborhood to try to solve a community problem?

(e) Submitted a letter or article for a magazine, newspaper, or online publication?

(f) Tried to change local policies in a place like a school, workplace, or neighborhood?

(g) Voted in an election?

(h) Wore a political campaign button, put a campaign sticker on your car, or placed a campaign sign in your window or in front of your house?

(i) Made a monetary donation to a political candidate, party or organization?

(j) Did volunteer work for a political campaign?

(k) Tried to talk to at least one person to explain why they should vote for or against a political party or candidate?

(l) Contacted a public official about an issue of concern to you?

(m) Allowed someone to live in your home or on your property for a period of time because they needed a place to live?[*]

(n) Gave food or money to someone who needed it?[*]

[*] Two items lacked face validity as indicators of civic engagement, did not load in a principal components analysis, and were not used in subsequent analyses.

APPENDIX B.
LIFHE COMMUNITY INTEGRATION SURVEY ITEMS

Now I'm going to read you a few statements and I'd like you to tell me how often you agree or disagree with them. Do you ALWAYS agree, SOMETIMES agree, FEEL NEUTRAL, SOMETIMES disagree, or ALWAYS disagree.

(a) I feel like part of this community, like I belong here.

(b) I know my way around this community.

(c) I know the rules in this community and I can fit in with them.

(d) I feel that I am accepted in this community.

(e) I can be independent in this community.

(f) I like where I am living now.

(g) There are people I feel close to in this community.

(h) I know a number of people in this community well enough to say hello and have them say hello back.

(i) There are things that I can do in this community for fun in my free time.

(j) I have something to do in this community during that main part of my day that is useful and productive.

NOTES

This research is supported in part by the president's Urban Research Enhancement Program, Wayne State University.

1. However, their panel design enables them to eliminate the effects of changes in cohort composition that might make older cohorts less well equipped to participate. For example, older cohorts are, on average, less educated than younger ones, and it may be this compositional difference, rather than aging itself, that influences lower participation rates among the elderly.
2. Unlike Verba and Nie (1972) our survey includes only one question about voting. Thus our classifications differ from theirs in that we have no separate voting mode; the one item asking whether the respondent voted in an election in the past year loads with the other campaign-related items.
3. For both these variables, we attempt to correct for the strong negative skew by substituting dummy variables based on the spiked category. Results are not substantially different from those obtained with the original variable, on which we base our reported findings.

WORKS CITED

Abramson, Paul R., and John H. Aldrich. 1982. "The Decline of Electoral Participation in America." *American Political Science Review* 76 (3): 502–21.

Bartels, L. M. 2000. "Partisanship and Voting Behavior, 1952–1996." *American Journal of Political Science* 44 (1): 35–50.

Berelson, Bernard, Paul F. Lazarsfeld, and William N. McPhee. 1954. *Voting: A Study of Opinion Formation in Presidential Campaign*. Chicago: University of Chicago Press.

Bobo, L., and F. D. Gilliam Jr. 1990. "Race, Sociopolitical Participation, and Black Empowerment." *American Political Science Review* 84 (2): 377–93.

Brady, Henry E., Sidney Verba, and Kay Lehman Schlozman. 1995. "Beyond SES: A Resource Model of Political Participation." *American Political Science Review* 89 (2): 271–94.

Burns, N., K. L. Schlozman, and S. Verba. 2001. *The Private Roots of Public Action: Gender, Equality, and Political Participation*. Cambridge, MA: Harvard University Press.

Caldeira, G. A., A. R. Clausen, and S. C. Patterson. 1990. "Partisan Mobilization and Electoral Participation." *Electoral Studies* 9 (3): 191–204. doi: 10.1016/0261-3794(90)90025-4.

Calhoun-Brown, Allison. 1996. "African American Churches and Political Mobilization: The Psychological Impact of Organizational Resources." *Journal of Politics* 58 (4): 935–53.

Campbell, Angus, Philip Converse, Warren Miller, and Donald Stokes. 1960. *The American Voter.* New York: John Wiley.

Campbell, David E., and Steven J. Yonish. 2003. "Religion and Volunteering in America." In *Religion as Social Capital: Producing the Common Good*, edited by Corwin Smidt, 87–106. Waco, TX: Baylor University Press.

Chapleski, Elizabeth. 2002. *Facing the Future: 2002 City of Detroit Needs Assessment of Older Adults.* Institute of Gerontology, Center for Urban Studies, Center for Healthcare Effectiveness Research. Detroit: Wayne State University.

Chappell, Neena L. 1999. "Volunteering and Healthy Aging: What We Know." For Volunteer Canada and Manulife Financial and Health Canada.

Cohen, Cathy, and Michael Dawson. 1993. "Neighborhood Poverty and African American Politics." *American Political Science Review* 87 (2): 286–302.

Craig, Stephen C., Richard G. Niemi, and Glenn E. Silver. 1990. "Political Efficacy and Trust: A Report on the NES Pilot Study Items." *Political Behavior* 12: 289–314.

Dawson, Michael C., Ronald Brown, and Richard Allen. 1990a. "Racial Belief Systems, Religious Guidance, and African-American Political Participation." *National Political Science Review* 2: 22–44.

———. 1990b. "Racial Belief Systems, Religious Guidance, and African-American Political Participation." In *Black Electoral Politics*, edited by Lucius Barker. New Brunswick, NJ: Transaction Publishers.

Dennis, Betty P., and Jane B. Neese. 2000. "Recruitment and Retention of African American Elders into Community-Based Research: Lessons Learned." *Archives of Psychiatric Nursing* 14 (1): 3–11.

Djupe, Paul A., and Christopher P. Gilbert. 2002. "The Political Voice of Clergy." *Journal of Politics* 64 (2): 596–609.

———. 2006. "The Resourceful Believer: Generating Civic Skills in Church." *Journal of Politics* 68 (1): 116–27.

Djupe, Paul A., Anand E. Sokhey, and Christopher P. Gilbert. 2007. "Present but Not Accounted For? Gender Differences in Civic Resource Acquisition." *American Journal of Political Science* 51 (4): 906–20.

Eldersveld, Samuel J. 1956. "Experimental Propaganda Techniques and Voting Behavior." *American Political Science Review* 50 (1): 54–165.

Eldersveld, Samuel J., and R. W. Dodge. 1954. *Personal Contact or Mail Propaganda? An Experiment in Voting and Attitude Change.* New York: Dryden Press.

Emig, A., M. Hesse, and S. Fischer. 1996. "Black-White Differences in Political Efficacy, Trust, and Sociopolitical Participation: A Critique of the Empowerment Hypothesis." Urban Affairs Review 32 (2): 264–76.

Finkel, Steve. 1985. "Reciprocal Effects of Participation and Political Efficacy: A Panel Analysis." *American Journal of Political Science* 29 (4): 891–913.

Finkel, Steven E., and Karl-Dieter Opp. 1991. "Party Identification and Participation in Collective Action." *Journal of Politics* 53: 339–71.

Fuchs, E., R. Shapiro, and L. Minnite. 2005. "Social Capital, Political Participation, and the Urban Community." In *Social Capital and Poor Communities,* edited by Susan Saegert, J. Phillip Thompson, and Mark R. Warren. New York: Sage.

General Accounting Office. 2008. "Elderly Voters: Some Improvements in Voting Accessibility from 2000 to 2004 Elections, but Gaps in Policy and Implementation Remain." Testimony before the Special Committee on Aging, United States Senate. Statement of Barbara D. Bovbjerg, Director, Education, Workforce, and Income Security, and William O. Jenkins, Director, Homeland Security and Justice.

Gerber, Alan S., and Donald P. Green. 2000. "The Effect of a Nonpartisan Get-Out-the-Vote Drive: An Experimental Study of Leafletting." *Journal of Politics* 62 (3): 846–57.

Gerber, Alan S., Donald P. Green, and Ron Shachar. 2003. "Voting May Be Habit-Forming: Evidence from a Randomized Field Experiment." *American Journal of Political Science* 47 (3): 540–50.

Gimpel, James G., and Jason E. Schuknecht. 2003. "Political Participation and the Accessibility of the Ballot Box." *Political Geography* 22 (5): 471–88.

Glenn, Norval. 1974. "Aging and Conservatism." *Annals of the American Academy of Political and Social Sciences* 415: 176–86.

Granovetter, Mark. 1985. "Economic Action and Social Structure: The Problem of Embeddedness." *American Journal of Sociology* 91 (3): 481–510.

Greeley, A. 1997. "The Other Civic America: Religion and Social Capital." *American Prospect* 32: 68–73.

Griffen, Julie A., Robin A. Hanks, and Sarah-Jane Meachen. 2010. "The Reliability and Validity of the Community Integration Measure in Persons with Traumatic Brain Injury." *Rehabilitation Psychology* 55 (3): 292–97.

Huckfeldt, Robert, and John Sprague. 1992. "Political Parties and Electoral Mobilization: Political Structure, Social Structure, and the Party Canvass." *American Political Science Review* 86: 70–86.

———. 1995. *Citizens, Politics, and Social Communication: Information and Influence in Political Campaigns.* Cambridge: Cambridge University Press.

Jackson, James S., Patricia Newton, Adrian Ostfield, Daniel Savage, and Edward L. Schneider, eds. 1988. *The Black American Elderly: Research on Physical and Psychosocial Health.* New York: Springer.

Jankowski, Thomas B., and John M. Strate. 1995. "Modes of Participation over the Adult Life Span." *Political Behavior* 17 (1): 89–106.

Jennings, M. Kent. 1979. "Another Look at the Life Cycle and Political Participation." *American Journal of Political Science* 23 (4): 755–71.

Jennings, M. Kent, and Gregory B. Markus. 1988. "Political Involvement in the Later Years: A Longitudinal Survey." *American Journal of Political Science* 32 (2): 302–16.

Kam, C. D. 2007. "When Duty Calls, Do Citizens Answer?" *Journal of Politics* 69 (1): 17–29.

Knack, S. 1994. "Does Rain Help the Republicans? Theory and Evidence on Turnout and the Vote." *Public Choice* 79 (1/2): 187–209.

Lawless, Jennifer L., and Richard L. Fox. 2010. *It Still Takes a Candidate: Why Women Don't Run for Office.* Rev. ed. Cambridge: Cambridge University Press.

Leighley, Jan E. 1995. "Attitudes, Opportunities, and Incentives: A Field Essay on Political Participation." *Political Research Quarterly* 48 (1): 181–209.

Manly, J. J., D. A Byrd, P. Touradji, and Y. Stern. 2004. "Acculturation, Reading Level, and Neuropsychological Test Performance among African American Elders." *Applied Neuropsychology: Adult* 11 (1): 37–46.

McClurg, Scott D. 2003. "Social Networks and Political Participation: The Role of Social Interaction in Explaining Political Participation." *Political Research Quarterly* 56 (4): 449–64.

McColl, Mary Ann, Peter Carlson, Jane Johnston, Patricia Minnes, K. Shue, Diane Davies, and T. Karlovits. 1998. "Definition of Community Integration: Perspectives of People with Brain Injuries." *Brain Injury* 12: 15–30.

McColl, Mary Ann, Diane Davies, Peter Carlson, Jane Johnston, and Patricia Minnes. 2001. "The Community Integration Measure: Development and Preliminary Validation." *Archives of Physical Medicine and Rehabilitation* 82: 429–34.

Milbrath, Lester W., and M. L. Goel. 1977. *Political Participation: How and Why Do People Get Involved in Politics?* 2nd ed. Boston: Rand McNally.

Musick, Marc A., and John Wilson. 2003. "Volunteering and Depression: The Role of Psychological and Social Resources in Different Age Groups." *Social Science and Medicine* 56 (2): 259–69.

Pew Research Center. 2009. "A Religious Portrait of African-Americans." *Forum on Religion and Public Life.* www.pewforum.org/A-Religious-Portrait-of-African-Americans.aspx. Accessed April 2, 2012.

Piven, F., and R. Cloward. 1988. *Why Americans Don't Vote.* New York: Pantheon Books.

Plutzer, Eric. 2002. "Becoming a Habitual Voter: Inertia, Resources, and Growth in Young Adulthood." *American Political Science Review* 96: 41–56.

Putnam, R. 2000. *Bowling Alone: The Collapse and Revival of American Community.* New York: Simon and Schuster.

Ramakrishnan, Subramanian, and Mark Baldassare. 2004. *The Ties That Bind: Changing Demographics and Civic Engagement in California.* San Francisco: Public Policy Institution of California.

Reese, L. A., and R. E. Brown. 1995. "The Effects of Religious Messages on Racial Identity and System Blame among African Americans. *Journal of Politics* 57 (01): 24–43.

Rosenstone, Steven J., and John Mark Hansen. 1993. *Mobilization, Participation, and Democracy in America.* New York: Macmillan.

Rule, Wilma L. B. 1977. "Political Alienation and Voting Attitudes among the Elderly Generation." *Gerontologist* 17: 400–404.

Schlozman, Kay Lehman, Sidney Verba, and Henry E. Brady. 2013. *The Unheavenly Chorus: Unequal Political Voice and the Broken Promise of American Democracy.* Princeton, NJ: Princeton University Press.

Sears, David O., and Sheri Levy. 2003. "Childhood and Adult Political Development." In *Oxford Handbook of Political Psychology*, edited by D. O. Sears, L. Huddy, and R. Jervis, 60–109. Oxford: Oxford University Press.

Shaffer, Stephen D. 1981. "A Multivariate Explanation of Decreasing Turnout in Presidential Elections, 1960–1976." *American Journal of Political Science* 25 (1): 68–95.

Shields, Todd G., Kay Fletcher Schriner, and Ken Schriner. 1998. "The Disability Voice in American Politics: Political Participation of People with Disabilities in the 1994 Election." *Journal of Disability Policy Studies* 9: 33.

Shingles, Richard D. 1981. "Black Consciousness and Political Participation: The Missing Link." *American Political Science Review* 75 (1): 76–91.

Smidt, Corwin E., John Green, James Guth, and Lyman Kellstedt. 2003. "Religious Involvement, Social Capital, and Political Engagement: A Comparison of the United States and Canada." In *Religion as Social Capital: Producing the Common Good*, edited by Corwin E. Smidt, 153–70. Waco, TX: Baylor University Press.

Strate, John M., Charles J. Parrish, Charles D. Elder, and Coit Ford III. 1989. "Life Span Civic Development and Voting Participation." *American Political Science Review* 83 (2): 443–64.

Tate, Katherine. 1994. *Black Faces in the Mirror: African Americans and Their Representatives.* Princeton, NJ: Princeton University Press.

Teixeira, Ruy A. 1992. *The Disappearing American Voter.* Washington, DC: Brookings Institution.

US Census Bureau. 2010. *State and County Quick Facts.* http://quickfacts.census. gov/qfd/states/26/2622000.html. Retrieved April 4, 2012.

Uslaner, Eric M. 1999. "Democracy and Social Capital." In *Democracy and Trust*, edited by Mark Warren. Cambridge: Cambridge University Press.

———. 2002. *The Moral Foundations of Trust.* Cambridge: Cambridge University Press.

Verba, Sidney, and Norman H. Nie. 1972. *Participation in America: Political Democracy and Social Equality.* New York: Harper and Row.

Verba, Sidney, Norman H. Nie, and Jae-on Kim. 1971. *The Modes of Democratic Participation: A Cross-National Comparison.* Beverly Hills, CA: Sage.

Verba, Sidney, Kay Schlozman, and Henry Brady. 1995. *Voice and Equality: Civic Voluntarism in American Politics.* Cambridge, MA: Harvard University Press.

Wald, Kenneth D., Dennis Owen, and Samuel S. Hill Jr. 1988. "Church as Political Communities." *American Political Science Review* 82: 531–48.

Wielhouwer, Peter W., and Brad Lockerbie. 1994. "Party Contacting and Political Participation, 1952–90." *American Journal of Political Science* 38 (1): 211–29.

Wolfinger, Raymond E., and Steven J. Rosenstone. 1980. *Who Votes?* New Haven, CT: Yale University Press.

12

"ACTIVE AGING" AS CITIZENSHIP IN POLAND

· · · · · · · · · ·

JESSICA C. ROBBINS-RUSZKOWSKI

INTRODUCTION AND METHODOLOGY

Political-economic transformations in Poland in recent decades, marked by the shift to a market economy in 1989 and EU membership in 2004, have brought about changes both in macrolevel political-economic structures and in microlevel experiences and understandings of citizenship. That is, changes in the state and nation happened concurrently with changes in individual lives and imaginations. The fall of state socialism meant not only the introduction of a multiparty political system, a democratically elected government, and the embrace of the free market, but also entailed transformations in Polish citizens' possible work, family, and life trajectories. As much interdisciplinary scholarship on Eastern Europe has demonstrated (e.g., Einhorn 1993), opposing the former socialist state sometimes corresponded with right-wing nationalism. In postsocialist Poland, it is common for far-right politicians to criticize the socialist past and look to other historical periods for models of morality—namely, the time of partitions (1772–1918). (In this light, the years under Soviet rule [1945–89] are often seen as the final partition.) Along with denouncing the socialist past, these politicians imagine the Polish nation as independent, ethnically homogenous, Catholic, and anticommunist. This ideology became especially prominent in 2005, when the president and prime minister were both from the Prawo i Sprawiedliwość

(PiS, or Law and Justice) Party, which won elections with an anticorruption, anticommunist platform. For PiS, citizenship in contemporary Poland is tied to "traditional" family values as taught by the Catholic Church and evident in patriarchal gender roles (see Graff 2009).

Since 1989, age has become a marker of citizenship and political affiliation. For example, elections of the past decade show distinct differences in voting patterns, wherein older Poles have voted overwhelmingly for the far-right nationalist Catholic party, and younger Poles have voted overwhelmingly for the center-right neoliberal EU-oriented party.[1] This disparity in voting patterns is common knowledge, and Poles of all ages mention the far-right conservatism of the oldest generations in conversation—often unkindly. The following brief examples from recent years show the extent to which age and generation are used to index political worldviews.

Before parliamentary elections in 2007 a widely circulated image depicted a large group of older women wearing characteristic wool caps (*moherowe berety*, or mohair berets) attending what is presumably a mass, with the caption "VOTE, or they'll do it for you!"[2] This image was meant to motivate younger people to vote and did so through a demonization of elderly women for their presumed politico-religious views. As part of a get-out-the-vote campaign, another ad urged, "steal your grandmother's identity card!" (thereby preventing her from voting). Crucially, it is not just older people who are seen as threatening, but specifically older *women*. In other words, older women come to stand in for all older people, and are thus associated with the conservative nationalist views of PiS and its media supporters, such as Radio Maryja.[3] Notably, it is when older women are seen as citizens that they become dangerous; one such older woman is harmless, but a large number of women attending a mass—a voting bloc— is dangerous.

More recently, controversies following the tragic plane crash in April 2010, which killed the Polish president and many top governmental officials, took on a generational contour. Many who protested the burial of the president and first lady in the crypts of Wawel Cathedral in the royal capital of Kraków were young, while those protesting the removal of a large cross in front of the presidential palace in Warsaw tended to be older.[4] This centrality of older generations to particular aspects of the national political scene contrasts with the marginalization of older people in most other spheres of life.

These political differences between young and old, however, have a complex relationship to the socialist past. In popular media and casual conversations, these political differences have come to suggest that older Poles are living in the socialist—and therefore backward—past, while younger Poles inhabit the present, modern world, from which Poland's future will develop.[5] These assumptions prevent older Poles from being coeval with their fellow citizens (Fabian 1983). In response to such marginalization, and with EU funding, NGOs and other organizations have developed a mission of transforming these "backward" older Poles into what some call "Euro-seniors"— that is, proper citizens of the EU. This mission takes place through a range of activities; especially common are courses in foreign languages, computer skills, health, and communication. Yet other continuing education institutions, Uniwersytety Trzeciego Wieku (UTW, or Universities of the Third Age), with different funding sources, have offered similar kinds of programming in Poland for over thirty years. And both types of institutions currently cultivate "*aktywność*," or "activity," among their participants as a morally desirable practice of aging. This has resonances with what is called "active aging," which has become increasingly popular and desirable among both gerontologists and American and Western European publics.[6] Indeed, the EU recently declared 2012 the "European Year for Active Ageing and Solidarity between Generations."

These types of binary contrasts between a progressive, forward-looking (Western) Europe and a "backward" regressive Eastern Europe have a long history (see Chirot 1989 for an analysis that relies on such a contrast; see Galbraith 2004 and Wolff 1994 for ethnographic and historical analyses of this contrast). Eastern Europeans have long been understood to have different forms of personhood (e.g., Dunn 2004) as well as different forms of nationality (Zubrzycki 2001; 2002).[7] Both types of distinctions posit a fundamental difference between Western and Eastern Europeans that is often rooted in conceptions of history, and specifically in Cold War oppositions of socialism and capitalism (though these distinctions in fact have a deeper history). Because these tropes of difference encompass not only citizenship but personhood as well, such Cold War oppositions affect not only the obviously political dimensions of people's lives, but also fundamental shared understandings about what it is to be a person.

Although the scholarship uses such distinctions as heuristic models rather than to explain literal differences, these models obscure the complexity of everyday lives and persons. Instead of throwing out such binaries altogether, however, I would like to hold them in the background of my analysis since Poles with whom I conducted fieldwork took up these categories themselves. That is, these are not only analytic distinctions, but also distinctions that Poles use to understand their worlds. Therefore I hope that by investigating the limits of such binaries I can work toward greater analytic and ethnographic clarity. In so doing, I draw on perspectives from kinship studies (Carsten 2000, 2007; Franklin and McKinnon 2001) showing that politics, history, memory, and lived experiences of relatedness must be analyzed together. By relatedness, I mean the processual formation and unraveling of kinship ties that need not be bound by blood or marriage. I argue that these educational institutions foster new forms of citizenship, relatedness, and personhood among older Poles that are gendered and historically contingent, but not easily identifiable with either socialist or capitalist world orders.

My goals in this chapter, then, are threefold: first, to sidestep the problematic binaries that so often dominate research on Eastern Europe; second, to think about the relationship between citizenship and personhood; and third, to ask what sorts of temporalities and scales characterize contemporary forms of citizenship.

This chapter is based on eighteen months of ethnographic research in Wrocław and Poznań, two cities in western Poland, from 2008 to 2010. Throughout, I refer to citizenship in its processual form as experienced in everyday life, as ethnographically rather than quantitatively evident (Brubaker et al. 2006).) In my fieldwork, I interviewed around one hundred Poles (mostly over the age of sixty) and conducted participant observation at medical and educational institutions in each city. In what follows, I describe two educational institutions, both in Wrocław—an NGO-run program called @ktywny Senior, or @ctive Senior, and the Uniwersytet Trzeciego Wieku (UTW, or University of the Third Age).[8]

I first describe @ktywny Senior and the forms of citizenship it assumes and engenders. I then describe the University of the Third Age and give a brief case study to show what sorts of complexities analyzing experiences of older persons themselves can reveal. For both cases, I will ask how participants' experiences and institutional ideals both construct and reflect historical continuities and ruptures in citizenship, thus elucidating possibilities for inclusion in the contemporary Polish nation-state.[9]

@KTYWNY SENIOR

During my fieldwork, I kept encountering the words *"aktywny,"* or "active," *"aktywność,"* or "activity," and *"aktywizacja,"* or "activation" (or perhaps "mobilization"). These words appeared in UTWs and in the popular press on aging, but were most prominent at @ktywny Senior, an EU-funded NGO pilot program that ran for several months in 2008 that aimed at returning retirees to the workforce.[10] While these words often refer to physical activity, they suggest "activity" in broader spheres of life as well (see Berkel and Møller 2002 for a discussion of wide-ranging "active social policies" in Europe).[11] The program was started by Marek Ferenc, a former manager of a health clinic, who was inspired to start it after visiting a friend in a retirement community in British Columbia, where he was struck by the contrast to the isolated lives of retirees in his own neighborhood in Wrocław. He learned about Sun City, Arizona, and wanted to bring similar principles to Poland; the @ktywny Senior program was his first attempt to change the ways that older people experience and understand aging.[12] The program targeted seniors living in the surrounding 1970s-era *blokowisko*, or socialist-era bloc apartments. Marek later told me that he chose this neighborhood, Popowice, because 22 percent of inhabitants were above sixty, as compared to a citywide average of 13 percent.[13]

In conjunction with a local primary-care clinic, he recruited people by offering free ongoing medical screenings to retirees, on the condition that they attend this program, consisting of classes on healthy aging, communication, and computer skills. The primary goal was to create *"aktywność,"* or "activity," through teaching such concepts and practices as *"odpowiedzialny styl życia"* ("a responsible lifestyle"), *"negatywne konsekwencje życia nieodpowiedzialnego"* ("the negative consequences of an irresponsible lifestyle"), and *"integracja społeczna"* ("social integration"). Responsibility is needed, he said, because older people in Poland expect the doctor to have full responsibility for their health, as well as for pills to fix all their problems. This sense of responsibility for oneself, even in spheres as seemingly far removed from citizenship as doctors' visits, is implicitly contrasted to the patriarchal responsibility of the socialist state for the health of its citizens.

In addition to hosting lectures on preventive health behaviors such as proper diet and fitness, the @ktywny Senior program also included classes teaching computer skills and workshops on communication, to teach people how to communicate in the "new"—that is, postsocialist, transnational, technology-focused—world. The changes in social relations that occur through this program are intended to have political and economic effect; an implicit goal of the program was to return retirees to the capitalist workforce.[14] In particular, the program was intended for people who were forced into early retirement after 1989, many of whom were women. In an interview, the director of the @ktywny Senior program said that these people were marginalized because they were not part of the "computerization" of society that happened in the 1990s and 2000s.

This focus on "activity" is part of a broader European trend of encouraging "active aging," meant to address demographic shifts toward older populations in Europe, which threaten the solvency of social welfare systems. For instance, the "old age dependency ratio" in Poland is one of the highest in Europe and is predicted to increase from nineteen in 2010 to thirty-six in 2030; that is, in 2010 there were one hundred working persons for every nineteen persons over age sixty-five, and this is predicted to increase to one hundred working persons for every thirty-six persons over age sixty-five in 2030.[15] *Aktywność* can be seen as a way to keep the aging population healthier for longer. The ideal *aktywny* person still works or volunteers, has a vibrant social life that involves non-kinship-based relations, pursues hobbies, speaks at least one foreign language, travels internationally, and has basic computer skills.[16] Key components of *aktywność* are independence, openness (to new skills and new social connections), self-reliance, and self-care, suggesting similarities to neoliberal ideals (see Ong 2003 for an account of neoliberal citizenship in a different ethnographic context). Significantly, care giving rather than receiving is valued, which has serious implications for those who experience illness and disability in old age.

While the economic utility of active older adults is fundamental to this project, the economic is never isolated from the social or biological. At the end of the @ktywny Senior program, participants were encouraged to create slogans to represent their experiences of aging. I was struck by one slogan in particular: "*seniorzy też ludzie!*" or "seniors are people too!" I asked about this slogan in interviews, and participants strongly identified with it. For instance, Jadwiga, a seventy-year-old woman who still worked (at the time of the interview, as a private security guard on an overnight shift) described feeling "*niepotrzebna*," or "unnecessary," to younger Poles. Grażyna, a sixty-two-year-old former engineer who now works as an "*opiekunka*," or "care-giver," for an older German man for part of the year, claimed that older people's knowledge is not valued and their work is not respected in Poland, even though older people provide financial assistance to their families. This slogan captured people's negative experiences and reaffirmed their humanity, evident in capacities to learn new skills and form new relations.

It is worth asking how a slogan could become so powerful and contain the possibility for such affirmations of citizenship and personhood. Certainly, the social process of creating these slogans was a key source of their meaning. Participants described @ktywny Senior as providing them with new friends and opportunities to socialize with people of their own age. However, it is also worth examining the meaning of the form of the slogans themselves. The group created over a dozen slogans, such as *Do przodu Seniorzy!* (Forward, seniors!), *Seniorzy górą!* (Seniors rule!), and *Twój ruch!* (Your movement!). I repeated these slogans to several Poles ranging in age from twenty to seventy, who do not know the @ktywny Senior program, and asked them to comment. They paused, giggled, and then said that these phrases sound like socialist slogans. Indeed, these phrases share the quick rhythms and optimistic, forward-looking affect of socialist-era slogans, such as the famous *"Proletariusze wszystkich krajów, łączcie się!"* (usually translated in English as "Workers of the world, unite!"). This formal similarity suggests that there is more continuity between the socialist past and the postsocialist present than the participants or organizers would like to recognize. Indeed, even the EU uses such language, as in the headline of a recent newspaper advertisement sponsored by the European Social Fund directed toward NGO staff and businessmen: *"NGO-sy, przedsiębiorcy, jednostki samorządu terytorialnego—łączcie się!"* ("NGO'ers, entrepreneurs, local government administrators—unite!")[17] In their efforts to become more like Western European or American older adults, the participants in @ktywny Senior and its organizers rely on cultural forms that resonate with the socialist past. In other words, as participants and organizers engage in activities they envision as part of a modern, capitalist society, they create and inhabit the discourse of the very world they are trying to escape.

Yet the seeming dissonance between the westward-looking efforts of participants at @ktywny Senior and the historical legacy of socialism becomes less relevant when considering how people create citizenship and moral personhood through forming new social relations. That is, although there is a seeming conflict in a westward-looking program that encourages socialist-era practices among its participants, this distinction becomes less relevant when considering the social relations that make it possible for older Poles to assert their personhood, and thus their citizenship. At the UTW, such changes in social relations are even more apparent.

UNIVERSITY OF THE THIRD AGE

The UTW in Wrocław was founded in 1976, only three years after the first ever University of the Third Age in Toulouse. There are now almost four hundred such universities in Poland, with approximately 90,000 participants, around 85 percent of whom are women.[18] In Wrocław, approximately 750 people attend the UTW, which is affiliated with the College of Pedagogy at the University of Wrocław and has a permanent space in the basement of that building. Open to retirees over age sixty at a cost of about $35 annually, the UTW offers a wide range of lecture series, seminars, classes, and workshops on a variety of topics, such as physics, languages, computers, dance, and sailing. Through lectures and published materials, the UTW encourages attendees to make aging a positive, active, and creative time through learning new disciplines and skills and forming new friendships. Although this goal is individual, the process through which this self-fulfillment occurs is fundamentally social.

The people who attend the UTW are those one would expect: retired teachers, engineers, accountants, health-care workers, and other professionals. They tend to be quite healthy, with few visible disabilities or impairments. These women—for they are mostly women—describe their lives as active, busy, and fulfilling. They say the UTW creates opportunities for them "to do something for themselves" ("*robić coś dla siebie*") for the first time in their lives, now that they do not have to work, take care of elderly parents, or raise their own young children. Retired women who attend the UTW consciously strive toward an ideal of elder personhood that is distinct from their past lives in which they focused on kin and professional obligations. This shift in emphasis away from maintaining traditional kin ties and toward building new relations echoes the experiences of participants in @ktywny Senior, and also resonates with modernist discourses about the role of civil society in democratic (and capitalist) societies.

At the UTW, growing old is explicitly theorized by institutional leaders. In the words of Walentyna Wnuk, a former director of the university, "*dobrego starzenia musimy się uczyć*," or "we have to learn how to age well" (Wnuk 2009). Currently an adviser to the mayor on issues related to seniors, she also participates in an international coalition of Universities of the Third Age. She organized trips to Brussels and Strasbourg for UTW students to meet their European Parliament representative and described these as transformative, because they changed the minds of people who opposed Poland's EU membership. Older Poles have to learn to be "open" rather than "closed," she said, contrasting the present to the socialist past. Through the UTW she aims to create a new model of aging and a new type of citizen and person— a "*Eurosenior*," or "Euro-senior"—who is appropriate to the contemporary world order. Underpinning these comments is a binary Cold War logic that opposes a closed, socialist Poland to an open, capitalist, free Western Europe. For Dr. Wnuk, the chance for Polish retirees to meet with their representative to the European Parliament or travel to Brussels is part of a teleology in which the West remains the ultimate goal. Yet the retirees who participate in these programs do not always evaluate them in terms of dreams of the West. Rather, the UTW provides participants with a way to form new kin ties that create a more local kind of personhood.

One retired teacher, Jolanta, who had attended the UTW for over eight years at the time I met her, described her experience as providing her with a "*druga rodzina*," or "second family." This "family" gave her support, companionship, and most importantly, she said, advice for coping with health problems. Although she learned about health problems from medical professionals who give lectures and courses on various topics (e.g., nutrition, *trening pamięci*, or memory training), Jolanta cited the support she received from her peers at the UTW as the most valuable. Jolanta began attending the UTW after she had been retired for ten years and both her children had moved abroad. Widowed, she became lonely and sought out the UTW as a way to overcome this loneliness. She spoke of having a strategy for aging, in which she tried to fill in what she had missed out on during her life; for example, she learned to swim at age seventy. After a life in which she prioritized her children, Jolanta now puts her own concerns first. Indeed, Jolanta now spends so much time with her "second family" that she does not have time for her kin. For example, she regrets that her visits to her daughter in England are only possible during breaks in the UTW's school year, and that her visits to her husband's or parents' graves are less frequent because of the time she spends at the UTW.

Jolanta is similar to many women with whom I spoke who sought out the UTW as a way to form new social relations to overcome the loneliness accompanying retirement, and often, widowhood. They describe retirement and aging as negative experiences that have been improved through participating in the UTW. Yet these improvements have come through cultivating new relations that can supplant old kin ties, rather than through greater engagement with international cultural groups, such as those led by the former director, or through the new skills and hobbies themselves. That is, the new possibilities of citizenship afforded by Poland's membership in the EU are not what participants of the UTW most value. Although many research participants did describe their joy at the opportunities for travel provided by open borders and for their children and grandchildren to work abroad, these did not seem to be the most meaningful aspects of their participation in the UTW. In other words, elements of personhood, rather than citizenship, mattered most for these retired women.

This relative de-prioritization of the EU could perhaps be explained by the prevalent understanding that Poland has always been part of Europe (Galbraith 2011), so EU membership was to be expected, or by the common vision that the EU poses a threat to Poland's national sovereignty (Golanska-Ryan 2006). However, the delight that UTW participants took in their travels was genuine, and most of my research participants at the UTW supported Poland's EU membership. But such satisfaction was of a qualitatively different sort, as evident in different tones of voice and emotional registers, than were explanations having to do with kin and social relations. That is, Jolanta's experience shows the UTW is most important to her for the changes it provides in her social world. By focusing analytic attention on the practices that research participants felt to be the most significant, a more complete understanding of the role of the UTW in transformation of citizenships in old age emerges.

Therefore, rather than look for connections between individual citizens and (trans)national organizations, I suggest following the hierarchies of value emerging through ethnographic research. By paying attention to the biographical and social context within which experiences of citizenship emerge, the category of citizenship takes on a fuller, richer meaning that better approximates the ways it is experienced. For Jolanta and others at the UTW, creating new ties of relatedness is what matters most. Rather than a relationship between an individual and a nation (or transnational group), then, citizenship could also include the social ties that are so important to older Poles. This experience-based approach could help to close the gap between categories of practice and categories of analysis, and thus could create a more complex understanding of the way citizenship is actually negotiated in daily life. Moreover, this broadened social world in which relations with peers become as important as family ties is part of both older Poles' and institutional leaders' understanding of what it means to be a "modern," European, older person. No longer limited to the role of the "*moherowe berety*" whose worlds are dominated by kin and religion, older people who participate in educational activities therein signify their desire for European citizenship.

CONCLUDING THOUGHTS

Both @ktywny Senior and the University of the Third Age in Wrocław encourage the fundamentally social practices of *aktywność* among its participants, and despite comments by institutional leaders about self-care and European travel, the participants themselves most value the formation of social relations that these institutions provide. Indeed, it is through these practices and ties of relatedness that new social worlds emerge in which older Poles can become legitimate persons and citizens. The significance of making and unmaking social relations throughout people's lifetimes suggests that static binary heuristics are insufficient to explain lived experiences of citizenship. Rather, the analytic lens of relatedness keeps social relations in the foreground and shows that the hierarchy of value of social relations might be shifting in contemporary Poland. That is, nonkin ties are increasingly encouraged and valued in certain contexts. Older women, who are culturally understood as the caretakers and emotional center of the family, explicitly cultivate relations that can be equally, or possibly more, meaningful than their traditional (natal and affinal) kin ties.[19]

Ethnographic research also brings to the fore the temporal and spatial dimensions of personhood and citizenship. Although intimate social relations are key to understanding citizenship, this is not to say that it is purely local. Rather, the horizons of these social relations can include the Polish nation and the EU, though only at certain times and moments. The organizers of @ktywny Senior and leaders of the UTW trying to develop their programs self-consciously reference the EU in contrast to the socialist Polish state of the late twentieth century. For these institutional leaders, older Poles are not only Polish but also European citizens. The transnational, rather than the national, is the locus of morality. Participants in these programs eagerly claim EU citizenship for the cultural pride and possibilities for mobility it offers, and the historical Polish nation continues to structure older Poles' opposition to the socialist past, especially for those who are sympathetic to the nationalist policies of the far right. Yet in the daily experiences of older Poles, maintaining and creating social relationships gives meaning to their lives. Could such a perspective that focuses on the social rather than the (trans)national alter Polish perceptions of the *moherowe berety*? How might the experiential and analytic importance of relatedness for older women at the UTW change current understandings of citizenship in Poland and Eastern Europe?

By considering the histories of the University of the Third Age, @ktyw-ny Senior, and ideas of "active aging," I have tried to disrupt the polarizing conversations that can surround discussions of age and citizenship in Poland. Indeed, these histories alter popular associations of older Poles with the "backward" socialist past by showing that socialism is not completely past; that is, these ideas of "activity," imagined to be so new and post-1989, actually resonate with elements of the socialist past through the repetition of certain cultural forms. Retired Poles find solace and regain a sense of worth and location within a community through creating the very types of slogans they once viewed as propaganda. The institutional history of Universities of the Third Age challenges the conventional pre- and post-1989 historiography by presenting a connection between France and Poland in the 1970s, recalling deeper historical links between Poland and Western Europe. These traces of historical connections reaching both eastward and westward confound a binary logic that continues to structure both experience and analysis. Such heuristics that divide East from West and past from present do not capture the more complex experiential and institutional histories that characterize the citizenship of older Poles. When combined with an attention to the social relations through which personhood and citizenship are created, historical analysis can thus shed light on the complex intertwining of past, present, and future imaginations of citizenship.

NOTES

1. These voting trends also vary by geography; people living in western regions and urban locations are more likely to vote for the center right, while those living in eastern regions and rural locations are more likely to vote for the far right.
2. "GŁOSUJ, albo one zrobią to dla Ciebie!"
3. "Maryja" is the particular spelling of "Mary" that refers to the Virgin Mary (thanks to Brian Porter-Szücs for this clarification). Radio Maryja is the flagship member of a media conglomerate run by the controversial Redemptorist

priest Father Tadeusz Rydzyk. Other media outlets include Telewizja Trwam (I Persist Television) and Nasz Dziennik (Our Daily).

4. See the December 16, 2011, edition of "This American Life," www.thisamericanlife.org/radio-archives/episode/453/transcript, accessed August 25, 2012, for an English-language description of the controversy that erupted after the plane crash in April 2010.

5. I use the term "older" both to preserve local conventions of talking about age (it is impolite to refer to someone as "*stary*," or "old," rather than "*starszy*," or "older"), and to reflect the wide range of ages included in this term. Newspaper sections targeted at older people advertise themselves as "for 50+," and many Poles consider themselves old at fifty. This lack of differentiation of life stages after age fifty is something I explore further in other writings.

6. Global worries about the health of aging populations are evident in WHO publications from the 1990s (e.g., Kalache 1995; Kalache and Kickbusch 1997). "Active aging" was used in formal statements during the 1999 International Year of Older Persons, and the meaning is discussed in more depth in WHO's 2002 policy brief (WHO 2002).

7. In anthropological work on personhood, this line of argument builds on research from South Asian and Melanesian contexts (e.g., Daniel 1984; Dumont 1980; Marriott 1976; Strathern 1988) and was produced in the first decade or so of postsocialism, in which differences between socialism and capitalism loomed large. Other research from this decade (e.g., Lampland 1995) shows continuities in personhood between socialism and capitalism, yet the binary remains central. Moreover, much work on postsocialist regions has used workplaces and laboring subjects as the most common sites and objects of research. Adding to the contemporary body of research in Eastern Europe (e.g., Fehervary 2002; Hann et al. 2002; Lampland 1995; Lemon 2008; Rivkin-Fish 2005) that attempts to step aside from such a binary frame, this chapter focuses on older people—that is, people who, for the most part, are no longer members of the workforce.

8. Sites not discussed in this chapter include a rehabilitation hospital run by Catholic nuns, a state-run home for the chronically physically disabled, and a day center for those with Alzheimer's disease.

9. Interestingly, there is no Polish-language equivalent for "nation-state." There is *naród*, or nation, and *państwo*, or state, but no one word joins the national and governmental senses of belonging implied by "nation-state."

10. Unfortunately, I did not learn about this program until after it happened, so I was only able to interview participants, not observe the actual program events.

11. Thanks to Karolina Szmagalska-Follis for this reference, and to Karolina, Elżbieta Goździak, and Aleksander Kobylarek for discussions of *aktywność*.

12. Although one of the major goals of @ktywny Senior is social integration, including intergenerationally, this goal seems to run contrary to the enforced age segregation of communities like Sun City (see www.nytimes.com/2010/08/29/us/29children.html).

13. Although I usually referred to my research participants using the formal *pan/pani*, Marek indicated in our first meeting that he prefers the informal address, *ty*, traditionally reserved for peers or close friends. This rarely happened among people who were more than ten or fifteen years older than I, as Marek was, and usually suggested an affinity with the supposed informality of the United States or United Kingdom. Unless otherwise indicated, all other names are pseudonyms. The Popowice apartment buildings were the first in Wrocław built with the prefabricated materials that became a hallmark of the Eastern European urban landscape in the 1970s and 1980s (Thum 2011, 165–66).

14. Indeed, one of the sponsors of the Local Activation Centers (the result of the pilot program @ktywny Senior) in Wrocław is "Kapitał Ludzki," or "Human Capital," part of the European Social Fund. Among its goals are: "improving the level of professional activity and ability of finding employment by persons who are unemployed and professionally passive, reducing areas of social exclusion, enhancing the adaptability of employees and enterprises to changes that take place in the economy, and popularization of education in the society at all educational levels with concurrent improvement of the quality of educational services and a stronger correlation between them and the needs of the knowledge economy." www.efs.gov.pl/English/Strony/Introduction.aspx, accessed August 10, 2011.

15. Data from Statistics in Focus, published by Eurostat, the primary statistical office of the European Commission. http://epp.eurostat.ec.europa.eu/cache ITY_OFFPUB/KS-SF-10-001/EN/KS-SF-10-001-EN.PDF, accessed October 14, 2011, pp. 6, 11.

16. This description of an ideal older person is based on information from interviews with the participants of @ktywny Senior as well as from the popular press (see Robbins-Ruszkowski 2013).

17. *Gazeta Wrocław*, insert to *Gazeta Wyborcza*, July 23, 2012, 4.

18. See a recent study of UTWs in Poland, "Zoom na UTW" ("Zoom to the UTW"), for a comprehensive overview of the contemporary situation of UTWs in Poland. www.zoomnautw.pl, accessed June 17, 2013.

19. In other work, I explicitly consider the connections between such shifts in relatedness and (trans)national politics, given the significance of women to the Polish nation. There is much literature on connections between Polish women and the Polish nation, imagined through Poland's distinctly Marian Catholic history (see Porter-Szücs 2011). Yet this is distinct from connections between women and the state; that is, to say that there is a strong link between women and the nation does not mean that there is an analogous connection between women and the state.

WORKS CITED

Berkel, R., van, and I. H. Møller, eds. 2002. *Active Social Policies in the EU: Inclusion through Participation?* Bristol: Policy Press.

Brubaker, R., M. Feischmidt, J. Fox, and L. Grancea. 2006. *Nationalist Politics and Everyday Ethnicity in a Transylvanian Town.* Princeton, NJ: Princeton University Press.

Carsten, J., ed. 2000. *Cultures of Relatedness: New Approaches to the Study of Kinship.* New York: Cambridge University Press.

———. 2007. *Ghosts of Memory: Essays on Remembrance and Relatedness.* Malden, MA: Blackwell.

Chirot, D. 1989. *The Origins of Economic Backwardness in Eastern Europe: Economics and Politics from the Middle Ages until the Early Twentieth Century.* Berkeley: University of California Press.

Daniel, E. V. 1984. *Fluid Signs: Being a Person the Tamil Way.* Berkeley: University of California Press.

Dumont, L. 1980. *Homo Hierarchicus: The Caste System and Its Implications.* Chicago: University of Chicago Press.

Dunn, E. 2004. *Privatizing Poland: Baby Food, Big Business, and the Remaking of Labor.* Ithaca, NY: Cornell University Press.

Einhorn B. 1993. *Cinderella Goes to Market: Citizenship, Gender, and Women's Movements in East Central Europe.* London: Verso.

———. 2006. *Citizenship in an Enlarging Europe: From Dream to Awakening.* New York: Palgrave Macmillan.

Fabian, J. 1983. *Time and the Other: How Anthropology Makes Its Object.* New York: Columbia University Press.

Fehervary, K. 2002. "American Kitchens, Luxury Bathrooms, and the Search for a 'Normal' Life in Post-Socialist Hungary." *Ethnos* 67: 369–400.

Franklin, S., and S. McKinnon, eds. 2001. *Relative Values: Reconfiguring Kinship Studies.* Durham, NC: Duke University Press.

Gal, Susan, and Gail Kligman. 2000. *The Politics of Gender after Socialism: A Comparative-Historical Essay*. Princeton, NJ: Princeton University Press.

Galbraith M. 2004. "Between East and West: Geographic Metaphors of Identity in Poland." *Ethos* 32: 51–81.

———. 2011. "'Poland Has Always Been in Europe': The EU as an Instrument for Personal and National Advancement." *Anthropological Journal of European Cultures* 20: 21–42.

Golanska-Ryan, J. 2006. "Strategies of Resistance in the Polish Campaign against EU Membership." In *Postsocialism: Politics and Emotions in Central and Eastern Europe*, edited by M. Svasek, 159–77. New York: Berghahn.

Graff, Agnieszka. 2009. "Gender, Sexuality, and Nation—Here and Now: Reflections on the Gendered and Sexualized Aspects of Contemporary Polish Nationalism." In *Intimate Citizenships: Gender, Sexualities, Politics*, edited by E. Oleksy, 133–46. New York: Routledge.

Hann, C. M., Caroline Humphrey, and Katherine Verdery. 2002. "Introduction: Postsocialism as a Topic of Anthropological Investigation." In *Postsocialisms: Ideals, Ideologies, and Practices in Eurasia*, edited by C. M. Hann, 1–28. London: Routledge.

Kalache, Alexandre. 1995. "Aging Well!" *World Health* 5: 21.

Kalache, Alexandre, and Ilona Kickbusch. 1997. "A Global Strategy for Healthy Ageing." *World Health* 4 (July–August): 4–5.

Lamb, S. 2000. *White Saris and Sweet Mangos: Aging, Gender, and Body in North India*. Berkeley: University of California Press.

Lampland, M. 1995. *The Object of Labor: Commodification in Socialist Hungary*. Chicago: University of Chicago Press.

Lemon, A. 2008. "Writing against the New 'Cold War.'" *Anthropology News* 49 (8): 11–12.

Marriott, M. 1976. "Hindu Transactions: Diversity without Dualism." In *Transaction and Meaning: Directions in the Anthropology of Exchange and Symbolic Behavior*, edited by B. Kapferer. Philadelphia: Institute for the Study of Human Issues.

Oleksy, E. 2009. "Citizenship Revisited." In *Intimate Citizenships: Gender, Sexualities, Politics*, edited by E. Oleksy, 1–13. New York: Routledge.

Ong, A. 2003. *Buddha Is Hiding: Refugees, Citizenship, the New America*. Berkeley: University of California Press.

Porter-Szücs, B. 2011. *Faith and Fatherland: Catholicism, Modernity, and Poland*. New York: Oxford University Press.

Rivkin-Fish, M. 2005. *Women's Health in Post-Soviet Russia: The Politics of Intervention*. Bloomington: Indiana University Press.

Robbins-Ruszkowski, Jessica C. 2013. "Challenging Marginalization at the Universities of the Third Age in Poland." *Anthropology and Aging Quarterly* 34 (2): 157–69.

Strathern, M. 1988. *The Gender of the Gift: Problems with Women and Problems with Society in Melanesia*. Berkeley: University of California Press.

Thum, Gregor. 2011. *Uprooted: How Breslau Became Wrocław during the Century of Expulsions*. Translated by Tom Lampert and Allison Brown. Princeton, NJ: Princeton University Press.

WHO. 2002. Active Ageing: A Policy Framework. WHO/NMH/NPH/02.8. www.who.int/ageing/publications/active/en/index.html.

Wnuk, Walentyna. 2009. "Późna dorosłość to czas pomyślny." *Kurier UTW: Nieregularnik Uniwersytetu Trzeciego Wieku* 16: 5. Wrocław: Uniwersytet Trzeciego Wieku.

Wolff, L. 1994. *Inventing Eastern Europe: The Map of Civilization on the Mind of the Enlightenment*. Stanford, CA: Stanford University Press.

Zubrzycki, G. 2001. "We, the Polish Nation: Ethnic and Civic Visions of Nationhood in Post-Communist Debates." *Theory and Society* 30: 629–68.

———. 2002. "The Classical Opposition between Civic and Ethnic Models of Nationhood: Ideology, Empirical Reality, and Social Scientific Analysis." *Polish Sociological Review* 3: 275–95.

13

FROM PERSONAL CARE
TO MEDICAL CARE

· · · · · · · · · ·

The Problem of Old Age and the Rise
of the Senior Solution, 1949–50

TAMARA MANN

INTRODUCTION

In 1949, old age, as a demographic problem, attracted federal attention.[1]
Fourteen years after the Social Security Act established sixty-five as a chronological mark for the aged, Oscar Ewing, the director of the Federal Security
Agency, invited a group of experts on aging to Washington, DC, to determine how the federal government should best approach "the problems which
arise with the aged population."[2] In an amorphous field, sparse with data,
specialists, and working options, two luminaries stood out: the self-trained
social worker Ollie Randall and the University of Chicago–trained sociologist Clark Tibbitts. The two arrived in Washington with careful articulations
of the proper definition of the elderly, the afflictions that beset them, and the
appropriate solutions.

At that time, the data exposed troubling trends. Americans were living
longer and reproducing less. In 1900, 3.1 million Americans, just 4.14 percent of
the total population, were over sixty-five. By 1950 the number would jump to

12.3 million, 8.1 percent of the population. Dips in birthrates, despite the baby boom, exacerbated this upward shift. Two—rather than five—children had become the norm, and this augured a dependency crisis, as familial, financial, and social responsibilities fell solely to the middle aged.[3]

As demographers described the problem of old age in terms of scale and dependency, a new class of doctors described the health afflictions of old age through research into degenerating or deformed cells (see Cowdry 1939). For them, the problem of old age was the affliction of chronic disease, the next frontier for a medical profession emboldened by sharp reductions in infant mortality; old age was not a social trend but a biological disease with potential medical cures.

Randall and Tibbitts incorporated, responded to, and challenged both of these models in their comprehensive visions of proper eldercare. The aged could not be fully described or treated as a set of data points, nor could physical disease be isolated from social context. While Randall and Tibbitts agreed on the scope and complexity of the problems, they offered productive differences on how the problems should be solved. Where Randall relied on a highly individualized local model, which I call personal care, Tibbitts believed that the problems required a centralized, or federal, solution. These differing solutions would eventually promote two definitions of old age, one based on need and the other based on chronology.

In the spring of 1949, it seemed that the continuum between Randall's personal care and Tibbitts's centralized care would set the intellectual parameters for a national discussion on the problems of and solutions to old age. Yet as Randall and Tibbitts stepped into the Federal Security Agency meeting, a third option was brewing. At the exact moment social workers and social scientists recognized the mounting problems of the elderly, the Truman administration, frustrated with thwarted attempts to pass government-sponsored health insurance, settled on the aged as the key to a new political strategy of incrementalism. Social Security beneficiaries, Ewing and others claimed, could be the first recipients in an incremental approach to bring health insurance to all. For Randall and Tibbitts the mounting numbers of the elderly was a social problem. For the Truman administration, it was a solution. This divide would eventually limit the content of the Randall-Tibbitts debate, establish a federally funded medical solution to the problems of old age, and entrench the chronological definition of senior citizen.

From the middle of the 1950s on, a new class of citizen would emerge on the national scene. They would be defined by their age—sixty-five and over—by their wants—Social Security and Medicare—and by a polarized public dialogue that pitted the young against the old. In the 1940s, reformers pushed an alternative conception of the hardships of old age and offered an intergenerational rather than generational vision of social problem solving and, in turn, citizenship.

OLLIE RANDALL AND PERSONAL CARE

Ollie Randall paid attention to words: *home, time, living, loss, illness,* and *independence.* She fixated on them, obsessed over how they were deployed, and imagined how they could best be put to use. A philosopher of care, her ideas came from a professional life devoted to the extreme and mundane hardships New York's elders faced.

Randall, a prolific writer and speech-giver, left her own story. Born on September 3, 1890, into a large extended family, she grew up in a household that valued both adventure and duty. By her own admission, her professional interests paid homage to her childhood. Her father came from a long line of Rhode Islanders, and in the late 1880s he ventured out West to try his hand at ranching, where he met her mother, a schoolteacher from Illinois. The family soon returned to Rhode Island. Mr. Randall took up work in the newspaper business and Mrs. Randall stayed home to raise their four girls. The family—great-grandparents, grandparents, parents, and children—lived on the same street.[4]

Responsibility mattered in the Randall household. Every morning, at precisely 10:00 a.m., Ollie would bring her great-grandmother her morning blend. She wrote, "I grew up in a family with a lot of older people in it. I counted on them and they counted on me."[5] At the time, multigenerational households were an American norm. As late as 1948 only 4.5 percent of elderly men and 3.3 percent of elderly women lived in institutions, while the vast majority moved in with their children (Pollak and Heathers 1948, 25).

In the first decade of the twentieth century, older people had yet to be recognized as a distinct category of the needy (see Katz 1986; Bremmer 1988; McCarthy 1990, 2001). Tossed in with other needy groups in local poorhouses, they were the nonspecific wards of religious societies and new scientific charities. Social workers, policy makers, health-care professionals, and charity workers all did not know how to deal with their particular plights. In her sixty-year career, Randall would change that. "When I started," she recalled, and "wanted to work with the old people they thought I was nuts. Nobody was bothering with old people."[6]

After graduating from Pembroke College, Randall secured a position at one of the few agencies in the country with a program for the elderly: the Association for Improving the Condition of the Poor (AICP) (see Brandt 1942). Within a few months she ran all of the organization's programs dedicated to elders. She loved the job and quickly took to her boss, who, in her estimation, "was not held down by . . . habits and all the rest of it."[7] At the agency, she tried to figure out which programs did and did not effectively serve their population, ensuring that the services responded to an actual rather than just a perceived need.[8] She described her position as follows: "if you're in social work working with people, your job is to know what those needs are. What the people need, not what you need."[9]

The employees of the AICP recognized, before the federal government did, that new labor practices in the early twentieth century would disproportionately affect the aged (at the time defined as anyone over forty) and consequently set up two programs, a sheltered workshop and a summer camp. At the Old Men's Toy Shop, AICP ensured "that individuals who were not able to compete in the labor market because they cannot cope with the demands of time or production" remained employed.[10] For three weeks every summer, the elderly the AICP cared for became "part of a large community of camps for girls, small children, and family groups" at Sunset Lodge.[11] The important idea, Randall pronounced, was that the elders "do as others do."[12] They lived with people of all ages and celebrated the summer the way other Americans wished to celebrate the summer at the time, outdoors.[13] While Randall enjoyed assisting in these programs, the two institutions she spearheaded, Ward Manor and Tompkins Square House, both defined her career and arguably transformed eldercare in the country.

In 1926, William B. Ward of the Ward Baking Company donated an estate in Dutchess County, New York, to the AICP for a permanent home for the elderly. Randall reminisced, "I'll never forget seeing Mr. Ward sit down and draw a check for $75,000. I never saw anybody do it before and I've never seen anybody do it since but that's what he did when he handed it over to us."[14] From its founding until 1945, Randall managed Ward Manor, which became a physical articulation of the values of its inhabitants rather than its founder or manager.

Randall recognized that her residents came to the Manor because they had nowhere else to go. Many suffered from debilitating financial and emotional loss, arriving at Ward Manor feeling useless and discarded. In addition to creating a physically adequate space, she wanted to restore in her residents the feelings of dignity and self-worth. To do so, she believed the Manor had to be self-governing. "What we tried to do," she related, "was to get self-government in the home for the old people. . . . But I mean they would take responsibility and be taking over. Because it was where they were living. And that hadn't been done in any home for the aged up to that time."[15] Participation, in this model, was not a choice but a requirement. Randall observed that residents suffered when they weren't truly needed. Hobbies and activities did not carry enough weight to give meaning and purpose to a resident's day. For this reason the Manor required that every well person "share in some of the work of the home to the extent of his physical ability."[16]

With the infrastructure for Ward Manor taken care of, Randall began her next project: a housing unit for semidependent living.[17] Responding to a dearth of housing, rising unemployment, and extended life years without a pension, Randall set out to create low-cost apartments that would suit the aging body. Her team "planned a house which would have rooms for sixty old people—furnished or unfurnished as desired; housekeeping or not as desired; elevator; plenty of plumbing; a dining room and cafeteria with food at cost, a recreation room, a roof garden."[18] Although the residents would not have access to in-house nursing care there would be "a resident hostess whose business it is to know whether anything is needed."[19] For all of this, the cost would only be $20 a month. For the site the team chose Tompkins Square Park—an area that even Randall agreed could be construed as questionable. She saw beyond the park's shady reputation to its given amenities. The park, she wrote, "has Wanamakers within walking distance; Christodora House, which opens all its doors to our family of tenants; churches of all denominations; library; bus which goes by the door; and it is a place which is real in the hearts of our local political leaders for every tenant is a potential voter."[20] The aged would be integrated into rather than set apart from the social, spiritual, and political life of the neighborhood. Randall believed in this project to such a degree that she actually moved in upstairs.

After creating two old-age homes, Randall came to be haunted by the word *home*. Institutional living, for most, is a last resort. It is the culmination of financial, physical, and familial loss, a desperate conclusion to a series of living arrangement mishaps. For this reason, Randall understood that there was something almost cruel in the title "home for the aged." "Home," she lectured in 1940, "is not merely a residence or a dwelling place to us—it is a place around which most of the precious memories of our life cluster, and one which we have shared at one time or another with loved ones of our families."[21] "Even at best," she continued, "a home . . . is an impersonal substitution for a very personal place—no matter how poor or how good it was, or how good our substitute may be."[22] The article before the noun mattered. Professionals working in the field had a mandate to make "a home" or "the home" work, and to do so they needed to focus their attention on making residents feel "at home."

Independence, Randall astutely realized, was always an illusion. "None of us is genuinely 'independent' of others." For Randall, this was an empowering and not a limiting discovery. Once one realized that independence was a helpful feeling rather than an empirical reality, then it was possible to "achieve for the old person a *sense* of independence in any setting."[23] Equally important to a sense of independence was a sense of meaningful association and usefulness. For this reason, she often said: "The household and not the house is the most important factor in an institution."[24] Randall's professional experience as a caretaker to New York's elderly within but especially outside their own homes informed how she defined old age.

While the passing of days, weeks, months, and years could externally mark numerical age, old age, Randall recognized, is something far more relative—experienced, despite the official demarcation, in the ephemera of subjective judgments. Aging, she pronounced, is a natural part of the process of living. What do "we really think," she asked, "when we let ourselves think of 'growing old?' Most of us instinctively avoid thinking of it at all, at least for ourselves, either consciously or unconsciously. Many shudder emotionally away from the bogey it presents." "We forget then," she continued, "that aging, or growing older, is happening to every human being each moment, each hour, and each day he is privileged to go on breathing. . . . Growing old is a natural process, as natural as growing into adolescence and into adult life."[25] No one has a problem with the *growing* part of this equation. The word *growing*, she noted, "implies constant change, and usually change for the better." The problem is the second part of the phrase, *old*. "So, growing old is generally conceived of as a process of growth up to the period of old age, the beginnings of which occur at different times in growth for every human being, but which, when it is reached, is considered to be a kind of 'dead end.'"[26] Old age, it seemed to Randall, was too often conceived as something outside of the flow of time, the static end of a life marked by change.

For Randall, the final stage of life was defined not by a lack of development but by a different set of developments. If adulthood could be understood as a period of attainment—such as money, spouses, and children—old age could be defined as the opposite: it was the stage of life marked by departure. "Old age," Randall writes, "is a period of losses—loss of family, of friends, of job, of health, of income, and most important of all, of personal status."[27] It doesn't begin at the same time for everyone. It begins when the losses trigger unexpected needs. Despite her better intentions, Randall often relied on an operative definition of old age that assumed a kind of emotional or physical disability. Rather than easily placing people inside or outside the category of the aged, Randall's definition pushed caretakers to see the final stage of life as a trajectory marked by profound individualism.

According to Randall, the ailments of old age come in two categories: the external and the internal. Among the former were the problems of financial insecurity, health failure, and lack of adequate living arrangements. Among the latter were the crises of social isolation, personal status, and self-worth. Aspects of these issues were timeless, having afflicted elderly men and women throughout history, but more often they were created and compounded by modern conditions of industrialization and urbanization.

By the late 1940s, life expectancy averaged approximately sixty-eight years. Industrial workers, retired at forty, had to contend with twenty-odd years of life without adequate funds for themselves and their dependents. Compounding professional losses came physical ones. Even without the trials of cancer or heart disease, eyesight, hearing, agility, and strength dwindled in old age, complicating the obligations of daily life and commonly tipping the family budget toward increasing health-care costs.

The financial burden of professional and physical loss challenged not only aged individuals but also their families. Randall lamented the trials of intergenerational conflict, which tended to spike when working adults had the dual burden of providing for both their parents and their children. Empathizing with the challenges of caretakers, Randall wrote: "There is nothing which taxes one's patience more than caring day in, day out, for the needs of the old person whose chances of progress to restoration of health are negligible or nonexistent, but whose daily needs continue on the same, if not on an increasingly demanding level. This is also true in those cases of mild mental affliction—which include loss of memory, lack of orientation, forms of suspiciousness which may develop into what we speak of as a persecution complex, and confusion which often creates intolerable disorder in the household."[28] For these families, she recognized, there were not enough options. Few places offered adequate and affordable institutional care and even fewer provided appropriate mental health services. Moreover, home care programs could rarely provide enough resources for older persons or their depleted caretakers. Health and proper housing were, therefore, two of the most critical problems facing elders and their families.

Still, Randall argued that the greatest afflictions of old age were not the external ones but the feelings of isolation and the uselessness that accompanied them. She recognized that the loss of community and purpose diminished an aged individual's sense of self. To fully explain this process, she focused on the issue of time.

"Time," Randall mused, "has a very new and different meaning for us as we near the end of the road. It has, strangely enough, a sharply reduced value, in that, as we have more of it to use personally as 'leisure time,' with less skill or practice in so using it, it becomes a kind of drug in the daily market of our lives. Time becomes synonymous with boredom. . . . The past is now longer than the future can possibly be."[29] "Killing time," she continued, "a common pastime among older people, is a murderous activity in more ways than one since it kills so much more than time. It kills initiative, interest, and in the end it can kill the personality of the person who indulges in the practice too often and too long."[30] To Randall, there is nothing meaningful, productive, healthy, or even deserved about a life bereft of purpose. When a person stops believing he is useful to others, she wrote, "he ceases to be important to himself."[31]

Weaving together the subjective emotional ailments with the material and physical ones, Randall ranked the problems of old age in the following order: the loss of personal status, financial strain, family friction, housing, illness, social isolation, and unfulfilled spiritual needs.[32]

Randall, never one to indulge in too much talk, had solutions. Old age could not be magically or medically ignored, cured, or perpetually staved off. It had to be dealt with, its inevitable hardships understood, and its unnecessary pains ameliorated. The problems of old age existed in shared contexts and required joint solutions; this was a societal problem, not a post-sixty-five problem. Four groups, according to Randall, had responsibilities in this area: middle-aged individuals, the family members of elders, public and private institutions, and finally the federal government.

Randall had an unwavering conviction that old age is "essentially one's own personal business."[33] In tandem with her notion that elders can only be understood and cared for as individuals, she believed that each individual had an obligation to prepare for his or her own old age. Americans must acknowledge that they will age, that they will lose abilities, and that they will die, in order to cultivate good habits that will serve themselves and their families in the later years. It is not society's job to do this, thought Randall; it is one's own. In this way, Randall presaged the Polish aging experts at the University of the Third Age described in Jessica C. Robbins-Ruszkowski's chapter in this volume.

It is "our personal business," Randall exclaimed, to "prepare intellectually for changing satisfactions as the years are added one by one. . . . If we think we'd like to read and want to derive pleasure from it when we have time, we should develop the habit of finding time for reading at last a half hour or an hour a day now."[34] Regarding our own health, she preached, "it is our personal business to know more than the mere diagnosis. . . . We should focus our attention not on how we are to die of it, but how we may live *with* it."[35]

The burdens of old age, Randall recognized, were rarely borne solely by the aged individuals, but also by their younger family members, who provided financial and emotional assistance. She recognized that while family living arrangements in the twentieth century had changed, religious and political ideals surrounding the family had not. She wrote, "In our Christian communities we have been taught early to 'Honor thy father and thy mother.' There is no finer precept for family life. Perhaps we need to re-examine, not the precept itself, but the manner in which it can find acceptable expression today."[36] The family, she argued, "is the fundamental unit of our society and our democracy," and yet it bears the "brunt of all the aspects of the industrial changes, the geographical shifts, and the general social apathy."[37] We don't need to change our definition of the family, she pressed, "but we may change our ideas of what is a natural living arrangement for members of a family, if the individuals who compose it are to be happy and self-sufficient persons in the community."[38]

Primarily, Randall believed that it was "the personal business" of the family to create a workable living arrangement. Ideally, elders should remain in their home, and caretakers should have ample support from the community. Circumstances, however, often make this arrangement both physically and emotionally impossible. It is at this point that responsibility shifts from the individual and family to the immediate community and larger government. Randall described the transition: "We are transferring upon our collective shoulders the burden, hitherto assumed largely by the family and the intimate community, of giving support to retired and destitute old people. We and other nations have, as a collectivity, assumed the responsibility of filial duty."[39]

The responsibility, thought Randall, once assumed had to be met. She wrote that the "speed with which middle age, if not old age, has overtaken us individually and collectively had caught everyone short. There is unpreparedness in every aspect of economic, social, and personal life for this dividend of years granted to us."[40]

For society, the issue was not old age per se, she noted, but the soaring number of elderly. To cope with this problem of scale, Randall recommended that nonprofits, foundations, and local governments begin a rigorous process of data collection in order to fully understand the mutual or conflicting needs of individuals as they related to employment, health, housing, and family life. To cope with a systemic problem, Randall believed one had to extend listening skills beyond the aged themselves. For this reason she wanted the data to reflect the holistic needs of the community rather than the particular needs of the elderly. For example, she urged family agencies to "discover what affect the presence or absence of older people in the family has upon the family."[41]

In tandem with data collection, she called for a serious reevaluation of the mental and physical capacity of those deemed aged. She wanted to refocus efforts away from the disabilities of aging to the abilities of the experienced. She wrote: "I cannot help but feel that what we are essentially saying to our older people is 'Get out of the way. We will see that you don't go hungry; we will treat you with a good deal of quite inexpensive deference, we will, perhaps, dole out a little to add to what we have you save up yourselves but, nevertheless, get out. Cultivate the art of growing old gracefully—whatever that means—but don't by any chance do anything useful enough to command a wage or a salary.'"[42]

Randall had a nuanced understanding of illness and disability. Patients don't need a diagnosis or straight prognosis, she claimed; what they need is a careful analysis of "the degree of need established by the degree of disability for the several types of services—medical care, physical care, including personal services and attendance as well as nursing care, services to meet social and emotional need."[43] The goal of care, she contended, must lie in "a fuller use of the individual patient himself, in spite of, or because of, his disability."[44] For this reason, Randall was wary of the new institutional entity called the nursing home, where disability became identity and purposeful work came to be replaced by days of waiting.

For Randall, the majority of the responsibility for the problems of old age fell to individuals, their families, and their communities. Still, she believed that the federal government had to continue its involvement and do a better job intervening. She wrote, "We have in the United States today one of the most effective and largest Social Security programs which has ever been developed. . . . However, if one scrutinizes it and analyzes it as to what it actually provides, you may agree with me that 'social security' is something of a misnomer, for what we have in fact is a program of 'economic security.'"[45] Randall believed that the federal government had "a moral and real responsibility for seeing that people do not rust out, but wear out gradually as active members of the communities in which they live."[46] If business or industry could not "find ways and means of providing sheltered opportunity for work to older people," then the government should "develop the machinery to profit by the productiveness of older persons who may be denied the chance to function in other settings."[47]

Randall arrived in Washington optimistic and cautious. She understood the magnitude of the problem, the real possibility of solving aspects of the crisis, and yet remained extremely modest about the kind of care that would work. She distrusted systems that could not accommodate particularities and bureaucratic institutions that lost sight of individual responsibility and agency. She called for a collective rethinking of the aged's position within the family, the local community, and the broader society.

CLARK TIBBITTS AND CENTRALIZED CARE

Clark Tibbitts excelled in meetings. He knew how to run them, participate in them, and organize them. He even knew how to make them productive. He was a statistics man, educated in the social sciences, and devoted to fixing problems at a macrolevel. In 1929 he received a PhD in sociology at the University of Chicago, studying under the luminaries William Ogburn and Ernest Burgess. He went on to a joint career as an academic and a policy analyst. His interest in aging came not from his family but from his academic and professional life. He believed that with the help of good research and good ideas, the federal government could solve major social issues, such as old age.[48]

Tibbitts did not begin his career interested in the elderly. Like many sociologists at the time, his early work focused on immigrant politics and urban blight with one eccentricity, a fascination with organized crime (see Gordon 1991; Sharpes 2009). During the Depression, Tibbitts left his post as a sociology instructor at the University of Michigan to become the coordinator of urban research at the Federal Emergency Relief Administration and later the field director of the National Health Survey for the US Public Health Service, where he first came across the afflictions of the elderly.[49]

The survey sought "to determine the amount of sickness experienced by the general population."[50] To begin, Tibbitts had to create an operative definition of sickness. He wrote: "Sickness itself is difficult to define. When is one sick and when not?" For the purpose of the study they settled on what he argued was a subjective definition: "those who were disabled or unable to perform their normal duties."[51] The ability or inability to "perform one's usual work is not an objective item," acknowledged Tibbitts.[52] Still, the canvassing pressed on and the staff managed to determine two categories of disease: the acute and the chronic. The acute diseases, such as scarlet fever and smallpox, "last only a short period and can be cured without much cost."[53] Not only could families economically carry the cost of care, but also medical advancements had widely reduced the number of acute disease cases.

Chronic disease was another matter. The "long" and "disabling experience" of cancer, heart disease, arthritis, diabetes, and crippling conditions required expensive treatment. Moreover, chronic disease threw the "breadwinners out of work" and demanded "constant attention." The whole family, Tibbitts lamented, "may have to organize around the sick person—young people who wish to get married . . . have to stay home to care for the parent."[54] Tibbitts observed that while medicine had eliminated many acute diseases, chronic diseases would continue to grow in importance. There were, he wrote, "more old people" and "city life doesn't provide care."[55]

Tibbitts also observed the correlation between poverty and poor health. He wrote: "Disabling illnesses of all kinds increase as income drops. There is 57 percent more disabling sickness among persons who are on relief than among persons in families having annual incomes of $3,000 or more. Chronic disease is 87 percent more frequent at the bottom than at the top of the income scale."[56] Not only did poverty reduce access to health care, but also this reduced access plunged families deeper into poverty. The plights of the parents, he knew, determined the financial and then the physical opportunities of the children. When, in 1938, the University of Michigan asked him to return to run the recently created Institute of Human Adjustment, Tibbitts had come to the conclusion that the problems of soaring numbers of elderly afflicted with chronic disease would pose a great burden to the United States.

In 1937, the estate of Horace and Mary Rackham made a $6 million bequest to the University of Michigan to found an institute dedicated to "applying the findings of science to those problems of human imbalance."[57] The institute would help foster social adjustment through social service centers with active research arms. It began operations with a speech clinic, a psychological clinic, a vocational guidance demonstration center, and a community center.[58]

The term *social adjustment* had purchase in 1937. By 1942 its overuse prompted Verne Wright in his broad literature review of the topic to lament, "many authors use the term 'adjustment' or 'social adjustment' but they rarely define it" (Wright 1942, 408). Ernest Burgess, Tibbitts's mentor at Chicago and later chairman of the Committee on Social Adjustment at the Social Science Research Council (SSRC), had an operative definition based on Josiah Stamp's *The Science of Social Adjustment* (1937). Burgess noted that Stamp had used the term to mean "societal adjustment," which has two components: the first is the "adjustment of society and its institutions to the changing situation. . . . The other half is the adjustment of individuals to the changes which are taking place and to the social situation."[59] From the outset Tibbitts and Burgess believed that aging in the United States was a problem of societal adjustment.

For eleven years, from 1938 to 1949, Tibbitts directed the institute and worked to establish the societal adjustment problems of the elderly as equal to those of children and adolescents. By 1943 Burgess, through his position at the SSRC, joined Tibbitts on his quest and his Committee on Social Adjustment focused its attention and funds on this question of "old people."[60] Their argument went as follows: Since the creation of Social Security, old age had become "recognized as a national responsibility," and yet there had been few if any "systematic studies" on older people outside of their need for economic assistance.[61] In short, older people had been studied as a category of the worthy poor but not as a comprehensive minority group. The committee decided to put together a subcommittee on adjustment in later maturity and invited Clark Tibbitts to participate and to assist in designing a research conference on the topic.

In 1948 the SSRC finally published a record of its early studies of maladjusted elders in *Social Adjustment in Old Age: A Research Planning Report*. The text opens with a defense of the project that places the problems of old age in line with the afflictions of other minority groups—such as African Americans, adolescents, or criminals—and goes on to relay the particular predicament of demographic realignment: "Thus the dynamics of a continuing decrease of the younger and a continuing increase of the older population groups constitute one of the characteristic demographic phenomena of our time—a phenomenon fraught with social implications" (Pollak and Heathers 1948, 2). The problems this demographic reality pose intensify with urbanization, "the reduction in living space per family unit, the resulting shift from a three-generation to a two-generation family system, and the increase in standards of living and care which are considered appropriate to make the fulfillment . . . [of] traditional obligations increasingly difficult" (Pollak and Heathers 1948, 3). This new social crisis, the report asserted, would benefit from a social scientific approach based on accurate descriptions rather than mere aspirations.

For this reason, SSRC scholars recommended accepting the definition of old age the Social Security Act imposed. The reality of age typing had to override the dream of its disappearance. Otto Pollak, the report's editor, wrote: "Hardly ever before has a culture permitted such a degree of chronologically exact age typing for all people. In our present-day culture . . . with its birth registration and frequent use of birth certificates, mathematical awareness of chronological age has led to a situation where age typing is based not so much on manifestations as on expectations of changes with age" (Pollak and Heathers 1948, 3). Pollak continues, "social research must recognize the existing social situation and use the existing society's definition of old age which is still predominantly chronological" (Pollak and Heathers 1948, 3). The only exception to this rule comes up in particular systems. For example, if age typing in industry defines the elderly as over forty then social scientists have an obligation to take on that definition while studying that system. Social science cannot, the argument goes, create optimal conditions without studying suboptimal ones first. Although possibly detrimental, age typing was the current social reality, and researchers had to assume its existence. The report does not mention whether or not academics would contribute to age typing by solidifying its presence with such studies.

With a chronological definition of old age in hand, the report goes on to describe the problems elders face: "Problems of old age arise therefore chiefly in two ways: (1) as the result of declining physical or mental capacities which make it difficult or impossible to satisfy one's needs in ways previously employed, and (2) the individual reaches the chronological age which places him in the old age group as defined by society" (Pollak and Heathers 1948, 40). The first condition focuses on loss that occurs naturally due to the biological process of aging. The second refers to the pressures imposed by or correlated with societal attitudes.

Tibbitts contributed to this formulation by focusing on how changes in societal attitudes could actually deter physical and mental deterioration. He wrote: "The generalized popular notion about older people appears to be that they are physically and mentally deteriorated; eager to withdraw from responsibility and from social participation at an arbitrary age." However, he continued, "the growing knowledge about older people has revealed . . . that mental decline may be greatly retarded through the exercise of mental capacities; that most people do not wish to withdraw from work or from their fellows; and that they wish to retain a large share of responsibility for their own management."[62] To keep older people mentally alert, in better health, and thus out of poverty, Tibbitts believed the federal government had to be involved in combating stereotypes and putting the elderly back to work. For this reason, adult education became the cornerstone of Tibbitts's answer to the problems of old age.

Tibbitts came to this solution through two professional endeavors at the institute: a survey of elders and the first adult-learning courses in the country. In tandem, these projects offered precision to his overall theory and led him to advance a particular ideal of government involvement in the problems of old age.

Following the conference, the SSRC and the institute partnered to launch a pilot study of the "Socio-Psychological Problems of Aging." This project, the first of its kind to have "older people identify the problems of aging in a free-interviewing situation," concluded that the elderly want, in the following order, financial security, physical health and comfort, living arrangements (ideally in their own homes), affection, activity, and religion.[63]

Financial and physical health, affection, and activity—four out of a list of six—could all be tackled, to some degree, by keeping elders intellectually and professionally engaged. As early as 1944 Tibbitts partnered with Wilma Donahue, head of the psychology clinic at the institute, to launch the first university courses that would be "given to older people themselves on the topic of problems, adjustments, and activities in later maturity and old age."[64] Tibbitts was immensely proud of these courses, as they proved that old age could be planned for and that the aged wanted to remain intellectually active. By 1949, Tibbitts, who within months would become an aging specialist within the Federal Security Administration (FSA), believed that the problem of social adjustment in old age could be alleviated through a federal reeducation campaign that would reach every sector of society.

In 1949, Randall and Tibbitts had arrived at similar ends through different means. The social worker and the sociologist would describe the problems of old age with the same words: housing, employment, intergenerational tension, and self-worth. Both believed that the problem of old age could only be solved within its broader social context. Yet beneath this surface, productive differences existed. While Randall saw the value of a single clearinghouse for data and best practices, she remained extremely wary of monolithic models of care that did not envision the aged as capable of self-governance or isolated their problems from other age groups. Tibbitts had a more optimistic vision of government involvement. For him, statistics accurately described a problem of such magnitude that specific federal intervention was necessary.

At the exact moment the SSRC and the Institute for Human Adjustment called for federal attention to the problems of old age, the Truman administration sought a political solution to the stalemate around universal health care. Thus while Randall and Tibbitts arrived at the FSA meeting hoping to alleviate the ailments of America's elders, the Truman administration was about to devise a plan to use the potential political clout of the elderly to push universal health care through Congress (see Poen 1996).

THE SENIOR SOLUTION TO THE PROBLEM OF UNIVERSAL HEALTH CARE

In 1942, *Fortune* magazine announced the American public's support for national health insurance as a whopping 74 percent (Corning n.d.; Cantril 1978). It seemed just a matter of time until the United States offered every citizen the right of health care. In 1944, President Roosevelt called for an "Economic Bill of Rights" proclaiming that every American had the "right to adequate medical care."[65] With Roosevelt's untimely death, Harry Truman took up the mantle and tried unsuccessfully to push national health insurance through the clenched jaws of the Republican Congress (for more on the fight for national health insurance see Munts 1967; Hirshfield 1970; Numbers 1978; Poen 1996; Hoffman 2001; Quadagno 2005; Starr 2011). After leaving office, Truman reflected, "I have had some bitter disappointments as President . . . but the one that has troubled me most, in a personal way, has been the failure to defeat organized opposition to a national compulsory health-insurance program" (see Poen 1996, ix).

The president's tepid approval ratings, the postwar Congress's conservative bent, and the powerful alliance of anti-national-health-insurance special interest groups combined to thwart health insurance legislation from 1945 to 1947. In 1948, the president resigned himself to the fact that national health insurance would have to be an "ultimate aim" rather than a proximate one (for more on the incremental approach see Marmor 2000; Kooijman 1999). A new tactic was required. The president asked Oscar Ewing, his new head of the Federal Security Administration (the implementation arm of the Social Security Act), to convene a National Health Conference and complete a ten-year health plan.[66] The medical community and the advocates of national health insurance would have to work together.

———

Oscar Ewing had the right amount of ambition. Born in Greensburg, Indiana, in 1889, he took up political posts as a point of duty. The valedictorian of Indiana University came from a long line of ardent Democrats and began running for office in high school. But more than political power, Ewing craved an interesting life filled with diverse people, ideas, and responsibilities. In college, he decided to major in philosophy to focus on how to "put things together and make sense out of . . . the meaning of the whole rather than breaking down the parts."[67] His proclivity for coherence and completeness helped him pull ideas and people together. As a student at Harvard Law School he earned the praise of his professors and peers, many of whom found themselves at the other end of the political spectrum. In his career as a lawyer, Ewing managed to move smoothly between the private and public sectors, representing railroads, pharmaceutical companies, and the aluminum industry while prosecuting high-profile criminals for such crimes as sedition and treason.[68]

In the early 1940s, Ewing's political astuteness and social adroitness propelled him into the position of consigliere to the Democratic Party. President Roosevelt appointed him assistant vice chairman of the Democratic National Committee, where, in the 1944 convention, he supported Senator Harry S. Truman for vice president. When Truman became president, he wanted Ewing to head the Federal Security Administration.[69]

Ewing took up the post of head of the Federal Security Administration in 1947 with little social policy experience. It was clear that Truman did not appoint him to the FSA for his professional experience as a social service administrator. Rather, he appointed him because he knew politics. Ewing recalled, "The Federal Security Agency was politically a very sensitive position. Its activities affected every man, woman and child in the United States, and the President wanted someone heading the Agency who would be alive to the political consequences of what might be done."[70] At the outset, Ewing had two goals: to help enact the administration's agenda and to "create a better image of President Truman."[71]

Ewing's fight for national health insurance came at the president's behest. The spar with Congress, Ewing observed, "took place before I was Federal Security Administrator, before I even got interested in national health insurance." "After I became Administrator," he continued, "I realized that President Truman was strongly in favor of national health insurance. . . . Accordingly, at the request of the President, I called a conference to consider the health problems of the country, not merely national health insurance but every phase of health problems that faced this country."[72] Ewing recognized that he had to turn the conversation away from health insurance to health care if he wanted to cultivate a productive conversation between organized opposed interests. His National Health Assembly was such a success that even the vitriolic head of the American Medical Association, Dr. Morris Fishbein—one of the greatest opponents of national health insurance—told Ewing that "it was the best conference that had ever been held in this country on health problems."[73] The conference presented Ewing and the Truman administration with a glimmer of hope. National health insurance as previously conceived might be off the table, but perhaps some kind of compromise, under the guise of health care, could be reached. Incidentally, the assembly recommended that the FSA, to better get a handle on the relationship between old age and chronic disease, look into the 'broader aspects of aging'" (Roderick 1984, 41).

Improbably, the famed publisher William Randolph Hearst Jr. put Ewing on the path to actually developing national health insurance for the aged. At some point in 1949, Ewing recalls, Hearst "invited me over for cocktails."[74]

> He and I were talking and he said, "I'm very much in favor of your idea for national health insurance. But the thing that worries me about it is that if anything went wrong, if it didn't work, the upheaval that would result would be catastrophic because we would have a completely different system of medicine." Then he added, "Isn't there some small segment of the problem that you could pick out, apply your health insurance program to it, use it as a pilot plan operation?" This suggestion made a great deal of sense and it started me on my search for a limited program.[75]

Ewing left the party and immediately called the three Social Security big wigs—Arthur Altmeyer, Wilbur Cohen, and Isadore Falk—"to ask them if there was some part of our program for national health insurance that we could put out, get it going and use as a pilot plant operation."[76] They trio hedged. Louis Pink, a dear friend and former client, handed Ewing the idea of the elderly. Pink, an insurance expert with New York Blue Cross/Blue Shield, suggested "that the Government try to do something for the over sixty-five group so that the health insurance companies would have some actuarial data that would enable them to insure the over sixty-five group. He said that without such actuarial data an insurance company wouldn't know what premiums to charge or what risks the insurance should cover."[77] When Ewing came back to Altmeyer with this idea, it seemed to him that the trio had already imagined this option. At the close of the 1940s, a new strategy for national health began to emerge; health insurance would mirror the history of voting: enfranchisement would be incremental, offered to one group at a time.

———

When Randall and Tibbitts arrived in room 5051 of the Federal Security Building on April 22, 1949, FSA assistant administrator John L. Thurston announced his desire that the day be a "cross between a seminar and a Quaker meeting."[78] The goal of this spirited and erratic discussion would be a "blueprint" for federal involvement in the problems of the aged. What began as a conversation soon turned into the first National Conference on Aging. Originally designed by Randall and Tibbitts to foster a productive national dialogue on the problems of, and solutions to, old age, the lasting results of the conference would be the demonstration, albeit nascent, of the growing power of America's aged (soon to be called senior citizens) and the marriage of this power with Oscar Ewing's old-age hospital insurance program, nicknamed Medicare.

In the decade following the conference, the American Association of Retired Persons (AARP), the National Council on the Aging (NCOA), and the National Council of Senior Citizens (NCSC) would come into being and build a vibrant political coalition designed to advance iterations of the Truman administration's Medicare program. Politicians soon realized the power of the elderly vote, recognizing, in political scientist Henry Pratt's words, that seniors "could be appealed to . . . on the basis of their own separate identity and self-interest" (Pratt 1976, 71).

With the rise of the senior citizen more than just political strategy changed. The conversation around the problems of old age grew ever more anemic; chronological age came to be an accepted way of dividing the old from the young, aging became a disease to be solved, and intergenerational coalitions, and solutions, dwindled in value. As Peter Levine comments in "Civic Renewal: Theory and Practice" (this volume), moral concepts are indispensable. When it came to old age policy in the 1950s, the moral questions Randall, Tibbitts, and other experts posed in the 1940s receded. In their stead, a policy solution came to dominate the conversation and establish the parameters of civic engagement for seniors. For a decade to come age-specific medical care would trump personal care as a solution to the problems of old age.

NOTES

1. Throughout this essay, I use a number of terms to describe old age, including the aged and the elderly. Rather than advocate for a particular word to describe this complex and historically contingent stage of life, I deploy the terms my sources use.
2. "Proceedings of the Committee on Aging, United States Public Health Service," April 22, 1949, folder 051.2, box 129, record group 235, Federal Security Agency, National Archives, College Park, MD.

3. "The Study of Adjustment in Old Age," 1944, folder 6139, box 499, series 1, subseries 82, Record Group 1, Social Science Research Council Archives, 1924–1990, Rockefeller Archives Center, Sleepy Hollow, NY, 1.

4. Ollie Randall, "Reminiscences of Ollie A. Randall, Transcript of Oral History Interview, 1981," Community Service Society Project, Columbia Center for Oral History, Columbia University, New York, NY, 1–5.

5. Ibid., 16.

6. Ibid., 14–15.

7. Ibid., 22–23.

8. Ibid., 24.

9. Ibid.

10. Ollie Randall to Mrs. Margaret Lighty, June 11, 1947, folder 10, box 1, Ollie Randall Papers, 1914–1975. Social Welfare History Archives, Elmer L. Anderson Library, University of Minnesota Libraries, Minneapolis, MN.

11. Randall, "Care of old folks now and in the future," November 9, 1938, folder 401, box 34, Ollie Randall Papers, 1914–1975, 10.

12. Ibid.

13. Ibid.

14. Randall, "Reminiscences of Ollie A. Randall," 29.

15. Ibid.

16. Ollie Randall to Mrs. Margaret Lighty, June 11, 1947, Ollie Randall Papers.

17. Ibid.

18. Randall, "Care of old folks now and in the future," Ollie Randall Papers, 10.

19. Ibid.

20. Ollie Randall to Mrs. Margaret Lighty, June 11, 1947.

21. Randall, "OAR talks to Department of Welfare Agencies," April 3, 1940, folder 402, box 34, Ollie Randall Papers.

22. Ibid.

23. Randall, "Importance of Living Arrangements," May 26, 1947, folder 403, box 34, Ollie Randall Papers.

24. Randall, "Diversional Interests for Our Aged Guests," April 25, 1938, folder 401, box 34, Ollie Randall Papers.

25. Randall, "The Psychological Aspects of Aging," May 28, 1947, folder 403, box 34, Ollie Randall Papers.

26. Ibid.

27. Ibid.

28. Ibid.

29. Ibid.

30. Ibid.

31. Randall, "Old Age and Old People," late 1940s?, folder 313, box 29, Ollie Randall Papers.

32. Ibid.

33. Randall, "Old Age as Personal Business," March 14, 1944, folder 402, box 34, Ollie Randall Papers.

34. Ibid., 11.

35. Ibid., 19.

36. Randall, "Old Age and Old People."

37. Randall, "Sociological Aspects of Aging," speech given at the annual AMA meeting before 1951, folder 315, box 29, speeches, Ollie Randall Papers, 2–3.

38. Randall, "Old Folks in the World of Today—In the Family," 1947?, folder 402, box 34, Ollie Randall Papers.

39. Randall, "The Aged: Then and There, Here and Now," 1941 or 1949, folder 412, box 36, Ollie Randall Papers, 6.

40. Randall, "Sociological Aspects of Aging," 1–2.

41. Ibid., 4.

42. Randall, "The Aged: Then and There, Here and Now."

43. Randall, "The Chronically Ill Who Live in the Community," 1948, folder 404, box 34, Ollie Randall Papers.

44. Ibid.

45. Randall, "Needs of the Aged," November 15, 1946, folder 402, box 34, Ollie Randall Papers, 4–5,

46. Randall, "Old Age as Personal Business."

47. Ibid.

48. Clark Tibbitts, "Biography, 2-1-51," box 4, Papers, Speeches, and Reprints: 1929–1982, Clark Tibbitts Papers, 1926–1985, Bentley Historical Library, University of Michigan: Ann Arbor, MI.

49. Ibid.

50. Tibbitts, "The Field Activities and Sampling Procedure of the United States Public Health Service National Health Survey," enclosed in letter from Clark Tibbitts to Professor R. D. McKenzie, November 1, 1937, box 4, Clark Tibbitts Papers.

51. Ibid.

52. Ibid.

53. Ibid.

54. Ibid.

55. Ibid.

56. Ibid.

57. Institute of Human Adjustment, "Graduate School Announcement," Date?, Clark Tibbitts Papers.

58. Ibid.

59. "Council Minutes September, 10–12, 1940," folder, 1250 box, 208, series I, Committee Projects, Record Group I, Committee on Social Adjustment, Social Science Research Council Archives: 1924–1990, Rockefeller Archives Center: Sleepy Hollow, NY.

60. "The Study of Adjustment in Old Age."

61. Ibid.

62. Clark Tibbitts, "Meeting the Needs of Older People: memorandum to Mr. John L. Thurston, Assistant Administrator for Programs, Federal Security Agency," June 21, 1949, box 4, Clark Tibbitts Papers.

63. Ibid.

64. Institute for Human Adjustment, *Annual Report*, box 1, Clark Tibbitts Papers, 6.

65. www.fdrlibrary.marist.edu/archives/address_text.html.

66. For more on the assembly see Oscar Ross Ewing in J. R. Fuchs, "Oral History Interview, Oscar R. Ewing," www.trumanlibrary.org/oralhist/ewing1.html, Harry S. Truman, Library Independence, Missouri, 188–90.

67. Ibid., 10.

68. Ibid.

69. Ibid.

70. Ibid.

71. Ibid.

72. Ibid.

73. Ibid.

74. Ewing dates this meeting to the fall of 1951. However, the scholar Jaap Kooijman discovered a letter from I. S. Falk to Ewing dating the meeting to 1949. I confirmed the existence of this letter, which does remark on Ewing's meeting with Mr. Hearst and their discussion of a limited national health insurance proposal. While it is unclear whether Ewing and Hearst met before or after the 1949 FSA meeting with Tibbitts and Randall, it is clear that Ewing settled on this approach before the group began planning the National Conference on Aging. I. S. Falk to Oscar Ewing, November 22, 1949, Falk Papers, box 69, folder 710, Yale Library, New Haven, CT; Kooijman 1999, 119.

75. Ewing, Fuchs, 218–19.
76. Ibid.
77. Ibid.
78. "Proceedings of the Committee on Aging, United States Public Health Service," April 22, 1949, folder 051.2, box 129, record group 235, Federal Security Agency.

WORKS CITED

Achenbaum, W. Andrew. 1978. *Old Age in the New Land: The American Experience since 1790*. Baltimore: Johns Hopkins University Press.

———. 1983. *Shades of Gray: Old Age, American Values, and Federal Policies since 1920*. Boston: Little, Brown.

———. 1986. *Social Security: Visions and Revisions*. New York: Cambridge University Press.

Brandt, Lilian B. 1942. *Growth and Development of AICP and COS: A Preliminary and Exploratory Review*. New York: Community Service Society of New York.

Bremmer, Robert H. 1988. *American Philanthropy*. Chicago: University of Chicago Press.

Cantril, Hadley, ed. 1978. Fortune Magazine survey, July 1942. In *Public Opinion, 1935–1946*. Westport CT: Greenwood Press.

Corning, Peter. n.d. "Social Security History." www.ssa.gov/history/corningchap3.html.

Cowdry, E. V. 1939. *Problems of Ageing*. London: Bailliere, Tindall and Cox.

Gordon, Scott. 1991. *The History and Philosophy of Social Science*. London: Routledge.

Hirshfield, Daniel S. 1970. *The Lost Reform: The Campaign for Compulsory Health Insurance in the United States from 1932–1943*. Cambridge: Harvard University Press.

Hoffman, Beatrix. 2001. *The Wages of Sickness: The Politics of Health Insurance in Progressive America*. Chapel Hill: University of North Carolina Press.

Katz, Michael B. 1986. *In the Shadow of the Poorhouse: A Social History of Welfare in America*. New York: Basic Books.

Kooijman, Jaap. 1999. *. . . and the Pursuit of National Health: The Incremental Strategy toward National Health Insurance in the United States of America*. Amsterdam: Rodopi, 1999.

Marmor, Theodore R. 2000. *The Politics of Medicare*. 2nd ed. Social Institutions and Social Change. New York: A. de Gruyter.

McCarthy, Kathleen D. 1990. *Lady Bountiful Revisited: Women, Philanthropy, and Power*. New Brunswick, NJ: Rutgers University Press.

———. 2001. *Women, Philanthropy, and Civil Society*. Bloomington: Indiana University Press.

Munts, Raymond. 1967. *Bargaining for Health: Labor Unions, Health Insurance, and Medical Care*. Madison: University of Wisconsin Press.

Numbers, Ronald L. 1978. *Almost Persuaded: American Physicians and Compulsory Health Insurance, 1912–1920*. Baltimore: Johns Hopkins University Press.

Poen, Monte M. 1996. *Harry S. Truman versus the Medical Lobby: The Genesis of Medicare*. Columbia: University of Missouri Press.

Pollak, Otto, and Glen Heathers. 1948. *Social Adjustment in Old Age; a Research Planning Report*. Social Science Research Council, Bulletin 59. New York: Social Science Research Council.

Pratt, Henry J. 1976. *The Gray Lobby*. Chicago: University of Chicago Press.

———. 1995. *Gray Agendas: Interest Groups and Public Pensions in Canada, Britain, and the United States*. 2nd ed. Ann Arbor: University of Michigan Press.

Quadagno, Jill. 1988. *The Transformation of Old Age Security: Class and Politics in the American Welfare State*. Chicago: University of Chicago Press.

———. 2005. *One Nation, Uninsured: Why the U.S. Has No National Health Insurance*. New York: Oxford University Press.

Roderick, Sue Schock. 1984. "The White House Conferences on Aging: Their Implications for Social Chance." PhD diss., University of Southern California.

Roosevelt, Franklin D. 1938–50. *The Public Papers and Addresses of Franklin D. Roosevelt*, 13 vols., edited by William D. Hassett. New York: Random House; New York: Harper, 40–42.

Sharpes, Donald K. 2009. *The Evolution of the Social Sciences*. Lanham, MD: Lexington Books.

Starr, Paul. 2011. *Remedy and Reaction: The Peculiar American Struggle over Health Care Reform*. New Haven, CT: Yale University Press.

US Federal Security Agency. 1951. *Man and His Years: An Account of the First National Conference on Aging*. Raleigh, NC: Health Publications Institute.

Wright, Verne. 1942. "Summary of Literature on Social Adjustment." *American Sociological Review* 7 (3): 408.

ARCHIVAL COLLECTIONS

Bentley Historical Library, University of Michigan, Ann Arbor
Clark Tibbitts Papers

Columbia University Oral Histories, Social Security Project: Oral History, 1965–68, Columbia University, New York, New York

Reminiscences of Oscar Ross Ewing, Peter A. Corning Interviewer

Reminiscences of Ollie Randall, Peter A. Corning Interviewer

Harry S. Truman Library and Museum, Independence, Missouri

Oscar R. Ewing Papers

Oral History Interview, Oscar R. Ewing

Rockefeller Archive Center, Sleepy Hollow, New York

Social Science Research Council Archives

Social Welfare History Archives, University of Minnesota Libraries, Minneapolis

Ollie Randall Papers

United States Government Documents: National Archives, College Park, Maryland

Records of the US Federal Security Agency, Record Group 23

CONCLUSION

··········

JESSICA C. ROBBINS-RUSZKOWSKI
AND RICHARD MARBACK

The contributors to this volume have engaged a range of citizenship issues through their attention to age, aging, and generational differences. What they have added to conversations about the nature of our membership in political communities is recognition of the temporal experience of citizenship, an experience shaped as much by memories of the past as by hopes for the future, memories and hopes that wax and wane as we age. The grouping of the essays in this volume into four sections highlights the temporality of the citizenship experience. The essays in the first section, "Age, Cohort, and Generation," demonstrate that children and youth of the same age do not share equally in their hope for the rights and responsibilities of citizenship. The essays in the second section, "Young Age, Globalization, Migration," and the third section, "Generational Disparities and the Clash of Cultures," of this collection describe how the hopes of youth cohorts are shaped by the hopes as well as the memories of earlier generations. Taken together the essays from these first three sections reveal that the formative citizenship experiences of youth are experiences of intergenerational influence through which forces of globalization, patterns of migration, and the clash of cultures flow. "Later Life, Civic Engagement, Disenfranchisement," the fourth and final section of essays, makes clear that the accumulated hopes and memories of a cohort of older citizens fuel their desire to continue to participate in the lives of their communities. Taken together the essays in this collection make clear: the rich human experience of civic membership—from cultivating prospects for it in youth to actualizing possibilities for it in old age—cannot be understood through a single disciplinary perspective. To best comprehend the generational dynamics of citizenship we must appeal to a variety of disciplinary perspectives, each of which adds something more to our comprehension of community membership across the human life span. In this summary conclusion we will elaborate what we see as several of the key themes the preceding essays raised and their implications for the direction of the interdisciplinary study of citizenship.

Perhaps the overarching theme to be pulled out of this collection is the role of time and temporality in experiences of citizenship. It is not only that experiences of community membership change as we age, it is also that the experiences of civic engagement can and do change from one generation to the next. The essays in this collection, by focusing on the specific experiences of specific generations, bring into clearer focus the temporal nature of our citizenship. What makes this a particularly important contribution is the fact that the experience of human time and temporality currently receives less attention in the interdisciplinary study of citizenship than do the spatial dynamics of location and movement. We can understand the privileging of spatiality as a dominant conceptual framework in light of the geographic formation of citizenship through the establishment of Westphalian state sovereignty. Another no less significant influence on the paradigms of citizenship studies has been the expansion of nation-state influences through colonization, conquest, and trade, an expansion that has depended centrally on the movement of people—citizens, displaced persons, immigrants, slaves—over vast distances. Current research on the diasporic condition—from Gayatri Spivak's (1988) critiques of the legacy of colonialism and Paul Gilroy's (1993) elaborations on the African diaspora to Jonah Steinberg's (2011) recent work on globalization and Isma'ili identity—continues to speak to the issues of spatial identification and displacement. Similarly, among others, Seyla Benhabib's (2004) efforts to define the terms of global citizenship through discussion of the status of migrants and guest workers draws necessary critical attention to spatial logics that continue to dominate citizenship identifications.

Because space, place, and movement continue to function as key categories in thinking about citizenship, those categories are not absent from the essays in this volume. Instead, the authors in this volume enrich these categories by drawing our attention to the temporal experiences of occupying and moving through spaces of citizenship. Notable in this regard, Yuki Oda, in "(Re)Claiming US Citizenship," shows how the complex and varying nationality policies for people with differing connections to Mexico and the United States—connections that have varied so greatly in the first half of the twentieth century—have created different generations of citizens. In other words, the temporality of generations is relative to US nationality policy, creating generations structured by varying experiences of inclusion and exclusion. Similarly in "Children, Postconflict Processes, and Situated Cosmopolitanism," Pauline Stoltz accounts for the individual hopes and possibilities of Indo-European migrants in the Netherlands, hopes and possibilities mediated through citizenship and shaped by social policies related to changing geopolitical interests. Finally, Youcef's contribution, "Old Beurs, New Beurs, and French Citizenship," shows how the inclusion of an older generation of North Africans, an inclusion premised on previous participation in geopolitical actions, is not inherited by a younger generation, a generation whose hopes for inclusion are dashed by changes in the French political landscape. In each of these essays, generational temporalities of inclusion and exclusion are directly related to the interests of nation-states and empires. The essays by Oda, Stoltz, and Youcef, taken together with other essays from this collection—most notably those of Enzo Colombo, John Hink, and Saeed Khan—document the ways that past inequalities one generation experienced become—for better and for worse—the inheritance of a future generation. These authors make the case that any nuanced account of the capabilities necessary and sufficient for civic participation must consider the dynamics of such intergenerational influences.

The point has significant implications. Once we introduce the need to attend to intergenerational influences and experiences in our reflections on citizenship, we are obliged to focus some measure of attention on the inherent dynamics of those intergenerational influences and experience. In this regard, Tamara Mann's essay, "From Personal Care to Medical Care," describes how over time the inclusive, intergenerational roots of social security in the United States have been transformed into a program that comes to rely on the different category of "senior citizens," a category that now gets taken for granted. What Mann demonstrates so effectively is that even inclusive, intergenerational policies can yield practices of distinction. We can take away from her insight the realization that our studies of citizenship must interrogate the historical production of even inclusive-seeming categories if we are to better conceptualize what it is to be a citizen over the course of a human life.

When we recognize that time and temporality are defining features of civic membership, we must acknowledge as well the intergenerational dynamics of inclusion/exclusion. As many of the chapters from this volume demonstrate, the study of power relations that has become so central to an analysis of the politics of citizenship must account for age and aging. If one of the goals we set for the study of our experiences of human community is to work against the inequalities of exclusion, then we must attend to the power relations that orient intergenerational interactions. Influences flow both ways across generations. On the one hand, older generations can experience exclusion from the full range of citizenship opportunities as younger generations take on for themselves the task of claiming their identities as citizens. And there is in current research on citizenship concern for what contributes to, as well as limits, the participation of older people in the civic life of their communities. On the other hand, when younger generations lay claim to citizenship opportunities they often do so in conflict with constraints on participation imposed by older generations. While this point has received less attention in current research, several contributors to this volume point out the importance of this intergenerational dynamic. As Richard Marback argues in "The Challenge of ANC Youth from the Soweto Uprising to Julius Malema," the current political divisions within the African National Congress in South Africa follow the lines of a generational divide between the older generation of Nelson Mandela and a younger generation radicalized by the 1976 Soweto uprising. Similarly, Youcef's contribution, "Old Beurs, New Beurs, and French Citizenship," can be read as describing the experiences of a younger generation of Arabs in France who struggle to assert their own civic identity against the identity of an older generation, both generations contending with their respective claims to French citizenship. Finally, in "Complicating Citizenship," Enzo Colombo explains how the children of immigrants in Italy approach the challenges of Italian citizenship equipped with attitudes and abilities quite different from those of their parents. As Colombo suggests, their claims to Italian citizenship tug against the pull of their parents' immigrant identities.

Our reflections so far lead us to the point where attention to generational dynamics and experiences contributes most to citizenship studies; that is, on the importance of the relationship between kinship and citizenship.

A focus on generations cannot but highlight the role of kinship relations. All too often, however, the study of civic engagement has been analytically isolated from the study of kinship; a major contribution of this book, then, is to work toward the integration of these two domains of analysis. Recent anthropological research on kinship has shown that this isolation is an artifact of scholarship rather than of experience (e.g., Carsten 2000, 2007; Collier and Yanagisako 1987; Franklin and McKinnon 2001; McKinnon and Cannell 2013a and 2013b). In other words, the categories of analysis within which scholars think about citizenship tend to assume that kinship is not important to such studies. To even speak of citizenship is to call up narratives of modernity and the so-called modern world, narratives in which the nation-state is a dominant form, and in which there is a presumed relationship between an individual and the collective (Handler 1988, in McKinnon and Cannell 2013a, 21–22). This individual/collective relationship prevents us from seeing other kinds of relations—namely, kin relations. Moreover, the individual citizen who has a relationship with the collective is assumed to be a bounded, autonomous, rational individual in the Western model. This idea of personhood underpins studies of citizenship, making it difficult even to ask questions about potential relationships between kinship and citizenship, since kinship and citizenship are presumed to be distinct. Indeed, the very labels "kin-based" and "state-based" that often accompany typologies of "premodern" and "modern" societies already contain assumptions about the significance—or insignificance—of kinship in certain kinds of societies (McKinnon and Cannell 2013a). The "domaining" that is central to the modernist project thus serves to occlude the importance of kinship relations from studies of citizenship.

Contrary to this tendency, a number of chapters in this volume make the case for politics and kinship being fundamentally interrelated to the study of citizenship. These chapters show us how we can productively interrogate the relationships between kinship and citizenship. In this regard, Jane Fiegen Green, in her essay, "Appreciation and Elevation of Labor," describes in detail how young women in nineteenth-century New England justified factory work as a means to achieving ideals of domestic femininity. In addition, Amy Grey, in "The Spectacle of a Farmer Bending Over a Washtub," makes clear how the Dawes Act was an attempt to break ties of Native American kinship in order to establish stronger connections between Native Americans and the state. She shows how such efforts involved Presbyterian missionaries cultivating new domestic habits among Native American children. In his essay, "He Wants to Take Them to Russia!" John Hink shows the further entanglements of politics and kinship by documenting the ideology of Cold War custody decisions that prioritized children's ties to the US state over their ties to kin. Jessica Robbins-Ruszkowski shows in "'Active Aging' as Citizenship in Poland" how new, nonkin ties can supplant kin ties through participation in forms of "active aging" among older people in Poland. Finally, Saeed Khan's essay, "The Negotiation of Citizenship among Pakistani Youth in Great Britain," demonstrates the importance of kin relations, especially as mediated through images of "the homeland" of Pakistan, images that are central in shaping understandings of identity and belonging among Pakistani British youth. We can take from these essays a reminder that connections between the spheres of politics and kinship are of central importance in contemporary debates on citizenship. In terms of an agenda for the study of citizenship, these essays encourage us to be more critical of Western and modernist presumptions regarding the isolation of civic bonds from the bonds of kinship, opening one possibility, as Khan suggests, for conceptualizing citizenship globally. By analytically holding together these often-isolated domains, we can begin to rethink the category of citizenship in terms that are more open to other, non-Western forms of sociality and belonging, thus making citizenship a more truly global category.

When we consider the intergenerational dynamics of civic inclusion/ exclusion as temporal experiences intimately intertwined with establishment of kinship relations across the span of a human life, we cannot ignore the potential for emotional connection. We experience our aging and our intergenerational interactions as deeply personal, and we experience the worth of our citizenship in emotional terms. Current research on citizenship has accounted for the emotional experience of civic attachment in terms of the concepts of patriotism and cosmopolitanism (e.g., Benei 2008; Nussbaum 2013), and historical research drawing on insights from postcolonial thought has shown the importance of sentiment to the construction, maintenance, and subversion of politics and power (e.g., Burgett 1998; Stoler 2001). A focus on aging and the bonds within as well as across generations adds another dimension to our growing understanding of the emotional experience of belonging to a political community, demonstrating both how emotional bonds of civic engagement can change within as well as across generations and how the emotional bonds shared among generations can influence community membership.

In "Is Participation Decline Inevitable as Generations Age?," by Jennie Sweet-Cushman, Mary Herring, Lisa J. Ficker, Cathy Lysack, Marc Kruman, and Peter Lichtenberg, and "Civic Renewal," by Peter Levine—as well as the contributions by Robbins-Ruszkowski, Colombo, Khan, and Marback, which have already been mentioned—emotions are both implicitly and explicitly central to experiences of citizenship. In Robbins-Ruszkowski's essay, structures of feeling about past and current world orders influence ideologies of belonging in contemporary Poland, such that older people are thought to belong to the past rather than the future. Colombo, Khan, and Marback explicitly discuss the role of emotions in their writings on generation and citizenship; in their essays, generational differences are key to structuring the emotions of citizenship. Colombo's essay shows how feelings of belonging and identification have generational contours, as the children of immigrants in Italy feel differently than their parents about their countries of origin and new homes. Khan shows how everyday discrimination fuels anger, mistrust, and isolation among Pakistani youth in Britain; this emotional experience is directly related to their nonparticipation in the civic life of Britain, and their identification with Pakistan. These essays on immigrants, migration, and citizenship demonstrate that emotions have critical scalar functions, connecting people to faraway lands and communities. By analyzing the role of protests in the 1960s and 1970s on different generations of political activists in South Africa, Marback shows how political events can differently structure feelings, which in turn affect citizenship. As Marback insightfully writes, for these activists, the very possibility of being open to hope—and disappointment—is a civic act about the kinds of future toward which they struggle. Highlighting the fragility of all social interactions, the contributions of Marback and Levine show that emotions of trust and loyalty are central to the practice of civic engagement. In this light, citizenship thus becomes a moral practice through which community and sociality are constituted.

Indeed, by foregrounding the generational dimension of citizenship, the category of citizen emerges as one that is fundamentally social and relational in nature. This is important to emphasize in the context of modernist assumptions discussed above that presume the primacy of individual-nation relations, and in the context of the rise of what we can loosely call neoliberal ideologies (but see Collier [2011, 9–12] for a critique of such loose categorizations), in which the withdrawal of the welfare state is linked to individualizing discourses that "responsibilize" health, education, and finances (Shamir 2008). Taking a generational perspective, however, emphasizes the fundamental interconnectedness of citizens and persons and thus encourages us to think in terms that explicitly challenge the assumed bounded nature of the individual. Adopting a generational perspective entails understandings of personhood as processual and formed throughout the lives of individuals through their relations and in collectives (Mauss [1938] 1985; [1925] 1990).

Acknowledging the emotional dimensions of citizenship—that citizens live their lives in interactions with others for whom they care—brings us into awareness of the fact that membership in human communities is always embodied. In this volume, citizenship as embodied activity is discussed most explicitly in the contribution of Sweet-Cushman, Herring, Ficker, Lysack, Kruman, and Lichtenberg, which shows connections between experiences of pain and disability and civic participation. This is not to suggest that embodied experience can be isolated from community belonging. Embodiment is always implicitly part of thinking about experiences of citizenship over the life course. Indeed, the "problems" of an aging population about which Mann writes, and which prompt the creation of a new category of citizenship (senior citizens), are directly related to aging bodies. This bodily dimension of citizenship is another key aspect of this book's contribution to decentering the modernist assumptions that inform citizenship studies, among them the distinction between "rational" thinking and "irrational" emotion. A generational perspective thus participates in recent developments in the study of citizenship that ground analysis in a phenomenological perspective on our embodied humanity (Ignatieff 2003; Turner 2006).

This collection as a whole contributes to the phenomenological turn in citizenship studies. This collection also advances the view that thinking in terms of generational awareness of citizenship best conceives the essence of what it is to be human, what it is to live out our lives from youth to old age in an ongoing process of discovering, asserting, sharing, and at times rejecting and reformulating our civic bonds with each other. The lived experience of our civic bonds to each other, within and across generations—as determined as they may be by the establishment and enforcement of national boundaries—are determined in ways we experience through relationships we share with those born before us as well as those born after us.

WORKS CITED

Benei, Véronique. 2008. *Schooling Passions: Nation, History, and Language in Contemporary Western India*. Palo Alto, CA: Stanford University Press.

Benhabib, Seyla. 2004. *The Rights of Others: Aliens, Citizens, and Residents*. Cambridge: Cambridge University Press.

Burgett, Bruce. 1998. *Sentimental Bodies: Sex, Gender, and Citizenship in the Early Republic*. Princeton, NJ: Princeton University Press.

Carsten, Janet, ed. 2000. *Cultures of Relatedness: New Approaches to the Study of Kinship*. New York: Cambridge University Press.

———. 2007. *Ghosts of Memory: Essays on Remembrance and Relatedness*. Malden, MA: Blackwell Publishing,.

Collier, Jane Fishburne, and Sylvia Junko Yanagisako, eds. 1987. *Gender and Kinship: Essays toward a Unified Analysis*. Stanford, CA: Stanford University Press.

Collier, Stephen J. 2011. *Post-Soviet Social: Neoliberalism, Social Modernity, Biopolitics*. Princeton, NJ: Princeton University Press.

Franklin, Sarah, and Susan McKinnon. 2001. "Relative Values: Reconfiguring Kinship Studies." In *Relative Values: Reconfiguring Kinship Studies*, edited by S. McKinnon and S. Franklin, 1–25. Durham, NC: Duke University Press.

Gilroy, Paul. 1993. *The Black Atlantic: Modernity and Double Consciousness*. Cambridge, MA: Harvard University Press.

Ignatieff, Michael. 2003. *Human Rights as Politics and Idolatry*. Princeton, NJ: Princeton University Press.

Mauss, Marcel. [1938] 1985. "A Category of the Human Mind: The Notion of Person, the Notion of Self." In *The Category of the Person: Anthropology, Philosophy, History*, edited by M. Carrithers, S. Collins, and S. Lukes, 1–25. Cambridge: Cambridge University Press.

———. [1925] 1990. *The Gift: The Form and Reason for Exchange in Archaic Societies*. Translated by W. D. Halls. New York: Norton.

McKinnon, Susan, and Fenella Cannell. 2013a. "The Difference Kinship Makes." In *Vital Relations: Modernity and the Persistent Life of Kinship*, edited by S. McKinnon and F. Cannell, 3–39. Santa Fe: School for Advanced Research Press.

———. 2013b. *Vital Relations: Modernity and the Persistent Life of Kinship*. Santa Fe: School for Advanced Research Press.

Nussbaum, Martha. 2013. *Political Emotions: Why Love Matters for Justice*. Cambridge, MA: Harvard University Press.

Shamir, Ronen. 2008. "The Age of Responsibilization: On Market-Embedded Morality." *Economy and Society* 37 (1): 1–19.

Spivak, Gayatri. 1988. "Can the Subaltern Speak?" In *Marxism and the Interpretation of Culture*, edited by C. Nelson and L. Grossberg, 271–313. Champaign: University of Illinois Press.

Steinberg, Jonah. 2011. *Isma'ili Modern: Globalization and Identity in a Muslim Community*. Chapel Hill: University of North Carolina Press.

Stoler, Ann Laura. 2001. "Tense and Tender Ties: The Politics of Comparison in North American History and (Post)Colonial Studies." *Journal of American History* 88 (3): 829–65.

Turner, Bryan. 2006. *Vulnerability and Human Rights*. University Park: Pennsylvania State University Press.

CONTRIBUTORS

ENZO COLOMBO is associate professor of sociology of cultural processes and sociology of intercultural relations at the University of Milan, Italy. His most recent book is *Children of Immigrants in a Globalized World: A Generational Experience* (with P. Rebughini) (2012).

LISA J. FICKER, PhD, received her doctorate in clinical psychology at Wayne State University in 2010. She is currently working as a research associate for both the Institute of Gerontology and the Merrill Palmer Skillman Institute for Child and Family Development at Wayne State University. She manages a variety of research projects across the lifespan, such as the Lifespan Investigation of Family, Health, and Environment (LIFHE) project.

JANE FIEGEN GREEN is a PhD candidate at Washington University in St. Louis. Her dissertation, "The Boundaries of Youth: Labor, Maturity, and Coming of Age in Early Nineteenth-Century New England," uses the experiences of young men and women during the transition from childhood to adulthood to understand how the nation adapted to the commercial economy.

AMY GREY is a PhD candidate at the University of Arizona. Her dissertation focuses on the ways that class, race, gender, and religion shape discourses about citizenship in the context of new educational projects in the American Southwest. She is also interested in how popular culture shapes conceptions of citizenship.

MARY HERRING teaches courses in political behavior, statistics, and gender politics at Wayne State University. Her research has appeared in the *American Political Science Review*, the *Journal of Politics*, the *Social Science Quarterly*, the *National Political Science Review*, and the *Policy Studies Review*. She is currently working on a study of adolescents' political discussion.

JOHN W. HINK JR. is an assistant professor of history at Concordia University, Nebraska. He received a PhD in history in 2012 from Northern Illinois University. His research examines challenges to birthright citizenship in the United States during the twentieth century.

SAEED A. KHAN is currently in the Department of Classical and Modern Languages, Literatures and Cultures at Wayne State University, where he teaches courses on Islamic and Middle East history, politics and culture, and is also a fellow at the Center for the Study of Citizenship. His area of research is the identity politics of Muslim diaspora communities in the United States, United Kingdom, and Europe. He is also adjunct professor in Islamic studies at the University of Detroit–Mercy and at Rochester College, co-teaching a course on Muslim-Christian diversity. He has taught Islam and world politics at Michigan State University–James Madison College and has been a lecturer at Henry Ford College and Eastern Michigan University. In addition, he is a founding member and a senior research fellow at the Institute for Social Policy and Understanding, a Michigan-based think tank promoting the study and analysis of US social and domestic policy. Most recently, Saeed has founded the Center for the Study of Trans-Atlantic Diasporas, a think tank and policy center examining and comparing the condition of ethnic immigrant groups in North America and Europe, consulting the US and UK governments and the EU on their respective Muslim communities. He is a regular contributor to C-Span, NPR, Voice of America, and the National Press Club, as well as newspapers and other outlets, and is also a consultant on Islamic and Middle East affairs for the BBC.

MARC W. KRUMAN, director of the Center for the Study of Citizenship, is also chair of the Department of History and professor of history at Wayne State University. He has taught American history at Wayne State since 1975. Professor Kruman is the author of two books—*Between Authority and Liberty: State Constitution Making in Revolutionary America* (1997) and *Parties and Politics in North Carolina, 1836–1865* (1983)—and numerous articles. He has been awarded the Andrew W. Mellon Faculty Fellowship in the Humanities at Harvard University and a National Endowment for the Humanities Research Fellowship. In 1999 he was a Fulbright Senior Lecturer at the University of Rome. At Wayne State University, Kruman has received the President's Award for Excellence in Teaching and the Board of Governors Faculty Recognition Award (twice). He is also coeditor, with Richard Marback, of the Series in Citizenship Studies at Wayne State University Press.

PETER LEVINE is the Lincoln Filene Professor of Citizenship and Public Affairs in Tufts University's Jonathan Tisch College of Citizenship and Public Service and director of CIRCLE, The Center for Information and Research on Civic Learning and Engagement. Levine is the author of *We Are the Ones We Have Been Waiting For: The Philosophy and Practice of Civic Renewal* (Oxford University Press, 2013) and six other books.

PETER A. LICHTENBERG, PhD, is the director of both the Institute of Gerontology and the Merrill Palmer Skillman Institute and the founding director of the Wayne State University Lifespan Alliance. Dr. Lichtenberg is also a professor of psychology and physical medicine and rehabilitation. He is a clinical psychologist and obtained his PhD at Purdue University. Nationally and locally Dr. Lichtenberg has served on many community boards and held office in several professional organizations, including chair of the Michigan Dementia Coalition 1999–2010. Dr. Lichtenberg was the chair of the Behavioral and Social Sciences Section of the Gerontological Society of America (2007), chair of the APA Committee on Aging (2008), and a member of the APA Presidential Task Force on Integrated Care for an Aging Population, and president of the Adult Development and Aging Section of the American Psychological Association in 2010. In 2011 Dr. Lichtenberg was the John Santos Award winner from the American Psychological Association Division of Adult Development and Aging (20) for sustained excellence in gerontology programs.

CATHY LYSACK, PhD, OT(C), is the deputy director of the Institute of Gerontology (IOG) and a professor in the Department of Health Care Sciences (Occupational Therapy) at the Eugene Applebaum College of Pharmacy and Health Sciences at Wayne State University, where she is currently acting dean. In gerontology, she is engaged in various research projects and codirects the NIA-funded T32 Predoctoral Training Program in Aging and Urban Health. In occupational therapy, Dr. Lysack teaches courses in research methods. Dr. Lysack also serves on the editorial boards of the *American Journal of Occupational Therapy*, the *Canadian Journal of Occupational Therapy*, and the *Journal of Applied Gerontology*. In 2007 Dr. Lysack was inducted into the American Occupational Therapy Foundation's Academy of Research for "having made exemplary contributions toward the science of occupational therapy." She has published more than forty peer-reviewed articles and numerous book chapters.

TAMARA MANN, PhD, is the John Strassburger Postdoctoral Fellow at Columbia University. Her dissertation, "Honor Thy Father and Mother," is on the history of old age and health policy in United States.

RICHARD MARBACK is a professor of English at Wayne State University. He is the author most recently of *Managing Vulnerability: South Africa's Struggle for a Democratic Rhetoric* (2012) and coeditor of *The Hope and the Legacy: The Past, Present, and Future of "Student's Right to Their Own Language"* (2004). He is also the author of over thirty articles and chapters on historical and contemporary issues in rhetoric and composition. He is currently at work on a booklength manuscript exploring the role played by the African concept of Ubuntu in fostering public discussion.

YUKI ODA is an assistant professor at the Faculty of Commerce, Chuo University (Tokyo, Japan). He specializes in modern U.S. history and immigration history. He received his Ph.D. from the Department of History, Columbia University with a dissertation titled "Family Unity in U.S. Immigration Policy, 1921-1978." He has published articles in *Journal of Pacific and American Studies* (2006) and *Italian Americana* (Web 2012).

JESSICA C. ROBBINS-RUSZKOWSKI is an assistant professor at the Institute of Gerontology and the Department of Anthropology at Wayne State University. Her research interests are aging, personhood and kinship, memory, morality, and political economy. Previous work has appeared in *Transitions and Transformations: Cultural Perspectives on the Life Course, Anthropology & Aging Quarterly*, and *Forum Oświatowe (Educational Forum)*.

PAULINE STOLTZ is associate professor in the Department of Culture and Global Studies at Aalborg University, Aalborg, Denmark and chief editor of *Nora—Nordic Journal of Feminist and Gender Research*. Currently she is involved in a research project on "Gender, race and generation in post-conflict processes."

JENNIE SWEET-CUSHMAN is assistant professor of political science at Chatham University where she also serves as assistant director at the Pennsylvania Center for Women and Politics. She recently completed her doctoral studies in the Department of Political Science at Wayne State University in Detroit, Michigan, where her research in political participation included work on the urban elderly as well as the elite participation of women in the United States and Africa.

ABDELDJALIL LARBI YOUCEF was born in Mazouna, Algeria. He graduated from ES Senia and the Sorbonne University. He currently teaches American History, 1492–Present at the University Abd El Hamid Ibn Badis, Mostaganem. His field of interest is American constitutional law.

INDEX

Arabs, Algerian: citizenship for, 232–33; in Great Wars, 230–31, 233; racial classification of, 232; veterans, 231. *See also* French Algerians

Arendt, Hannah, 20

Aristotle, on social organization, 3

Arizona Territory, Presbyterian missionaries in, 70–71

Armenia, Soviet: expatriation to, 95

Armenian Orthodox Church, on *Choolokian* case, 98

ARY (Pakistani television), 117, 119

assimilation: compulsory, 122; as form of participation, 146; and multiculturalism, 122; self and other in, 123

assimilation, British, 122–23; for Pakistani youth, 122

assimilation, Native American, 68, 69; adaptive, 81–82, 85–86; under Dawes Act, 72, 73; versus extermination, 69, 71, 85; in federal Peace Policy, 69; reformers' interest in, 79; religious training in, 78–80; role of education in, 71–72, 79, 85; at Tucson Training School, 77

Association for Improving the Condition of the Poor (AICP), 290

Austin, Mary Hunter, 85

Azan, Paul, 231

baby boomers, civic participation among, 243–44

Bacri, Jacob: brokering of French debt, 229–30

Bagley, Sarah, 63n13

Balderrama, Francisco E., 203n4

Baldwin, Clive, 9

Bartlett, Ruth, 8

Baulieu, Paul-Leroy: *Algérie et Tunisie*, 232

Benhabib, Seyla, 121; *Another Cosmopolitanism*, 164, 168; on moral learning, 165; on postnationalism, 128n3;

situated cosmopolitanism of, 158, 163–65, 173–77, 179

Beurs, 238n1

Beurs, New: challenges to French authority, 228, 237–38; French citizenship of, 237–38; Jus Soli of, 237. *See also* youth, French Algerian

Beurs, Old: citizenship hopes among, 228, 236–37; during Glorious Thirty, 236; social exclusion of, 236

Bhimji, F., 125–26

Biko, Steve: on antiapartheid movement, 210; black consciousness movement of, 209, 215–16; on Mandela's generation, 212

Billman, Howard, 69; assimilationist goals of, 78; educational beliefs of, 70, 79; evangelism of, 78, 79, 82; on gendered labor, 67–68, 73, 79–80, 86; on Native American curriculum, 69; Progressive views of, 72, 76; support of farming, 74–75

birth certificates, US: delayed, 201–2

birth registration, US: gaps in, 198; standardization of, 201

black consciousness movement (South Africa), 209, 215–16, 217; Mandela on, 216, 220; at South African universities, 218

blackfeet (Algerians), 234–35, 238n2

Blinken, Samuel M.: in *Choolokian* case, 94–97

Board of Immigration Appeals (BIA), 195, 196, 198, 200, 206n29; on recovery of citizenship, 206n26; residence requirement rulings, 205n19

Bohman, J., 167–68

Booth, Wayne: *Modern Dogma*, 5

Boualam, Saïd: *Mon pays, la France!*, 235–36

boys, sexual violence against, 173

Boy Scouts, Native American culture among, 85

of, 51–52; cross-gendered alliances
among, 55; and cult of domesticity,
48–49; in intergenerational cohort,
57; in liminal positions, 61; literary
compositions of, 48; maturity for, 51,
55–56; obstacles to adulthood, 48, 49,
55; publications by, 47–61; pursuit of
knowledge, 50; women, 44–45, 47, 53.
See also working class
YouthBuild USA, 30
Yuval-Davis, Nira, 162, 165

Zeisel, Hans, 39n15
Zukin, Cliff, 5
Zuma, Jacob, 11; and Dalai Lama visit,
223; economic policies of, 222–23
Zwelonke, D. W., 211